GENESIS

ALLAN KARDEC

Spiritist Alliance for Books/Spiritist Group of New York
http://www.sgny.org
*E-mail:*sab@sgny.org

Original Title: La Genèse - Les Miracles et les Prédictions Selon le Spiritisme – Allan Kardec

Cover photo: The Whirlpool Galaxy in the constellation of Canes Venatici (Photograph taken by NASA and the Hubble Heritage Team STScI/AURA)
Cover Design and edition: Crisley Thomé, Wenderson Pereira Diniz Maria de Fátima Melo Salvo.
Logo design: Flavia Portugal

Editorial Production: **Editora** Sociedade Espírita Paulo de Tarso
Paulo de Tarso
Rua 104, Travessa Eurípedes Barsanulfo n° 140 CEP 74080-350, Setor Sul, Goiânia - Goiás - Brasil.

Printed in Brazil

Library of Congress number: TXu1-103-989

Main entry under title:
Genesis – The Miracles and Predictions According to Spiritism
1. Religious Philosophy 2. Spiritist Doctrine 3. Christianity
Kardec, Allan, 1804
ISBN 0-9742332-0-X

The **Spiritist Group of New York (SGNY)** is a not-for-profit organization, which has the sole aim to promote and disseminate the Spiritist Doctrine in English, as codified by Allan Kardec.

The group was officially established on April 12th, 2001. However, some of its participants have been earnestly fostering the dissemination of the Spiritist Doctrine in the United States and in the United Kingdom for about ten years.

As a result, a number of its founders and participating members have founded the **Spiritist Alliance for Books (SAB)**, which is an organization that aims to unite people from all over the world who are willing to volunteer in the effort of translating spiritist books (which were originally written in other languages) into English.

GENESIS

THE MIRACLES AND THE PREDICTIONS
ACCORDING TO SPIRITISM

ALLAN KARDEC

SPIRITIST ALLIANCE FOR BOOKS

This English translation is based on the French original (Nouvelle Edition conforme a L'Edition Originale - Union Spirite Française et Francophone).

PREFACE TO THE ENGLISH EDITION

It was a heartfelt happiness, indeed, for all of us when we came upon Mr. W. J. Colville's out of print version of *"Genesis,"* an English translation of the French book written and published by Allan Kardec in January of 1868. Our first discovery and viewing of this publication occurred on an exceedingly significant date for mankind, and particularly for us, residents of New York City. The date of our finding, incredibly enough, was September 11, 2002, exactly one year to date of the tragedy that struck our city and shook the world.

This finding has motivated us to scrutinize the text, and has served as the basis of our endeavor to publish a new version of *"Genesis"* in English, thus completing the series of five books that comprise the set of the Spiritist Doctrine presented by Allan Kardec.

Our commitment to this new publication stems from our intense desire to present as faithful a translation of the original French version as possible. In order to achieve this goal, we meticulously followed Kardec's French version, to insure the accuracy and thoroughness of the final product. In spite of having included a more relevant and effective footnote support to bridge the gap between XIX Century and modern science, the reader may rest assured that the original text presented by the author has been methodically preserved.

We sincerely hope that this book will help to enlighten all readers and bring joy to the many other hearts that until today had not been able to enjoy such an important work, due to its unavailability to the English speaking public.

A task of this magnitude could only be accomplished through the efforts and dedication of tireless workers who we would like to acknowledge for their excellent contribution:

Eliene Brito, Louis Day, Dean Whorton, Milena Whorton, Marie Levinson, Crisley Thomé, Edward Christie, Luciana dos Santos, Marcia Lacerda, Henrique de Sá, Suzanne Erickson and João Korngold.

We thank our spiritual guides for being ever present at our side, through the entire process and completion of this work, as well as for the trust they have bestowed upon us in making it possible for the first English translation of *Genesis* to reach our hands.

Jussara Korngold
Spiritist Alliance for Books
New York, May 2003

INTRODUCTION

This new work is one step more in the advancement in the effects and applications of Spiritism. As its title indicates, its object is the study of three points diversely commented upon and interpreted even to this day, - "Genesis, Miracles, and Predictions" in their relations with the recently known laws which are revealed through the observation of spiritual phenomena.

Two elements, or we may say two forces, govern the universe, - the spiritual element and the material one. By the simultaneous action of these two principles are developed some special phenomena, which are naturally rendered inexplicable if one should take away one of its two constituent elements, oxygen and hydrogen.

Spiritism, in demonstrating the existence of the spiritual world and its relations with the material world, furnishes the key to a multitude of unknown phenomena, which are considered as inadmissible by a certain class of thinkers. The record of such facts abounds in the Scriptures; and it is in default of knowledge concerning the laws that govern them that commentators of the two opposing parties moving always in the same circle of ideas, - some abstracting positive gifts from science, others from the spiritual principle, - have not been able to arrive at any rational solution.

The solution is found only in the reciprocal action between spirit and matter. It takes away, it is true, the great part of the supernatural character of these facts. But which is the more valuable method: to admit them have sprung from the laws of nature, or to reject them entirely? Their absolute rejection removes the base from the edifice; while their admission as facts, suppressing only accessories, leaves the base intact. This is why Spiritism leads so many people to a belief in truth, which they formerly considered utopian ideas.

This work is then, as we have said before, a complement of

the applications of Spiritism to this special point of a view. The materials were ready, or at least elaborated a long time since; but the moment for their publication had not arrived. It was necessary at first that the ideas which were to form the base should arrive at maturity; and moreover, it was necessary to take advantage of circumstances. Spiritism has neither mysteries nor secret theories. It can bear the full light of day so that everyone can judge of it by a knowledge of its laws; but everything has to come in its own time in order to win its way. A solution given lightly, prior to the complete elucidation of the question, would be a retarding force, rather than a means of advancement. In the matter in question the importance of the subject makes it a duty to avoid all precipitation.

Before entering into the subject, it has appeared necessary to us to define distinctly the respective roles of spirits and men according to the new doctrine. These preliminary considerations, which discard all ideas of mysticism, form the subject of the first chapter, entitled "Character of the Spiritist Revelation." We call serious attention to this point, because it is in a measure the knot of the question.

Notwithstanding the work incumbent upon human activity in the elaboration of this doctrine, the initiative belongs to the spirits; but conclusions are not drawn from the personal opinion of none of them. The truth can only be the resultant of their collective and concordant teachings. Without this united testimony, a doctrine could not lawfully be called the doctrine of the spirits; it would be merely that of one spirit, and would possess only the value of a personal opinion.

General concordance in teaching is the doctrine's essential character, the condition even of its existence. It is evident that all principles which have not received the consecration of general agreement can only be considered as a fractional part of this same doctrine, merely as a simple, isolated opinion for which Spiritism cannot assume the responsibility.

It is the concordant, collective teaching of the spirits who have passed beyond which constitutes the logical criterion, giving strength to the spiritual doctrine and assuring to it perpetuity. In order to change it, it would be necessary that the universal experience and teachings of spirits should change, and that one day they would contradict what they have previously declared. Considering that it has its source in the teachings of the spirits, in order for it to fail would be necessary the cessation of the existence of the spirits. This established, it must prevail over every personal system which has not, like it, roots extending in all directions. *The Spirits' Book* has seen its credit consolidate, because it is the expression of a collective thought. In the month of April, 1867, it accomplished its first decennial period. In this interval, the fundamental principles which form its base have been successively completed and developed by following progressive teachings of the spirits; but not one of its declarations has received contradiction through the trial. All without exception have remained firm, stronger than ever; while, among all the contradictory ideas with which persons have tried to oppose them, not one has prevailed, because on all sides the spiritual teaching was confirmatory. This characteristic result we can proclaim without vanity, as its merit is not attributable to us.

Similar circumstances have presided at the editing of our other works. Thus we have been able in all truth to tell the public that they are in accordance with Spiritism itself, owing to their conformity with the general teachings of the spirits. In this volume we can present under similar conditions the complement of the precedents, with the exception, however, of some theories yet hypothetical, which we have taken care to indicate as such, and which ought not to be considered as other than individual opinions until they have been confirmed. If they be contradicted, the responsibility of them does not rest upon the general doctrine.

Yet the constant readers of the *"Revue Spirite"[1]* will have observed that most of the ideas only outlined in preceding articles are enlarged upon and developed in this last work. The "Revue" is often for us a trial-ground, destined to sound the opinions of men and spirits upon certain principles, before admitting them as constituent parts of the doctrine.

---

[1] *"Revue Spirite," a valuable French spiritist periodical.*

CONTENTS

Chapter I
CHARACTER OF THE SPIRITIST DOCTRINE

1. Can one consider Spiritism as a revelation? If it be such, what is its character? Upon what is its authenticity founded? By whom, and in what manner has it been given? Is the doctrine of Spiritism a revelation in the liturgical sense of the word? That is to say, is it in all points the product of occult teaching from on high? Is it absolute or capable of mystifications? In conveying to men perfect truth, would not revelation have the effect of hindering them from employing their faculties, since it would save them the work of research? What can be the authority of the teachings of the spirit if they are not infallible, and superior to those of humanity? What is the utility of the morality that they preach if this is other than that of the Christ whom men acknowledge? What are the new truths that they bring to us? Has man need of a revelation and can he find himself and in his conscience all that is necessary to lead him aright? These are the questions which are important for us to focus.

2. Let us define at first the sense of the word. "Revelation," *to reveal*, derived from the word "veil," from the Latin *velum*, signifies literally to take away the veil, and, figuratively, to uncover, to make the acquaintance of a secret or unknown fact. In its most general sense it is employed with reference to every unknown thing which is brought to light, to every new idea which is given to man.

Indeed, all the sciences which have revealed the mysteries of nature are revelations; and one can well say that there is for us a constant revelation. Astronomy has revealed to us the astral universe of which we were ignorant; geology, the formation of the Earth; chemistry, the law of affinities; physiology, the functions of the organism, etc. Copernicus, Galileo, Newton, Laplace, and Lavoisier are revealers.

3. The essential character of all revelation must be truth. To reveal a secret is to make known a fact. If the thing is false, it is not a fact, and consequently not a revelation. All so-called revelation contradicted by facts is not revelation even if attributed to God. He not being able to tell an untruth or to deceive, we know it cannot emanate from him. It is necessary to consider it as merely a human conception.

4. What is the attitude of the professor to his pupils if it is not that of a revealer? He teaches them that which they do not know, that which they would have neither the time nor the possibility to discover for themselves, because science is the collective work of centuries, and of a multitude of men who have each contributed the results of their observations, by which those who come after them profit. Teaching is, then, in reality the revelation of certain scientific or moral, physical or metaphysical truths given by men who know them, to others who know them not, and who, without their aid would have remained ignorant of them.

5. But the professor teaches that which he has learned; he is a revealer of the second order. The man of genius teaches that which he has found for himself; he is the primitive revealer; he carries the light which from one place to another, makes itself known. Where would be humanity without the revelations from men of genius who appear from time to time?

But what are men of genius? Why are they men of genius? Whence do they come? What becomes of them? Let us observe that the greater part of them is born with transcendent faculties, and innate knowledge that a little work suffices to develop. They belong really to humanity since they are born, live and die like mortals. Where, then, have they obtained this knowledge which comes so mysteriously to them? Will one say with the materialist that chance has given to them cerebral matter in greater quantity and better quality? In this case they would have no more merit than one vegetable greater and more savory than another.

Will one say that God awarded spiritists with a more favored soul or mind than those of common men? – A supposition also entirely illogical, since it accuses God of partiality. The only rational solution of this problem is in the pre-existence of soul, and in a plurality of existences. The man of genius is a spirit which has lived a longer time, who has consequently acquired more and progressed more, than those who are less advanced. In becoming incarnate he brings to Earth what he knows; and, as he is much wiser than others without the necessity of learning, he is that which one calls a man of genius. But that which he knows is the fruit of an anterior work, and not the result of divine preference. Before entering anew into Earth-life, he has an advanced spirit. He is reincarnated; it may be for the purpose of benefiting others, or possibly for the opportunity of acquiring more knowledge himself.

Men progress incontestably by themselves by means of their intelligence; but, left to their own forces, progress is very slow, if they are not aided by more advanced minds, as the scholar is by his professors. All nations have among them men of genius who appeared at diverse epochs to impel and draw men from their inertia.

6. If we admit the solicitude of God for his creatures, why should we not also admit that the spirits are capable, by their energy and superior knowledge, to assist humanity to advance; that they are reincarnated at the desire of God, with the view of aiding progress in a definite manner; that they receive a mission as an ambassador receives one from his sovereign? Such is the role of the great geniuses. What come they to do, if not to teach to men truths of which they are ignorant, and of which they would not acquire the knowledge during still longer periods of time, had they not come to give the stepping-stone by which men are enabled to elevate themselves more rapidly? These geniuses who appear at different epochs like brilliant stars, leaving after them a long, luminous track for humanity, are missionaries, - or, better, Messiahs. The new facts they bring to light, be they of a physical or philosophical order, are revelations.

If God ordains revealers of scientific truths, he can, for a stronger reason, create them for moral truths, which are an essential element of progress, such as the philosophers whose ideas have lived through the ages.

7. In the special sense of religious faith, revelation informs us more particularly of spiritual facts which man cannot know of himself, that he cannot discover by means of his senses, and of which the knowledge is given him by God or by his messengers in direct word or by inspiration. In this case revelation is always made to favored men, designated under the names of prophets or Messiahs; viz., ambassadors, - missionaries having a mission to transmit truths to men. Considered from this point of view, revelation implies absolute passivity. One accepts it without examination, without discussion.

8. All religions have their revealers; and, although all are far from having known the whole truth, they sustained their claim for being providential. They were appropriate to the time and place where they lived, to the particular genius of the people to whom they spoke, and to whom they were relatively superior. Notwithstanding the errors of their doctrines, they have at least awakened minds. By so doing they have sown seeds or germs of progress, which later unfolded, or will yet blossom into the brighter light of Christianity. It is then wrong to anathematize the name of orthodoxy; for the day will come when all beliefs, however diverse in form, but which in reality repose upon the same fundamental principles, God and the immortality of the soul, will form themselves into a grand and vast unity, when reason shall have triumphed over prejudice.

Unhappily, religious systems through all time have been instruments of domination. The role of prophet has tempted the ambitious among those in subordinate positions. A multitude of pretended revealers, or Messiahs, who, by reason of the prestige of this name, have taken advantage of credulity to satisfy their pride, their cupidity, or their indolence, finding it easier to live at the expense of their dupes than in any other way. Christian religion has been a shelter for these parasites. In this subject let us call serious attention to Chap. XXI of *"The Gospel According to Spiritism," "There will be false Christs and false prophets."*

9. Are these direct revelations from God to men? This is a question which we dare not settle either affirmatively or negatively in an absolute manner. The thing is not radically impossible; but nothing gives certain proof of it. That which need not be doubted is that the spirits nearest God in perfection enter into his thoughts, and can transmit them. As to incarnated revealers, according to the hierarchical order to which they belong and to the degree of their personal knowledge, they can draw their instructions from their own knowledge, or receive them from spirits more elevated, from messengers ordained of God. The former, speaking in the name of God, have been taken for God himself.

These kinds of communications are not strange to those who are acquainted with spiritual phenomena between incarnates and discarnates. Instructions can be transmitted by diverse means, - inspiration pure and simple, by the hearing of the word, by seeing spirit-teachers in visions or apparitions, be it in dreams or in a state of wakefulness, of which one finds many examples in the *"Bible,"* the Gospel, and in the sacred books of all nations. It is then, rigorously exact to say that the greater part of revelers are inspired mediums, hearing or seeing. It does not follow that all are revelers, and still less intermediaries direct from God or his special messengers.

10. Pure spirits alone receive the word of God, with the mission of transmitting it; but one knows now that all spirits are far from being perfect, and there are those who give false appearances. That is why St. John has said. "Dear friends, do not believe every spirit, but test the spirits to see whether they are from God, because many false prophets have gone out into the world." (I John IV,1).

There are serious, true, and deceitful communications, examples of which are found in Apocryphal Scriptures. *The essential character of divine revelation is eternal truth. All revelation attained with error, or subject to change, cannot emanate from God.* It is truth that the law of the Decalogue still maintains all its original importance; while other Mosaic laws that are essentially transitory, often in contradiction with the law of Sinai, are the personal and political work of the Hebrew legislator. The customs of the people becoming milder, their laws improved. These laws have of themselves fallen into disuse, whilst the Decalogue has remained standing like a beacon-star to humanity. Christ has made it the base of his edifice, whilst he has abolished the other laws. If they had been the work of God, they would have remained standing. Christ and Moses are the two great revealers who have changed the face of the world, and there is the proof of their divine mission. A work purely human could have no such power.

11. An important revelation is being given at this present epoch. It is that which shows to us the possibility of communication with beings of the spiritual world. This knowledge is not new, without doubt; but it had remained until our day in a state of dead letter; that is to say, without profit for humanity. Ignorance of the laws which ruled these communications has stifled them by superstition. Man was incapable of drawing from them any salutary deduction. It was reserved for our day to rescue them from their ridiculous accessories, to comprehend the power, and to cause to shine the light which is destined to illuminate the future.

12. Spiritism, having taught us of the invisible world which surrounds us and in the midst of which we live without doubt, the laws which govern it, its connection with the visible world, the nature and state of the beings who inhabit it and tracing the destiny of man after death, is a veritable revelation in the scientific acceptance of the word.

13. By its nature, the spiritual revelation has a two fold character: it is at the same time a divine and a scientific revelation. It is the first in that its coming is providential, and not the result of the initiative and premeditative design of man. The fundamental points of the doctrine being the fact of the teaching given by spirits commissioned by God to enlighten men concerning things whereof they were ignorant, - things they could not learn by themselves and which it is important for them to know today, as they are ready to comprehend them. It is the second because it informs us that this teaching is a privilege granted to no one individual, but that it is given to all the world by the same means (or in the same way) that those who transmit and those who receive it are not passive beings, excused from the work of observation and research; that they are not called upon to abnegate their judgment and their free will, that their control of themselves is not interdicted but on the contrary, recommended; and, finally, that the whole doctrine *has not been enunciated in every part, nor imposed upon blind belief,* but is deduced by the work of man, by the observation of facts that the spirits place before us. The instructions that they give to us to compel us to study, comment, compare, until we arrive at a knowledge of consequences and applications. In short, *that which characterizes the spiritual revelation is the divine source from which it proceeds: - that the initiative belongs to the spirits and that the elaboration is the work of man.*

14. As a mean of elaboration, Spiritism proceeds in exactly the same course as the exact sciences; that is to say, it implies the experimental method. Some facts of a new order present themselves, which cannot be explained by known laws. It teaches us to observe, compare, analyze them, and from effects, arrive at causes; it reveals the laws which govern them; it then deduces the consequences, and seeks for useful applications; *it establishes no one preconceived theory.* Thus it has not presented as a hypothesis either the existence or intervention of spirits, neither the existence of the perispirit, or reincarnation, or any one principle of the doctrine. It has proved the existence of spirits in the beyond, and with it the other principles connected with the spiritual life. These are not facts which are revealed after a theory has been formed to confirm them; but the theory has subsequently arisen to explain the facts, and make a summary of them. It is rigorously exact to declare that Spiritism is a science of observation, and not the product of the imagination. Not until its studies were based on experimental methods did the sciences begin to make serious progress. Although it was believed that this method could only be applied to matter, it is just as well applied to metaphysical things.

15. Let us cite an example: there happens in the world of spirits a very singular occurrence, and one that assuredly no one would have imagined. It is that some spirits think they are still incarnated. However, the superior spirits, who know it well, do not tell us, in response to our anticipation, "There are some spirits who believe that they still live in the Earth-life, who have preserved their tastes, their habits, and their instincts." We have invoked the manifestation of this category of spirits in order that we may observe them. Having then seen spirits uncertain of their state, or affirming that they were yet of this world, attending to their ordinary occupations, the example has proved the fact. The multiplicity of similar facts has proved that it was not an exception, but one of the phases of spirit-life. We have been permitted to study all the varieties and causes of this singular illusion; have recognized that this situation is characteristic of those but little advanced morally, and that it is peculiar to certain kinds of death; that it is not necessarily of very short duration, but can continue for months and even years. It is thus that theory is born of observation. It is the same of all other principles of the doctrine.

16. Just as science, properly speaking, has for object the study of the laws of material principles, the special object of Spiritism is the knowledge of the laws of spiritual principles. As this latter class of principles is one of the forces of nature, as it acts incessantly and reciprocally upon the material principles, the result of it is that knowledge of one cannot be complete without knowledge of the other; that separated, they are incomplete; that science without Spiritism finds itself utterly powerless to explain certain phenomena by laws of matter alone; - while Spiritism without science would lack support and control. The study of the material laws should precede that of the spirituality, as it is matter that first touches the senses.

If Spiritism had appeared before the scientific discoveries, it would have been rejected, as is the case with all that comes before its time.

17. All sciences are joined to and succeed one another in rational order. One is born of the other, according as they find support in anterior knowledge and ideas. Astronomy, one of the first which might have been cultivated, has remained in the infancy of its errors till the moment when physics came to reveal the law of the forces of the natural agents. Chemistry, being unable to do anything without physics, must come next in succession, in order that they should walk together, and learn upon one another. Anatomy, physiology, zoology, botany, and mineralogy have been recognized as veritable sciences only by the aid of the lights carried by physics and chemistry. Geology, born of yesterday, without astronomy, physics, chemistry, and others, would have failed to possess true elements of vitality. It could not be born until they had been recognized.

18. Modern science has done justice to the four primitive elements of the ancients, and from observation to observation it has arrived at the conception of *one generative element alone* in all the transformations of matter; but matter by itself is inert, it has neither life, thought, nor sentiment; its union with the spiritual principle is a necessity. Spiritism has not invented this principle, but was the first to demonstrate it by undeniable proofs. It has studied it, analyzed it, and revealed it in evident action. To *the material element* it has come to add *the spiritual element. The material and spiritual elements* are the two living principles or forces of nature. By the indissoluble union of these two elements, we can explain without difficulty a crowd of facts hitherto inexplicable.[2] In its essence simply, and as having for object the study of one of these two constituent elements of the universe, Spiritism lays forcible hold of the

---

[2] The word element is not herewith taken to mean simple elementary body, consisting of primitive molecules, but to mean a constituent part of a whole. Accordingly, it can be said that the spiritual element has

greater part of the sciences, and, above all, after they had
exhibited their powerlessness to explain all things by the laws
of matter alone.

19. Spiritism is accused by some to be in alliance with
magic and sorcery; but men forget that astronomy has for her
elder sister astrology, which is not totally discarded from
among the beliefs of today; that chemistry is the daughter of
alchemy, with which no scientific man would dare to occupy
himself today. No one denies, however, that there were in
astrology and alchemy the germs of truth, from which have
sprung actual sciences; and, that, notwithstanding its ridiculous
formulas, alchemy has revealed the law of affinity between
material bodies. Astrology was supported by its knowledge
of the position and movement of the stars it had studied, but,
owing to ignorance of the true laws which ruled the mechanism
of the universe, the stars were, for ordinary people, mysterious
beings ruling the destinies of men, superstition lending to them
a moral influence and prophetic meaning. When Galileo,
Newton, and Kepler had demonstrated the laws from which
the telescope had withdrawn the veil, and given to men that
glance into the depths of space which certain people
considered so indiscreet, the planets appeared to us as simple
worlds, similar to our own; and all the lattice-work of the
marvelous crumbled away.

It is the same with Spiritism in regard to magic and
sorcery; the two latter were supported truly by spiritual
manifestations, as astrology was upon the movement of the
stars. In the ignorance of the laws which rule the spiritual world,
however there were joined to these communications ridiculous
practices and beliefs, to which modern Spiritism, the fruit of
experience and observation, has done justice. Assuredly the
distance which separates Spiritism from magic and sorcery is
greater than that which divides astronomy from astrology, and

an active part in the economy of the universe; as one can say that both,
the civil and the military elements are part of the statistics of a
population; or that the religious element partakes in the education; or
that there exists both the Arab and the European elements in Argelia.

chemistry from alchemy. The desire to confound them proves that one knows not the first thing about them.

20. The simple fact that is possible to communicate with beings of the spiritual world opens up to us incalculable consequences of the highest gravity and importance. Here a new world is revealed to us, and one which is so much the more important in that it awaits all men without exception! Knowledge concerning it cannot fail to produce, in a general sense, a profound modification in the customs, character, habits, and beliefs which exert so great an influence upon man's social life. It has caused a revolution in ideas, a revolution so great and powerful that it is not circumscribed to any one people, much less to one caste, but reaches simultaneously the heart of all classes, all nationalities, all civilizations.

For the best of reasons, Spiritism is considered the third grand revelation. Let us see wherein the revelations differ, and how they are attached to one another.

21. Moses, as a prophet, has revealed to men the knowledge of the only true God, Sovereign Master of all things. He has promulgated the law of Sinai, and laid the foundation of true faith. As a man he has been the legislator of the people, through whom this primitive faith has exerted an influence over all the Earth.

22. Christ, taking from the ancient laws all that is eternal and divine, rejecting only that which was transitory, because purely disciplinary and of human conception, also adds a revelation of the future life of which Moses had not spoken, - with its retributions and recompenses which await all mankind after physical dissolution. (See *"Revue Spirite,"* 1861, pp. 90 and 280).

23. The most important part of the revelation of Christ, the primary source, the cornerstone of his whole doctrine, is the entirely new character he ascribes to divinity. God is no more the vindictive, jealous, and terrible God of Moses, the cruel and unmerciful God who bathes the Earth with human blood, who orders massacre and extermination of

nations, without excepting women, children, and the aged;
who chastises those who spare the victims. He is no more
the unjust God who punishes a whole community for the
faults of its chief, even punishing the innocent instead of
the guilty, visiting the sins of the fathers upon the children,
but a merciful God, sovereignly just and good, full of
tenderness and mercy, who pardons the repentant sinner,
and *rewards everyone according to his works.* He is no more
the God of a favored people, *the God of armies,* presiding
at combats in order to sustain his own cause against the
gods of other nations, but the common Father of humanity,
who extends his protection over all his children, and calls
them all his own. He is no more the God who recompenses
or punishes by giving or withholding earthly goods, who
makes glory and good fortune to consist in conquering rival nations, and placing them in a state of slavery, or in the
multiplicity of progeny; but he is the God who says to men:
"Your true country is not of this world; it is in the celestial
kingdom; it is there that the lowly in heart shall be elevated,
and the proud abased." He is no more the God who makes
a virtue of vengeance, ordering us to exact "an eye for an
eye, a tooth for a tooth," but the God of mercy, who says,
"Forgive if you would be forgiven; return good for evil; do
to others what you would have them do to you." He is no
more the exacting and tyrannical God who imposes the most
rigorous laws upon us in regard to the ceremonies by which
he desires to be adored, who is offended with the
inobservance of a formula, but the great and good God
who is honored not by the form or ceremony, but by the
sincere, heartfelt thought. He is no more the God to be
feared, but the God to be loved.

24. God being the pivot of all religious beliefs, the base
of all civilizations, *the character of all religions conform to
the idea they give of God.* Those which make him vindictive
and cruel think they honor him by acts of cruelty, by butcheries
and tortures; those who make him a partial and jealous God
are intolerant, over-scrupulous in forms, according as they

believe him to be more or less tainted with weaknesses and human errors.

25. The whole doctrine of Christ is founded upon the character he attributes to divinity. With an impartial God, perfectly just, good, and merciful, he has been able to make of the love of God and charity toward one's neighbor the express conditions of salvation, and to say, "Love the Lord your God with all your heart and with all your soul and with all your mind. This is the first and greatest commandment." And the second is like it: Love your neighbor as yourself. All the Law and the Prophets hang on these two commandments. Upon this belief alone he has been able to base the principle of the equality of men before God, and of universal fraternity. Yet, would it be possible to love this God of Moses? No; one could but fear him.

This revelation of the true attributes of divinity, joined to that of the immortality of the soul and of man's future life, deeply modified the mutual relations of men, imposed upon them new obligations, caused them to view the present life under another light. It effected a marked change for the better in the manners and social relations of humanity. It is incontestably, in its consequences, the most important point in the revelation of Christ, of which one can never fully appreciate the importance. Sad to say, it is the point least commented upon, - the one which has been misconstrued in a greater degree than all his other teachings.

26. However, Christ adds, "All this I have spoken while still with you. But the Consoler, the Holy Spirit, whom the Father will send in my name, will teach you all things and will remind you of everything I have said to you. And I will ask the Father, and he will give you another Consoler to be with you forever" (John, 14: 16, 25 and 26). If Christ did not impart all the truth which he was capable of giving, he thought it better to leave some truths in shadow until men should be capable of comprehending them. From his own acknowledgement, his teachings were then incomplete. Since

he announces the coming of the spirit who should add unto
them, he prophesied that they would deviate from his teachings;
in a word, that they would deteriorate from that which he had
done for them, but everything he declared should be
reestablished. Now, one *reestablishes* only that which has been
defective.

27. Why did he call the new Messiah, the *Consoler?*
This significant name, without ambiguity, is a revelation in
itself. It predicted that men would have need of consolation,
implying that there was an insufficiency of consolation in the
new belief being formed. Scarcely ever has Christ been so
clear and explicit as in these last words, which have gained
the particular attention of but few people, perhaps because
teachers have failed to place them in the right light to deepen
their prophetic sense.

28. If Christ has not been able to develop his teachings
in a complete manner, it is because men were so ignorant, and
they could acquire knowledge only with time. He talked of
things which appeared to them visionary and unreal in their
undeveloped state. In order to complete his mission, it was
only necessary to explain and develop truths already given. It
was unnecessary to add new truth; for the germ of all was
found in his words; the key was needed which should unlock
their meaning.

29. But who dares to attempt to change the meaning of
the Holy Scriptures? Who has the right? Who possesses the
necessary light, if not the theologians?

Who will dare to undertake it? Science first, which asks
permission of no one to make known the laws of nature. It
crushes under its feet the most beloved errors and prejudices.
What man has this right? In this age of intellectual
emancipation and of liberty of conscience the right of
examination belongs to the entire world; and the scriptures
are no more the holy ark upon which one fears to lay a finger
in the expectation of being crushed thereby. We need not
contest the Theologians of the Middle Ages, and particularly
the Fathers of the Church, who were brilliant in regards to

special necessary knowledge. They were not, however, strong enough to condemn as heresy the movement of the Earth and belief in the antipodes; but, from all known periods of the world's formation till the present time, they have thrown the anathema at every new revelation.

Men have not been able to explain the scriptures by the exclusive aid of that knowledge which they, mixed with false or uncertain ideas, possessed concerning the laws of nature, revealed later by science. That is the reason why theologians themselves have really mistaken the sense of certain words and facts in the Gospel. Determined, at any price, to find the confirmation of a preconceived thought, they remained always in the same circle, without changing their point of view, in such manner that they saw only that which they wished to see. Wise theologians as they were, they could not comprehend facts depending upon laws of which they knew nothing.

But who could judge between the diverse and often contradictory interpretations given outside of theology? As new facts and laws are revealed, we will be enlightened in the logic and good sense and use these to distinguish utopia systems from those based in reality. Now science has revealed certain laws; Spiritism brings others to light. Collectively they are indispensable to the correct understanding of the sacred texts of all religions, - those of Confucius and Buddha equally with those of Christianity. As to theology, it cannot know how to judiciously plead an exception for the contradictions of science, since it is not always in accord with itself.

30. Spiritism, taking its starting-point at the words of Christ, as Christ has taken his from Moses, is a direct consequence of his doctrine.

To the vague ideas of the future life it adds a revelation of the existence of the invisible world which surrounds us and occupies all space; thus defining the belief, by giving it body, consistence, and a reality to the idea.

It defines the connection between the soul and the body, and raises the veil which conceals from men the mysteries of life and death.

By Spiritism man knows whence he comes, where he goes, why he is upon the Earth, why he suffers temporarily, and can see, above all, the justice of God.

He learns that souls progress unceasingly through a series of progressive existences until they shall have attained to that degree of perfection in which God only reigns.

He learns that all souls, having the same starting-point, are created equal, with the same opportunity to progress in virtue of their own free will, that all are of the same essence, and that there is between them only a difference of accomplished progress; that all have the same destiny, and will attain the same end more or less promptly according to their labor and desire to progress.

He learns that there are no disinherited ones, no lost souls, neither one more favored than another; that God has not created some favored ones who are excused from the work which is imposed upon others to facilitate their progression; that there are no creatures perpetually condemned to unhappiness and suffering; that those designated under the name of demons are spirits yet undeveloped and imperfect, who do wrong in the world of spirits as they did here upon Earth, but who will advance and improve their condition; that the angels are not beings distinct from the rest of creation, but spirits who have attained that height through the same earthly sufferings and temptations as others undergo; that thus there are not varied creations of different classes among intelligent humanity, but that all creation springs from the great law of unity which rules the universe, and that all beings gravitate towards a common end, which is perfection, without one being favored at the expense of the others, all holding the thread of their destiny in their own hands.

31. By the communications that man can now establish with those who have left the Earth, he receives not only the material proof of the existence and individuality of the soul, but he comprehends the solidarity which joins the living and the dead in this world, and those of this world with those of other worlds. He knows their situation in the world of spirits; he follows them in their migrations; he can testify of their joys and sorrows; he knows why they are happy or unhappy and the end which awaits all, according to the good or evil they accomplished. These communications introduce him to a future life, which he can observe in all its phases and conditions. The future is no more a vague hope; it is a positive fact, a mathematical certitude. Thus he has no more fear of death; it is for him a deliverance, the gate of true life.

32. By the study of the situation of the spirits, one learns that happiness or unhappiness in the spiritual life is experienced according to the degree of perfection or imperfection one has obtained; that each one suffers the direct and natural consequences of his own faults; in other words, that he is punished where he has sinned; that these consequences last as long as the cause which has produce them; that thus the culprit would suffer eternally if he persisted eternally in his fault, but that suffering ceases with repentance and reparation. Now, as our joy and sorrow are within our own grasp, each one can, by virtue of his free will, prolong or shorten his sufferings, as the sick suffers from his excesses as long as he indulges in them.

33. If reason repels, as incompatible with the goodness of God, the idea of everlasting punishment, perpetual and absolute, often inflicted for one fault alone, - the tortures of hell, which no repentance, however ardent or sincere, can lessen, - it acknowledges this distributive impartial justice which is extended to all; never shutting the door of return to goodness, and extending unceasingly the helping hand to the shipwrecked one, instead of allowing him to sink without aid into the abyss.

34. The plurality of existences, of which Christ established in the Gospel, though merely touching upon it, is one of the most important laws revealed by Spiritism, as it reveals its reality and necessity for one's progress. By this law can be explained all the apparent anomalies which human life presents, - its differences of social position; the premature deaths, which, without reincarnation, would render abridged lives useless for souls; the inequality of intellectual and moral aptitudes, owing to the antiquity of the spirit, who has lived a longer or a short time, and has become more or less learned and progressed, and who, being reborn, brings into requisition the knowledge of anterior existences. (See item n° 5)

35. With the doctrine of the creation of a soul at every birth, one falls necessarily into the belief in beings favored of God. Men are strangers to one another. Nothing unites firmly; the ties of family are purely physical. They are not solidarities of a past in which they did not exist. With the doctrine of nothingness after death or annihilation all relationships of life cease; there are no unions for the future. By reincarnation they form solidarities of the past and the future, their connection perpetuating itself in the spiritual and material world. Fraternity has for base the changeless laws of nature. Goodness has an objective existence, while there is no reversal of inevitable consequences.

36. With belief in reincarnation, the prejudices of races and castes fall dead, since the same spirit can be reborn rich or poor, lord or beggar, master or subordinate, free or enslaved, man or woman. Of all the arguments brought against the injustice of servitude and slavery, against the subjection of the weaker to the rule of the stronger, there is no one of them which expresses so logically the reason therefore as the law of reincarnation. If, then, reincarnation is founded upon a law of nature which is the source of universal brotherhood, it is based upon the same law as that of the equality of social rights and of freedom.

37. Take away from man the free, independent spirit surviving matter, and you make of him an organized machine, without will or responsibility, without other restraint than the civil law, simply an intelligent animal. Expecting nothing after death, nothing hinders him from augmenting the joys of the present. If he suffers, he has in perspective only despair and annihilation for refuge. With certainty of a future, of seeing again those whom he has offended, all his ideas change. Had

Spiritism only drawn man from the sad doubt of a future life, it would have done more for his moral improvement than all the disciplinary laws which have bridled him sometimes, but changed him never.

38. Without pre-existence of the soul, the doctrine of original sin is not only irreconcilable with the justice of God, who would render all men responsible for the fault of one, but is senseless; while the penalty cannot be justifiable, because the soul did not exist at the epoch where it is pretended its responsibility commenced. With pre-existence and reincarnation man carries into his new incarnation the germ of his past imperfections, the defects of which he has not been cured, which betray themselves in his native instincts, in his propensity for this or that vice. It is his veritable original sin, to the consequences of which he is naturally submitted, but with this capital difference: that he carries the burden of his own faults, and not that of the fault of another. This difference at one and the same time consoles, encourages, and honors sovereign equity, each separate existence offering to man the means of making reparation for sins committed, and of progress either by overcoming some imperfection, or by acquiring some fresh knowledge until he becomes sufficiently purified to have no more need of earthly experience, when he will live exclusively a glorious, eternal life of spirit.

For the same reason, he who has progressed morally upon rebirth carries his moral qualities with him just as he who had progressed intellectually carries his intelligent ideas with him. The former is identified with goodness, which he practices without effort, without calculation; that is to say, without thinking about it. While he who is obliged to combat low tendencies is always in a battle with them. The first is already conqueror, the second on the way to victory. There is, then, *original virtue, as there is original knowledge, and original sin*, or, more correctly, *imperfection*.

39. Experimental Spiritism has studied the properties of spiritual fluids, and their action upon matter. It has demonstrated the existence of a fluidic body, in which the ancients had a partial belief, designated by St. Paul under the name of "*spiritual body*;"[3] that is to say, the gaseous body of the soul, which remains after the destruction of the material body. It is known today that this envelope is inseparable from the soul; that it is one of the constituent elements of a human being; that it is the vehicle for the transmission of thought; and that during earthly life it serves as a connection between spirit and matter. This spiritual body or perispirit, plays such an important part in the organism and in a multitude of productions, that there needs to be allied to physiology and psychology.

40. The study of the properties of the perispirit, of the spiritual fluids, and of the physiological attributes of the soul, opens new horizons to science, and gives the key to a great number of unknown phenomena, the laws which rule them being until now unknown. Phenomena are denied by materialism because they are linked with Spiritism, and, because called by another name than miracles or supernatural occurrences, are ignored by those of supernatural belief. Among others are the phenomena of double sight, visions of objects at a distance, natural and artificial somnambulism, psychic effects of catalepsy and lethargy, prescience, presentiments, apparitions, transfigurations, the transmission of thought, fascination, instantaneous cures, obsessions and possessions, etc. In demonstrating that these phenomena repose upon laws as natural as the electrical, and that there exist normal conditions in which they can be reproduced, Spiritism destroys the empire of the marvelous and supernatural, and consequently the source of the greater part of superstition. If it founds a belief in the possibility of certain things regarded by some as chimerical, it precludes one from

---

[3] **Note of SAB**: "It is sown in dishonor, it is raised in glory; it is sown in weakness, it is raised in power;" "It is sown a natural body, it is raised a spiritual body. If there is a natural body, there is also a spiritual body." (1 Corinthians 15: 43, 44).

believing in others of which it has demonstrated the impossibility and irrationality.

41. Spiritism, very far from denying or destroying the Gospel, on the contrary comes to confirm, explain, and prove it. By the new laws of nature that it reveals, it throws light upon the obscure points of the teachings of Jesus, upon all that he has done and said, in such a way that those to whom certain parts of the Gospel were formerly unintelligible, or seemed *inadmissible*, comprehend them without trouble by the aid of Spiritism, accept them, and better understand their importance as they are able to separate the reality from the allegory. Christ appears to them in a grander light. He is no longer simply a philosopher: he is a divine Messiah.

42. Besides the moral power that Spiritism wields is the importance that it gives to all actions of life. It points with its finger at the consequences of goodness and wickedness; gives moral force and courage; gives consolation in afflictions by inducing unalterable confidence in the future, by the thought of having near one the beings that one has loved, the assurance of seeing them again, the possibility of speaking to them, the certainty that all one has accomplished, all one has acquired, of intelligence, science, or morality *till the last hour of life,* nothing is lost, that all yields advancement. One finds that Spiritism realizes all the promises of Christ in regard to the Consoler that he promised to send. Now, as it is the Spirit of Truth who presides over the great work of regeneration, the promise of his coming is thus accomplished as he is, in fact, the true *Consoler.*[4]

---

[4] Many fathers of families deplore the premature death of children on account of the education for which they have made great sacrifices, and say that it is totally lost. With a belief in Spiritism, they do not regret these sacrifices, and would be ready to make them, even with the certainty of seeing their children die; for they know that, if the latter do not receive the benefits of such education in the present life, it will serve, first, to advance them as spirits, then as so much of intellectual property for a new existence, so that when they shall return they will

43. If to these facts one adds the unheard of rapidity of the propagation of Spiritism, notwithstanding all which has been done to combat it, one cannot deny that its coming is providential, since it triumphs over all the forces of allied human antagonism. The facility with which it is accepted by such a large number of persons, and that without constraint, without other pressure than the power of the idea, proves that it responds to a need, - that of believing in something after the belief in nothing, which skepticism caused; and consequently it has come at the right time.

44. Afflictions are many in number. It is not then surprising that so many men accept a doctrine which comforts them in preference to one which gives no reasonable hope of a future; for it is to the unhappy more than to the happy of Earth that Spiritism addresses itself particularly. The sick person welcomes a physician with more joy then he who is well. Now, the afflicted are the sick patients, and the Consoler is the physician.

You who combat Spiritism, if you desire that one leaves it to follow you, give something more than it supplies, and something better; cure soul's wounds more surely; give more consolation, more satisfaction to the heart, more legitimate hopes, greater certitudes; paint for the future a more attractive picture, more rational; but think not to gain your end, you with the perspective of annihilation, you with the alternative of the flames of hell, or useless, sanctimonious, perpetual contemplation!

---

have intellectual capital which will render them more apt in gaining new knowledge. Examples of this are those children who are born with innate ideas, who know, as one might say, without the trouble of learning. If, as fathers, they have not the immediate satisfaction of seeing their children put this education to profit, they will enjoy it certainly later, be it as a spirit or earthly beings. Perhaps they can be again the parents of the same children that they call happily endowed by nature, and who owe their aptitude to a former education; as also, if some children do wrong on account of the negligence of their parents, the latter may have to suffer later by troubles and grieves which will be caused by them in a new existence. (*"The Gospel According to Spiritism,"* chap. 5, n° 21: Premature Deaths.)

45. The first revelation was personified in Moses, the second in Christ, the third in no one individual. The two first are individuals; the third is collective, which is an essential character of great importance. It is collective in the sense that it has been made in favor of no one person: consequently, no one can be called the prophet of it. It has been given simultaneously in all parts of the Earth to millions of persons, of all ages, of all faiths, of all conditions, from the lowest to the highest according to the prediction given by the author of the Acts of the Apostles: "In the last days, God says, I will pour out my Spirit on all people. Your sons and daughters will prophesy, your young men will see visions, your old men will dream dreams. Even on my servants, both men and women, I will pour out my Spirit in those days, and they will prophesy." (Acts, Chap. II, v. 17, 18) It has not sprung from any one special civilization, but serves as a rallying point for all.[5]

46. The two former revelations, being the product of a personal teaching, have been forcibly localized; that is to say, they have taken place in the locality from which knowledge has extended gradually; but centuries were necessary in order for it to reach the extremities of the globe, and even then without encompassing it altogether. The third has the peculiarity, that, not being personified in one individual, it is rained down simultaneously upon thousands of different points, which have become centers or focuses of radiation.

---

[5] Our special role in the grand movement of ideas which is produced by Spiritism, and which is already operating, is that of an attentive observer who studies facts to seek their cause, and to draw from them definite results. We have confronted all those whom we could possibly gather around us; we have compared and commented upon instructions given by the spirits from all parts of the globe; then we have arranged the whole methodically. In a word, we have studied, and given to the public the fruit of our researches, without attributing to our labors other value than of a philosophical work deduced from observation and experience, never desiring to put ourselves in the place of a chief of doctrine, or desiring to thrust our ideas upon any one. In publishing them, we have used a common right, and those who have accepted

These centers multiplying themselves, their rays meet again little by little, like circles formed by a multitude of stones thrown into the water, in such a manner that in a given time they will have covered the entire surface of the globe.

Such is one of the causes of the rapid propagation of the doctrine. If it had surged upon a single point, if it had been the exclusive work of one man, it would have formed a sect around him; but a half century might have passed before it have passed the limits of the country where it would have taken root, while Spiritism, after a period of ten years, had planted its beacon-lights from pole to pole.

47. This unheard of circumstances in the history of teachings gives to it exceptional force, and an irresistible power of action. Indeed, if anything checks it at one point in one country, it is literally impossible to curb it in all points in all countries. For one place where it will be disregarded, there will be a thousand where it will flourish. As no one can reach it in an individual, one cannot attain to the spirits who are the source of it. Now, as spirits are everywhere, it is impossible that they could be made to disappear from the globe. They are always appearing; and the belief in them reposes *upon a fact in nature*, and one cannot suppress a law of nature. This fact alone should convince those who are not quite persuaded to become believers ("*Revue Spirite*," February, 1865, p. 38: "*Perpetuity of Spiritism*").

48. However, these different centers might have remained for a long time isolated from one another, situated as are some in far distant countries. A connection was necessary between them, which should place them in

---

them have done so freely. If these ideas have found numerous sympathizers, it is that they have had the advantage of responding to the aspirations of a great number; of this we are not vain, as their origin belongs not to us. Our greatest merit is that of perseverance and devotion to the cause we have espoused. We have only done that which others also can do. That is why we have made no pretension of being a prophet or Messiah, and do not believe ourselves such.

communion with their brothers in belief by teaching them that which was done elsewhere. This union of thought, which would have been impossible to the Spiritism of antiquity, is accomplished by the numerous publications which are now found everywhere; which condense, under a unique, concise, and methodical form, the teaching given everywhere through multiplied methods of expression, and in diverse languages.

49. The two first revelations could have only been the result of a direct teaching; they were imposed on the mind by the authority of the word of the Master, men being too undeveloped to join in the work of their elaboration.

Let us remark at the same time a very sensible shade of resemblance between them, important to the progress of morals and ideas; it is that they were given to the same people in the same locality, but at in interval of nearly eighteen hundred years. The doctrine of Moses is absolute, despotic; it admits no discussion, but imposes itself upon all people by force. That of Jesus is essentially that of counsel and advice; it is freely accepted, and gains its advocates by persuasion; it is discussed by the living person of its founder, who disdains not to argue with its adversaries.

50. The third revelation comes at an epoch of emancipation and of intellectual maturity, where developed intelligence cannot agree to play a passive role; where man accepts nothing blindly, but wishes to see where one conducts him; to know the why and the how of everything. It claims to be at the same time the product of a teaching, and the fruit of labor, of research, and of free examination. *Spirits teach us only that which is necessary to put us in the way of truth; but they abstain from revealing to man that which he can discover by himself,* leaving to him the care of discussing, controlling, and submitting all to the crucible of reason, leaving him often to learn the lesson at his own expense. It gives to him the principal, the materials from which to draw the interest and to put it in use. (See item n°13).

51. The elements of spiritual revelation having been given simultaneously at a multitude of points to men of all social conditions and of different degrees of knowledge, it is very evident that observations could not have been made everywhere with the same effect; that the sequences drawn from them, the relation of the laws which govern this order of phenomena, - in a word, the conclusion which ought to establish ideas, - could proceed only from the harmony and correlation of facts. Now, every isolated center, circumscribed in a limited circle, seeing most often only a particular order of manifestations, sometimes in appearance contradictory, having communications generally with the same category of spirits, and, moreover, blocked by the local influences and by the spirit of party, finds it materially impossible to embrace the whole, powerless to join isolated observations to a common principle. Each one judging facts according to his knowledge and his anterior beliefs, or by the particular opinions of the spirits manifesting, there would soon be as many theories and systems as centers, of which no one would be complete, in default of elements of comparison and of control. In a word, each one would remain content with his partial revelation, believing it to include all the truth, for want of knowledge that in a hundred other places one could obtain more or better.

52. It is well to observe further, that nowhere has spiritual teaching been given in a complete manner. It touches upon so great a number of observations, upon subjects so diverse, requiring knowledge and special mediumistic aptitudes, that it is simply impossible to unite at the same point all the necessary conditions. Teaching having become collective, and not individual, the spirits have divided the labor by disseminating the subjects of study and observation, as in certain factories different parts of the object manufactured are divided among different workman.

Revelation is thus partially given in diverse places, and by a multitude of intermediaries; and it is in this manner still to be followed up, for all is not revealed. Every center finds in the other centers the complement of that which obtains, and it is only the joining together of all the instructions which can constitute the doctrine of Spiritism.

It is, moreover, necessary to group the facts gleaned, in order to see their corresponding similarity, to gather the different documents, instructions given by spirits upon all points and all subjects, in order to compare them and analyze them by studying their analogy and difference. Communications being given by spirits of all orders more or less clearly, it is necessary to learn the degree of confidence reason would accord to them; to distinguish the systematic, individual, and isolated ideas from those which had the sanction of the general teaching of the spirits; to separate the utopian from the practical; to cut away those which were notoriously contradictory, judged by positive science and healthy logic; to utilize the errors even the information given by spirits of the lowest sphere, for a knowledge of the invisible world; and to form of it a homogeneous whole. In a word, a center of elaboration is necessary, independent of all preconceived ideas, of all prejudice of sect, *resolved to accept a self-evident truth*, though it be contrary to one's personal opinion. This center forms itself by the force of things, and *without premeditated design.*[6]

---

[6] The first work which took a philosophical view of the doctrine was *"The Spirits' Book."* It deduced moral sequences from facts, which had approached all parts of the belief, in touching upon the most important question that it raised, has been since its appearance, the rallying-point towards which the individual works have spontaneously converged. It is worthy of note that from the publication of this book dates the era of the Spiritist philosophy, previously coming under the head of curiosities of experience. If this book (*"The Spirits' Book"*) has gained the sympathies of the majority, it is because it was the expression of the sentiments of this same majority, and that it responded to its aspirations. It is also because each one found there the confirmation, and a rational explanation of that which he in particular obtained. If it had disagreed with the general teachings of the spirits, it would have received no favor, and would have promptly fallen into oblivion. Now, around whom is one to rally? It is not man, who is nothing by himself, only a master-workman, who dies and disappears, but around an idea which perishes not when it emanates from a source superior to man.

53. From this state of things rises a double current of ideas; some going from the extremity to the center, others returning from the center to the circumference. It is thus that the doctrine has promptly marched towards unity, notwithstanding the diversity of sources from which it has emanated; that the divergent systems have little by little fallen, on account of their isolation, and failure to obtain the sympathy of the majority. A communion of thought is now established between different centers. Speaking the same spiritual language, they comprehend and sympathize with one another from one end of the world to the other.

The spiritists have been found to be stronger; they have battled with more courage; they have marched with a more assured step, now that they are no more alone, and have found a support, a link which attaches them to the great family. The phenomena of which they were witnesses are no longer strange, abnormal, contradictory, since they are found to agree with the general laws of harmony; since, glancing at it as a whole, they see the grand humanitarian *object*.[7]

This spontaneous concentration of scattered forces has given place to an immense connection, a unique monument to the world, a living picture of the true history of modern Spiritism; reflecting, at the same time, partial works, the multiplication of sentiments which has developed the doctrine, the moral results, the devotion and the weakness, - precious archives for posterity, who will be able to judge men and things by authentic documents. In the presence of these unexceptional testimonies, what will become in the time of all false allegations, defamations of envy and jealousy?

[7] A significant testimony, as remarkable as touching, of this communion of thought which is established between spiritists by conformity of belief, are the prayerful demands which come to us from far-distant lands, from Peru to the extremities of Asia, from persons of diverse nationalities and religions, whom we have never seen. Is it not the prelude of the establishment of the one great church which is preparing itself, the proof of the firm stand Spiritism is taking everywhere?
It is remarkable that of all the societies formed with premeditated intention of withdrawal by proclaiming divergent principles, - as those

But how is one to know if a principle is taught everywhere, or if it is the result of an individual opinion only? Isolated societies not having the knowledge of that which was said elsewhere, it was necessary that a central one should gather all the information, ascertain the opinion of the majority, and send the knowledge to all.[8]

54. There is no science which has in all its parts proceeded from the brain of one man. All, without exception, are the product of successive observations, leaning upon preceding ones, as upon a known point, in order to arrive at an unknown one. It is thus that the spirits have proceeded with Spiritism. That is why their teaching is gradual. They approach questions only in proportion and in measure, as the principles upon which they ought to lean are sufficiently elaborated, and as opinion is prepared to assimilate them. It is

---

who, by reason of self-love or otherwise, wishing not to have the appearance of sustaining the common law, have believed themselves strong enough to go alone, to have enough light to pass as consoler, - not one has succeeded in establishing a long-lived or popular idea; all have died out or vegetated in the shade. How could it be otherwise, since, in order to distinguish themselves, instead of endeavoring to give the greatest amount of benefit to the world, they rejected those principles of the doctrine which give to it the most powerful attraction, those which are the most consoling, encouraging, and rational? If they had comprehended the power of the moral elements which alone induce unity, they would not have been rocked in a chimerical illusion; but, mistaken their little circle for the universe, they have seen in the adherents only a society which could easily be overthrown by one entertaining contrary opinion. They strangely misapprehended the essential character of the doctrine, and this error could lead only to deception. In place of destroying unity, they destroyed the connection which could give them strength and life. (See *"Revue Spirite,"* April, 1866, pp.106 and 111: Spiritism without Spirits; Independent Spiritism.)

[8] Such is the object of our publications, which can be considered as the result of this. All opinions are discussed there; but the questions are arranged as principles only after having received the sanction of the controls, who alone can give them lawful strength and affirmation.

remarkable that, each time particular centers have wished to approach premature questions, they have obtained only contradictory responses, and never conclusive ones. When, however, the favorable moment arrives, the instruction is given universally at nearly the same moment of time.

There is, at the same time, between the march of Spiritism and that of the sciences, a capital difference. It is that the latter have attained their present advancement only after long intervals of time, whilst only a few years have sufficed for Spiritism, not to gain the culminating point, but at least to gather a sum of facts to constitute a doctrine. That is obtained by innumerable manifestations of spirits, who, by the will of God, manifest simultaneously; each one bringing the contingent of their knowledge. The result is, that all parts of the doctrine, instead of being successively elaborated during many centuries, have been concocted almost simultaneously in a few years, and that this has sufficed to group them in order to form a whole.

God has willed it thus, firstly, in order that the edifice should progress more rapidly; secondly, in order that it should have a permanent and immediate control in the universality of the teaching, each part having value as well as *authority* only by its connection with the whole; all becoming harmonious, finding their place in the general edifice, and each one arriving in due time.

In confiding, not to one spirit alone, the care of the promulgation of the doctrine, God has willed that the lowest, as well as the highest among the spirits, as well as among men, should carry each his stone to the edifice, in order to establish between them a structure of cooperative solidarity, which has failed to all doctrines springing from one source alone.

That is why we do not accept, without due thought, any one theory; therefore the doctrine proceeding from general instructions is not the product of a preconceived system. It is largely this fact which gives it strength, and assures its future.

On the other hand, every spirit, the same as every man, having only a limited sum of knowledge, they were incapable of treating ex-professo the innumerous questions which Spiritism touches. That is why the doctrine, in order to fulfill the desires of the Creator, could not be the work of one spirit alone, nor of one medium. It could proceed only from the united work of the many, - the one controlled by the other.[9]

55. A later character in the spiritual revelation, which is drawn from the conditions in which it is produced, is that, leaning upon facts, it is, and ever must be, essentially progressive, like all sciences based upon observation. In its essence it is allied to science, which, being a revelation of the laws of nature by a certain order of facts cannot be contrary to the will of God, the author of these laws. *The discoveries of science glorify, instead of demeaning God. They destroy only that which men have built upon the false ideas they have formed of God.*

Spiritism is based then only upon absolute principle, - that which is demonstrated by proof, or that which results logically from observation. Touching all the branches of social economy, to which it lends the aid of its own discoveries, it will assimilate itself always with all progressive doctrines, of whatever order they may be. It has arrived at a state *of practical truth*, and discarded the utopian ideas which would have destroyed it. In ceasing to be that which it is, it would deceive in regard to its origin and its providential object. *Spiritism, marching hand in hand with progress, will never be overthrown, because, if new discoveries should demonstrate that it is in error upon a point, it would modify itself in regard to it. If a new truth is revealed, it accepts it.*[10]

---

[9] See in *"The Gospel According to Spiritism,"* Introduction, item 6, and "Revue Spirite," April, 1864, p. 90: Authority of the Spiritual Doctrine; Universal Control of the Teaching of the Spirits.

[10] In face of so clear and categorical declarations as those herein present in this chapter, all allegations of tendencies to absolutism and autocracy of the principles fall down, as well as all the false assimilations that

56. What is the utility of the moral doctrine of the spirits, since it is no other than that of Christ? Has man need of a revelation? And can he find all that within himself which is necessary to guide him?

God has without doubt given to man a guide in his conscience, which says to him, "So in everything, do to others what you would have them do to you." This moral philosophy is certainly inscribed in the heart of man; but do all know how to read it there? Have men never misconstrued these wise precepts? What have they done with the ethics of Christ? Do those who teach them practice them? Have they not become a dead letter, a beautiful theory, and good for others but not for one's self? Would you reproach a father for repeating a hundred times the same instructions to his children if they did not profit by them? Why should God do less than a father of a family? Why should he not send from time to time special messengers to men, charged with recalling them to their duties, and with reinstating them in that "narrow path" from which they have wandered, with opening the eyes of those who are blind to wisdom, as the most advanced men are sent as missionaries to the savage and barbarous?

The spirits teach no other morality than that of Christ, for the reason that there is no better. But, then, of what good is this instruction, since it teaches that which we know? One could say the same of the ethical teachings of Christ, which were taught five hundred years before he lived by Socrates and Plato in almost identical words; also by all moralists who repeat the same thing under many forms and words. *The spirits come simply to augment the number of moralists*, with the difference, that, manifesting themselves everywhere, they are heard in the hut as well as in the palace by the ignorant as well as the learned.

---

some forewarned or not well informed people lend to the doctrine. These declarations, however, are not new; we have been repeating them many times in our writings, so that no doubt persists in respect to them. Moreover, they mark the true role that fits us, the only one we desire: of being a simple worker.

That which the teaching of the spirits adds to that of Christ is the knowledge of the laws which bind the living to the dead, which complete the vague ideas which he gave of the soul, its past and future, and which the laws of nature give as sanction to his doctrine. By the aid of the new lights carried by Spiritism and the spirits, man comprehends the solidarity which binds all beings together. Charity and fraternity become social necessities. Man does from conviction that which he did only for duty's sake; and this is better when men will practice the moral teachings of Christ.

Then alone will they be able to say that they have no more need of incarnate or discarnate moralists; then God will send them no more of them.

57. The latter is one of the most important questions which is based upon the title of this chapter: what is the authority of the spiritist revelation, since it emanates from beings whose light is limited, and who are not infallible?

The objection would be serious if this revelation consisted only of the spirit instructions, - if we should hold it as from them exclusively, and accept it with closed eyes. It is without value until man carries to it the cooperation of his knowledge and judgment, as the spirits are constrained from putting it in the way of deductions which he can draw from observation of facts. Now, the manifestations in their innumerable variety are facts. Man studies them, and seeks in them the law. He is aided in this work by spirits of all orders, who are *collaborators* rather than revealers in the usual sense of the word. He submits their sayings to the control of logic and good sense. In this way he benefits by some special knowledge which is derived from their position, without abdicating the use of his own reason.

The spirits being none other than the souls of men, in communicating with them *we do not go away from humanity*, which is a capital circumstance to consider. Men of genius who have been the beacon-lights of humanity have come to us from the spirit world, as they have re-entered it on quitting the Earth. Since spirits can communicate with men, these same geniuses can give us instructions under a spiritual form, as they have done in a corporal one. They can instruct us after death, as they did in life. They are invisible, instead of visible, which is all the difference. Their experience and knowledge ought not to be less; and if their word, like that of man's, had authority, it ought not to have less because that they are in the land of spirits.

58. But there are not only superior spirits which manifest: there are also those of all orders. This is necessary in order to initiate us into the true character of the spiritual world, by showing it to us in all its phases. By this means the relations between the visible and invisible world are more intimate, the connection is more evident. We see more clearly whence we came, and where we go. Such is the essential object of these manifestations. All spirits, in whatever degree to which they may attain, teach us something; but, as they are more or less enlightened, it is left to us to determine whether they are good or evil, and to profit by their teaching as it permits. Now all, whomsoever they may be, can teach and reveal to us facts of which we are ignorant, and which but for them we should never know.

59. Wise, incarnated spirits are powerful individualities, - indisputably so; but their action is restrained and necessarily slow in propagating itself. Allowing that one among them should come alone, - be it even Elias, Moses, Socrates, or Plato, - to reveal to us in these latter days the state of the spiritual world, which one among them would have proved the truth of his assertions in this time of skepticism? Would not men have regarded him as a dreamer or utopist? And, admitting that his teachings were accepted as the absolute truth, centuries would pass away before they would be accepted by the masses. God in his wisdom has not obtained it thus; he has willed that the instruction be given by the *spirits themselves*, and not by the incarnates, in order to convince men of their existence, and that it might take place simultaneously over all the Earth, which may have been to propagate it the more rapidly, or that we might find in the coincidence of the teaching a proof of its truth, each one having thus the means of convincing himself.

60. The spirits come not to free man from work, study, or research; they bring no ready-made science; they leave him to his own strength in that which he can discover for himself. The spirits know perfectly well today that for a long time experience has demonstrated the error of the opinion which attributed to spirits the possession of all knowledge and wisdom, and that it was sufficient to address one's self to the first spirit which came; in order to know all things. After leaving the Earth, spirits occupy one out of many spiritual planes, as upon Earth there are superior and vulgar persons. Many spirits then know scientifically and philosophically less than certain men; they tell no more, and often less, than they know. As among men, the most advanced can teach us more, and give us more judicious advice, than those less advanced. *To demand counsel of spirits is not to address supernatural powers, but persons like ourselves, - those to whom we would turn for counsel in their earthly life, as parents, friends, and individuals more enlightened than ourselves.* Here is an important fact for those who are ignorant of Spiritism, and have formed a false idea of the nature of the world of spirits and of the condition of affairs beyond the tomb.

61. What is then the utility of these manifestations, or, as we may say, this revelation, if the spirits know no more than ourselves, or if they do not tell us all they know?

Firstly, as we have said, they abstain from giving us that which we can acquire through labor. Secondly, there are facts which they are not permitted to reveal, because we are not sufficiently advanced to receive them. But, aside from this, the conditions of their new existence extend the circle of their perceptions. They see that which they saw not upon Earth, freed from the trammels of matter. Delivered from the cares of the corporeal life, they judge things from a more elevated point, from a healthier one; their perspicuity embraces a broader horizon; they perceive their errors, and rid themselves of human prejudices.

It is in this that the superiority of spirits over incarnates consists; therefore their counsel will be, according to their degree of advancement, more judicious and disinterested than that of the incarnates. Conditions are found by which they can instruct us in principles of which we are ignorant. Until now men had created only suppositions in regard to the future. That is why beliefs upon this point have been divided into systems so numerous and so divergent, - from a belief in nothing to fantastic ideas of hellfire and paradise. Today we have ocular demonstration; the actors themselves from the life beyond the tomb, who alone can give us knowledge of it, come to tell us what it is. These manifestations serve, then, to give us knowledge of the invisible world which surrounds us, of which, without them, we should not be aware of the existence. This knowledge alone should be considered of the highest importance, even supposing that the spirits were incapable of teaching us anything more.

If you should go into a strange country by yourself, would you reject the teachings of the most humble peasant whom you chanced to encounter? Would you refuse to interrogate him about the state of the land because he was only a peasant? You would not expect from him, certainly, intelligence of a very high character; but such as it is, and in his sphere, he will be able, upon certain points, to give you better than a wise man who does not know the country. You will draw from his indications sequences which you could not do of yourself. He will have been at least a useful instrument for your observations, had he served only to make known to you the customs of the peasants. It is the same in connection with the spirits, where the lowest can teach us something.

62. A common incident will explain the matter better.

A ship loaded with emigrants departs for a far-distant locality. It carries men of all conditions, the relatives and friends of whom remain at home. One learns that the ship has been wrecked. No trace remains of it; no news is obtained in regard to its fate. It is thought that all passengers have perished; and mourning is in all the families. However, the entire company, without the loss of a single soul, has landed upon an unknown soil, which is abundant and fertile, where all live happily under favoring skies; but their friends are ignorant of their fate. Now, one happy day another ship reaches their shore; it finds all the shipwrecked ones safe and well. The happy news spreads with lightning-like rapidity. Each one says, "Our friends are not lost;" and they give thanks to God. They cannot see each other; but they correspond, exchange testimonies of affection, and joy succeed to sadness.

Such is terrestrial life and life beyond the grave before and after modern revelation. The latter, like the second ship, carries to us the good news of the survival of those who are dear to us, and the certitude of one day rejoining them. Doubt in regard to their fate and our own exists no more; discouragement is effaced by hope.

But other results are added to enrich this revelation. God, judging humanity mature enough to penetrate the mystery of its destiny and to contemplate with composure new marvels, has permitted the veil between the known and the unknown worlds to be raised. The fact of the manifestations has nothing supernatural about it: *it is the spiritual humanity that comes to talk to humanity in the flesh, and to say to it:*

"We exist; nothingness exists not. Behold that which we are, and that which you will be; the future is the same for you as to us. You walk in darkness; we come to throw light upon your way, and to prepare it before you. Terrestrial life was all you could comprehend, because you saw nothing beyond. We come to say to you, in showing the spiritual life to you, the earthly life is as nothing. Your sight was arrested at the tomb; we come to show you the splendid horizon beyond it. You knew not why you suffer upon Earth; now, in suffering you see the justice of God. Goodness was unfruitful for the future; it will have henceforth an object, and will be a necessity. Fraternity was only a beautiful theory; it is now firmly established as a law of nature. Under the empire of the belief that death ends all, immensity is void, egotism reigns master among you, and your watchword is, "Each one for himself." With certitude of the future, infinite space is peopled with infinitude. Emptiness and solitude do not exist; solidarity joins all beings both this side and beyond the tomb together. It is the reign of charity with the device, "One for all and all for one." Instead of bidding an eternal farewell to dear friends at the close of life, you will now say, "Good bye till I see you again."

Such are the results of the law of the new revelation. It has come to fill the void which incredulity has deepened, to revive hope where it is withering into doubt and a perspective of annihilation, to give to everything a reason for existing. Is this result, then, without importance because the spirits come not to solve scientific problems, and to give to the indolent the means of enriching themselves without trouble? However, the fruits which man ought to gather from it are not only those for a future life; he will extract good from the transformation that these new beliefs ought to work in his character, his tastes, his tendencies, and, in pursuance of which, upon his habits and social relations. In putting an end to selfishness, pride, and incredulity, the way is paved for the blessing, which is the reign of God announced by the Christ.[11]

---

[11] The use of the article before the word Christ (originating from the Greek Christos, anointed), employed in the absolute sense is more correct, as this word is not the name of the Messiah of Nazareth, but a quality considered substantial. One would then say: Jesus was Christ; he was the Christ announced. The death of the Christ, and not of Christ. Conversely, one can say: the death of Jesus and not of the Jesus. Together the two words Jesus Christ form one single noun. For this same reason one can say: The Buda Gautama acquired the dignity of Buda due to his virtues and his austerities; the life of the Buda. Just as one can say: army of the Pharaoh, and not of Pharaoh; Henry IV was king, the title of king; the death of the king, and not of king.

Chapter II
GOD

Existence of God – The Divine Nature – Providence – The View of God

EXISTENCE OF GOD

1. God being the first cause of all things, the starting point of all, the pivot upon which the edifice of creation reposes, is the subject to be considered before any other.

2. It is by elementary principle that one judges a cause by its effect, when one sees not the cause.

If a bird cleaving the air receives a deadly shot, one judges that a ball, sent by a skilful hand, struck it, although one may not have seen the marksman. Is it then always necessary to have seen a thing before knowing that it exists? In everything it is by observing effects that we arrive at the knowledge of causes.

3. Another principle, also elementary, and passed into an axiom by force of truth, is that all intelligent effect must have an intelligent cause.

If one inquired who was the inventor of such an ingenious piece of mechanism, the architect of such a monument, the sculptor of such a statue, or the painter of such a picture, what would one think of him who should reply that it was done without the help of anyone? When one sees a superior work of art or of industry, they say that that is probably the work of a man of genius, because it is evident that a high intelligence has presided at its conception. One judges, nevertheless, that a man has done it, because one knows that it is not above human capacity; but no one will say that it proceeded from the brain of an idiot or of an ignorant, and still less that it is the work of an animal, or the product of chance.

4. Everywhere one recognizes the presence of man by his works. The existence of the pre-diluvium man is proved not only by human fossils, but also, with as much certitude, by the presence in the soil of this epoch, of utensils made by man. A fragment of a vase, a carved stone, a weapon, a brick, will suffice to attest their presence. By the rudeness or by the perfection of the work one will recognize the degree of intelligence or of advancement of those who have accomplished it. If, then, finding yourself in a country inhabited exclusively by barbarians or savages, you should discover a statue worth of Phidias, you would not hesitate to say, that, savages being incapable of having made it, it must be the work of an intelligence superior to theirs.

5. In looking around one's self upon the works of nature, observing the foresight, the wisdom, the harmony, which preside in all things, one recognizes that there is a power superior to the highest flights of human intelligence, since the greatest genius of the Earth would not know how to create a blade of grass. Since human intelligence cannot produce them, it proves that they are the product of an intelligence superior to that of humanity, unless we say that effects are without cause.

6. To this some oppose the following argument:

Works said to be produced by nature are the product of material forces, which are agitated mechanically by following the laws of attraction and repulsion. Particles of inert bodies are aggregated and disintegrated by the power of these laws. Plants are born, sprout, grow, and multiply always in the same manner, each one of its kind, by virtue of these same laws; each subject being like that from which it sprung. The growth, florescence, fructification, and coloring are subordinate to some material cause, such as heat, electricity, light, humidity, etc. It is the same with animals. Even stars are formed by attraction of particles, and move perpetually in their orbits by the effect of gravitation. This mechanical regularity in the employ of natural forces does not imply a free intelligence. Man moves his arms when he desires and as he desires, but he who would move them in the same manner from his birth to his death would be an automaton. Now, the organic forces of nature, considered as a whole, are, in some respects, automatic.

All that is true; but, these forces are effects which must have a cause, and no one has pretended that they constitute the divinity. They are material and mechanical; they are not intelligent of themselves, we all know, but they are set at work, distributed, and appropriated to the needs of everything by an intelligence, which is not that of man. The useful appropriation of these forces is an intelligent effect, which denotes an intelligent cause. A clock moves with an automatic regularity, and it is this regularity which constitutes its merit. The force which makes it act is material and not intelligent; but what would this clock be if an intelligence had not combined, calculated, and distributed the employment of this force in order to make it move with precision? Because we cannot see intelligence, and because it is not in the mechanism of the clock, is it rational to conclude that it does not exist? One judges it by its effects.

The existence of the clock attests the existence of the clockmaker; the ingenuity of its mechanism is a proof of the intelligence and knowledge of its maker. When ones sees one of these complicated clocks which mark the hour in order to give you the knowledge of which you have need, has it ever occurred to anyone to say, "There is a very intelligent clock?"

Thus, it is in the mechanism of the universe: *God does not show himself, but he makes affirmation of himself in his works.*

7. The existence of God is then an acquired fact, not only by revelation, but by the material evidence of facts. The most barbarian people had not had a revelation; yet they instinctively believe in a superhuman power. The savages themselves, do not escape logical consequences; they see things which are beyond human power, and they conclude that they are produced by a being superior to humanity. Are they not more rational than those who presume that such things were created by themselves?

THE DIVINE NATURE

8. It has not been permitted to man to sound the inmost nature of God. *We still lack the inner knowledge of our own sense of being, which can only be acquired by means of a complete purification of the Spirit; only then will we be able to comprehend God.* But if we cannot penetrate his essence, his existence being given as premise, we can, by the power of reason, arrive at the knowledge of his necessary attributes; for, in seeing that which he cannot be without ceasing to be God, we judge that what he must be. Without the knowledge of the attributes of God, it would be impossible to comprehend the work of creation. It is the starting point of all religious beliefs; and the fault of most religions is that they have made their dogmas the beacon-light to direct them. Those which have not attributed to God all power have made many gods; those which have not endowed him with sovereign goodness have made of him a jealous, angry, partial, and vindictive God.

9. *God is supreme and sovereign intelligence.* The intelligence of man is limited, since it can neither make nor comprehend all that exists; that of God, embracing infinity, must be infinite. If we supposed it to be limited to a certain point, then it would be possible to conceive a being still more intelligent, capable of comprehending and doing that which the other was not able to do. This search would continue indefinitely.

10. *God is eternal*: that is to say, he has had no beginning, and he will have no end. If he had had a commencement, he must have sprung from nothingness. Now, nothingness being nothing, can produce nothing; or, if he could have been created by another being anterior to himself, then this other being would be God. If one could suppose of him a commencement or an end, one would then be able to conceive a being having existed before him, or being able to exist after him, and thus one after the other even to infinitude.

11. *God is unchangeable.* If he were subject to change, the laws which govern the universe would not have any stability.

12. *God is immaterial*; that is to say, his nature differs from all that which we call matter: otherwise he could not be immutable, for he would be subject to the transformations of matter.

God has not a form appreciable to our senses: if he had, he would be matter. We say, the hand of God, the eye of God, the mouth of God, because men knowing him only by themselves, takes themselves as a term of comparison of all that which they comprehend not. Pictures representing God as an old man with a long beard, covered with a mantle, are ridiculous: they have the disadvantage of lowering the Supreme Being to the level of poor humanity. It is but one step from that to endow him with the passions of humanity, and to make of him a jealous and angry God.

13. *God is all-powerful.* If he had not supreme power, one could conceive of a being more powerful; thus from one to another, till one could find a being that no other could surpass in power, and it is the latter who would be God.

14. *God is sovereignly just and good.* Providential wisdom in divine laws is revealed in small as well as in great things, and this wisdom gives no room to doubt either his justice or his kindness.

The infinitude of a quality excludes the possibility of a contrary one which would lessen or annul it. A being infinitely good could not have the smallest particle of wickedness; a being infinitely bad could not have the smallest particle of goodness, - just as an object could not be absolutely black with the faintest shade of white, neither one absolutely white with the slightest spot of black.

God would not then be both good and bad; for possessing neither one nor the other of these qualities in a supreme degree, he would not be God. All things would be submitted to caprice, and he would have stability in nothing. It is then only possible to be infinitely good or infinitely bad. If he were infinitely bad, he would do nothing good. Now, as his works testify of his wisdom, of his goodness, and of his solicitude for us, it is necessary to conclude that being unable to be at the same time good and bad without ceasing to be God, he must be infinitely good.

Sovereign kindness and goodness imply sovereign justice; for if he acted unjustly or with partiality in one instance, or in respect to any one of his creatures, he would not be sovereignly just, and consequently not perfectly good.

15. *God is infinitely perfect.* It is impossible to conceive of a God without an infinitude of perfections, without which he could not be God; for one would always be able to think of a being possessing that which was wanting in him. In order that no one being surpass him, it is necessary that he be infinite in all.

The attributes of God being infinite, are neither susceptible of augmentation nor of diminution. Without that they would not be infinite, and God would not be perfect. If one could take away the least part of one of his attributes, he would no longer be God, since it would be possible for a more perfect being to exist.

16. *God is unique.* The unity of God is the result of absolute infinitude of perfection. Another God could not exist except upon one condition, that of being equally infinite in all things; for, if there were between them the slightest difference, the one would be inferior to the other, subordinate to his power, and would not be God. If there were between them absolute equality, there would be for all eternity one same thought, one wish, one power; thus confounding their identity, and there would be in reality only one God. If each one had special attributes, the one would do that which the other would not, and then there would not be between them perfect equality, since neither one nor the other would have sovereign authority.

17. It is ignorance of the principle of infinite perfection of God which has engendered polytheism, the worship of all people in early times. They attribute divinity to all power which seemed to them above humanity. Later, reason led them to join these diverse powers in one alone; then, as men have gradually comprehended the essence of the divine attributes, they have taken away from their creeds the beliefs which denied them.

18. After all, God cannot be God except on condition of not being surpassed in anything by another being; for them the being who should surpass him in whatever it might be, were it only by a hair's breadth, and would be the true God; for it is necessary that God be infinite in all things.

It is thus that the existence of God being proved by his works, one arrives, by a simple logical deduction, to determine the attributes which characterize him.

19. God is then *the Supreme and Sovereign Intelligence. He is unique, eternal, immutable, immaterial, all-powerful, sovereignly just and good, infinite in all his perfection,* like no other.

Such is the base upon which the universal edifice reposes. It is the beacon-light whose rays illuminate the entire universe, and which alone can guide man in the search for truth. In following it he will never go astray; and, if he is often led astray, it is for want of having followed the route which was indicated to him.

Such is the *infallible* criterion of all philosophical and religious doctrines. Man has a rigorously exact measure in the attributes of God with which to judge him; and he can say with certitude that *all theory, all principle, all dogma, all beliefs, all practices which are in contradiction with anyone of these attributes, which should tend not necessarily to annul it, but simply to weaken it, cannot be of the truth.*

In philosophy, in psychology, in ethics, in religion, there is no truth in that which departs one iota from the essential qualities of divinity. Perfect religion must be that of which *no article of faith* is in opposition with these qualities; all the dogmas must sustain the proof of this control without conflicting with it in any particular.

.

PROVIDENCE

20. Providence is the solicitude of God for all his creatures. God is everywhere. He sees all, he presides over all, even to the smallest thing; in this, providential action consists.

"How can God, so grand, so powerful, so superior to all, interfere with the pettiest details, occupy himself with the most trifling thoughts and actions of each individual? Such is the question upon which unbelief alights, from which it concludes, that, in admitting the existence of God, his action should extend only to the general laws of the universe; that the universe operates to all eternity by virtue of these laws, to which every creature is subject in his sphere of activity without a need for the incessant cooperation of Providence."

21. In their actual state of inferiority men can only with difficulty comprehend the infinite God, because they are themselves narrow and limited in their views of him. They imagine him to correspond to their ideas; they represent him as a circumscribed being and make of him an image according to their ideal. Our pictures, which paint him with human features, contribute not a little to establishing this error in the mind of the masses, who adore him in form more than in thought. He is to the greater part of humanity a powerful sovereign upon an inaccessible throne, lost in the immensity of the heavens; and, because their faculties and perceptions are limited, they do not comprehend that God can, or deigns to, interfere directly in little things.

22. In his impotence, how is man to comprehend the essence even of divinity? He can form of it only an approximate idea by the aid of comparisons, necessarily very imperfect, but which can at least show him the possibility of that which at first sight seems to him impossible.

Let us suppose a fluid subtle enough to penetrate all bodies; this fluid, being without intelligence, acts mechanically by material force alone. But if we suppose this fluid to be endowed with intelligence, with sensitive and perceptive qualities, it will no more act blindly, but with discernment, will, and liberty; it will see, hear, and feel.

23. The properties of the perispiritual fluid can give us only an idea of it. It is not intelligent of itself since it is matter; but it is the vehicle of the thought, the sensations, and perceptions of the spirit.

The perispiritual fluid is not the thought of the spirit, but the agent and intermediate of this thought. It is in a manner, *impregnated* by the life of him who transmits it; and, in the impossibility of isolating it where we are; he seems to be one with the fluid, as sound and air seem to be one and the same in such a way that we can, as it were, materialize it. We say, for instance, the air is sonorous; we, in taking the effect for the cause, say that the fluid becomes intelligent.

24. Let it be so or not with the thought of God, - that is to say, let it act directly, or by the intermediation of a fluid; for the facility of our intelligence, let us represent it under the concrete form of an intelligent fluid filling the universe, penetrating all parts of creation, - *Nature in its entirety is plunged in the divine fluid.* Now, by virtue of the principle that the parts of a whole are of the same nature, and have the same properties as the whole, each atom of this fluid, if one can express it thus, possessing thought, - that is to say, the essential attributes of divinity, this fluid being everywhere, - all is submissive to its intelligent action, to its foresight, to its solicitude; there is not a being, however inferior he may be, that is not in a measure penetrated by it. We are thus constantly in the presence of divinity. Not one of our actions can escape his notice. Our thoughts are in incessant contact with his thoughts; and reason tells us that God reads the profoundest depths of our hearts. We are in him, as he is in us, according to the word of Christ.

In order to exercise his watchful care over all his creatures, it is not necessary for God to look at them from the height of immensity. Our prayers, in order to be heard by him, have not to traverse space, not to be spoken with a reverberating voice; for, being ever at our side, our thought are perceived by him. Our thoughts are like the tones of a bell, which make all the molecules of the ambient air vibrate.

25. Far from us is the thought of materializing divinity. The image of an intelligent universal fluid is evidently only a comparison, but adapted to give a more just idea of God than the pictures which represent him with a human face. Its object is to make us comprehend the possibility of the presence of God everywhere, and of his occupying himself with everything.

26. We have always before our eyes an example which can give us an idea of the manner in which the action of God can be exercised over all beings, even to the inmost recesses of their hearts, and, consequently, how the most subtle impressions of our soul reach him. It is drawn from spiritual teaching on this subject.

27. "Man is a little world, of which the director is the spirit, and the principle directed is the body. In this universe the body will represent a creation whose spirit is God. (You comprehend that there can be here only a question of analogy, and not of identity.) The member of his body, the different organs which compose it, - its muscles, its nerves, its veins, its joints, - are so many material individualities localized in special parts of the body, if one can so speak. Although the number of this constitutive parts, so varied and different by nature, is considerable, it is not to be doubted, however, that he cannot move, that no action whatever can occur in any particular part, without the consciousness of the spirit in regard to it. Are there diverse sensations in many places simultaneously? The spirit feels them all, discerns them, analyses them, assigns to each its cause and place of action through the perispiritual fluid.

A similar phenomenon takes place between creation and God. God is everywhere in nature, as the spirit pervades all the body. All the elements of creation are in constantly rapport with him, as all the particles of the human body are in immediate contact with the spiritual being. There is, then, no reason why phenomena of the same order should not be produced in like manner in the one case as in the other.

A member is agitated: the spirit feels it; a creature thinks:

God knows it. All the members move: the different organs are put in vibration, the spirit feels every manifestation, distinguishes them, and localizes them. The different creations, different creatures, are agitated, think, act diversely, and God knows all that which passes, assigns to each one that which is peculiar to him.

One can deduce from it equally the solidarity of matter and of intelligence, the solidarity between all beings of the world, that of all worlds, and, indeed, that of all creations of the Creator." – Quinemant: Société de Paris, 1867.

28. We comprehend the effect, which is much. From the effect we mount to the cause, and we judge of the cause by the grandeur of the effect; but its inmost essence escapes us, like that of the cause of a multitude of phenomena. We know the effects of electricity, of heat, of light, of gravitation; we form calculations in regard to them: however, we are ignorant of the inmost nature of the principle which produces them. Is then, more rational to deny divine principles because we do not comprehend it?

29. Nothing hinders us from admitting a principle of sovereign intelligence, a center of action, a principal focus, beaming always, inundating the entire universe with its beams, like the sun with its light. But where is this focus? That is what no one can tell. It is probable that God is no more confined to a certain point than is his action, and that he traverses incessantly the regions of space without limit. If common spirits have the gift of ubiquity, this faculty in God must surely be unlimited. Admitting that God does fill the universe, one can suppose that this focus has no necessity for transporting itself, but that he appears at each point were sovereign will desires to be. From which we can infer that he is everywhere, but in no one place especially.

30. Before these unfathomable problems we must feel our smallness. God exists: we cannot doubt it. He is infinitely just and good: this is his essence. His care extends itself to all; we comprehend it. He can then desire only our good: that is

why we should have confidence in him. This is the essential
part of it: for the rest, let us wait until we are worthy of
understanding him.

VIEW OF GOD

31. Since God is everywhere, why do we not see him?
Upon leaving the Earth, shall we see him? Such questions are
daily posed.

The first is not difficult to solve. Our material organs
have limited perceptions, which render them powerless to see
certain things, sometimes even material objects. Thus certain
fluids escape our view, as also that of our analytical instruments.
However, we do not doubt their existence. We see the effects
of the pestilence; but we do not see the fluid which transports
it. We see bodies move under the influence of gravity; but we
do not see this force.

32. The spiritual essence of things cannot be perceived
by material organs; it is only by the spiritual vision that we
can see spirits, and the substances of the immaterial world.
Our soul alone can then have perceptions of God. Does it see
him immediately after death? Communications from beyond
the tomb can alone inform us. By them we learn that the
privilege of seeing him is granted only to the purest souls,
and thus very few possess the necessary degree of ethereality
upon leaving their terrestrial envelope. Some common
comparisons will make this the more easily comprehended.

33. He who is in the depth of a valley surrounded by a
thick fog does not see the sun; but at a higher point, by aid of
the increased light, he judges that the sun is shining. If he
climbs the mountain, in proportion as he rises, the fog becomes
thinner, the light more and more brilliant; but he does not as
yet see the sun. When he commences to see it, it is as yet
veiled; for the least vapor suffices to conceal its splendor. It is
only after rising above the lowering mist, only in an
atmosphere of perfect purity, that he sees it in all its brightness.

Thus it is with the soul. The perispiritual covering,

although invisible and impalpable to us, who are still too gross for certain perceptions, is in truth, a veritable substance. This covering becomes spiritualized itself in proportion as the soul becomes elevated by morality. The imperfections of the soul are like veils which obscure its light. Every imperfection when removed leaves one veil less; but it is only after becoming completely purified that it enjoys the full plenitude of its faculties.

34. God being the divine essence by excellence, can be perceived in all his splendor only by spirits who have arrived at the highest degree of ethereality. If imperfect spirits do not see him, it is not that they are farther away from him than are others. They and all natural things are submerged in the divine fluid, as we are in the light, only their imperfections are veils which hide him from their sight. When the fog shall have disappeared, they will see him resplendently shine. To attain this vision, there will be no necessity for climbing, nor of seeking him in the depths of infinitude. The spiritual sight being rid of the moral taints which obscure it, they will see him in every place; for he is everywhere to be found. He must be as truly upon the Earth as elsewhere, if he is everywhere.

35. It takes time for the spirit to purify itself; and the different incarnation are the alembics in the depths of which is left each time some impurity. In quitting his mortal envelope man is not instantaneously despoiled of his imperfections. That is the reason why some see no more of God after death than while living on Earth; but, in proportion as spirits become purified, they have a more distinct intuition, if they do not see God, they comprehend him better: the light is less vague. Thus, when spirits say that God forbids them to respond to this question, it is not that God appears to them, or speaks to them, in order to direct them to do, or prohibit them for doing, such and such things. No; but they feel him: they receive the emanation of his thought, as we feel in respect to spirits who envelop us in their fluid, although we do not see them.

36. No man can see God with fleshly eyes. If this favor were accorded to anyone, it would only be in that trance state when the soul is as much redeemed from the trammels of matter as is possible during incarnation. Such a privilege would only be accorded to advanced souls incarnated for a mission here, and not in expiation for sin. But, as spirits of the most elevated order shine with dazzling splendor, it is possible that spirits less elevated, incarnate or discarnate, struck with the splendor which surrounds them, have believed that they have seen God himself, as one sees sometimes a minister taken from his sovereign.

37. Under what appearance does God present himself to those who are rendered worthy of such a favor? Is it under any form, - as a human figure, or as a focus of beaming light? This is something that human language is powerless to describe, because there exists no point of comparison which can give an idea of it. We are like blind men whom men seek in vain to instruct concerning the appearance of the light of the sun. Our vocabulary of knowledge is limited to our needs, and to the circle of our ideas. Just as that of the savage could not possibly depict the marvels of civilization, so that of people of the highest culture is too poor to describe the splendors of the heavens, our intelligence too limited to comprehend them, while our too feeble sight would be dazzled by their brightness could we see them, as they are.

Chapter III
GOOD AND EVIL

**Source of goodness and wickedness – Instinct and
Intelligence – Destruction of living beings by one another.**

SOURCE OF GOODNESS AND WICKEDNESS

1. God being the origin of all things, and his nature being
all wisdom, justice and goodness, all which proceeds from
him, must be imbued with these attributes; for that which is
infinitely wise, just, and good, can produce nothing
unreasonable, wicked, or wrong. The wickedness which we
observe cannot then be derived from him.

2. If wickedness was the province of a special being
who is called Satan, he must be either equal to God, and for
all eternity as powerful, or he must be his inferior.

In the first case, there would be two rival powers in
constant contention, each one seeking to overthrow the work
of the other, and constantly thwarting each other. This
hypothesis is irreconcilable with that unity of purpose which
reveals itself in the arrangement of the Universe.

In the second case this being, being inferior to God,
would be subordinate to him. Not being able to exist for all
eternity like him, without being his equal, he would have had
a commencement. If he has been created, God must have been
his creator. Thus God would have created a bad spirit, which
is impossible if he be infinite goodness. (See *"Heaven and
Hell"* chap. X, *"The Demons"*)

3. However, evil exists, and it has a cause.

Evils are of many kinds; there are firstly, physical and
moral evils, then the evils that men can evade, and those that

are independent of human will. Among the latter are classed the natural plagues.

Man, whose faculties are limited, cannot compass or understand all the designs of the Creator. He studies things at the point of view of his personality by artificial interests, and by conditions that he has created, and which are not in the order of nature. That is why he finds oftentimes wrong and injustice in that which he would know to be just and admirable if he could see its cause, its end and definite results. In seeking the reason for being and utility of everything, he will surely discover that all bears the imprint of infinite wisdom, and he will bow before the wise power even in things which he fails to comprehend.

4. Man has received a share of intelligence by which he can avert, or at least greatly palliate the effects of all natural plagues. The more knowledge he acquires, the farther he advances in civilization, the less disastrous these plagues will be. With a wisely provident social organization he will be able to neutralize the consequences of them, and in time, evade them entirely. Thus for these plagues which annoy us now, but which have their use in the general order of nature, God has given to men, in the faculties by which he has endowed his mind, the means of paralyzing their effects in the future.

It is thus that he renders healthy insalubrious countries; that he destroys pestilential miasmas; that he fertilizes waste lands and applies himself to preserve them from inundation; that he constructs healthier habitations, stronger to resist winds so necessary for the purification of the atmosphere; that he is sheltered from the inclemency of the weather. It is thus that necessity has created science by the aid of which he improves the condition of the habitable parts of the globe, and augments the general well-being.

5. The evils to which men are exposed by ignorance are a stimulant for the exercise of their intelligence, for all their moral and physical faculties, by inducing them to seek for means to shelter themselves from them. If man had nothing to fear, no necessity would incline him to seek for anything better:

he would become benumbed in the inactivity of his mind; he would invent nothing and discover nothing. *Pain and suffering are incentives which spur men onward, in the march of progress.*

6. But the most numerous evils are those which men create by their own vices, - those which spring from their pride, from their selfishness, from their ambition, from their cupidity, from their excess in all things. Hence the cause of wars, calamities, dissensions, injustice, oppression of the feeble by the strong, and of the greater part of diseases.

God has established laws full of wisdom, which are only for the good of men. All that is necessary to man's welfare is his obedience to them. His way is traced out for him by his conscience. The divine law is engraved upon his heart. Moreover, God reminds him incessantly by his messiahs and prophets, by all incarnates who have received the mission of enlightening him, of moralizing him, of improving his condition, and in these latter days by the multitude of discarnates who manifest on all sides, - *if man conformed himself rigorously to the divine laws, he would evade, without doubt, the severest evils, and would live happily upon the Earth.* If he doesn't obey them, it is by virtue of his free will; and he must submit himself to the consequences. ("*The Gospel According to Spiritism,*" Chap. 5, items 4, 5, and 6)

7. But God, full of goodness, has placed the remedy by the side of evil; that is to say, he brings good out of its opposite. There comes a time where an excess of moral wickedness becomes intolerable, and makes man realize the need of a change of life. Instructed by experience, he is impelled to seek a remedy in goodness, always by the effect of his free will. When he enters the better path, it is by the influence of his own desire, and because he recognizes the inconveniences of the other way. This necessity is a compulsion to improve himself morally, in view of being happier. This brings with it the natural consequence of bettering his material condition also (see item n°5).

8. One can say that evil *is the absence of good, as cold is the absence of heat. Wickedness is no more a distinct attribute than cold is a special fluid. One is the negative of the other.* Where good exists not, there is necessarily evil. Not to do wickedly is already the commencement of good. *God desires only good; from man only comes evil. If there were in the universe a being charged with evil, man would not be able to evade him; but man, having the cause of wrong-doing within HIMSELF, having at the same time his free-will, and for his guide the divine laws, he can avoid it if he desires to do so.*

Let us take a common fact as a comparison. A landowner knows that at the extremity of his field is a dangerous place, and those who might venture there would be wounded, or perish. What means does he employ to prevent accidents? He places near the place a notice forbidding people to pass there on account of danger. Such is the law: it is wise and provident. If not withstanding the warning, an imprudent person pays no heed, and passes beyond it, thereby injuring himself, whom can he blame if not himself?

Thus it is with all evils; man could evade them if he would obey the divine laws. God, for example, has placed a limit to the gratification of wants: man is warned by satiety. If he passes beyond this limit, he does it voluntarily. The illness, infirmities, and death, which may be the consequence of it, are then occasioned by his own fault, and not that of God.

9. Wickedness being the result of imperfections of man and man being created by God, will they not say that God had at least created, if not evil, the cause of evil? If he had made man perfect, evil would not exist.

If man had been created perfect, he would be carried by fate in the way of goodness. Now, by virtue of his free will, he is carried by fate neither to the good nor bad; God having decreed that he should submit to the law of progress, and that this progress should be fruit of his own labor, in order that he should have the merit of it, as well as be responsible for his evil deeds, which he can always avoid by the use of his will.

The question then is to know what is in man the source of propensity to evil.[12]

10. If one studies all the passions, and even all vices, one sees that they have their origin in the instinct of self-preservation. This instinct is strongest with animals, and with primitive men, who approached nearest the animal existence. It governed them entirely, because they had not the moral sense for a counterpoise, having not been born into the intellectual life. The instinct is weakened in proportion as intelligence is developed, because the latter rules matter.

The spirit is destined for the spiritual life: but in the first phases of its corporeal existence it has only material needs to satisfy; and to this end the exercise of the passions is a necessity for the preservation of the species and of the individual, materially speaking. But, passed beyond this period, he has other needs, - needs at first partly moral and partly material, then exclusively moral. It is then that the spirit rules matter. If he throws of the yoke, he advances on his providential way; he approaches his final destiny. If on the contrary, he allows himself to be ruled by the senses, he is held back on his upward progress by assimilating himself with the brute. In this situation *that which was formerly good, because it was a necessity of his nature, becomes an evil, not only because it is no more a necessity, but because it has become hurtful to his spiritual well-being.* Similarly, that which is considered a good quality in a child becomes an imperfection in the adult. Evil is thus relative, and the responsibility therefore proportionate to the degree of advancement.

---

[12] The error consists in presuming that the soul leaves the hands of the Creator already in a state of perfection, whereas it is the opposite: God wants our perfection to be the result of our own labor, through a gradual purification of the Spirit. He further wishes the soul - which is endowed with free will - to be able to choose between good and evil, and that its final goals should be attained at the price of activity, and by resisting evil. If He had created the soul as perfect as Himself, by securing its eternal beatitude right from his hands, he would have created it not after his image, but after his own self. (Bonnamy, *"The Reason of Spiritism,"* chapter VI).

All passions have thus their providential utility; if not
so, God has made some things intrinsically useless and hurtful.
It is only abuse which constitutes the evil, and man abuses by
virtue of his free-will. At length, awakened to the knowledge
of his own share in it, he chooses freely between the good
and the bad.

INSTINCT AND INTELLIGENCE

11. What is the difference between instinct and
intelligence? Where does one end and the other commence?
Is instinct a rudimental intelligence or a distinct faculty, - an
exclusive attribute of matter?

*Instinct is occult power which incites organic beings
to spontaneous and involuntary acts in relation to their
conservation.* In instinctive acts there is neither reflection,
contrivance, nor premeditation. Thus the plant seeks air, turns
itself towards the light, directs its roots towards water and
the nutritious soil; the flower opens and closes its petals by
turns, according to its needs; climbing plants wind
themselves around supports, or cling to them by their tendrils.
It is by instinct that animals are apprised of that which is
useful or injurious to them, that they are directed, according
to the season, towards propitious climates; that they construct,
without preliminary lessons, with more or less art, according
to species, soft places of rest and of shelter for their progeny,
machinery by which they snare their prey by which they are
nourished, that they handle dexterously weapons of defense
with which they are provided; that the sexes are brought
together, that the mother produces offspring, and that the
little ones seek her breast for nourishment. With man instinct
rules at the outset of life. It is by instinct the infant makes his
first movements, that he seizes his nourishment, that he cries to express his wants, that he imitates the sound of the
voice, that he tries to speak and to walk. With the adult, even,
certain acts are instinctive: such are spontaneous movements
to escape a danger, to remove one's self from peril, to

maintain one's equilibrium; such are, also, the blinking of the eyelids to temper the brilliance of the light, the mechanical opening of the mouth to breath, etc.

12. *Intelligence is revealed by voluntary, reflective, premeditated, united actions, according to the fitness of circumstances.* It is incontestably an exclusive attribute of the soul.

All mechanical action is instinctive; that which denotes reflection and contrivance is intelligent. One is free; the other is not.

Instinct is a sure guide which never deceives; intelligence, solely because it is unrestrained, is sometimes subject to error.

If the instinctive action has not the character of the intelligent one, it reveals, nevertheless, *an intelligent cause*, essentially provident. If one admits that instinct has its source in matter, it is necessary, also, to admit that matter is intelligent, - surely wiser and more foreseeing than the soul, since instinct does not deceive, whilst intelligence does.

If one considers instinct to be rudimental intelligence, why is it, in certain cases, superior to reasoning intelligence - that it makes possible the execution of things that the latter cannot produce?

If it is the attribute of a special spiritual principle, what becomes of this principle? When instinct is effaced, this principle must also be destroyed. If animals are only endowed with instinct, their future is without issue; their sufferings have no compensation. This would be in conformity with neither the justice, nor the goodness of God. (Chap. II, n°19).

13. According to another system, instinct and intelligence have one and the same principle alone. Having arrived at a certain degree of development, this principle, which at first had only the qualities of instinct, is subject to a transformation which imparts to its free intelligence.

If this were true, for the intelligent man who loses his ability to reason, and is guided exclusively by instinct, his intelligence would regress to its primitive state; and, upon recovering his ability to reason, his instinct would, once again, turn back into the state of intelligence; this cycle would repeat itself, alternatively, for each bout of rage encountered. This is not admissible.

Incidentally, intelligence and instinct are frequently present, side-by-side, in the same action. For instance, upon walking a man's legs move in an instinctive way; mechanically, he places one foot before the other, without thinking of it. However, when he wants to accelerate or lessen his pace, lift up his foot, or deviate it in order to avoid an obstacle, there is calculation and combination involved; he acts here with a deliberate purpose. *The involuntary impulsion of the movement is the instinctive act; whereas the calculated direction of the movement is the intelligent act.* A carnivorous animal is compelled by its instinct to gain nourishment from meat; but the precautions it takes, its foresight of possible eventualities - which varies according to the circumstances - in order to capture his prey, are acts of intelligence.

14. Yet, a last hypothesis, which, however, is perfectly allied to unity of principle springs from the essential provident character of instinct, and agrees with that which Spiritism teaches us concerning the connection between the spiritual and the corporeal world.

One knows now that discarnated spirits have the mission of watching over incarnated ones, of whom they are the guides and protectors; that they surround them with their fluidic effluvia; that man acts often in an unconscious manner under the influence of these effluvia.

One knows, besides, that instinct itself, which produces actions without the aid of reason, predominates in children and in general with those persons whose intellect is feeble. Now, according to this hypothesis, instinct can neither be an attribute of the soul nor of matter. It does not belong properly to any living being, but must be the effect of the direct action of invisible protectors who supply the deficiency to imperfect intelligence by inciting them to necessarily unconscious actions for the preservation of life. It is like the leading-string by which one supports the infant learning to walk; and, in the same manner, as one discontinues gradually the use of the string in order that he may learn to stand without help, the spirit-protectors leave their protégées to themselves when the latter can be guided by their own intelligence.

Thus, instinct, far from being the product of a rudimental and imperfect intelligence, is ever the result of an unknown power *in the plenitude of its strength* supplying knowledge to a feebler understanding, impressing the latter to act unconsciously for his own good in a way impossible to him were it not for this impression; or it may be that a being of riper information, becoming temporarily trammeled in the use of his powers, - the first takes place with man in his infancy, the second in cases of idiocy and mental affections.

It has passed into a proverb that there is a God for children, fools and drunkards; for children, fools, and drunkards are always kept from harm. This belief is truer than one would think. This God is none other than the spirit-protector who watches over the one incapable of protecting himself by his own reason.

15. In this set of ideas one must go still farther; for this theory, however rational it may be, does not solve the difficulties of the question.

If one observes the effects of instinct, one remarks, in the first place, a unity of view, and, as a whole, a certainty of results which ceases to exist when instinct is displaced by free intelligence. Moreover, in the appropriation of instinctive faculties, so certain and so constant in the needs of every creature, one recognizes a profound wisdom. This unity of sight could not exist without a unity of thought. Consequently, by the multiplicity of acting causes, or by following the progress which is always accomplished by individual intelligences, there is between them a diversity of operation and of will wholly incompatible with this so perfectly harmonious a unity produced since the beginning of time, and in all places with a regularity and mathematical precision never at fault. This uniformity in the result of instinctive faculties is a fact which forcibly implies *unity of cause*. If this cause were inherent in every individuality, there would be as many varieties of instincts as of individuals from the plant to man. A general uniform and constant effect must have a general uniform cause. An effect revealing wisdom and providence must result from a wise and provident cause. A wise and provident cause being necessarily intelligent, cannot be exclusively material.

As we find not in created beings, incarnated or discarnated, the necessary qualities to produce such a result, it is necessary to go higher, - that is, to the Creator himself. The reader is referred to the explanation given of the means whereby one can conceive of providential action (chap. II, n°24). If one imagines all beings permeated with the divine effluence, severely intelligent, he will comprehend the provident wisdom and unity of sight which presides in all the instinctive movements conducing to good of each individual. This solicitude is so much the more active as the individual has fewer resources within himself, due to his possession of intelligence. This is why it shows itself in a greater and more absolute degree in animals than in men.

In the light of this theory one understands that instinct is always a sure guide; the maternal instinct, the noblest of all; that which materialism lowers to the level of attractive forces of matter, finds itself re-enthroned and ennobled. Reason readily perceives that it is not desirable that it should be delivered over to the capricious action of that intelligence known as free will. *Through the maternal organism God himself watches over his newly born creatures.*

16. This theory, however, does not destroy the role of the spirit-protectors, whose concurrence is a fact proved by experience; but it is necessary to remark, that the action of the latter is essentially individual, that it is modified by the qualities proper to the protector and his charge, and that it never has the uniformity and generality of instinct. God, in his wisdom, himself conducts the blind; but he leaves to free intelligence the work of guiding clear-seeing ones, that each may be responsible for his own acts. The mission of the spirit-protectors is a duty voluntarily accepted, and which is for the guardian spirits a means of advancement according to the manner in which they fulfill it.

17. All these analysis of instinct are necessarily hypothetical and no one of them is sufficiently authentic in character to be given as a definite solution. The question will certainly be solved some day, when many will have attained to a power of observation revealing truths yet beyond our grasp. Until then it is necessary to submit these diverse opinions to the crucible of reason and logic, and wait until more light breaks. The solution which approaches the nearest to the truth will be necessarily that which harmonizes the best with the attributes of God; that is to say, to sovereign goodness and justice (see chap. II, n° 19).

18. Instinct being an unerring guide, when spirits resort to outward intelligence in the primary periods of their development, they are confounded sometimes by effects. There is, however, between these two principles a difference which it is necessary to consider.

Instinct is a sure guide, and always a good one. At a given time, it may become useless, but never hurtful. It is weakened by the predominance of intelligence.

The passions in the first expressions of the soul have this in common with instinct: they are guided by an equally involuntary force. They are born more particularly to supply the needs of the body, and depend more than instinct upon the organism. That which distinguishes them above all else from instinct, is that they are individual, and do not produce, as does instinct, general and uniform effects. We see them, on the contrary, varied in intensity of nature according to individual development. They are useful as stimulants; that is, until the awakening of the moral sense, which, in the case of a passive being, transforms him into a rational being. From this moment they become not only useless, but hurtful to the development of the spirit, whose upward progress they hold back; they are weakened by the development of reason.

19. The man who would constantly act instinctively might be very good, but would let his intelligence sleep. He would be like a child who would not quit his leading-strings, refusing to use his limbs. He who masters not his passions can be very intelligent, but at the same time very impure. *Instinct annihilates itself; passions are governed only by the effort of the will.*

THE DESTRUCTION OF LIVING BEINGS BY ONE ANOTHER

20. The reciprocal destruction of living beings by one another is a law of nature which, at first sight, seems in no way reconcilable with the goodness of God. One asks why he has made it necessary for them to nourish themselves by destroying each other.

For him who sees things only in a material light, whose vision is limited to the present life, this appears indeed an imperfection in the divine plan, because they judge of divine perfection from their point of view. Their own judgment is their measure of his wisdom, and they think that God does not know as well as themselves. Their short-sightedness not permitting them to judge of the whole, they do not comprehend how a real good can result from an apparent evil. The knowledge of the spiritual principle, considered in its veritable essence and by the grand law of unity, which constitutes the full harmony of the universe, can alone give to man the key to this mystery, and show to him the providential wisdom and harmony precisely where he saw only an anomaly and contradiction.

21. *The true life of the animal, as well of the man, is no more in the body than it is in the clothing; it is in the intelligent principle that pre-exists and survives the body.* This principle has need of a body in order to develop itself by the work of controlling brute matter. The body is employed in this work, but the spirit is not thereby injured; on the contrary, it comes out of the strife every time stronger, more lucid and more capable. What matters if the spirit changes more or less frequently its envelope? It is no less a spirit. It is as absolutely as though a man should renew his clothings a hundred times a year: he would still be the same man.

By the constant spectacle of destruction, God teaches man of how little worth is the material envelope, and excites in them the idea of the spiritual life by making them desire it as compensation.

But some will say: Could not God arrive at the same result by other means, without obliging living beings to destroy each other? If all is wisdom in his works, we ought to suppose that his wisdom is no more defective in this particular than in any other. If we cannot comprehend it, it is necessary to ascribe the seeming folly to our lack of advancement. Each time we can try to seek the reason by taking this for our watchword: *God must be infinitely just and wise.* Let us, then, seek for his justice and wisdom in all things, and let us bow before that which surpasses our understanding.

22. The first reason which presents itself for this destruction – a purely physical utility, it is true – is this: organic bodies are supported only by the aid of organic matter. This matter alone contains the nutritive elements necessary to their sustenance. The bodies which are instruments of action for the intelligent principle, having need of incessant renovation, Providence makes them serve for their mutual support. That is why beings are nourished by one another. It is thus that body is nourished by body: but the spirit is not changed; it is only despoiled of its envelope.[13]

23. This is outside moral considerations of a more elevated order.

The battle is necessary to the development of the spirit. It is in battle that it exercises its faculties. He who attacks another that he may nourish himself, and he who defends himself to preserve his life, making an assault upon intelligence, thereby augments his own intellectual strength. As he must contend against stratagem, displaying intelligence, thereby both augment their intellectual force. One of the two succumbs.

---

[13] See *"Revue Spirite"* August 1864, Extinction of the Races.

But what is it that the stronger or more skillful has in reality taken away from the feebler? His vestment of flesh, - nothing else. The spirit, which is not dead, will take another body.

24. With inferior beings in creation, with those in whom the moral sense does not exist, where instinct has not been replaced by intelligence, the struggle would have for incentive only the satisfaction of a material necessity. Now, one of the most imperious physical needs is that of food. They struggle, then, only to sustain life; that is to say, to seize prey, or to defend themselves from attack, for they cannot be actuated by a more elevated object. It is in this first period that the soul is elaborated and tried by the vicissitudes of life.

There is a period of transition where man is scarcely distinguishable from the brute. In the first periods of his existence animal instincts rules; and the battle has still for its incentive the satisfaction of material wants. Later, the animal instinct and moral sentiment are counterbalanced. Then struggles are no more simply for nourishment, but for the satisfaction of ambition, pride, and love of dominion; it is still necessary to destroy. But, accordingly as moral sense gains ascendancy, moral sensibility becomes developed; the desire to destroy diminishes, at length it becomes effaced and odious to him. Man has a horror of blood.

However, a struggle is always necessary to the development of the spirit. After having arrived at a point which appears to us the culminating one, he is still far from being perfect. It is only at the price of activity that he acquires knowledge by experience, and as he is despoiled of the last vestiges of animality; but then the effort, no longer brutal and bloody as it formerly was, becomes purely intellectual. Man struggles against difficulties, but no more with beings of his own species.[14]

---

[14] Without prejudging the consequences that one could take from this principle, we simply wanted to show, with this explanation, that the destruction of living beings, one by another, does not, by any means, lessen the divine wisdom, and that everything follows a sequence within

the laws of nature. However, this chain is completely void if we disregard the spiritual principle. Our constant regarding of matter alone leads us to a multitude of unanswered questions. The materialistic doctrines bring within them the seeds of their own destruction. For once they are faced with their own antagonism of mankind's aspirations of universality and its moral consequences; they will be seen as agents of dissolution, causing them to be repelled by society. Secondly, they face their reluctance to comprehend one's needs to become familiar with all that is brought forth by progress. Intellectual development leads man to search for answers. Well, as little as he may reflect, it will not take him long to recognize the inability of materialism to explain everything. One would question if a doctrine that upholds man's most vital questions as enigmas could ever prevail, considering that it does not satisfy the heart, reason, or intelligence. The progress of ideas will defeat materialism, just as it has already destroyed fanaticism.

Chapter IV
THE SCIENTIFIC NOTE IN GENESIS

1. The history of the origin of nearly all ancient nations is mingled with that of their religion: that is why their first books have been religious works; and as all religions are allied to the spirit of things, which is allied to that of humanity, they have founded upon the arrangement and formation of the universe explanations limited by the knowledge of the times, and the founders of their systems. The result is that the first religious books have been the first scientific treatises, as they have also been the only code of civil laws.

2. In primitive times, means of observation being very imperfect, the first theories upon the system of the universe were stained with grave errors; but, if opportunities for investigation had been as complete as they are today, men would not have known how to take advantage of them. They could only be the fruit of successive developments, and repeated studies of the laws of nature. By measure, as man has advanced in the knowledge of these laws, he has penetrated the mysteries of nature, and rectified ideas which he had conceived concerning the origin of things.

3. Man has been impotent to solve the problem of creation until science has given him the key to it. It has been necessary that astronomy should open the doors of boundless space, and permit him to gaze into its infinite depths; that by the power of calculation he could determine with rigorous precision the movement, position, the volume, the nature, and the role of the celestial bodies; that natural physics should reveal to him the laws of gravitation, of heat, of light, and of electricity; that chemistry should teach of the transformations of metal, and mineralogy of the materials which form the surface of the globe;

that geology should teach man to read in terrestrial beds the gradual formation of this same globe; and that botany, zoology, paleontology, anthropology, should come to initiate him into the science of the affiliation and succession of organized beings. By the aid of archeology he has been able to trace the progress of humanity through the ages. All sciences, in a word, complete one another: they carry their indispensable contingent for the knowledge of the history of the world. Without them man would have for his guide only his first hypothesis.

Before man was in possession of these means of investigation, all commentators on Genesis whose reason rebelled at material impossibilities, continued to revolve in the same circle of ideas, with no power to depart from them. Science has come to the rescue by attacking the old edifice of belief, opening a way whereby the whole aspect has changed entirely. Once the conducting thread is found, the difficulties are promptly met. In place of an imaginary Genesis, we have a positive, and in some respect an experimental Genesis. The field of the universe is extended into the infinite. We behold that the Earth and the stars form themselves gradually in obedience to the eternal and immutable law, which testifies far more fully to the grandeur of God than a miraculous creation suddenly originating from nothing by a sudden act of divinity after ages of inaction.

Since it is impossible to comprehend Genesis without the help of science, one can say most truthfully *that it is science who has been elected to constitute the true Genesis according to the laws of nature.*

4. Have we reached in the nineteenth century a sufficient power of scientific attainment to solve all the difficulties of the problem of Genesis? [15]

No, assuredly not; but one thing is certain, that all the principal errors are destroyed, and the most essential foundation laid for undeniable principles. The yet uncertain points are, properly speaking, only minute portions, which,

---

[15] **Note of SAB**: This assertive is still true in our days.

whatever the future may bring forth, cannot impair the whole. Notwithstanding all the resources of which it has been able to avail itself, there is an important element still wanting, without which the work can never be complete.

5. Of all ancient histories of the creation of the world and the human race that which approaches nearest to modern scientific revelation, notwithstanding the errors which it contains - some of the latter being now distinctively pointed out by the finger of science - is incontestably that of Moses. Some of these errors are such more in appearance than in reality, as they spring from false interpretation of certain words, whose primitive significance is lost as they pass from language to language by means of translation into different tongues, or whose meaning is changed with the customs of the nations particularly the allegorical form peculiar to the Oriental style, of which the literal sense was taken to the exclusion of the spiritual.

6. The Bible contains statements that our reason, which has been developed by science, will not allow us to accept; and also others which seem strange and repugnant to us, because they are connected with customs which are not ours. But, notwithstanding this, it would be wrong not to recognize the grand and beautiful thoughts which it contains. Allegory holds a conspicuous place in it, and under its veils conceals sublime truths, which appear, if one seeks for them, in the foundations of ideas contained in them.

Why has this veil not been sooner lifted? On one side it has been for the want of light which science and healthy philosophy alone could give, and, on the other, the belief in the absolute immutability of a creed, consequent upon a too blind respect for the letter, to which reason bent blindly, fearing that science might not accord with the lattice-work of beliefs which were built upon their literal sense. On account of the antiquity of these beliefs, it has been feared that, if the first ring of the chain should be broken, all the meshes of the network would at length separate. Commentators, therefore, have shut their eyes when doubt arose. But we cannot evade danger by shutting our eyes to it. When the foundation of a building falters, is it not more prudent to immediately replace defective stones by good ones, rather then to wait out of respect for the age of the edifice until there is no remedy for the evil other than its reconstruction from the foundation?

7. In pursuing our investigations, even into the bowels of the Earth, and into the blue depths of the sky above us, science has demonstrated in an undeniable manner the errors of the Mosaic Genesis taken in its literal sense, and the material impossibility of things having taken place literally as they are there represented to have done. It has thus given severe shocks to some ancient doctrines. The orthodox faith is disturbed; it believes that its very cornerstone is removed by the adoption of these new ideas. But which is most likely to be right, science marching prudently and progressively over the solid ground of figures and observation, without affirming anything before the proof of it is at hand, or history written at an epoch when means of observation were absolutely lacking? Should we believe the person who affirms that two and two make five, and refuses to verify it, or he who says two and two make four, and proves it?

8. But then it is objected, if the Bible is a divine revelation from God, how can it contain mistakes? While, if it be not a divine revelation, then has it no authority? Religious beliefs may thus be destroyed for want of a foundation.

It must be one thing or the other; either science is wrong, or theology is right. If theology is right, then an opinion contrary to its cannot be a true one. There is no revelation superior to the authority of facts.

If God, who is truth, could seduce men from the path of rectitude either knowingly or unconsciously, he would no longer be God. If, then, facts contradict the words which are attributed to him, the logical conclusion is, that he has not pronounced them, or that they have been misconstrued.

If religion suffers in some respects by these contradictions, the wrong must not be ascribed to science, which cannot agree with unreasonable statements, but to men for having prematurely founded absolute dogmas, which have been made a question of life and death, upon hypothesis susceptible of being overthrown by experience.

We must resign ourselves to the sacrifice of some things, whether we desire to or not; we cannot do otherwise. As the world progresses, the will of a few persons cannot arrest it in its onward march. The wiser way is to follow it, and accommodate ourselves to the new state of things, rather than to cling to old beliefs which are crumbling to pieces, at the risk of falling with them.

9. Were it desirable to impose silence upon science out of respect to texts of scripture regarded as sacred, it would be as impossible to do so as to stop the movement of the Earth. No religious systems have ever gained anything by sustaining manifest errors. The mission of science is to discover the laws of nature. Now, as these laws are the work of God, they cannot be contrary to religions founded upon truth. To hurl anathemas at progress, calling it a hindrance to religion, is to go contrary to the will of God. There is scarcely anything so useless; for all the anathemas in the world will not hinder science in its progressive work of bringing truth to light. *If religion refuses to accompany science, it is left alone.*

10. Stationary religions can alone dread scientific discoveries. Scientific truths are only destructive to the systems of those who allow themselves to be distanced by progressive ideas by wrapping themselves in the absolutism of old beliefs. These persons have such a narrow idea of divinity that they do not comprehend that to assimilate themselves with the laws of nature revealed by science is to glorify God in his works; but in their blindness they prefer to do homage to the spirit of evil. *A religion which would be in no one point contradictory to the laws of nature would have nothing to fear from progress, and would be invulnerable.*

11. Genesis comprises two divisions, - the history of the formation of the material world, and that of humanity in its dual (corporal and spiritual) principle. Science is limited in its researches by laws which rule matter. In dealing with man it has studied only his bodily envelope. And concerning this it has been enabled to give an account with incontestable precision of the main parts of the mechanism of the universe and of the human organism. This important point attained, it has been further able to complete the Genesis of Moses, and to rectify the defective parts of it.

But the history of man, considered as a spiritual being, is attached to a special order of ideas, which is not, properly speaking, in the domain of science, and which the latter, for this reason, has not made the subject of its investigations. It belongs more particularly to philosophy, which has formulated upon this point only contradictory systems, from genuine spirituality to the denial of the spiritual principle, and even of God, without other foundation than the personal ideas of human authors. It has thus left the question undecided for want of sufficient light to answer it.

12. This, however, is the most important question for man, for it is the problem of his past and future; that of the material world affects him only indirectly. It is the most important of all knowledge to learn of man's origin, what becomes of him, if he has lived before, if he will continue to live on forever, and what end is in store for him.

Upon all these questions science is mute. Philosophy gives opinions only, and these often diametrically opposed to each other; but at least it permits such questions to be discussed, which indices many people to range themselves on its side in preference to that of dogmatic theology, when allows of no discussion on the subject.

13. All religions are in accord with each other in the acknowledgement of such first principles as the existence of the soul, at the same time not demonstrating it. They agree neither in belief concerning its origins, its past history, or its future destiny, and above all, in that which is the most essential, the conditions upon which its future happiness depends. The greater part of them accept pictures of the future imposed on

them by the belief of their adepts, which can be supported
only by blind faith, unable to endure a serious examination;
the destiny which they accord to the soul being allied in their
dogmas to ideas of the material world, and the mechanism of
the universe universally entertained in primitive times, are
irreconcilable with the actual state of knowledge. Being able
to lose only by examination and discussion, their devotees
deem it better to proscribe both.

14. From these different faiths touching the future of
man, doubts and incredulity arise. However, incredulity leaves
a painful void. Man regards with anxiety the unknown future
upon which he must sooner or later enter. The idea of
annihilation chills him. His conscience says to him that beyond
the present there is something for him. But what? His developed
reason forbids him any longer to accept the histories which
have quieted his early days, which have put conscience to
sleep by his taking the allegory for a reality. What is the
meaning of this allegory? Science has torn away the corner of
the veil; but it has not revealed that which it is most important
for man to know. He interrogates it, but in vain; it answers
nothing in a convincing way to calm his apprehensions. He
finds everywhere affirmation hurling itself against negation,
without more positive proofs on one side than on the other.
*Incertitude concerning things of the future life has made many
men reject the duties of the material life with a kind of frenzy.*

Such is the inevitable effect in transitional epochs. The
edifice of the past is crumbling away, and that of the future is
not yet constructed. Man is like an adolescent who has lost
the innocent belief of his early years, and has not yet obtained
the knowledge of a riper age; he has only vague aspirations,
which he knows not how to define.

15. If the spiritual question regarding man has remained
till our day in a theoretical condition, it is because direct means
of observation have failed to establish the material theory of
the world, and the field has remained open to the varying
conceptions of the human mind; while man has not known
the laws which rules matter and has not been able to apply the

experimental method, he has erred from system to system concerning the mechanism of the universe and the formation of the Earth. It has been in the moral as in the physical order of things; in the attempt to establish ideas, men have failed in the essential element, - the knowledge of the laws of the spiritual principle. This knowledge was reserved for our epoch, as the discovery of the laws of matter has been the work of the two last centuries.

16. Until now the study of the spiritual principle, the study of metaphysics, has been purely speculative and theoretical. In Spiritism it is all experimental. By the aid of the medianimic faculty, more developed in our day, - far more generalized and better studied, - man is found possessed of a new instrument of observation. Mediumship has been for the spiritual world that which the telescope has been for the astral, and the microscope for the world of infinitesimalities. It has allowed exploration of it, study, and one might say vision, of its connection with the corporeal world - of the distinction in the living man between the intelligent and the material being; for they can now be seen to act separately. Once in relation with the inhabitants of the spirit-world, one has been able to follow the soul in its ascending march, in its migrations, in its transformation. At length the study of the spiritual element is made practical; this was wanting to all preceding commentators on Genesis; thus their inability to comprehend it, and rectify its errors.

17. The spiritual and material worlds, being in constant contact, are inseparable from each other. Both have their part to play in Genesis. Without the knowledge of laws which rule the former, it is as impossible to create a complete Genesis as it would be for a sculptor to give life to a statue. At this day only, though neither material nor spiritual science has said its last word, man possesses the two necessary elements to throw light upon this immense problem. These two keys are necessary in order to arrive at even an approximate solution.

Chapter V
SYSTEMS OF THE ANCIENT AND MODERN WORLD

1. The first idea that man forms of the Earth, of the movements of the stars, and of the constitution of the universe, must be, in the commencement of his observations, entirely based upon the testimony of the senses. In his ignorance of the most elementary laws of physics, and of the forces of nature, having only his limited sight as a means of observation, he was able to judge only by appearances.

As he beheld the sun appear in the morning outside of the horizon and disappear in the evening on the other side, he naturally concluded that it revolved around the Earth, whilst the latter remained stationary. If it had been suggested to him that the contrary was the truth, he would have replied that that was impossible; for would he not have declared that we see the sun change its position, and we do not feel the Earth move?

2. The few facts known then by voyagers, whose journeys rarely exceeded the limits of their tribe or of the valley in which they dwelt, would not permit of their establishing a spherical Earth. In what way could they arrive at the conclusion that the Earth is a ball? Men would not have been able to support this assertion; and, in supposing it inhabited on its entire surface, how would they have supposed it possible to live in opposite hemispheres, the head down and feet up? The fact would have appeared less possible when the rotational movement of the globe should have been explained. When one sees in our day, when the law of gravitation is known, people relatively enlightened, unable to give an account of this phenomenon, is it astonishing that men in the early ages had not even suspected it?

The Earth to them was a flat surface, circular as a millstone, extending out of sight in the far horizon, hence arose the saying yet in use: "Going to the end of the world." Its limits, its thickness, its interior, its inferior surface that which was beneath them, was unknown to them.[16]

3. The heavens, appearing to be concave in form constituted, according to common belief, a real vault, the lower borders of which rested on the Earth and marked the end of it, — a vast dome, the space of which was filled with air. With no idea of the infinity of space, incapable even of conceiving it, men imagined this vault formed of solid matter; whence the name of *"firmament"* which has survived such a belief, and which signifies *firm, enduring* (from the Latin *firma mentum*, derived from *firmus*, *"firm"*, and from the Greek *herma, hermatos*, a prop, or supporter, or fulcrum).

4. The stars, of the nature of which they had no suspicions, were to them simply luminous points, small and large, attached to the vault like suspended lamps, disposed on one surface only, consequently all at the same distance from the Earth, in the manner in which they are represented in the interior of certain cupolas, which are painted blue in imitation of the azure hue of the sky.

Although today ideas are changed, the usage of the ancient expressions is retained. We say yet, for example, "the starry vault;" "under heaven's arch."

5. The formation of clouds by the evaporation of the waters of the Earth was then equally unknown. They did not suspect that the rain which falls from the sky arose in vapor

---

[16] Hindu mythology taught that the sun was "divested in the evening of its light, and traversed the sky during the night with an obscured face. Greek mythology represented the car of Apollo as drawn by four horses. Anaximander of Miletus maintained in concord with Plutarch, that the sun was a chariot tilled with a very brilliant fire, which escaped through a circular opening. Epicurus gave as his opinion that the sun was lighted in the morning, and extinguished at night in the waters of the ocean. Others thought that it was made of pumice-stone heated to a state of incandescence. Anaxagoras regarded it as a heated iron of the

from the Earth; for they did not see the water arise. Whence the belief in large and small bodies of water from celestial and terrestrial sources, from reservoirs situated in lofty regions, — a supposition which accorded perfectly with the idea of a solid vault capable of maintaining them. The larger bodies of water, escaping through fissures in the sky, fell in rain; and the rain fell gently or came in torrents, according to the size of these openings.

6. The complete ignorance of the whole universe, and of the laws which rule it, of the nature, constitution, and destination of the stars, which seemed, besides, so small compared with the Earth, would necessarily make the latter to be considered as the principal object in creation, and the stars as accessories created solely to give light to its inhabitants. These prejudices are cherished by some to this day, despite the discoveries of science, which have altered the aspects of the world for mankind. Many people believe still that the stars are ornaments of the sky, placed there to please the eye of man.

7. They delayed not to perceive the apparent movement of the stars in a body from east to west, rising in the evening, and going down in the morning, preserving their respective positions. This observation had for a long time no other result than that of confirming the idea of a solid vault carrying the stars along in its rotary movement.

These first simple ideas have made, during long secular periods, the foundation of religious beliefs, and have served as a base for all ancient cosmogonies.

---

magnitude of the Peloponnesus. Strange to relate, the ancients were so invincibly determined to consider the apparent size of this body as real, that they persecuted this rash philosopher for having attributed such magnitude to the torch of day, that Pericles was obliged to exercise all the power of his authority to save him from condemnation to death, and commute the latter to a sentence of exile." (Flammarion: *"Studies and Lectures upon Astronomy,"* p. 6.) If they held such ideas in the fifth century, before the Christian Era, in the most flourishing times of Greece, we cannot be astonished at those entertained by men in earlier times on the system of the universe.

8. Later they discovered, by the direction of the movement of the stars, and their periodical return in the same order, that the celestial vault could not be simply a hemisphere resting upon the Earth, but a hollow sphere, in the center of which was the Earth, flat at the utmost convex, and inhabited only upon its upper surface. This was a progressive idea.

But upon what rested the Earth? It would be useless to relate all the ridiculous suppositions born of the imagination. That of the Indians, who declared it was supported by four white elephants, the latter standing on the wings of a vulture; is sufficient for an example. Wise people avowed that they knew nothing about it.

9. However, a general opinion, extending into pagan theogonies, appointed *the lower place*, otherwise called the depths of the Earth, or under it — they knew not much about it — for the sojourn of the reprobates, and called it hell; and in *celestial heights*, beyond the region of the stars, they fixed the home of the blessed. The word "hell" is now used, although it should have lost its etymological signification, since geology has dislodged the place of eternal sorrow from the center of the Earth, and astronomy demonstrated that there are neither upper nor lower directions in space.

10. Under the clear sky of Chaldea, India, and Egypt, cradle of the most antique civilization, one could observe the movement of the stars with as much precision as the absence of special instruments permitted. They saw at first that certain stars had a movement of their own independent of the rest, which caused them to no longer believe that they were attached to the vault. They called them wandering stars or planets, in order to distinguish them from fixed stars. They calculated their movements and periodical returns.

In the diurnal movement of the starry spheres they observed the immovableness of the polar star, around which others described, in twenty-four hours, oblique or parallel circles, smaller or greater, according to their distance from the central star. This was the first step towards the knowledge of the obliquity of the world's axis. Moreover, long voyages enabled them to observe the change of aspect in the sky according to latitudes and seasons. The elevation of the polar star above the horizon varying with the latitude, suggested the idea of the roundness of the Earth. Thus little by little they arrived at more accurate ideas of the system of the world.

Towards the year 600 B.C., Thales of Miletus, Asia Minor, became convinced of the sphericity of the Earth, the obliquity of the ecliptic, and the cause of the eclipses.

A century later Pythagoras of Samos discovered the diurnal movement of the Earth upon its axis, its annual movement around the sun, and connected the planets and comets to the solar system.

One hundred and sixty years B.C., Hipparchus of Alexandria, Egypt, invented the astrolabe, calculated and predicted the eclipses, observed the spots on the sun, ascertained the tropical year and the duration of the revolutions of the moon.

However precious these discoveries were for the progress of science, they were nearly two thousand years in becoming popularized. These new ideas, having then as a means of diffusion only a few rare manuscripts, which remained in the possession of some philosophers who taught them to privileged disciples, the masses of the people, whom they dreamed not of enlightening, profited nothing by them, but continued to cherish old beliefs.

11. Towards the year 140 of the Christian Era, Ptolemy, one of the most illustrious men of the Alexandrian school, combining his own ideas with common beliefs, and a few of the more recent astronomical discoveries, composed a system, which one can call a compound of beliefs, which took his name, and during a period of nearly fifteen centuries was solely adopted in the civilized world.

According to the theory of Ptolemy, the Earth is a sphere in the center of the universe, and is composed of four elements, — earth, water, air, and fire. This is the first region, called "*elementary.*" The second, called "*the ethereal,*" comprised eleven heavens, or concentric spheres, turning around the

Earth; viz., that of the moon, those of Mercury, Venus, of the sun, Mars, Jupiter, Saturn, of the fixed stars, of the first crystalline heaven (a solid transparent sphere), of the second crystalline sphere, and at last of the outer circle, of primitive mobility, which, by its motion, was supposed to carry around all those within it, causing them to make a revolution every twenty-four hours. Beyond these eleven spheres was the Empyrean, or highest sphere, "abode of the blessed," thus named from the Greek *pyr* or *pur*, which signifies "fire," because they believed this region to be resplendent with light like fire.

The belief in many superposed heavens or spheres has prevailed for a long time; but they varied in regards to number. The seventh was generally regarded as the highest, whence the expression, "to be carried to the seventh heaven." St. Paul said that he had been elevated to the third heaven.

Independent of the general motion, the stars had, according to Ptolemy, some particular movements of their own, greater or less according to their distance from the center. The fixed stars made a revolution in 25,816 years. This last computation denotes knowledge of the precession of the equinoxes, which is actually accomplished in about 25,868 years.

12. At the commencement of the sixteenth century, Copernicus, a celebrated astronomer, born at Thorn, Prussia, in 1472, and who died in 1543, reproduced the ideas of Pythagoras. He published a system which, confirmed each day by new observations, was favorably received, and was not long in proving that of Ptolemy to be unreliable. According to this system, the sun is the center; the planets describe circular orbs around this body of light; the moon is a satellite of the Earth.

A century later, in 1609, Galileo, born at Florence, invented the telescope.[17] In 1610 he discovered the four

---

[17] **Note of SAB**: Dutch spectacle-maker Hans Lippershey is credited with inventing the first telescope in the year 1608, when he discovered

satellites of Jupiter, and calculated their revolutions. He recognized that the planets have no light like the stars, but that they receive light from the sun; that they are spheres similar to the Earth. He observed their phases, and determined the duration of their rotation upon their axes. He thus gave, by material proofs, a definite sanction to the system of Copernicus.

From this period the belief in superposed heavens was extinguished. The stars are innumerable suns, probable centers of as many planetary systems. The planets were recognized as worlds similar to the Earth, and like it, without doubt, inhabited. The sun was believed to be a star, and the center around which the planets, which are subject to it, revolve.

The stars are no more confined to a zone of the celestial sphere, but are irregularly disseminated in limitless space. Those which appear to touch each other are immeasurable distances apart. The smallest, in appearance, are the farthest from us; the largest, those which are nearest, are hundreds of thousands millions of miles distant from us.

The groups which have gained the name of *constellations* are only apparent assemblages caused by

---

that a distant object appeared to be much closer when viewed through a concave lens and a convex lens held in front of each other. He mounted the lenses in a tube to make the first crude refracting telescope.

Science historians credit Italian scientist Galileo with the first use of the telescope for scientific observations of astronomical objects. In 1609, using a homemade telescope that could magnify objects to 20 times the size seen by the naked eye, Galileo discovered four moons orbiting the planet Jupiter. By the end of the following year, he had used his telescope to resolve the Milky Way Galaxy into countless stars, see dark spots on the Sun, and map the face of the Moon. The rapid rate of these discoveries and the extraordinary new insights they offered are unique in the history of astronomy.Soon after, telescopes started getting longer, because the ways to improve the focusing abilities of telescopes were either to lengthen the telescopes or to use mirrors — and a "reflecting telescope" using mirrors wasn't invented until Newton did so in the 1670s. Source: http://encarta.msn.com

distance, perspective effects, such as appear to the view of him who is placed at a fixed point from lights dispersed over a vast plain, or the trees of a forest. But these assemblages do not in reality exist. If one could be transported into the region of one of these constellations by measure, as one would approach, the form would disappear, and new groups would design themselves to the sight.

Since these groups do not really exist, the signification that a common superstitious belief attributes to them is illusory, as they have only as groups an imaginary existence.

In order to distinguish the constellations, names have been given to them, such as these of: *Lion, Bull, Twins, Virgin, Balance, Goat, Crab, Orion, Hercules, Great Bear or Chariot of David, Little Bear, Lyre,* etc.; and they have been represented by figures corresponding to these names, but which in every case have but fanciful connection with the apparent forms of the starry groups. We should then seek in vain for these figures in the sky.

The belief in the influence of the constellations, particularly those which constitute the twelve signs of the Zodiac, comes from the idea attached to the names they bear. If that which is called Lion had been named Donkey or Lamb, people would have attributed to it a totally different influence.

13. Galileo and Copernicus destroyed the old cosmogonies. Astronomical knowledge advanced: it could not retrograde. History records the difficulties these men of genius had to encounter through prejudice, especially through the sectarian spirit of the times, which was interested in the maintenance of errors upon which the priesthood had founded beliefs considered unchangeable. The invention of an optical instrument has been the means of destroying the trelliswork of the beliefs of many thousands of years. Nothing could prevail against a truth which could be demonstrated to man's vision. Thanks to the art of printing, the public gained a knowledge of the new ideas; and while some recognize their truth, and took part in the struggle for truth, it soon became necessary to combat, not simply a few individuals, but general opinion, which would take its part in the contest for truth.

How grand the universe is compared with the narrow proportions our forefathers assigned to it! How sublime God's work when we see its accomplishment according to the laws of nature! But only with the aid of time, and the affords and devotion of men of genius, were the sealed eyes opened, and the bandage of ignorance removed.

14. Henceforth the way will be open for numerous and illustrious wise men to enter upon the completion of the outlined work. Kepler, in Germany, discovered the celebrated laws which bear his name, and by the aid of which he discovered that planets describe not circular orbs but ellipses, of which the sun occupies one of the focuses. Newton, in England, discovered the law of universal gravitation. Laplace, in France, created celestial mechanics. In short, astronomy is no more a system founded upon conjecture and probability, but a science established upon the most rigorous bases of arithmetic and geometry. Thus one of the cornerstones of Genesis is laid, approximately 3,300 years after Moses.

Chapter VI
GENERAL URANOGRAPHY[18]

Space and Time — Matter — Laws and Forces — First Creation — Universal Creation — Suns and Planets — Satellites — Comets — The Milky Way —Fixed Stars — Deserts of the Space — The Eternal Succession of Worlds — The Universal Life — The Plurality of Worlds.

SPACE AND TIME

1. Many definitions of space have been given. The principal one is this: space is the extent which separates two bodies; from which certain sophists have inferred, that, where no body is, there can be no space. Doctors of theology have taken this idea as the base of their belief, that there is necessarily an end to space, alleging that bodies limited to a certain number cannot form an infinite succession, and that where bodies no longer exist is also the end of space. Yet another definition of space is: the place where worlds move, the void where matter acts, etc. Let us leave, in the treatises where they repose, all these definitions, which define nothing.

---

[18]. This chapter is an extract, word for word, from a series of communications dictated to the Spiritual Society of Paris, in 1862 and 1863, under the title of Uranographical Studies, and signed, GALILEO, M. C. F. Medium. (These are the initials of the name Camille Flammarion)
Note of SAB: Chapters 6-11 include discussions on various scientific disciplines such as physics, chemistry, cosmology, geology and oceanography.
Science provides us with an understanding of our material existence by means.

Space is one of those words which represents a primitive and axiomatic idea, self-evident, to which the diverse definitions which are given serve only to obscure its meaning. We all know what space is; and I desire only to establish its infinity in order that our subsequent studies may find no barrier opposing itself to the investigation of our ideas.

Now, I say that space is infinite for this reason: that it is impossible to suppose any limit to it, and that, notwithstanding the difficulty of gaining a conception of infinitude, it is, however, easier to think of going eternally through space, than to decide upon a stopping-place in it beyond which no more space extends.

In order to grasp as far as is possible with our limited faculties the infinitude of space, let us suppose ourselves departing from Earth, lost in the midst of infinitude, towards any point in the universe, and that with the exceeding celerity of an electric spark, which traverses thousands of leagues in a second. Scarcely have we left our globe, having passed over millions of miles, we find ourselves in a place whence our Earth will appear to us only under the aspect of a pale star. An instant after, following always the same direction, we shall arrive near the far-distant stars, which you can scarcely distinguish from your terrestrial station; and whence not only the Earth is lost to our sight in the heavenly depths, but also your sun's splendor is eclipsed by the distance which separates us from it. Propelled incessantly at the same

---

of reason and testing: how it originated, what are its present conditions, and what might be its ultimate fate. Spiritism attempts to reconcile this understanding with the need to find meaning in our lives: what is its purpose, how do we conduct our lives, and how to understand life's vicissitudes. Many of the scientific theories explained in the following chapters were current in the mid 1800's and are therefore outdated. These chapters are significant, however, because they show, right from Spiritism's outset, the desire to embrace both science's restless inquiry into our material existence with the moral teachings and guidance found in the Bible and the teachings of Jesus Christ.

lightning speed, we pass over planetary systems at every step as we advance in space, over islands of ethereal light, over starry ways, and glorious places where God has scattered worlds profusely, as he has sown plants on terrestrial prairies.

Now it is only a few minutes since we took our departure from Earth, and already hundreds of millions of millions of miles separate us from Earth, thousands of worlds have been displayed to our sight, and yet listen! We have in reality advanced but one step in the universe.

If we continue for years, ages, thousands of centuries, hundreds of millions of earthly periods of time, to transverse incessantly with the same lightning speed the fields of space, on whatever side we may go, toward whatsoever point we may direct ourselves from this invisible grain which we have quitted, and which is called Earth, the same immensity of space will be ever before us. This is space.

2. Time, like space, is a self-evident fact. One can make a better estimate of it by establishing its relation to the infinite whole.

Time is the succession of things. It is bound to eternity in the same manner as things are joined to infinitude. Let us suppose ourselves at the beginning of our world, at that primitive epoch where the Earth was not held in equilibrium by the divine impetus; in short, at the commencement of Genesis. Time has not arisen from the mysterious cradle of nature, and no one can tell at what epoch of the ages we are, since the pendulum of the centuries is not yet in motion.

But, silence! The first hour of a newborn Earth resounds through the air, and henceforth are *night* and *morning*. Beyond Earth eternity remains impassive and immovable, although time marches with steady feet in other worlds. Upon Earth time is enthroned, and during a series of generations, years and centuries of it will be counted.

Let us now transport ourselves to the last day of this world, to the hour when, its power for good being paralyzed by age and decay, it will be effaced from the book of life never more to reappear. Here the succession of events is arrested, the terrestrial movements which measure time are interrupted, and time is ended with them.

This simple exposition of natural things which give birth to time, perpetuate it, and then allow it to be extinguished, suffices to show that, seen from the point where we must place ourselves for our studies, time is a drop of water which falls from the cloud into the sea of which the fall is measured.

There are as many different and contradictory times as there are worlds in the vast expanse. Beyond worlds, eternity alone replaces these ephemeral inheritances and quietly fills with its light immovable the immensity of the heavens. Immensity and eternity without limits, — such are the two grand properties of universal nature.

The eye of the observer who traverses untiringly the immeasurable distances of space, as well as that of the geologist who peers into the secrets of the ages, descending even into the depths of a yawning eternity, where they will some day be engulfed, act in concert, each in his way, to acquire this double idea of infinitude, duration, and extent.

Now, in preserving this order of ideas, it will be easy for us to conceive that time being only connected with transitory things depending wholly upon things which can be measured, if, taking the terrestrial centuries for units, we piled them thousands upon thousands in order to form a colossal number, this number will never represent more than a moment in eternity, just as thousands of leagues joined to thousands of leagues are only a speck in boundless extent.

Thus, for example, time being unknown in eternity, and the ages being totally distinct from the ethereal life of the soul, we could write a number as long as the terrestrial equator, and suppose ourselves aged by this number of centuries, without making our soul one day older; and, adding to this uncountable number of ages a series of similar numbers as long as from here to the sun, or still more yet, imagining ourselves to live during the prodigious succession of circular periods represented by the addition of those numbers when we should have passed through them, the incomprehensible accumulation of years which would weigh upon our heads would be as though they were not: an entire eternity would always be before us.

Time is only a comparative measure of the inheritance of transitory things. Eternity is susceptible of no measure as regards duration of time: it owns no beginning or end; the present only belongs to it.

If centuries upon centuries are less than a second compared with eternity, what comparison does the duration of human life bear to it?

MATTER

3. At first sight nothing would appear so profoundly varied, so essentially distinct, as the diverse substances which compose the world. Among the objects in art or nature which daily pass before our eyes, are there two objects which can be accused of a perfect identity? Is it not only a parity of composition? What dissimilarity at the point of view of solidity, of compressibility, of weight and multiple properties of bodies, between atmospheric gas and a thread of gold, between the aqueous molecules in the clouds, and those of the mineral which forms the bony framework of the globe! What diversity between the chemical tissue of the varied plants which decorate the vegetable kingdom, and that of the no less numerous representatives of animal life upon Earth!

However, we can state as an absolute and fundamental truth, that all substances known and unknown, however dissimilar they may appear, either in view of their constitution or in regard to their reciprocal action, are only different forms through which matter presents itself, only varieties into which it is transformed under the direction of the innumerable forces which govern it.

4. Chemistry, of which the progress has been so rapid since the epoch in which I lived, thus far still relegated to the secret domain of magic by its own supporters, — this new science, which one can justly consider the child of this century is, we observe, uniquely based, far more solidly than its elder sisters, upon the experimental method. Chemistry, I say, has had fair play with the four primitive elements which the ancients agreed to recognize in nature. It has shown that the terrestrial element is only a combination of diverse substances varied to infinitude; that the air and water are equally decomposable, that they are the product of a certain number of equivalents of gas; that fire, far from being itself a principal element, is only a state of matter resulting from the universal movement to which it is submitted, and is of a sensible or latent combustion.

In return it has found a considerable number of principles until then unknown, which have appeared to form, by their determined combinations, diverse substances, different bodies, that it (chemistry) has studied by following certain laws, act simultaneously, and in given proportions, in the works operated in the grand laboratory of nature. These principles it has named *simple bodies*, indicating by that that it considers them primitive and indecomposable, and that by no known operation can they be reduced to parts relatively more simple than themselves.[19]

5. But there, where the appreciation of man is checked even when he is aided by the most impressionable of his artificial senses, the work of nature continues; there, where the common man accept appearance for reality, is where the practitioner raises the veil, and distinguishes the beginning of things. The eye of him who has detected the mole of nature's action sees alone under the constitutive materials of the world *the primitive cosmic matter*, simple and alone, varied in certain countries at the epoch of their birth, divided into solidarities during their life, which at length have become disjointed, and received into the receptacle of life's boundless whole by decomposition.

---

[19] The principal simple bodies are: among non-metallic bodies, oxygen, hydrogen, nitrogen, azoth, chlorine, carbon, phosphorus, sulphur, and iodine; among metallic bodies are gold, silver, platinum, mercury, lead, pewter, zinc, iron, copper, arsenic, sodium, potassium, calcium, aluminum, etc.

6. It is of these questions that we ourselves, spirits, lovers of science, speak when we assert that the opinions we express are merely conjectural. Upon these questions I will either keep silent, or prove my knowledge. To those who then would be tempted to see in my words only a dangerous theory, I will say: learn, if possible, by investigation, the multiplicity of the operations of nature, and you will recognize, that, if one admits not the unity of matter, it is impossible to explain not only the science of the suns and spheres, but without going so far, the germination of a seed in the Earth or the production of an insect.

7. If one observes such a diversity in matter, it is because the forces which have presided at its transformations, the conditions in which they are produced being unlimited in number, the various combinations of matter must be unlimited also.

Then the substance that one desires to comprehend belongs properly to fluids; that is to say, imponderable bodies, or it may be those dressed with the ordinary properties of matter. There is in all the universe only one primitive substance — the cosmic matter, or cosmos of uranography.

LAWS AND FORCES

8. If one of those unknown beings who spend their ephemeral existence in the depths of the dark regions of the ocean, if one of those polygrastic animals, one of the nereids, miserable animalcules, who only know the ichthyophagous fish and the submarine forests, received suddenly the gift of intelligence, the faculty of studying their world, and of establishing a reasonable idea of that living nature which develops in their midst, and of the terrestrial world which is not now included in the field of their observation.

If by the marvelous effect of some new power this strange race of beings should be lifted out of their unbroken darkness to the surface of the sea, not far from the fertile banks of an isle covered with luxuriant vegetation, to the genial sun, dispenser of a beneficent warmth, — what judgment would they pass? What theories of universal creation would be theirs, — theories to be soon effaced by larger appreciation, but by theories still as relatively incomplete as the first? Such is, O man! an image of all your speculative science.[20]

9. Now, as I come to treat of the laws and forces which rule the universe, I who am, like you, a being relatively ignorant of real science, notwithstanding the apparent superiority which is given me over my Earthly brothers, the opportunity which is mine of studying questions in nature which is withheld from them in their position, my object is only to expose to you a general idea of universal laws, without explaining in detail the methods of operation, and nature of the special forces dependent upon them.

There is an ethereal fluid which pervades space and penetrates bodies. This fluid is ether, or *primitive cosmic matter*, generatrix of the world and beings. There are inherent forces in ether which preside at the metamorphoses of matter — the necessary and immutable laws which rule the world. These multiple forces, indefinitely varied according to the combinations of matter, localized according to masses or bulk, diversified in their modes of action according to circumstances and places, are known upon Earth under the names of *weight, cohesion, affinity, attraction, magnetism, and active electricity*; the agent of the vibratory movements, those of *sound, light, heat*, etc. In other worlds they are presented under other aspects, offer other characters unknown in this, and in the immense extent of the heavens an indefinite number of forces are developed upon an unimaginable ladder, the grandeur of which we are as incapable of estimating as the crustacean

---

[20] Such is the state of those who deny the spiritual world, when, after having been despoiled of their fleshly envelope the horizons of this world are revealed to their vision, they comprehend the emptiness of the theories whereby they attempted to explain everything by matter alone. However, these horizons hold yet for them mysteries which are successively unveiled as they are raised to greater heights of wisdom by purification; but on their entrance into this new world they are first to recognize their blindness, and how far they were from the truth.

animal in the depth of the ocean is of understanding the universality of terrestrial phenomena.[21]

Now, just as there is but one simple primitive substance generatrix of all bodies, but diversified in its combinations, even as all forces depend upon a universal law diversified in its effects, and which in the eternal decrees has been everywhere imposed upon creation in order to constitute harmony and permanent stability.

11. Nature is never opposed to itself. The coat-of-arms of the universe has for its only device: unity - variety. In climbing the ladder of the worlds, one finds unity in harmony in all creation. At the same time there is an infinite variety in this immense garden of stars. In passing through the degrees of life from the lowest being even to God, the great law of continuity is recognizable. In considering the forces in themselves, one can find a series whose result, mingling with the generatrix, is the universal law.

You cannot appreciate this law to the full extent, since the forces which represent it in your field of observation are restrained and limited. However, gravitation and electricity can be regarded as a large application of the primordial law which reigns beyond the heavens.

---

[21] Should we bring to this all that we know, we should not comprehend more fully that which escapes our senses than the blind man so born comprehends the effects of light and the use of eyes. Therefore, there can be in other places properties of cosmic fluid and combinations, of which we have no idea, of effects appropriated to needs unknown to us, giving place to new and other modes of perception. We do not, for example, comprehend how we can see without bodily eyes and without light; but who says that there exist no other agents than the light affecting special organisms? The somnambulic sight, which neither distance, material obstacles, nor darkness can arrest, offers us an example? Let us suppose that in some world the inhabitants are normally that which our somnambulists are exceptionally, they will have no need of the light or of eyes like ours, and they will see that which we cannot see. It is the same with all other sensations: the conditions of vitality and perceptibility, sensations and needs vary according to places.

All these forces are eternal, — we will explain this word, — universal as the creation. Being inherent in the cosmic fluid, they necessarily act in all things everywhere, modifying their action by their simultaneous working or their succession, predominating here, effacing themselves farther on; powerful and active at certain points, latent or secret at others, but finally preparing, directing, preserving and destroying worlds in their diverse periods of life, governing marvelous works of nature, wherever they are exerted, assuring to creation eternal splendor.

THE FIRST CREATION

12. After having considered the universe under general points of view, its composition, its laws, and its properties, we can extend our studies to the mode of formation which gave light to worlds and beings. We would descend then to the creation of the Earth particularly, and to its actual state in the universality of things, and from whence, taking the globe as a starting-point and for relative unity, we would proceed with our planetary and sidereal studies.

13. If we have well considered the connection, or rather the opposition, of eternity to time, — if we are familiar with the idea that time is only a relative measure in the succession of transitory things, whilst eternity is essentially immovable and permanent, and that it is susceptible of no measurement as regards duration of time, — we should comprehend that there is no commencement or end to it.

On the other side, if we could form a just idea — although necessarily a very feeble one — of the infinitude of divine power, we could comprehend how it is possible that the universe has always been, and always will be; how God's eternal perfections always spoke of him before worlds were born. Before time was born, immeasurable eternity received the divine word, and impregnated space eternal as itself.

14. God, who has always existed, has created through all eternity, and could not be otherwise, for, however far back is the epoch that our imagination can reach for the supposed limits of creation, there will always exist an eternity beyond that limit. Weigh well this thought, — an eternity during which the divine hypostasis, the infinite volition, had been absorbed in a mute, inactive, and unfruitful lethargy, an eternity of apparent death for the eternal Father who gives life to beings; of indifferent speechlessness for the Word which governs them, of cold and selfish sterility for the spirit of love and of vivication.

Let us better comprehend the grandeur of divine action, and its perpetuity under the semblance of an absolute being! God is the sun of beings: he is the light of the world. Now, the appearance of the sun gives birth instantaneously to floods of light, which fill all space. So does the universe, born of the Eternal, raise us in thought to unimaginable periods of infinite duration, even to the time of the "*Fiat lux*" in the beginning.

15. The contemplation of the absolute beginning of objects raises us to their Creator. Their successive appearance in the domain of existence constitute the order of perpetual creation.

What mortal is there who knows how to reveal the unknown and superbly veiled magnificence which lay under the darkness of the ages, which was developed in those ancient times when none of the marvels of the present universe existed? At this primitive epoch, where the voice of the Lord was making itself heard, the materials which were in the future to assemble symmetrically to form themselves into the temple of nature were found on the bosom of the infinite void, when at the sound of this mysterious voice, which every creature venerates as a mother's, when the morning stars harmoniously sang together!

The world was in its cradle; it was not yet established in its strength and plenitude of life. No; the creative power never contradicts itself; and, like all things, the universe was born a child. Invested with laws previously framed, and by initial impulsion inherent in its formation, primitive cosmic matter gave birth successively to whirlwinds, to agglomerations of diffuse fluid, to masses of nebulous matter, infinitely modified and divided, in order to form in the immeasurable regions of space different centers of simultaneous or successive creations.

By reason of forces which predominate over each other,

and by ulterior circumstances which presided at their developments, these primitive centers became each the focus of a special life. Those least disseminated in space, and riches in acting forces and principles, commenced from that time their particular astral life. Others occupying unlimited space grew very slowly, or divided themselves anew into other secondary centers.

16. In carrying ourselves back only a few millions of centuries beyond this present epoch, our Earth did not exist. Our solar system had not yet commenced the evolutions of planetary life; and yet splendid suns illuminated the ether. Already inhabited planets gave life and existence to a multitude of beings who have preceded us in our earthly career. Opulent productions of an unknown nature, and marvelous heavenly phenomena, had developed, under the gaze of others eyes, pictures of boundless creation, and even more. Already some splendors, which had caused the hearts of other mortals, at one time, then to palpitate with the thought of infinite power, were effaced; and we poor little beings who come after an eternity of life has passed, we believe ourselves contemporaneous with creation!

Yet again let us comprehend nature better. Let us know that eternity is both before and behind us, that space is the theater of an unimaginable succession and simultaneity of creations. The nebula we scarcely distinguish in the far-distant heavens are agglomerations of suns in process of formation; others are milky ways of inhabited worlds; others the seat of catastrophe and decay. Let us know that even as we are placed in the midst of an infinitude of worlds, even as we are in a double infinitude of anterior and ulterior durations, that universal creation is not for us alone, and that we must not consider this, our little globe, as an isolated formation.

Universal Creation

17. After mounting as high as we can, despite our weakness, toward the concealed source whence worlds flow like drops of water in a river, let us consider the march of successive creations, and their serial developments.

Primitive cosmic matter comprises the material fluid and vital elements which unroll the magnificence of all the universes throughout eternity. It is the fruitful mother of all things, the first grandmother, and, still more, the eternal generatrix. It has not disappeared, this substance from which sidereal spheres are produced; it is not dead, this power, for it brings incessantly new creations into light, and incessantly receives the reconstituted principles of worlds which are effaced from the eternal book of life.

Ethereal matter more or less rarefied, which descends among the interplanetary spaces, — this cosmic fluid which fills the world more or less rarefied in immeasurable regions, rich in agglomerations of stars more or less condensed, where astral heavens do not yet shine forth more or less modified by diverse combinations according to locality in space, — is none other than the primal substance in which primitive forces reside, from which nature draws all things.[22]

18. This fluid which penetrates bodies is like an immense ocean. In it resides the vital principle which gives birth and life to beings, perpetuating it upon every globe according to its condition. It is a principle in a latent state, which slumbers when no existence calls for it. Every mineral, vegetable, animal, or other — for many other natural kingdoms exist, the existence of which you do not suspect — knows how, by virtue of this universal vital principle, to appropriate the conditions of its existence and of its duration.

The molecules of the mineral have their share of this life, as well as the seed and the germ, and group themselves, like an organized being, into symmetrical forms, which constitute individualities.

---

[22] If one inquires what the principle of these forces is, and how it can be even in the substance which produces it, we would reply that mechanics offers us numerous examples. The elasticity which makes a spring unbend, — is not that in the spring itself, and does it not depend upon the mode of the aggregation of molecules? The body which obeys a centrifugal force receives its impulsion from the primitive movement which has been impressed upon it.

It is very important to comprehend this idea: that primitive cosmic matter was invested not only with laws which assure the stability of worlds, but also with the universal vital principle which causes spontaneous generations upon every world, in proportion as conditions for the successive existence of beings manifest themselves, when the time comes for the appearance of children of life, during the creative period.

Thus universal creation is accomplished. It is then true to say that, the operations of nature being the expression of the divine will, God has always created, and creates unceasingly, and always will create.

19. Until now we have passed over in silence the subject of the spiritual world, which also is a part of creation, and accomplishes its destiny in accordance with the august decrees of the Master.

I can give only very limited information concerning the mode of the creation of spirits, on account of my own ignorance; and I must still keep silent upon some matters into which I have been permitted to search.

To those who are religiously desirous of obtaining knowledge, and who are humble before God, I will say (while I implore them not to base any one system prematurely on my words), that the spirit does not receive divine illumination until the time when free will and conscience are given him to grasp the idea of his high destiny; i.e., until he has passed through a series of inferior existences, during which the realization of his individuality is slowly elaborated. This only dates from the day when the Lord impresses upon his forehead his august seal; then, the spirit takes rank as human.

Again, I beg of you, do not build upon my words dogmatic theories like those so sadly celebrated in the history of metaphysics. I would a thousand times prefer to keep silent forever concerning questions so far above our ordinary meditations, than expose you to a misconstruction of the sense of my teachings, and so engulf you through my imperfection in the inextricable labyrinths of deism or fatalism.

THE SUNS AND THE PLANETS

20. Once upon a time in the history of the universe, lost among the myriad worlds, cosmic matter was condensed into the form of an immense nebula. This nebula was animated by the universal laws which govern matter. By virtue of these laws, and notably by the molecular force of attraction, it took the form of a spheroid, the only one which can originally be taken by a mass of isolated matter in space.

The circular movement, produced by gravitation exactly equal in all the molecular zones toward the center, soon modified the primitive sphere in order to conduct it from movement to movement toward the lenticular form. We speak of the whole of the nebula.

21. New forces surged in the train of this rotary movement — centripetal and centrifugal force — the first tending to draw every particle to the center, the second tending to cause the recession of every atom from it. Now, the movement accelerating itself, according to the condensation of the nebula and its radius, augmenting as it approaches the lenticular form, the centrifugal force, incessantly developed by these two causes, soon predominated over the central attraction the same as a too rapid movement of a sling breaks the cord, and throws the projectile to a distance.

Thus, the predominance of centrifugal force detached the equatorial circle of the nebula, and with this ring formed a new mass, isolated from the first, but nevertheless in submission to its empire. This mass has conserved its equatorial movement, which, modified, became its movement of translation around the solar body. Moreover, its new state gave to it a rotary movement around its proper center.

22. The nebulous generatrix which gave birth to this new world is condensed, and has resumed the spherical form; but the primitive heat developed by its different movements weakening it only by very slow degrees, the phenomenon we have just described will reproduce itself often during a long period, while this nebulous mass will not become dense or solid enough to oppose an efficacious resistance to the modifications of form, which successively impress its rotary movement.

It will then not have given birth simply of one astral body, but to hundreds of worlds detached from the central focus, issued from it by the mode of formation already presented. Now, each one of these worlds, invested like the primitive world with natural forces presiding at the creation of the universe, will engender in succession new globes gravitating henceforth around it, as it gravitates in concurrence with its brothers around the focus of their existence and life. Each one of these worlds will be a sun, a center of a whirling body of planets, successively escaped from its equator. These planets will each receive a particular life, although dependent upon their astral generator.[23]

23. Planets are thus formed of masses of condensed

---

[23] **Note of SAB**: Theories of Origin: Current theories connect the formation of the solar system with the formation of the Sun itself, about 4.7 billion years ago. The fragmentation and gravitational collapse of an interstellar cloud of gas and dust, triggered perhaps by nearby supernova explosions, may have led to the formation of a primordial solar nebula. The Sun would then form in the densest, central region. It is so hot close to the Sun that even silicates, which are relatively dense, have difficulty forming there. This phenomenon may account for the presence near the Sun of a planet such as Mercury, having a relatively small silicate crust and a larger than usual, dense iron core. (It is easier for iron dust and vapor to coalesce near the central region of a solar nebula than it is for lighter silicates to do so.) At larger distances from the center of the solar nebula, gases condense into solids such as are found today from Jupiter outward. Evidence of a possible pre-formation supernova explosion appears as traces of anomalous isotopes in tiny inclusions in some meteorites. This association of planet formation with star formation suggests that billions of other stars in our galaxy may also have planets. The high frequency of binary and multiple stars, as well as the large satellite systems around Jupiter and Saturn, attest to the tendency of collapsing gas clouds to fragment into multi-body systems. Source "Solar System," Microsoft® Encarta® Online Encyclopedia 2002 - http://encarta.msn.com © 1997-2002.

matter, but not yet solidified, detached from the central mass by the action of centrifugal force, and taking, by virtue of the laws of motion, the spheroid form more or less elliptic, according to the degree of fluidity they have maintained. One of these planets is the Earth, which, before being cooled and invested with a solid crust, must have given birth to the moon by the same mode of astral formation to which it owes its own existence. The Earth henceforth inscribed in the book of life, a cradle of creatures whose feebleness is protected under the wing of Divine Providence, a new cord in the infinite harp which must vibrate in its place in the universal concert of worlds.

SATELLITES

24. Before the planetary bodies have attained a degree of coolness sufficient for solidification, smaller bodies, veritable liquid globules, are detached from some in the equatorial plane, — a plane in which the centrifugal force is the greatest, — and which by virtue of the same laws have acquired a movement of translation around their planetary generatrix, like theirs around their central astral generator.

Thus the Earth has given birth to the moon, the body of which, being smaller, has cooled in a shorter time. Now the laws and forces which presided at its detachment from the terrestrial equator and its movement of translation in this same plane, act in such a way, that this world, in place of being invested with the spheroid form, takes that of an ovoid globe; that is to say, having the elongated form of an egg, the center of gravity in the inferior part.

25. The conditions by which the distinctive form of the moon was effected would permit it scarcely to quit the Earth, and constrain it to remain perpetually suspended in its sky like an ovoid figure, of which the heaviest parts form the lower face turned toward the Earth, and of which the least dense parts occupy the summit, which is the side opposed to the Earth, elevating itself towards the heavens. This is the reason that this body presents continually the same face to us. It can be likened, in order to better comprehend its geological state, to a globe composed of cork, of which the base, turned towards the Earth, is formed of lead.

Hence two essentially distinct natures are found upon the surface of the lunar world, — one without any possible analogy with ours, for fluid and ethereal bodies are unknown to it; the other, relatively analogous to the Earth, since all the least dense substances are found upon this hemisphere. The first, perpetually turned towards the Earth, is without atmosphere or water, except maybe at the boundaries of this sub-terrestrial hemisphere; the other, rich in fluids, is perpetually opposed to our world.[24]

26. The number and condition of the satellites of every planet have been carried according to the special conditions of their formation. Some have given birth to no secondary body,

---

[24] This entirely new theory of the moon explains, by the law of gravitation, the reason why this body always turns the same face toward the earth. Its center of gravity, instead of being in the center of the sphere, is to be found upon one of the points of its surface, and, consequently, attracted to the Earth by a greater force than are the lighter parts. The moon produces the effect of figures called Poussahs, which constantly stand upright upon their base, while the planets, whose centers of gravity are at equal distances from the surface, turn regularly upon their axes. The vivifying fluids, gaseous or liquid, on account of their specific lightness, would be found accumulated in the superior hemisphere constantly opposed to the Earth. The inferior hemisphere, the only one we see, must be destitute of them, and consequently incapable of sustaining life, whilst life would reign on the other. If, then, the upper hemisphere be inhabited, its inhabitants have never seen the Earth, unless by excursions into the other hemisphere, which would be impossible for them, since it lacks the necessary conditions of vitality. However rational and scientific this opinion may be, as it has not yet been confirmed by any one direct observation, it can be accepted only as an hypothesis; and as such it serves as a beacon-star to science. But one has to agree that up to the present, it is the sole satisfactory explanation of the particularities presented by this satellite.
[25] **Note of SAB**: In 1877, two satellites of Mars were discovered: Phobos and Deimos.

— Mercury, Venus, and Mars[25], for instance; whilst others have formed one or many, like the Earth, Jupiter, Saturn, and others.

27. In addition to its satellites, or moons, the planet Saturn presents a special phenomenon of the ring, which seems from afar, to surround it like a white aureole. This formation is to us a new proof of the universality of the laws of nature. This ring is surely the result of a separation which took place in primitive times in the equator of Saturn, just as an equatorial zone has been thrown off from the Earth, and formed its satellite. The difference consists in this that the ring of Saturn was found formed in all its parts of homogeneous molecules, probably already in a certain state of condensation, and enabled in this manner to continue its rotary movement in the same way, and in a time nearly equal, to that which revolves the planet. If one of the points of this ring had been denser than another, one or many agglomerations of substance would have been suddenly expelled, and Saturn would have counted many satellites more. Since the time of its formation, this ring has been solidified, as well as the other planetary bodies.[26]

---

[26] **Note of SAB**: The rings of Saturn have puzzled astronomers ever since they were discovered by Galileo in 1610 using the first telescope. The puzzles have only increased since Voyagers 1 and 2 imaged the ring system extensively in 1980 and 1981. In addition to the images, several Voyager instruments observed occultations of the ring system with radial resolution as fine as 100 meters. The rings have been given letter names in the order of their discovery. The main rings are, working outward from the planet, known as C, B, and A. The Cassini Division is the largest gap in the rings and separates Rings B and A. In addition a number of fainter rings have been discovered more recently. The D Ring is exceedingly faint and closest to the planet. The F Ring is a narrow feature just outside the A Ring. Beyond that are two far fainter rings named G and E. The particles in Saturn's rings are composed primarily of water ice and range from microns to meters in size. The rings show a tremendous amount of structure on all scales; some of this structure is related to gravitational perturbations by Saturn's many moons, but much of it remains unexplained.
Source: http://ringmaster.arc.nasa.gov/saturn/saturn.html

COMETS

28. Wandering stars far more truly than the planets which have received this etymological designation, the comets should be the guides leading us over the limits of the system, to which the Earth belongs, carrying us into the far-away regions of sidereal space.

But, before exploring by the aid of these travelers of the universe the celestial domains, it will be well for us to become acquainted as much as possible with their intrinsic nature and their role in the planetary economy.

29. Men have often seen in these wandering stars growing worlds, elaborating in their primitive chaos conditions of life and existence which are bestowed upon inhabited worlds; others have imagined these extraordinary bodies to be worlds in a state of destruction, and their singular appearance has been made the subject of erroneous opinions concerning their nature. Astrology has taught that they foretell coming disasters, and that they were messengers decreed by Divine Providence to warn the astonished and trembling Earth.

30. The law of variety is applied in such great profuseness in the works of nature, that one demands how naturalists, astronomers, or philosophers have invented so many systems in order to link comets to planetary bodies, and in order to see in them only stars more or less advanced in development or decay. The pictures which nature is ever presenting ought, however, amply to suffice for the removal from the observer's mind of all search for parallels which do not exist, and leave to the comets the modest but useful role of wandering stars serving as advance-guards for solar empires; for the celestial bodies are found in many forms other than planetary. Comets have not, like the planets, to fulfill the mission of affording an abiding place for humanity. They travel in successive journeys from sun to sun, enriching themselves sometimes on their route by planetary fragments reduced to a vaporous state, bringing to their focuses the vivifying and renovating principle that they cast upon terrestrial bodies (Chap. IX, n° 12).

31. If one of these bodies should approach our little

globe in order to transverse its orbit, and return to its apogee situated at an immeasurable distance from the sun, let us follow it in thought, in order to visit with it the sidereal countries. To do so we must leap over the prodigious expanse of ethereal matter, which separates the sun from the nearest stars; and observing the combined movements of this body, that one could well believe lost in this desert of infinitude, we should find there still an eloquent proof of the universality of nature's laws, which are exercised in distances the extent of which the most fervid imagination can hardly conceive.

There the elliptic form is exchanged for the parabolic; and the tail is lessened at the point of transition to only a few yards, while at its perigee it would extend many millions of leagues. Perhaps a more powerful sun, more important than the one it has just quitted, will exert over this comet a greater attraction, and will receive it into the ranks of its own subjects; and then the astonished children of your little Earth will wait in vain for the return they had prognosticated by imperfect observations. In this case, we, whose thought has followed the wandering comet into those unknown regions, will encounter then a new nation never seen before by terrestrial eyes, unimaginable by spirits who inhabit the Earth, inconceivable even to their thought; for it will be the theater of unexplored marvels.

We have arrived at the astral world in this brilliant universe of vast suns which shine in infinite space, and which are the brilliant flowers of the magnificent garden of creation. Until we arrive there, we can never know what the Earth really is.

THE MILKY WAY

32. During some beautiful starry, moonless nights, everyone has observed this beautiful white light which traverses the heavens from one extremity to the other, and which the ancients have named "The Milky Way" on account of its milky appearance. This diffuse light has long been explored by the aid of the modern telescope; and this road of powdered gold, or this spring of milk of antique mythology, has been transformed into a vast field of unknown wonders. The researches of observers have led to a knowledge of its nature, and have shown that, where the unaided vision could behold only a feeble light, millions of suns, more important and larger than that which illuminates the Earth are to be found.

33. The Milky Way indeed is a country sown with solar or planetary flowers which shine in its vast extent. Our sun and all the bodies accompanying it make a part of these radiant globes of which the Milky Way is composed; but notwithstanding the sun's gigantic dimensions relative to the Earth, and the vastness of Earth's empire, it occupies, however, only an unappreciable place in this vast creation. One can count thirty millions of similar suns revolving in this boundless region, apart from one another by distance more than a hundred thousand times as great as that of the terrestrial orbit.[27]

34. One can judge, by this approximation, of the extent of this sidereal region, and of the relation which unites our system to the universal whole of the systems which occupy it. We can thus judge of the comparative smallness of the solar domain, and much more of the infinitesimality of our little Earth. How, then, are the people who inhabit it to be considered?

When I say diminutiveness of our little Earth, our assertions apply not only to its material form and to the physical extent of the bodies which we study, but still more, and above all, to the moral state, to the degree to which they have attained in the universal hierarchy of beings. In this latter phase creation is shown in all its majesty, creating and propagating everything by the solar world, making manifestations of life and intelligence in each one of the systems which surround it on every side.

35. One becomes acquainted only in this way with the position occupied by our sun, or by the Earth in the starry expanse. These considerations will acquire greater weight still

---

[27] More than three trillions four hundred billions of leagues.

if we reflect that the Milky Way seen from afar represents only an imperceptible and inappreciable point in the immensity of the sidereal creations. Millions like it exist in space. It is a stellar nebula. If it appears to us richer and more immense than others, it is for this sole reason that it surrounds us, and develops itself in its extent under our very eyes; whilst the others, lost in unfathomable depths, are scarcely to be seen.

36. Now, if one remembers that the Earth, comparatively speaking, is nothing or almost nothing in the solar system, that the latter is nothing or nearly nothing in the Milky Way, this latter is nothing or nearly nothing in the universe of nebula, and this universe itself a very little thing in the midst of the vastness of infinitude, one will begin to comprehend what the terrestrial globe is.

FIXED STARS

37. Those bodies called "fixed stars," and which constellate the two hemispheres of the firmament, are not isolated from all exterior attraction as is generally supposed; on the contrary, they belong to one and the same agglomeration of stellar bodies. This agglomeration is no other than the nebula of which we form a part, the equatorial plane of which as displayed in the sky has received the name of "Milky Way." All the suns which compose it are conjointly responsible: their collective influences react perpetually upon one another, and universal gravitation re-unites them all in one family.

38. Among these different suns, the greater number are, like our own, surrounded by secondary worlds, which they illuminate and make fruitful by the same laws which preside in the life of our planetary system. Some of them, like Sirius, are thousands of times more magnificent in dimensions and in grandeur than ours, their role are more important in the universe, whilst a very great number of planets very superior to ours surround them. Others are very dissimilar in their astral functions. Thus a certain number of these suns, veritable twins of the sidereal order, are accompanied by their brothers of the same age, and form in space binary systems, to which nature has given entirely different functions than those which belong to our sun.[28] There the years are measured no more by the same periods, neither are the days measured by the same suns; and these worlds lighted by a double luminary have received a share of conditions of existence unimaginable to those who have not emerged from this little terrestrial globe.

Other stars without attendants, deprived of planets, have received the best elements of habitability which are given to any of them. The laws of nature are diversified in this immensity; and, if unity is the watchword of the universe, infinite variety is no less the eternal attribute.

39. Notwithstanding the prodigious number of these stars and their systems, in spite of the immeasurable distances which separate them, they all belong to the same stellar nebula which the most powerful telescopic vision can scarcely traverse, and which the boldest conceptions of the imagination can scarcely attain unto, — a nebula which, nevertheless, is only a unit in the order of nebula which compose the astral world.

40. The stars which they call *fixed* are not immovable in space. The constellations which they have imagined to be in the vault of the firmament are not really symbolical creations. The distance from the Earth and the appearance of the universe measured from this station are the two causes of this double optical illusion (Chap. V, n° 12).

---

[28]This is what we call in Astronomy binary stars (double stars). They are two suns, one revolving around the other, as a planet does around its sun. What a strange and magnificent show the inhabitants of these worlds, comprised of these systems illuminated by double suns, should enjoy! But also, how different the conditions of life should be there! In a latter communication, the spirit of Galileo affirms: "There are, indeed, more complex systems in which different suns, one facing the other, perform the role of satellites. Marvelous effects of light are then produced for the inhabitants of the globes they illuminate. In fact, despite the apparent proximity of one to the other, inhabited worlds can revolve amongst them and receive alternatively the waves of diversely colored light, in whose union comprises the white light.

41. We have seen that the totality of the stars which shine in the azure dome is enclosed in a cosmic agglomeration, in the same nebula which you call Milky Way; but, although all belong to this same group, all of the stars are no less animated by their own translation movement in space. Absolute repose exists nowhere. They are regulated by the universal laws of gravitation, and revolve in space under the incessant impulsion of this immense power. They revolve, not in routes traced by chance, but following certain orbits of which the center is occupied by a superior star. In order to render my words more comprehensible, as an example, I will speak specially of your sun.

42. One knows, by modern observations, that the sun is not fixed or a central point, as they believed it to be in the early days of modern astronomy, but that it advances in space, drawing with it its vast system of planets, satellites, and comets.

Now this march is not casual: it does not wander about in the infinite voids, to be lost far away from the regions assigned to it, its children, and subjects. No; its orbit is measured, concurrently with other suns of the same order as itself, and surrounded like itself with a certain number of inhabited worlds, it gravitates around a central sun. Its movement of gravitation, the same as that of other suns (its brothers), is inestimable by annual observation; for a great number of earthly centuries would hardly suffice to mark the time of one of these astral years.

43. The central sun, of which we have just spoken, is itself a globe, comparatively speaking, secondary to another still more important one, around which it is perpetually traveling with a slow and measured march in company with other suns of the same order.

We might contemplate this successive subordination of suns to suns till our imaginations became weary of ascending through such a vast a hierarchy; for, let us not forget that they can count in round numbers thirty millions of suns in the Milky Way[29], subordinate to one another, like the gigantic machinery of an immense system.

44. And these stars, so innumerable, live, each and every one, a conjointly responsible life. For nothing in the economy of your little terrestrial sphere lives a lonely, detached life, which rule extends to the whole boundless universe.

These systems upon systems would appear from afar, to the eye of the philosophical investigator who could comprehend the picture developed by space and time, like pearl and gold dust blown into whirlwinds by the divine breath which makes sidereal worlds fly through the heavens like grains of sand through the desert.

More immovability, more silence, more night! The great spectacle which would then display itself before our eyes would be the real creation, immense and full of that ethereal life which the all-seeing eye of the Creator embraces in its boundless vision.

But until now we have spoken only of a nebula. Its millions of suns, its myriads of inhabited Earths, form, as we have said before, only an island in the infinite archipelago.

Deserts of Space

45. An immense wilderness, without limits, extends beyond the agglomeration of stars, of which we have just spoken, and surrounds it. Solitudes succeed to solitudes, and immeasurable plains extend through the far reaching expanse. Masses of cosmic matter are found everywhere isolated in space like islands in a vast archipelago. If one can appreciate,

---

[29] **Note of SAB**: The Milky Way, the large, disk-shaped aggregation of stars, or galaxy, that includes the Sun and its solar system In addition to
the Sun, the Milky Way contains about 400 billion other stars. There are hundreds of billions of other galaxies in the universe, some of which are much larger and contain many more stars than the Milky Way. Source "Milky Way," Microsoft® Encarta® Online Encyclopedia 2002 - http://encarta.msn.com © 1997-2002.

in some measure, the enormous distance which separates the mass of stars, of which we form a part, from the collections nearest to them, it is necessary to know that these stellar islands are disseminated sparsely in the vast ocean of the heavens, and that the extent of space dividing them is immeasurably greater than their respective dimensions.

Now, we must remember that the stellar nebula measure, taken as a unity, a thousand times the distance between the nearest stars; that is to say, some hundred thousand trillions of leagues. The distance between them being much vaster could not be expressed in numbers comprehensible by your minds. The imagination alone, in its highest conceptions, is capable of attaining to this prodigious immensity. These mute solitudes, destitute of all appearance of life, can give one the idea, in some measure, of this relative infinity.

46. This celestial desert, however, which surrounds our sidereal universe, and which appears to extend like the distant confines of our astral world, is embraced by the infinite power of the Almighty, who, beyond these heavens of our heavens, has developed the screen of his unlimited creation.

47. Beyond these vast solitudes, indeed, world radiate in untold magnificence, as well as in regions accessible to human investigation. Beyond these wildernesses splendid oasis float in the limpid ether, and incessantly renew beautiful scenes of activity and life. There, in the far-away distance, are displayed aggregations of cosmic substance utterly beyond the range of the telescope through the transparent regions of our heavens. These nebula that you call diffuse, and which appear to you like clouds of white dust lost in the unknown depths of ethereal space, when revealed, develop new worlds, whose strange and varied conditions, when compared with those inherent in your globe, endow them with modes of life of which your imagination cannot conceive, nor your studies explain. There creative power shines resplendently in all its plenitude before him who comes from regions occupied by your system. Other laws are there in activity, whose forces rule the manifestations of life; and the novel routes we follow in these strange regions open up to us unknown perspectives.[30]

THE ETERNAL SUCCESSION OF WORLDS

48. We have seen that one primordial and general law alone has been given to the universe in order to insure eternal stability, and that this universal law is perceptible to our senses by means of the many modes of operation we call the directing forces of nature. We are going to show today that the harmony of the entire universe, considered under the double aspect of eternity and of space, is assured by this supreme law.

49. Indeed, if we go back to the primitive origin or first agglomerations of cosmic substance, we must remark that, already under the empire of this law, matter is submitted to the necessary transformations which develop from the germ

---

[30] Diffuse nebula is the name given in astronomy to a nebula whose clusters of stars, as of yet, are unidentifiable. At first they had been considered as an agglomeration of cosmic matter in the process of condensation to form worlds. Presently however this appearance is thought to be due to its distance, and that with powerful enough instruments they would all be definable.

Though imperfect, a familiar comparison can give us an idea of the definable nebula: They are like groups of sparkles projected by fireworks, at the moment of explosion. To us, each of the sparkles would represent a star, and the set would be the nebula, or the group of stars drawn together in a point of space, subjected to a common law of attraction and of movement. Seen from a distance, these sparkles are barely distinguishable and its group has the appearance of a small cloud of smoke. This comparison is not exact, as it refers to a mass of condensed cosmic matter.

Our Milky Way is one of these nebula; we count approximately 30 million stars or suns in it (see footnote n° 29). It occupies no less than some hundreds of trillion leagues of extension, even though it is not the largest. Let us suppose that only an average of 20 inhabited planets revolves around each sun; this would give us an approximate total of 600 million worlds, for our group alone.

to the ripe fruit, and that, under the impulsion of diverse forces of this law, the Earth climbs over the ladder of its periodical revolutions. At first the fluidic center of motion, generator of worlds, thence the central and attractive nucleus of spheres which have been cradled on its bosom.

We know already that one law presides throughout the history of cosmos. That which it is important for us to know now is that it presides equally at the destruction of astral bodies; for death is not only a metamorphosis for living beings, but a transformation for inanimate matter. If it is correct to say, in the literal sense, that all life is amenable to the scythe of death, it is also just to add that all substance must of necessity submit to the inherent transformations of its constitution.

50. Here is a world that from its cradle has passed through all the succession of years allotted to it by its special organization; the interior focus of its existence is extinguished: its elements have lost their original virtue.

If we could transport ourselves from our nebula to another, there we would feel like we were in the middle of our own Milky Way, though with skies full of stars in a way completely different than ours. Despite its colossal dimensions, from a distance this Milky Way would appear to us as a small lenticular speck, lost in infinity. Before reaching the nebula, we would feel like the traveler who leaves a city and travels through a vast uninhabited country, before arriving at another city. We would have traversed incommensurable spaces, devoid of stars and worlds, that which Galileo called "deserts of the space." As we advanced, we would see behind us a fleeting view of our nebula. While ahead of us we would see that (galaxy) in whose direction we were heading to, becoming more and more clearer, similarly to the mass of sparkles from the fireworks. By transporting ourselves in thought to regions of the space located ahead of the archipelago of our nebula, we would see all around us millions of similar and diverse forms of archipelagos, each of them encompassing millions of suns and hundreds of millions of inhabited worlds.

All of that which can help us to associate ourselves with the vastness of the extension and of the structure of the Universe is useful to enhance our ideas, so restricted by ordinary beliefs. God grows before our eyes, as we better understand the greatness of these works, while recognizing

The phenomena of nature which claimed for their production the presence and action of forces found in this world, henceforth cannot present themselves, because the lever of their activity can no longer sustain them.

Now, what would one think if this extinguished Earth, without life, should continue to gravitate in celestial space without an object and pass like a useless cinder in the whirlwind of the heavens? Can any of us think it should remain inscribed in the book of universal life when it is only a dead letter denuded of meaning? No; the same laws which have elevated it above the dead chaos, and which have adorned it with the splendors of life, the same forces which have governed it throughout its adolescence, which have supported its first steps in existence, and which have conducted it to a ripe old age, preside at the disintegration of its constituent elements, in order to render it in the laboratory from which creative power draws unceasingly the means of general stability. These elements return to this common mass of ether in order to assimilate with other bodies, or to help in the formation of other suns. And this death will neither be a useless event to this or to its sister planets. It will renew in other regions other creations of a different nature; and there, where some systems

---

our own inferior place. As seen, we are far from the belief implemented by the Mosaic Genesis, which makes our small imperceptible Earth God's chief creation, and its inhabitants, the sole objects of his concern. We comprehend the vanity of those who believe that all in the universe was made for them, and of those who dare to discuss the existence of the Supreme Being. Some centuries from now it will be a motive of wonder that a religion made to glorify God, has demoted him to such miserly proportions; and has repelled and considered as being conceived by the spirit of evil the discoveries which could have no other result but that of augmenting our admiration for the divine omnipotence, upon initiating us to the grandiose mysteries of the creation. It will be a motive of even greater astonishment when it becomes known that such teachings were repelled, for they should have emancipated the spirit of mankind and oppose the preponderance of those who claimed to be God's representatives on Earth.

of worlds have vanished, will soon be born a new and more brilliant garden of flowers, more beauteous and fragrant still.

51. Thus the real and effective eternity of the universe is assured by the same laws which direct the operations of time. Thus worlds succeed to worlds, suns to suns, without the immense mechanism of the heavens ever reaching the limit of its gigantic resources.

There, where your eyes admire the splendid stars under the vault of night, — there, where your mind contemplates the magnificent radiance, resplendent in far-distant space — through countless ages, the finger of death has extinguished these splendors. Long ago void has succeeded to this radiance, and received new creations yet unknown. It takes millions of years for the light of these stars to reach us, by reason of their immense distance from us; and the rays that we receive today are those that were sent in our direction a long time before the formation of this Earth. We continue to admire them long ages after their extinction.[31]

What are the six thousand years of historic humanity compared with the measureless ages before them? Seconds to your ages! What are your astronomical observations compared with the actual state of the universe? The shadow eclipsed by the sun.

---

[31] Here there is an effect of the time the light takes to cross the space. Scientists have defined the speed of light in a vacuum to be exactly 299,792,458 meters per second (about 186,000 miles per second). Since the mean distance of the Earth from the sun is 149,503,000 km (92,897,000 mi), it takes approximately 8 minutes and 30 seconds from the sun to Earth. From this results that a phenomenon that takes place on the surface of the sun will only be perceived eight minutes later; and for the same reason, we will see it only eight minutes after its disappearance. If, due to its distance, the light of a star takes a thousand years to reach us, we cannot see this star until a thousand years after its formation. (For complete explanation and description of this phenomenon, see the *"Revue Spirite"* of March and May of 1867, pgs. 93 and 151; clarifications from *"Lumen,"* by M. C. Flammarion).

52. Here, then, as in our other studies, let us recognize that Earth and man are as nothingness compared to that which is; and that the most colossal operations of our minds extend yet only near unto the confines of an immensity and eternity of existence in a universe which will have no end.

And when measureless periods in our immortality shall have passed over our heads, when the actual history of the Earth will appear to us like a vaporous shadow in the depth of our remembrance, when we shall have inhabited during countless ages all the multiple degrees of our cosmological hierarchy, when the most distant domains shall have in future, ages been passed through by innumerable peregrinations, we shall have still before us an unlimited succession of worlds, — an unending eternity for perspective.

UNIVERSAL LIFE

53. This immortality of souls, of which the system of the physical world is the base, has appeared to be imaginary in the eyes of certain thinkers. They have ironically styled it the immortal traveler, and failed to comprehend that the soul possessed immortal life before this world was made. However, it is possible to make them comprehend all the grandeur of it, — I would say, nearly all the perfection of it.

54. That the works of God are created for thought and intelligence, that the worlds are the abodes of beings who contemplate them, and who discover under their veil the power and wisdom of Him who formed them, is no longer doubtful to us; but that the souls who people them are harmoniously linked together is what is important for us to understand.

55. Human intelligence, indeed, does not really take it in the existence of these radiant globes which scintillate in space as simple masses of inert matter without life. It scarcely dreams that there are in these far-distant regions magnificent twilights and splendid nights, fruitful suns and days full of light, valleys and mountains where the multiple productions of nature have been developed in all their luxuriant pomp, and that a realm so admirably adapted to the enfoldment of every potency of the soul should remain forever destitute of conscious life.

56. But to this eminently just idea of creation it is necessary to add that of the unity of humanity; and it is in this that the mystery of the future exists.

One and the same human family has been created throughout the universe of worlds; and the ties of a fraternity yet unappreciated on your part bind you to these worlds, and they to you. *If these astral bodies which harmonize in their vast systems are inhabited by intelligences, it is not by beings unknown to one another, but by beings marked in the forehead with the same destiny, who needed to encounter one another for the discharge of their functions of life, which cannot be discharged apart from their mutual sympathies.* There is one great family of spirits populating the celestial worlds. There is one grand radiance of the eternal spirit embracing the expanse of the boundless universe, and which remains as a primal and final type of spiritual perfection.

57. By what strange aberration could we refuse belief in the immortality of the vast regions of ether, when we enclose it within an inadmissible limit and an absolute duality? Ought not, then, the true system of the universe to precede the true dogmatic doctrine, and science the theology? Will it deviate as to the point of establishing its base upon metaphysics? The reply is readily given, and shows us that the new philosophy will be triumphantly enthroned upon the ruins of the old, because its base will be victoriously elevated above ancient errors.

THE PLURALITY OF WORLDS

58. You have followed us in our celestial excursions, and you have visited with us the immense regions of space. We have seen suns succeed to suns, systems to systems, and nebula to nebula. The splendid harmonious panorama of cosmos has been unfolded before our eyes, and we have received a foretaste of the idea of infinitude, which we can comprehend in all its extent only in a future state of perfection. The mysteries of ether have unveiled their secret hitherto incomprehensible, and we have conceived at least an idea of the universality of things. It is important now to pause and reflect.

59. It is well, without doubt, to have recognized the smallness of the Earth, and mediocre importance in the hierarchy of worlds. It is wise to have lowered the human arrogance so dear to us, and to have become humiliated in the presence of absolute grandeur; but it will be much more satisfactory to interpret with the moral sense the spectacle to which we have been witnesses. I desire to speak of the infinite power of nature, and of the idea which we ought to form of its mode of action in the diverse extend of the universe.

60. Habituated, as we are, to judge of things by our poor little sojourn here, we imagine that nature has not been able to act, or ought not to act in other worlds, except in accordance with the rules which we have recognized here below. Now it is precisely in this respect that it is important to reform our judgment.

Cast your eyes upon any region whatsoever of your globe, and upon anyone of the productions of its nature. Do you not recognize there the seal of an infinite variety, and the proof of an unequalled activity? Do you not see upon the wing of the little canary-bird, upon the petals of an opening rosebud, the fascinating fecundity of this beautiful nature?

When your studies are applied to the winged beings which cleave the air, — when they descend to the violet of the woods, to the depths of the ocean, — in all and everywhere you read this universal truth: All-powerful nature acts according to place, time, and circumstances. It is a unit in its general harmony, but a multiple in its productions; it handles a sun as a drop of water; it peoples an immense world with living beings, with the same facility as it opens the egg deposited by the autumn insect.

61. Now, if such is the variety that nature has been able to depict in all places on this little world, so narrow, so limited, what can you imagine of its action in larger worlds, so great in extent, which far more fully than the Earth attest her unknown perfection?

Do you not then see, around each one of the suns in space, systems similar to your planetary system? But you do not see that these planets support the three kingdom of nature that develops around you. For, as no two human faces are exactly similar, this same prodigious, unimaginable variety has been displayed in the abodes of ether which float on the breasts of space.

Since animated nature commences with the zoophyte and ends with man, since the atmosphere feeds terrestrial life, since the liquid element is incessantly renewed, since your seasons are succeeded in this life by the phenomena which divide them, do not conclude that the millions on millions of worlds which roll in space are similar to this: far from it. They differ according to the diverse conditions which have been developed on them, and according to their respective roles in the drama of the universe: they are varied gems in an immense mosaic, diversified flowers in a super garden.

Chapter VII

GEOLOGICAL OUTLINE OF THE EARTH

Geological Periods – Primitive State of the Globe –
Primary Period – Transition Period – Secondary Period –
Tertiary Period – Deluge Period – Post-Deluge Period –
Birth of Man.

GEOLOGICAL PERIODS

1. The Earth carries within it the evident traces of its formation. One can follow the phases of it with a mathematical precision in the different rocks which compose its framework. The whole of these studies constitute the science of *geology*, a science born of this century, and which has thrown light upon the much controversial question of its origin, and of that of the living beings which inhabit it. Here there is no point upon which one can hang a hypothesis. It is the rigorous result of the observation of facts, and into the presence of facts doubt is forbidden to enter. A history of the formation of the globe is written in the geological beds of the Earth in a clearer manner than in books hitherto written, because it is Nature itself who speaks and not the imagination of men that created systems. Where one sees the traces of fire, one can say with certitude that fire has existed; where those of water are seen, one says with no less certainty that water has been there; where one sees those of animals, one infers that animals have lived there.

Geology is therefore a science of observation: it draws conclusions only from that which it sees. Upon doubtful points it affirms nothing. It utters only debatable opinions concerning phenomena, of which the definite solution awaits more complete observations. *Without the discoveries of geology, as well as those of astronomy, the genesis of the world would still lie in legendary shadows.* Thanks to it, today man knows the history of his habitation; and the trelliswork fables which surrounded his cradle is crushed, never to rise again.

2. Everywhere where stony cavities exist, natural excavations, or apertures opened by man, one observes that which is called *stratifications*, or superposed beds. The rocks which present this phase are designated *stratified rocks*. These beds, of a very variable thickness, sometimes of only a few hundred inches, sometimes a hundred yards and more, are distinguished from one another by the color and nature of the substances of which they are composed. Works of art, the boring of wells, the exploding of quarries, and, above all, mines, have given the means of observation to a considerable depth.

3. The beds are generally homogeneous; that is to say, that each one is formed of a similar substance, or of diverse substances which have co-existed, and have formed a compact whole. The line of separation isolating them from one another is always distinctly defined as in the different parts of a ship. No part is seen mingled or lost in another, each remains within its own respective limits. Such is the case, for example, in the colors of the prism or the rainbow.

By these characters, observers decided that they had been successively formed, deposited upon one another by different causes and conditions. The deepest have naturally been formed first, and those nearest the surface subsequently. The last of all, that which is found on the surface, is the bed of vegetable which owes its properties to the destruction of organic matter which produces plants and animals.

4. The lower beds, placed under the vegetable, have received in geology the name of rocks, a word which in this acceptation implies not always the idea of a stony substance, but signifies a resting-place of some mineral substance. Some are formed of sand, of clay or loam, of chalk or pebbles; others of stones, properly speaking, of greater or lesser hardness, such as sand-stone, marbles, chalk, limestone, millstone, coals of the Earth, asphalt, etc. They say that the power of a rock depends upon its thickness.

By the inspection of the nature of these rocks or beds, one recognizes by certain signs, that they are produced by heated substances sometimes vitrified by the action of fire, others, by terrestrial substances deposited by water. Some of these substances have remained disintegrated, as sand; others at first in a pasty state, under the action of certain chemical agents or other causes, have become hardened, and have acquired in time the consistence of stone. Superposed stony beds show successive deposits. Fire and water have then played their parts in the formation of the materials composing the solid framework of the globe.

5. The normal position of terrestrial or stony beds producing aqueous deposits is horizontal. When one sees these immense plains, often extending as far as the eye can see in a perfectly horizontal line, united as if leveled by a roller, or depths of valleys as smooth as the surface of a lake, one can be certain that at some distant epoch these places have been for a long time covered by tranquil waters, which, in retiring, have left the beds dry upon which they were deposited during their sojourn. After the retreats of the waters, these beds have become covered with vegetation. If in place of fertile, muddy clay or chalky ground, which afford nourishment for soil, the waters had deposited only siliceous sand without aggregation, we should find here dry and sandy plains constituting waste lands and deserts. The deposits left by partial inundation and those which form the alluvium at the mouth of rivers, give us a faint idea of this.

6. Although the horizontal is the most normal and usual position of these aqueous formations, one sees, often to a considerable extent in mountainous districts, rocks, which indicate by their nature that they were formed by water in an inclined, and sometimes even in a vertical position. Now, as according to the laws of the equilibrium of liquids and weights, the aqueous deposits can be formed exclusively upon horizontal planes, it is therefore supposed that those which rest on inclined planes are drawn into the lower depths by currents, and by their own weight. It is evident that these deposits have been raised by some force, after their solidification and transformation into stone.

From these considerations we can conclude with certitude that all these stony beds composed of aqueous deposits, in a perfectly horizontal position, have been formed during the succession of ages by tranquil waters; and that, whenever they are found in an inclined position, the Earth has been violently agitated and subsequently broken up by general or partial earthquakes of more or less importance.

7. A characteristic fact of the highest importance for the unexceptional testimony it furnishes, consists in fossil remains of vegetables and animals encountered in innumerable varieties in the different beds; and as those remains are even found in the hardest stones, it is necessary to conclude that the existence of these beings antedates the formation of these stones. Now, if we consider how many centuries must have been spent in this hardening process, which has eventually brought them to the condition in which they have been from time immemorial, one is forced to the conclusion that the time of the advent or organized beings upon the Earth is lost in the night of unknown ages, and that it is consequently very far behind the dates assigned by "Genesis."[32]

8. Among these vegetable and animal fossils are those which have been penetrated throughout by siliceous or calcareous substances, which have transformed them into

---

[32] Fossil, from the Latin fossilia and fossilis, derived from fossa, "ditch," and from fodere, "to dig or plough the earth." This word is used in geology to signify bodies, or the remains of organized bodies, belonging to creatures that lived in prehistoric times. It is equally applied to mineral substances bearing traces of the presence of organized beings, such as the imprints of vegetables or of animals. The word "fossil," in a more general acceptation, has been substituted for that of petrifaction, which applies only to bodies transformed into stone by the infiltration of siliceous or calcareous substances in the organic tissues. All the petrifactions are necessarily fossils, but all fossils are not petrifactions.

stone, of which some have the hardness of marble: these, properly speaking, are petrifactions. Others have simply been enveloped by matter in a soft state, and a few of them are found in a perfect state in the hardest stones. Others have left only imprints, but of a distinct perfect delicacy. In the interior of certain stones the imprint of feet have been discovered, also the form of fingers and nails, from which it is concluded that some animal has produced them.

9. The animal fossils are but little comprehended. One finds sometimes the solid and resisting parts, such as bones, scales, and horns. Sometimes these are complete skeleton, but more frequently only detached portions of which it is easy to recognize the production. By the inspection of a jaw or a tooth, one sees immediately whether it belongs to a herbivorous or carnivorous animal. As all the parts of an animal have a necessary correlation, the form of the head, of a shoulder-blade, of a bone of the leg, or a foot, suffices to determine the size, the general form, and the mode of life of the animal.[33] The terrestrial animals have an organism clearly separating them from aquatic animals. Fish and shell-fish fossils are excessively numerous; shell-fish alone sometimes forming entire beds of great thickness. By their nature, one quickly determines whether they are marine or fresh-water animals.

10. The masses of pebble-stone rock, which in certain places constitute important rocks, are unequivocal indication of their origin. They are rounded like the pebble-stones on the seashore, an unmistakable sign that they have been

---

The formation with which stony beds are covered, when they are plunged into waters charged with calcareous substances, such as those of the Saint-Allyre stream, near Clermont, in Auvergne, France, are not properly speaking, petrifactions, but simple incrustations. Monuments inscriptions and other objects produced by human effort belong to the science of archeology.

[33] At the point to which George Cuvier has carried the science of paleontology, one bone alone suffices often to determine the race, species, and form of an animal, also its habits, by which it can be entirely reconstructed.

subjected to the effects of waters. The countries where they are found buried in large quantities have most certainly once been occupied by violently agitated waters.

11. Rocks of diverse formations are also characterized by the nature of the fossils they enclose. The most ancient ones contain vegetable and animal remains, which have entirely disappeared from the surface of the globe. Certain more recent species have completely disappeared, but have preserved an analogy, which differs only in size and slightly in form. Others, of which we see the last representations, are tending evidently to disappearance in a near future, such as the elephant, rhinoceros, hippopotamus, etc. Thus, as the terrestrial beds approach our epoch, the animal and vegetable species they contain approach those animals and vegetables which still exist.

The perturbations and inundations which have taken place upon the Earth since its origin have completely changed the conditions of vitality, and have made entire generations of living beings disappear.

12. By interrogating the nature of the geological beds, one knows in the most positive manner if, at the epoch of their formation, the country which encloses them was occupied by the sea, by lakes, or by forests and plains peopled with terrestrial animals. If, then, in the same country one finds a series of superposed beds containing alternately marine and fresh-water fossils many times repeated, it is an unexceptionable proof that this same country has been many times encompassed by the sea, covered by lakes, and become dry again.

And how many centuries upon centuries certainly, thousands of centuries perhaps has it required to accomplish each period of this? What a powerful force must have been required to displace and replace the ocean, to raise mountains! How many physical revolutions, violent commotions, the Earth has passed through before becoming what it has been through historic ages! And they try to make us believe that the formation of the Earth took less time than is necessary to propagate a plant!

13. The study of the geological beds attests, as has previously been stated, to successive formations, which have gradually changed the form of the globe, and divided its history into many epochs. These epochs constitute that which is called geologic periods, the knowledge of which is necessary to establish a true Genesis. Geologists count six principal periods, which they have designated as follows: first the primary, second the transition, third the secondary, fourth the tertiary, fifth the deluge, sixth the post-deluge or present period. Rocks formed during the duration of each period are called thus: primitive, transition, secondary rocks, etc. One says that such and such rocks, such and such fossils, are found in rocks of such and such periods.

14. It is essential to remark that the number of these periods is not absolute, and that it depends upon system of classification. One does not comprehend, in the six principal periods designated above, all which are marked by notable and general change in the state of the globe; but observation proves that many successive formations have been produced during the history of each. That is why they are divided into periods, characterized by the nature of the rocks, which bear twenty-six general and very characteristic formations, without counting those which are produced by modifications due to purely local causes.

PRIMITIVE STATE OF THE GLOBE

15. The depression of the poles and other conclusive facts are certain indications that the Earth had been originally in a fluid or soft state. This state could have been caused by matter having been liquefied by fire or softened by water.

It is proverbially said: "There is no smoke without fire." This true proverb is an application of the principle: "There is no effect without a cause." For the same reason one can say: "There is no fire without a focus." Now, by facts which pass under our eyes, there is not only smoke produced, but also very real fire which must have a focus. This fire coming from the interior of the Earth, and not from on high, the focus must be within; the fire being permanent, the focus must be equally so.

The heat which is augmented by measure as it penetrates the interior of the Earth, and which at a certain distance from the surface attains a very high temperature; the hot springs, so much warmer according to the depth from which they come. Fires and masses of heated and burning substances, which escape from volcanoes with vast upheavings, or by crevasses produced by earthquakes, can leave no doubt concerning the existence of an interior fire.

16. Experience demonstrates that the temperature has been raised one degree by every thirty yards of depth: whence it follows that at a depth of three hundred yards the augmentation is ten degrees, at three thousand yards, one hundred degrees, a temperature of boiling water; at thirty thousands yards, seven to eight leagues (from twenty-one to twenty-four miles), one thousand degrees; at twenty-five leagues (seventy-five miles), more than thirty-three hundred degrees, a temperature at which no known material can resist fusion. From there to the center there is still a space of more than fourteen hundred leagues (forty-two hundred miles), may be twenty-eight hundred leagues (eighty-four hundred miles), in diameter, which must be occupied by molten substances.

Although this is only a conjecture judging cause by effect, it has all the elements of probability; and one arrives at this conclusion, that the Earth is still an incandescent mass covered with a solid crust of twenty-five or more leagues (seventy-five miles) in thickness, which is scarcely the one hundred and twentieth part of its diameter. Proportionally speaking, it must be much thinner than the thinnest rind of an orange.[34]

---

[34] **Note of SAB**: Earth's radius is about 6,371 km and the radius of the core is about 3,486 km (the inner core radius is about 1,217 km; a little more than two-thirds of the radius of the Moon). Although the interior of Earth is only a few tens of miles beneath our feet, it is more difficult to reach than the surface of Pluto or even a nearby star! The deepest mines in the world are only three to four kilometers deep. The deepest well ever drilled only penetrates 12 kilometers into the interior. Since it is 6371 kilometers to the center of Earth, comparatively speaking,

For the rest, the thickness of the terrestrial crust is very variable in many places; for there are some countries, especially volcanic territories, where the heat and flexibility of the soil indicate that it is much thinner. The high temperature of hot springs is also an indication of close vicinity to the central fire.

17. It is then evident that the primitive state of the softness or fluidity of the Earth must have been caused by the action of heat, not by water. The Earth was then originally an incandescent mass. In consequence of the caloric rays, it became liquefied. It has been gradually cooled, and the cooling process has naturally commenced on the surface, which has become hardened, whilst the interior has remained in a fluid state. One can thus compare the Earth to a block of coal coming red from the furnace, the surface cooling by contact with the air, although, if one breaks it, the interior is found to be yet burning.

18. At the epoch when the terrestrial globe was an incandescent mass, it contained not one atom more or less than it does today. Only under the influence of this high temperature, the greater part of the substances composing it, and which we see under the form of liquids and solids, earth, stones, metals,

---

we have not even been able to get through the skin of the peach because the high pressures and temperatures of the surrounding rock cause the metal of even the strongest drills to quickly weaken and deform. At depths of 100 kilometers, rock flows like butter, and any hole we could form would quickly close. Near the surface of Earth, both temperatures and pressures are low, so rock behaves like cold wax: they crack and crumble. As we delve into Earth's depths, temperatures and pressures rise quickly. At only a depth of 50 kilometers (about 30 miles), temperatures are already near 1000 degree F. (500 degree C) and pressures are near 200,000 psi (pounds per square inch). Estimates of the temperatures in the deep interior of Earth range from about 4000 deg. C to about 7000 deg. C, which is about as hot as the surface of the Sun. (The rock and iron at these temperatures remain as solids and liquids instead of gases because of the very high pressures in Earth's interior.) The mantle accounts for about 84% of Earth's volume but the core contains almost 70% of the planet's mass. Source:htpp://www.cotf.edu

and crystals, were found in a very different state. They have only been submitted to a transformation. In consequence of the cooling process and mixtures, the elements have formed new combinations. The air, considerably inflated, became extended to an immeasurable distance. All the water forcibly reduced to vapor was mingled with the air. All the substances susceptible of volatilization – such as metals, sulphur, carbon – were there found in a gaseous state. The state of the atmosphere was then in no way comparable with its present condition. The density of all these vapors gave it an opacity through which no ray of sunlight could penetrate. If a living being could have existed on Earth at this period, he would have had for light only the sinister brightness of the fires beneath his feet, the burning atmosphere, and not even the existence of the sun would be noticed.

PRIMARY PERIOD

19. The first effect of the cooling process was to solidify the outermost surface of the melted mass, and to form there a resisting crust, which, thin at first, little by little thickened. This crust constitutes the stone called "granite," of an extreme hardness, named thus by reason of its granulated appearance. The three principal substances found there are feldspar, quartz or crystal rock, and mica. This last has a brilliant metallic tint, although it is not a metal.

The granite-bed is then the first ever formed upon the globe, which it entirely envelops, and of which it constitutes in some sort the bony framework. It is the direct product of melted matter consolidated. Upon it and in the cavities that its violently agitated surface presented are successively deposited the beds of other rocks subsequently formed. That which distinguishes this from later formations is the absence of all stratification; that is to say, it is in its whole extent a compact and uniform mass, and not divided by different kinds of beds. The effervescence of incandescent substances must have produced numerous and profound crevasses through which this substance was expelled.

20. The second effect of the cooling process was to liquefy certain vaporous substances in the air, which were precipitated to the surface of the ground. There were then shower and lakes of sulphur and bitumen, veritable stream of iron, copper, lead, and other heated metals infiltrating themselves into the fissures which constitute today the metallic veins and arteries of the Earth.

Under the influence of these different agents the granite surface experienced successive decomposition. Combinations were formed which resulted in primitive rocks distinct from the granite rocks, but in confused masses, and without regular stratifications.

Then came the waters, which, falling upon a burning soil, vaporized anew, fell again and again in torrents until the temperature permitted them to rest upon the soil in a liquid state.

At the formation of the granite rocks the regular series of geologic periods commence. To the six principal periods it is proper to add that of the primitive incandescent state of the globe.

21. Such was the aspect of this first period, a veritable chaos of all the elements mingled together seeking their position where no living being could possibly exist, as one of its distinctive characters in geology at this time is the absence of all traces of vegetable and animal life.

It is impossible to decide upon the duration of this primary period: no more can we of the ones that follow. But, judging from the time necessary for a cannon-ball of given volume heated to the red-white heat to become sufficiently cool to allow of a drop of water resting upon it in a liquid state, it has been calculated, that, if this cannon-ball were of the magnitude of the Earth, more than one million years would be necessary.

Transition Period

22. At the commencement of the transition period the solid granite crust had thickened only a little, and offered but a feeble resistance to the effervescence of the burning substance which it covered and repressed. Numerous rents were made, by means of which the interior land was thrown out. The soil presented considerable inequalities of surface.

Waters not very deep covered nearly all the surface of the globe, with the exception of elevated lands formed of rocks frequently submerged at their base.

The air gradually became purged from the heavier gaseous substances, which, while condensing by the cooling process, were precipitated to the surface of the ground, then drawn into and dissolved by the waters.

At this epoch it is necessary to understand "cooling process" in a relative sense; that is to say, in connection with the primitive state; for the temperature must have still been burning.

The thick aqueous vapor which was raised on all sides from the immense liquid surface fell in abundant and warm rains, obscuring the air. Soon, however, the rays of the sun began to shine through this foggy atmosphere.

One of the last substances of which the air has been purged, because it is naturally in a gaseous state, is carbonic-acid gas, which then formed one of its constituent parts.

23. At this epoch beds of earthly sediment began to form, deposited by waters charged with lime and other matters peculiar to organic life.

Then appeared the first living beings of the vegetable and animal kingdom. At first few in number, one finds more and more frequent traces of such as one penetrates more and more deeply into the beds of this formation. It is to be remarked, that everywhere life is manifested as soon as conditions are propitious to vitality, and that each species is born as soon as the proper conditions of its existence are produced.

24. The first organized existences which appeared upon the Earth were vegetables of the least complicated organization, designated in botany under the names of cryptogams, acotyledonous plants and monocotyledonous plants, such as lichens, mushrooms, mosses, ferns, and herbaceous plants. One does not now see trees with woody trunks, but only those of the palm species, whose sponge-like trunks are analogous to the stems of herbs.

The animals of this period, which have succeeded to the first vegetation, are exclusively marine. These were at first polyps, radiates, zoophytes, animals whose rudimentary and simple organizations approach most nearly to vegetable forms. Later came fishes and shellfish, the species of which do not exist now.

25. Under the empire of heat and humidity and in consequence of the excess of carbonic acid dispersed into the air – a gas improper for the respiration of terrestrial animals but necessary to the plants – the exposed terrains were quickly covered with a pungent vegetation while at the same time aquatic plants multiplied on the surface of marshes. Plants, which in our day are simple herbs a few inches high, attained a prodigious height and magnitude; there were then forests of tree-like ferns from eight to ten yards in height, and of proportionate magnitude; plants called wolfsfoot, and a kind of moss of the same size, equisetum arvense,[35] four or five yards high, which we hardly see now. At the end of this period pines or fir-trees began to appear.

26. In consequence of the displacement of the waters, the grounds which produced these masses of vegetation were many times submerged, covered again with terrestrial sediment, during which those which had become dry appeared in their turn with a similar vegetation; thus there were many successive generations of vegetables destroyed and renewed again. The animals being aquatic suffered nothing from these changes.

These remains accumulated during a long series of years, and formed beds of great thickness. Under the actions of heat, of humidity, of pressure, exercised by subsequent terrestrial deposits, and, without doubt, also various chemical agents, such as gas, acids, and salts, products of a combination of primitive elements, these vegetable substances were

---

[35] A marsh-plant commonly called horsetail.

submitted to a fermentation converting them into coal. The coal-mines are, then, the direct result of the decomposition of a mass of vegetables accumulated during the transition period. That is why they are found in almost every country.[36]

27. The fossil remains of the luxuriant vegetation of this epoch are being discovered today under the ice of the polar regions, as well as in the torrid zone: therefore it is necessary to conclude, that, since vegetation was uniform, the temperature also must have been equally so. The poles were then not covered with ice as now: then the Earth drew its heat from itself, from the central fire which equally heated all the solid bed, then too thin to offer to it successful resistance. This heat was much greater than that conveyed by the solar rays, enfeebled as they were by the density of the atmosphere. Later on, when the central heat could exert only a feeble influence upon the surface, that of the sun preponderate; and the Polar Regions, receiving only oblique rays giving very little heat, became covered with ice. One understands that at the epoch of which we speak, and for a long time after, ice was unknown upon the Earth.

This period has been a very long one, judging from the number and thickness of the coal-beds.[37]

SECONDARY PERIOD

28. With the transition period the colossal vegetation and animals which characterized this period disappeared.

---

[36] Turf is produced in the same manner by the decomposition of vegetable matter in marshy grounds; but with this difference, being much more recent and formed under different conditions, it has not had time to carbonize.

[37] In the Bay of Fundy (Nova Scotia), M. Lyell found upon a coal-bed four hundred yards in thickness, sixty-eight different levels, presenting evident traces of many forest soils, the trunks of the trees of which were still garnished with their roots (L. Figuier). Supposing that it takes one thousand years to form each of these levels; it must have taken sixty-eight thousand years to form this coal-bed alone.

Perhaps it was caused by a change in atmospheric conditions, or on account of inundations having destroyed all which had life on Earth. It is probable that the two causes have contributed to this change; for, by a study of the rocks which mark the end of this period, we find signs of great earthquakes, upheavings, and eruptions which have thrown upon the Earth great quantities of lava, and also notable changes which have appeared in the three kingdoms.

29. The secondary period is characterized, under the mineral kingdom, by numerous and important beds, which attest a slow formation in the waters, and mark very different characteristic epochs.

Vegetation is less rapid and less colossal in growth than in the preceding period, caused no doubt by the diminution in heat, and humidity, and by modifications experienced by the constitutive elements of the atmosphere. To herbaceous and pulpy plants were joined those with woody stalks and, properly speaking, also the first trees.

30. Animals are still aquatic or amphibious at this time; animal life upon the Earth seeming to have made but little progress. A great quantity of shell-covered animals have been developed in the seas by the formation of calcareous substances; also new fishes of a more perfect organization than those of the previous period have appeared, also the first of the whale tribe. The most characteristic animals of this period are monstrous reptiles, among which are found:

The *ichthyosaurus*, a species of lizard-fish, which attained ten yards in length, the jaws of which, being of a prodigious length, were armed with one hundred and eighty teeth. Its general form was a little like the crocodile, but without the scaly breastplate; its eyes were as large as the head of man; it had fins like the whales, and spouted water into the air like them.

The *plesiosaurus* was another marine animal, as large as the ichthyosaurus, the excessively long neck of which was bent like that of the swan, which gave to it the appearance of an enormous serpent attached to the body of a turtle or tortoise.

It had the head of a lizard and the teeth of a crocodile. Its skin must have been smooth; for no trace of scales, or carapaces, have been found.[38]

The *teleosaurus* approaches nearer the actual crocodiles, which appear to be the diminutive descendants of it. Like them it had a scaly breastplate, and lived at times upon the Earth as well as in the water. Its body was about ten yards in length, allowing three or four for the head alone. Its enormous mouth had an aperture two yards in length.

The *megalosaurus* was a great lizard and a kind of crocodile from fourteen to fifteen yards in length, essentially carnivorous, nourishing itself with reptiles, small crocodiles, and tortoises. Its formidable jawbone was armed with teeth like a double bladed pruning or garden knife bent round behind in such a way, that, once having entered into their prey, it was impossible for the latter to disengage themselves.

The *iguanodon* (iguana), the largest lizard which had appeared upon the Earth, measured from twenty to twenty-five yards from the head to the extremity of the tail. Its snout was surmounted by a horn formed of bone, similar to the iguana of our day, from which it seem to have differed only in size; the latter having a body not a yard in length. The form of the teeth prove that it was herbivorous, and the feet that it was a land animal.

The *pterodactyl*, was a strange animal of the size of a swan, being like a reptile in body, with the head of a bird. Its toes, which were of a prodigious length, were united with a fleshy membrane like that of the bat, which served it as a parachute when it precipitated itself from the height of a tree or rock upon its prey. It had no horny beak like birds; but the jawbones were as long as half its body, and were garnished with teeth terminating in a point like a beak.

31. During this period, which must have been very long as the number and importance of the geological beds

---

[38] In 1823 the first fossil of this animal was found in England. Later on, this same type of fossil was also found in France and in Germany.

attest, animal life developed largely in the watery elements, in like manner to vegetation in a previous period. The purer air, more conducive to respiration, permits some animal to live upon the Earth. The sea has been many times displaced, but without violent commotion. With this period disappeared in their turn those races of gigantic aquatic animals, replaced later by analogous species, less disproportionate in form, and of infinitely smaller size.

32. Pride has influenced man to say that all animals were created for his purposes and for his needs. But what is the number of those which directly serve him, which he has been able to subject, compared to the incalculable number of those with which he has never had and will never have any connection? How is it possible to sustain a similar thesis in presence of these innumerable species which alone have populated the Earth for thousands and thousands of centuries before he came here himself, and which have disappeared? Can one say that they have been created for his profit? However, these species all had their utility in life. God would not create them for nothing in order to give himself the pleasure of destroying them; for all had life, instincts, and the capacity for misery and happiness. What then was the object? It must have been a sovereignly wise one, though we are still unable to comprehend it. Perhaps the secret will one day be given to man, in order to humble his pride; but in the meantime how many ideas crowd upon us in presence of these new horizons into which we are permitted to gaze, and which display to us the imposing spectacle of this creation, so majestic in its slow and mighty developments, so admirable in its foresight, so punctual, precise, and invariable in its results.

TERTIARY PERIOD

33. With the tertiary period commences for the Earth a new order of things. The aspect of its surface is completely changed; the conditions of vitality are profoundly modified, and approach the present state of the Earth. The first part of this period is signalized by an arrest in animal and vegetable productions. Everything bears traces of an almost entire destruction of living beings, and then appeared successively new species, the better organization of which is adapted to the locality where they are called to live.

34. During preceding periods the solid crust of the globe, by reason of its thinness, presented, as has been said, a pretty feeble resistance to the action of the internal fire. This envelope, easily broken, permitted melted substances to be freely expelled to the surface of the Earth. After having acquired a certain thickness, this did not take place. Burning substances compressed on all sides, like boiling water in a closed vessel, would end in an explosion. The granite mass, violently broken at many points was riddled with crevasses, like a cracked vase. Upon the line of *these crevasses* the solid crust was raised and reformed, formed peaks, chains of mountains, and their ramifications. Certain parts of the envelope which were not rent where simply piled up, whilst upon other points excavations and depressions were produced.

The surface of the Earth became during the tertiary period very unequal. The waters, which until this time had covered in a nearly uniform manner the greater part of its extent, flowed down into the lowest places, leaving vast continents of dry land, or summits of isolated mountains, which formed islands.

Such is the great phenomenon which has been accomplished in the tertiary period, and which has transformed the aspect of the globe. It was not produced instantaneously or simultaneously at all points, but successively at epochs more or less remote from one another.

35. One of the first consequences of these uprisings has been, as has been said, the inclination of the primitively horizontal beds of sediment, and which have remained everywhere in this horizontal position where the soil has not been overthrown. It is in the flanks and in the vicinities of the mountains that these inclinations are steeper.

36. In countries where the beds of sediment have preserved their horizontal position, in order to reach that of the first formation, it is necessary to pass through all the others, often to a great depth, at the end of which one invariably finds the granite rock. But, when these beds have been elevated into mountains, they have been carried above their normal level, sometimes to a very great height, in such a way that, if one makes a vertical trench upon the side of the mountain, they are shown in all their thickness, superposed like the different layers of a building.

This explains why quite large beds of marine shell fossils are often found on high elevations of land. It has been generally recognized that at no epoch the sea has been able to attain such a height; for all the water on the Earth is not sufficient for it, and would not be even were it a hundred times greater in volume. Some might say that the quantity of water had diminished; but then the query would come. What had become of it? The uprisings which are now incontestably demonstrated by science explain completely and logically the marine deposits which are found upon certain mountains.[39]

37. In places where the uprising of the primitive rock has produced a complete rent in the soil, perhaps by its rapidity, perhaps by form, height, or volume of the raised mass, the granite has appeared bare like a *tooth which pierces the gums*; the beds which were covered, elevated, upheaved, and recovered have been brought to life; whilst rocks belonging to the most ancient formations, and which were found in their primitive position at a great depth, form now the soil of certain countries.

38. The granite mass, dislodged by the effect of the earthquakes, has left in some places fissures through which the melted substances have escaped: the volcanoes. The volcanoes are like chimneys to this immense furnace, or better still, like *escape-valves*, which, in providing an exit for the great excess of burning substances, preserve them from terrible

---

[39] Beds of marine shell fossils were found five thousand meters above the sea level, in the Andes of South America.

commotions, whence one can infer that a large number of active volcanoes is a source of safety to the whole Earth.

One can form an idea of the intensity of this fire by learning how volcanoes opened in the midst of an ocean are not extinguished by the immense waters which cover and penetrate them.

39. The uprisings of the Earth in one solid mass have necessarily displaced the waters which have flowed back into hollow places, become deeper by the uprising of emerged rocks and by depressions; but these same low depths have been raised in their turn sometimes in one place, sometimes in another, and have repelled the waters, which have flowed elsewhere successively until they have found a stable resting place.

The successive displacements of this liquid mass have violently agitated the surface of the Earth. The waters, in passing away, have drawn portions of rocks of anterior formation, brought to light by the earthquakes; denuded mountains which were recovered, and brought to light their granite or calcareous base. Deep valleys have been hollowed out, and others filled in.

There are, then, mountains formed directly by the action of the central fire: they are principally granite mountains. Others are due to the action of the waters, which, in drawing mellow Earth and soluble matters after them, have hollowed out valleys around a calcareous or other resisting base.

The substances drawn by running waters have formed the beds of the tertiary period, which are easily distinguished from the preceding ones less by their composition, which is nearly the same, than by their disposition.

The beds of the primary, transition, and secondary periods, formed upon a slightly undulating surface, are nearly uniform over all the Earth. Those of the tertiary period, to the contrary, formed upon a very unequal base and by the procession of the waters, have a more local character. Everywhere, by digging to a certain depth, one finds all the anterior beds in the order of their formation; whilst the tertiary rocks are not found everywhere, nor all the beds of the latter.

40. During the earthquakes which took place at the commencement of this period, one finds that organic life has been arrested, which is proved by the absence of fossils in these rocks. But, as soon as a calmer state was restored, vegetables and animal re-appeared. The conditions of vitality being changed, the atmosphere becoming purer, new species, with more perfect organization, were formed. As regards structure, the plants differed very little from those of our time.

41. During the two preceding periods the Earth uncovered by water was of very small extent, marshy and frequently submerged: that is why the animals were all either aquatic or amphibious. The tertiary period, in which vast continents have been formed, has been characterized by the appearance of terrestrial animals.

Just as the transition period has brought forth colossal vegetables, and the secondary period monstrous reptiles; the tertiary period has produced gigantic mammals animals, such as the *elephant, rhinoceros, hippopotamus, paleotherium, megatherium, dinotherium, the mastodon, mammoth*, etc. The two latter elephant varieties were 5 to 6 meters tall, and their tusks would reach 4 meters long. It has produced birds as well, some of the species of which are living now. A few of the animals of this period have survived subsequent inundations. Others that have been designated by the generic term, *"pre-diluvium animals,"* have completely disappeared, or have been replaced by analogous species, in form lighter and smaller in which the original types have been merely outlined: such are the felisspeloea, a carnivorous animal about the size of the bull, having the anatomical characteristics of tiger and lion; *the cervus megaceron*, a variety of deer of which the horns, three yards in length were separated by three to four yards from their extremities.

DELUGE PERIOD

42. This period has been marked by one of the greatest inundations which have ever visited the globe, which changed once more the aspect of its surface, and destroyed completely a multitude of living species, of which only few remains have been found. Everywhere are left traces which attest its generality. The water, violently driven from its bed, has surrounded continents, drawing with them Earth and rocks, denuding mountains, and uprooting forests of a century's growth. The new deposits which they have formed are designated in geology "*diluvial terrains.*"

43. One of the most significant traces of this great disaster are rocks called "erratic blocks." Thus are named granite rocks that are found isolated in plains reposing upon tertiary beds, and in the midst of diluvial rocks, sometimes many hundred of miles from mountains whence they have been torn. It is evident that they can have been transported so great a distance only by the violence of a current.[40]

44. A no less characteristic fact, and one the cause of which is not yet explained, is that among the diluvial rocks are found the first aerolites. It is, then, at this epoch that they began to form. The cause which produced them did not previously exist.

45. It is toward this epoch that the poles commenced to be covered with ice, and the glaciers were formed on the mountains, which indicates a notable change in the temperature of the globe. This change must have been sudden; for, had it operated gradually, animals, such as the elephant, which live now only in warm climates, and which are found in great numbers in a fossil state in the polar territories, would have had time to withdraw little by little, to the more temperate regions. Everything goes to prove that they have been suddenly seized by great cold, and enveloped in ice.[41]

---

[40] It is one of these blocks, evidently by its compositions coming from the mountains of Norway, which serves as the pedestal to the statue of Peter the Great at St. Petersburg.

[41] In 1771, the Russian naturalist Pallas found in the midst of the ice from the North the entire body of an elephant fossil, covered with its skin, still maintaining part of its flesh. In 1799, another elephant fossil

46. This was, then, the veritable universal deluge. Opinions are divided as to the cause which produced it; but, whatever they may have been, the fact no less exists.

It is generally supposed that a sudden change took place in the position of the axes of the Earth, by which the poles were displaced, whence a general projection of the water upon the surface. If this change had come about gradually, the waters would have been displaced by degrees without agitation; whilst everything indicates a violent and sudden commotion. While in ignorance of the veritable cause, one can give only hypothesis.

The displacement of the waters can have been occasioned only by the uprising of certain parts of the solid crust, and the formation of new mountains on the bosom of the waters, like that which took place at the commencement of the tertiary period; but, beyond there having been a general inundation, this would explain nothing of the sudden change of the temperature of the poles.

47. In the agitation caused by the displacement of the waters, many animals have perished; others, in order to escape inundation, have withdrawn to the high elevations, into caves and crevasses, where they have perished in masses, perhaps by famine, perhaps by devouring one another, or by the flowing of the water into the places where they have taken refuge, and from whence they could not escape. Thus is

---

was found and described by the naturalist Adams. It was equally immersed in a huge block of ice, near the mouth of the Lena River, in Siberia. The people who lived in the neighborhood (Jakoutes) tore its flesh apart to feed their dogs. Its skin was covered with a long mane and the neck was covered with thick fur. The head, not including the tusks, measured more than 3 meters and weighed more than 400 pounds. Its skeleton is at the museum of Saint Petersburg. On the island and on the beaches of the glacial ocean large quantities of tusk are found, which constitute objects of considerable commerce under the name of ivory fossil, or ivory from Siberia.

explained the cause for the great quantity of bones of animals, carnivorous and otherwise, which are found mixed-up in certain caves, named by reason of this "*bone caverns*." They are found most frequently under the stalagmites. In a few of them the bones seem to have been drawn there by the current of the waters.[42]

POST-DELUGE OR PRESENT PERIOD – BIRTH OF MAN

48. The equilibrium once re-established on the surface of the globe, animal and vegetable life promptly resumed their course. The consolidated soil had taken a firmer position; the purer air agreed with more delicate organs. The sun, which shone with all its splendor through a limpid atmosphere, produced with its light a less suffocating, more vivifying atmosphere than that of the interior furnace. The Earth was inhabited by less ferocious animals; the more succulent vegetables offered a finer alimentation. All at length was prepared for the new host which must come to inhabit the Earth. It was then that man appeared, the last created being, he whose intelligence henceforth must concur with the general progress by progressing himself.

49. Has man existed on the Earth only since the deluge period? Or did he appear before this epoch? This question is a disputed one now; but its solution, whatever it may be, is only of secondary importance, as it would change none of the established facts, neither it negate the appearance of the human species on Earth prior to the date assigned by the Biblical Genesis, by many thousands of years.

---

[42] A great number of similar caverns have been discovered, of which some are quite extensive. There exist some in Mexico which are many miles in extent. That of Adelsberg, in Carniola, Austria, is no less than nine miles. One of the most remarkable is the Gailenreuth, in Wurtemberg. There are many in France, England, Germany, Sicily, and other countries of Europe.

The reason why it has been thought that the advent of man was posterior to the deluge is, because no authentic traces of his appearance previous to this have been found. The bones discovered in diverse places, and which have been thought to belong to a supposed race of pre-diluvium giants, have been recognized as the bones of quadrupeds.

That which is beyond doubt is, that man did not exist either in the primary, transition, or secondary periods, not only because no traces of him are found, but because conditions were not prepared for his appearance. If he has appeared in the tertiary period, it must have been towards the end, and then men must have been very few in number.

Besides, the deluge period, having been short, has not produced notable changes in climacteric and atmospheric influences. Animals and vegetables were about the same before as after. It is then, not a material impossibility that the advent of man took place before this great inundation. The presence of the monkey at this period adds to the probability which recent discoveries appear to confirm.[43]

Whether or not man has appeared before the great universal deluge, it is certain that his career as a human being has never really commenced to outline itself until the post-deluge period, which is specially characterized by his presence.

---

[43] See : *"l'Homme antédiluvien* and *Des outils de pierre,"* by Boucher de Perthes ; *"Discours sur les révolutions du globe,"* by Georges Cuvier, with remarks from Dr. Hoefer.

Chapter VIII
THEORIES OF THE EARTH

**Theory of Projection – Theory of Condensation
Theory of Incrustation – The Spirit of the Earth**

THEORY OF PROJECTION

1. Of all the theories touching the origin of being, that which has received the most credit in recent days is that of Buffon, perhaps by reason of the place its author held in the scientific world, perhaps because knowledge on the subject was slender at the time.

By seeing all the planets moving in the same direction and in the same plane from the occident to the orient, from west to east, going over orbits of which the inclination does not exceed seven and a half degrees, Buffon concluded, by this uniformity, that they must all move in obedience to the same cause.

According to him, the sun being an incandescent melted mass, he supposed that a comet, having been hurled obliquely against it, by knocking against its surface, had detached a portion, which, projected into space by the violence of the shock, became divided into many fragments. These fragments have formed planets, which have continued to move circularly, by the combination of centripetal and centrifugal force, in the way communicated by the direction of the original shock; i.e., in the plane of the ecliptic.

Planets must then be parts of the incandescent substance of the sun, and consequently incandescent themselves at their commencement. They have been submitted to a cooling and consolidating process during a period of time proportionate to their volume; and, when the temperature has permitted, life has appeared on their surface.

In consequence of the gradual lowering of the central heat, the Earth would arise in a given time to a completely cool state; the liquid mass would be entirely frozen; and the air, more and more condensed, would finally disappear. The lowering of the temperature, rendering life impossible, would lead to the diminution, then to the disappearance, of all organized beings. The cooling process which has commenced at the poles would pass successively from one country to another until it reached the equator.

Such is, according to Buffon, the present state of the moon, which, smaller than the Earth, should be now an extinguished world, whence life is henceforth excluded. The sun itself will some day end in the same manner. According to his calculation, it must have taken the Earth about seventy-four thousand years to arrive at its present temperature, and in ninety-three thousand years it must see the end of organized nature.

2. The Theory of Buffon - Contradicted by more recent discoveries in science, is now almost entirely abandoned for the following reasons:

1. For a long time it was believed that comets were solid bodies, which, coming in collision with planets, would destroy them. According to this hypothesis the supposition of Buffon was not improbable; but is now known that they are formed of a gaseous, condensed substance, rarefied enough, however, to allow of stars of less magnitude being visible through their nucleus. In this state, offering less resistance than the sun, a violent shock capable of projecting afar a portion of its substance is an impossible thing.

2. The incandescent nature of the sun is equally a hypothesis, as nothing yet discovered confirms it. The results of observation all point, however, in an opposite direction. Although its nature as yet has not been quite determined upon, the means of observation are very much improved, and thus it can be much better studied. It is now generally admitted by scientists that the sun is a globe composed of a solid substance, surrounded by a luminous atmosphere, which is not in contact with its surface.[44]

3. In the times of Buffon the six planets familiar to the ancients were the only ones discovered, - Mercury, Venus, Earth, Mars, Jupiter, and Saturn.[45] Since then there have been discovered a number, of which the three principal – Juno, Ceres, and Pallas – have an inclined orbit of thirteen, ten, and thirty-four degrees respectively, which does not accord with the movement of unique projection.[46]

4. The calculations of Buffon upon the cooling process have been recognized as completely wrong since the discovery of the law of the diminution of heat by M. Fourier. Therefore, not only seventy-four thousand years have been necessary to develop the present temperature of the Earth, but rather millions of years.

5. Buffon has considered only the central heat of the globe, without taking into account that of the sun's rays. Now it is recognized by scientific facts, rigorously founded upon experience that, by reason of the thickness of the terrestrial crust, the internal heat of the globe has for a long time played only an insignificant part in regulating the temperature of the surface. The variations to which the atmosphere is submitted are periodical and due to the preponderating action of the solar heat (see chap. VII, n° 25). The effect of this cause being permanent, whilst that

---

[44] One will find a complete dissertation, according to modern science, upon the nature of the sun and comets in "Studies and Lectures upon Astronomy," by Camille Flammarion.

[45] **Note of SAB**: Uranus, the first planet discovered in modern times, was discovered by William Herschel while systematically searching the sky with his telescope on March 13th, 1781. Neptune - Eighth planet from the sun was discovered on Sept 23rd 1846. Adams and Le Verrier are jointly credited with Neptune's discovery. Pluto - Ninth planet, and farthest, from the sun was discovered by Clyde W. Tombaugh on February 18th, 1930.

[46] **Note of SAB**: The asteroids Juno, Ceres, and Pallas are located between the orbit of Mars and Jupiter.

of the central heat is hardly anything, the diminution of the latter can bring to the surface of the Earth no sensible modification in order that the Earth should become uninhabitable by the general cooling process: the extinction of the sun would be necessary.[47]

THEORY OF CONDENSATION

3. The theory of the formation of the Earth by the condensation of cosmic matter is that which now prevails in science as being that which is best justified by observation, which solves the greatest number of difficulties, and which leans more than all others upon the grand principle of universal unity. It is that which has been previously described in chap. VII, *"General Uranography."*

The two theories, as we perceive, lead to the same result, - the primitive state of incandescence of the globe ceasing, the formation of a solid crust, the existence of the central fire, and the appearance of organic life as soon as the temperature renders it possible. They differ in the mode of formation of the Earth; and it is probable that, if Buffon had lived in our day, he would have had other ideas.

Geology takes the Earth at the point where direct observation is possible. Its state anterior to this can be only conjectural. Now, between two hypothesis, good sense teaches that it is necessary to choose the one sanctioned by logic, and which best agrees with observed facts.

THEORY OF INCRUSTATION

4. We mention this theory only from memory, not because it has any scientific value, but only because it has

---

[47] For details on this subject, and for the law of the diminution of heat, see *"Letters upon the Revolution of the Globe"* by Bertrand pages 19 and 307. This work, which was written with simplicity and without a spirit of system, offers, in terms of modern science, a geological study of great interest.

some few adherents even today who have been seduced by it. The following is an abstract of it:

"God, according to the Bible, created the world in six days, four thousand years before the Christian era. This is what geologists contest by the study of fossils, and by numerous incontestable evidences of decay, which carries the origin of the Earth back a million of years. However, the scriptures have told the truth, and the geologists also; and it's a simple peasant[48] who makes them agree by teaching us that our Earth is a very recently incrustrated planet, composed of very ancient materials.

"After the appearance of the *unknown planet*, after its having arrived at maturity in the place we now occupy, the spirit of the Earth received the order to bring together its satellites, in order to form our present globe according to the laws of progress. Four of these bodies alone consented to the association proposed to them, the moon alone persisted in its autonomy; for *the globes have all their free will*. In order to proceed with this fusion, the spirit of the Earth directed toward the satellites a magnetic attractive ray, which entranced all the animal, vegetable, and mineral properties which they brought to the community. To the operation there were no witnesses save the spirit of the Earth and the great celestial messengers who aided in this work by opening the globes in order to unite their contents. The joining together having been accomplished, the water ran into the voids left by the absence of the moon. The atmospheres were mingled; the awakening or resurrection of the entranced germs commenced. Man was the last object which was awakened from the magnetic sleep, saw around him the luxuriant vegetation of a terrestrial paradise, with animals feeding in peace around him. All that could be performed in six days with workmen as powerful as those which God had charged with this commission. The planet Asia brought us the yellow race, which belongs to the most ancient civilization; Africa, the black race; Europe, the white; and America, the red. The moon would perhaps have brought the green or blue.

---

[48] M. Michel of Figagneres (Var), author of the *"Key of Life."*

Thus certain animals of which we find the remains may never have lived upon this present Earth, but may have been found in the portions received from other worlds which have decayed. Fossils, found in climates where they would not have been able to exist lived, no doubt, in very different zones upon globes where they were born. Such remains, as are found at the poles with us, must have existed at the equator on their own globes.

5. This theory has against it the most positive results of experimental science, added to which it leaves out entirely the question of origin, which it pretends to solve. It tells well how the Earth should be formed, but does not instruct us how the four worlds which constitute this have been formed.

If such things have taken place, why is it that we find no trace of this immense union in any depth which has been explored? If each one brought its own peculiarities of materials, then Asia, Africa, Europe, and America would each have a geology peculiar to themselves, *which is not so.* On the contrary, the first granite uniform crust of a homogeneous composition is in all parts of the globe *without a breach of continuity.* Then the geological beds of the same formation are identical in their constitution; everywhere in the same order superposed, continuing, without interruption, from one side to the other of the seas of Europe, Asia, Africa, and America, and conversely. These beds are witnesses to the transformations of the globe, attesting that these transformations have been accomplished over its entire surface, and not upon one part alone. It shows us equally well the periods of the appearance, existence, and disappearance of the same species of animals and vegetables in different parts of the world; the fauna and flora of these remote periods, marching everywhere simultaneously under the influence of a uniform temperature, changing in character everywhere according as the temperature is modified. Such a state of things is irreconcilable with the theory of the formation of the Earth by the additions of many different worlds.

One would naturally inquire: What would become of the sea, which occupies the void left by the moon, if the latter had desired to join its sisters? Also what would become of the Earth if the moon should some day take a fancy to join the others, take its place, and expel the sea.

6. This belief has gained some adherents, because it seemed to explain the presence of the different races of men upon the Earth, and their localization; but, since these races have been able to germinate upon separate world, why would they not be able to have germinated upon different points of the same globe? That is trying to solve a difficulty by one much greater. Indeed, however great the rapidity and dexterity with which this operation may have been performed, this adjunction could not have been made without violent commotion. The more rapid it had been, the more disastrous had been the inundations. It seems then impossible that beings in a simple cataleptic sleep could have slept through it, awaking peacefully after all was over. If these beings were only germs, of what did they consist? How could perfectly formed beings be reduced to the state of a germ? The question would always arise: How were they developed anew? The miracle of a miraculous formation would again be brought forth, but by a method less poetic and grand than the biblical Genesis; whilst natural laws give an explanation of its formation much more complete, and above all more rational, deduced from experience and observation.[49]

The Earth's Soul

7. The Earth's soul represents the main theme in the theory of incrustation; let us see if the following idea gives us a better foundation.

---

[49] When such ideas are added to a cosmogony, one wonders if the rest of it reposes upon a rational basis. The agreement which they pretend to establish by this system between the biblical "Genesis" and science is altogether an illusory idea, since it is contradicted by science itself. The author of the letter above, a man of great learning, having been for a time seduced by this theory, soon saw the vulnerable side, and delayed not to combat it with the arms of science.

Organic development is always in accordance with the development of the intellectual principle. The organism completes itself upon the multiplication of the soul's faculties. In all beings, from the polyp to the man, the organic scale follows constantly the progression of intelligence. Neither could it be otherwise, as the soul needs an instrument adequate to the importance of the functions it should carry out. What good would be the intelligence of the monkey to an oyster, without the necessary organs for its manifestation? If then, the Earth were an animated being, serving as body to a special soul, due to its constitution, this soul would have to be even more rudimental than that of the polyp, as the Earth does not have the same vitality as that of the plant. According to the role that has been attributed to this soul, one makes of it a being that is endowed with reason and a most complete free will; in short, a superior Spirit. This is not rational, as never a Spirit would have been so poorly divided and imprisoned. The idea of the soul of the Earth, understood in such sense should then be classified among the systematic and chimerical conceptions.

More rationally one would understand the soul of the Earth to be the collectivity of Spirits in charge of developing and directing its constituent elements, which would already suppose a certain degree of intellectual development; better still, to a Spirit to whom is assigned the highest direction of the moral destinies and the progress of its inhabitants. Such a mission cannot be developed by other than a being eminently superior in wisdom and knowledge. In this case, this Spirit is not the soul of the Earth per say, since it is neither incarnate in it, nor subjugated to its material state; rather it will be a leader placed at its direction, analogous to a general who is placed at the direction of an army.

A Spirit in charge of such an important mission, as the governing of a world, could not have caprices, or else God would be very imprudent for entrusting the execution of his laws to beings capable of transgressing them due to their bad will. Or, if we follow the doctrine of incrustation, it would be due to the ill will of the Moon's soul that one attributes the reason of the Earth's incompleteness. These are ideas that are refutable by their own selves. (*"Revue Spirite"* of September of 1868, pg. 261).

Chapter IX

REVOLUTIONS OF THE GLOBE

General or Partial Revolution – Age of the Mountains – Biblical Deluge – Periodical Revolutions – Future Cataclysms – Increase or Diminution of the Volume of the Earth.

GENERAL OR PARTIAL REVOLUTION

1. The geological periods mark the phases of the general aspect of the globe by the succession of its transformations. But with the exception of the deluge period, which bears the marks of sudden commotions, all others have been accomplished slowly, and without sudden transition. During all the times that the constituent elements of the globe have been seeking their true positions, changes have been general. Once the base consolidated, only partial modifications are produced upon the surface.

2. Besides general revolutions, the Earth has undergone a great many local perturbations, which have changed the aspect of certain countries. As for the others, two causes have led to them, - fire and water.

By fire; sometimes by volcanic eruptions, which have desolated whole districts, turning villages and their inhabitants into beds of ashes; by earthquakes, or by uprisings of the solid Earth crust, making the water flow back upon the lower countries, or by depressions of this same crust in certain places over greater or less extents, where the waters have been precipitated, leaving other territories bare. Thus islands have appeared on the bosom of the ocean, while others have disappeared; thus portions of continents have separated, and formed islands; thus arms of land in the ocean, becoming dry, have united islands to continents.

By water; - sometimes by overflows, or the retreat of the sea from certain shores; by uprisings, which have arrested the course of the water, lakes have been formed; by overflows and inundations, or the alluvia formed at the mouth of rivers. This alluvial deposit, by obliging the sea to flow back, has created new countries: such is the origin of the Delta of the Nile, in Lower Egypt; of the Delta of the Rhone, or Camargue.

AGE OF THE MOUNTAINS

3. By the inspection of territories disturbed by the uprising of mountains, and beds which form long chains, one can determine their geological age. By the geological age of mountains, it is not necessary that we understand it as the number of the years of their existence, but the period during which they have been formed, and consequently their relative antiquity. It would be an error to suppose that this antiquity is by reason of their elevation, or of their exclusively granite nature, considering that the mass of granite, while being thrown up, can have perforated and separated the superposed beds.

It has thus been ascertained by observation that the mountains of Vosges, of Bretagne, and of the Côte d'Or, in France, which are not very high, belong to the ancient formations. They date from the transition period, and are anterior to the coal deposits. The Jura has been formed near the middle of the secondary period. It is contemporary with gigantic reptiles. The Pyrenees have been formed later, - at the commencement of the tertiary period. The Mont Blanc, and the group of Western Alps, are posterior to the Pyrenees, and date from the middle of the tertiary period. The Eastern Alps, which comprise the mountains of the Tyrol, are more recent still; for they were not formed until the end of the tertiary period. Some mountains of Asia are posterior to or contemporary with the deluge period.

These uprisings must have been due to great local

perturbations and inundations, - greater or less according to the extent of the displacement of waters, and the interruptions and changes of course of rivers.[50]

BIBLICAL DELUGE

4. The biblical deluge – designated also the great Asiatic deluge – is a fact which cannot be contested. It must have been occasioned by the uprising of a portion of the mountains of that country, similar to the phenomenon in Mexico. That which supports this theory is the existence of an inland sea, which formerly extended from the Black Sea to the Arctic Ocean, which has been attested by geological observations. The Ocean of Azov, the Caspian Sea, whose water are brackish, although not in communication with any other sea, the Sea of Aral, and the innumerable lakes scattered over the immense plains of Tartary and the steppes of Russia, appear to be remains of this ancient sea. Then, by the uprising of the Caucasian Mountains, a part of these waters have flowed back

---

[50] The last century offers a remarkable example of a phenomenon of this kind. Six days journey from the city of Mexico was found in 1759 a fertile and well-cultivated country, where grew an abundance of rice, corn, and bananas. In the month of June frightful earthquakes agitated the soil, and the trembling continued two whole months. In the night of Sept. 28 and 29 the earth experienced a violent commotion; a territory of many miles in extent was slowly raised, and attained a height of five hundred feet upon a surface of thirty square miles. The earth undulated like ocean-waves in a tempest. Millions of hillocks alternately rose and fell. At length a gulf, nearly nine miles in extent opened. From it proceed smoke, fire, burning stones and ashes, which were thrown to a prodigious height. Six mountains rose from this yawning gulf, among which the volcano Jorullo was raised to about five hundred and fifty yards, or thirteen hundred and seventy-five feet, above the former plain. At the moment the earthquake commenced, two rivers, - the Cuitimba and the Rio San Pedro, - flowing behind, inundated the whole plain occupied now by the Jorullo; but a gulf opened, and swallowed them. They reappeared in the west, very far away from their ancient bed. (Louis Figuer: *"The Earth before the Deluge,"* p.370).

northward to the Arctic Ocean, and another portion to the south toward the Indian Ocean. These inundated and ravished Mesopotamia in particular, and all the country inhabited by the ancestors of the Hebrews. Although this deluge extended over a considerable surface, it is well understood today that it has been only local in its extent; that it has not been due to rain: for, however abundant and continuous rains had been for sixty days, the calculation proves that the quantity of fallen water could not possibly have been sufficient to cover all the Earth even to the tops of the highest mountains.

But men were then acquainted with only a very small portion of the globe, and had no idea of its configuration. As soon as the inundation had encompassed all know countries, it was for them a universal flood. If, to this belief, one adds the hyperbolical form and imagery peculiarly Oriental in style, one cannot be surprised at the exaggeration in the biblical recital.

5. The Asiatic deluge was evidently posterior to the advent of man upon the Earth, since the memory of it has been preserved by tradition only in the memory of the inhabitants of this part of the world, who have consecrated it in their theogonies.[51]

It is equally posterior to the great universal deluge which has marked the present geological period; and, when they

---

[51] The Indian legend about the diluvium states, according to the Book of Vedas that Brahma, transformed into a fish addressed the pious monarch Vaivaswata telling him: "The time for the dissolution of the Universe has arrived; shortly, everything existent upon the earth will be destroyed. You need to build a ship in which you will board, after you have gathered and loaded the seeds of all plants. You will wait for me, for I will be with you at the ship; you will recognize me because, as a sign, I will have a horn on my head." The saint obeyed; he built a ship in which he boarded and, using a strong cable, tied it to the fish's horn. For many years the ship was towed with great speed through the darkness of a frightful thunderstorm, landing finally at the top of the Himawat (Himalaya) mount. Brahma then instructed Vaivaswata to create all beings in order to populate the Earth.

The analogy between this legend and Noah's biblical report about the deluge is evident. From India this legend made its way to speak of pre-diluvium men and animals, geologists make reference to this first cataclysm.

PERIODICAL REVOLUTIONS

6. Besides its annual motion around the sun, which produces the seasons; its rotary movement upon itself in twenty-four hours, which produces day and night, - the Earth has a third movement, which is completed in about twenty-five thousand years (or, more exactly, 25,868 years), which produces the phenomenon designated in astronomy "*the precession of the equinoxes*" (Chap. V, n° 11).[52]

This movement, which it would be impossible to explain in a few words without figures and without a geometrical demonstration, is described by a waved curve very nearly circular, which has been compared to the movement of a dying spinning-top, in consequence of which the axis of the Earth, changing in inclination, described a double cone, of which the summit is at the center of the Earth, and the bases embrace the surface circumscribed by the polar circles; that is to say, an amplitude of twenty-three and a half degrees of radius.

7. The equinox is the time when the sun enters the equinoctial points, - viz., March 21 and Sept. 22; the former being called the vernal or spring equinox, and the latter the autumnal: therefore the sun is exactly on the equator twice a year.

But, in consequence of the gradual change in the obliquity of the axis, the obliquity of the ecliptic is brought about. The time of the equinox is found each year to have advanced a few minutes (twenty-five minutes seven seconds).

Egypt, along with a multitude of other beliefs. Being that the book of Vedas antecedes that of Moses, the narrative it contains about the deluge cannot be a copy of the latter. Rather, it is possible that Moses, who had learned the doctrines of the Egyptian priests, may have taken his information from them.

[52] **Note of SAB**: According to recent studies, the precession of the equinoxes has a periodicity of 24,000 years. Source: James R. Fleming – www.colby.edu/sts/st215/6.2view/index.htm.

It is this advance which is called the *precession of the equinoxes* from the Latin *proecedere*, to march before," *derived from proe*, signifying *"before*," and *cedere*, signifying *"to go away*."

These few minutes, after a long time, make years. The result is that the equinox of the springtime, which now arrives in March, will arrive in a given time in February, then in January, then in December; and then the month of December will have the temperature of March, and March that of June, and so on in succession, until, returning to the month of March, it will be found as at present, which will be 25,868 years from now. Then it will recommence the same revolution indefinitely.[53]

8. It results from this conical movement of the axis that the poles of the Earth do not constantly regard the same points in the heavens; that the polar star is not always the same; that the poles are gradually more or less inclined toward the sun, and receive from it more or less direct rays. Whence it follows that Iceland and Lapland, for example, which are under the polar circle, will, in a given time, be able to receive the solar rays as though they were in the latitude of Spain or Italy; and that, in the extreme opposite position, Spain and Italy will have the temperature of Iceland and Lapland; so in succession at every renewed period of 25,000 years.[54]

---

[53] The procession of the equinoxes leads to another change, that which has been brought to pass in the signs of the Zodiac. The earth going around the sun in a year, according as it advances, the sun finds itself every month opposite a new constellation; these are twelve in number; viz., Taurus, Aries, Pisces, Aquarius, Capricorn, Sagittarius, Scorpio, Libra, Virgo, Leo, Cancer, Gemini. These are the signs of the Zodiac they form a circle in the plan of the terrestrial equator. According to the month of the birth of an individual, they say that he was born under such a sign: whence the prognostications of astrology. But, in consequence of the precession of the equinoxes, it happens that the months do not correspond to constellations as they did two thousand years ago. For instance, a person born in July is not now born in the sign Leo, but in that of Cancer: thus falls the superstition attaching to signs (chap. V, n° 12).

[54] The gradual displacement of the isothermal lines, a phenomenon recognized by science in such a positive way as the displacement of the sea, is a material fact that supports this theory.

9. The consequences of this movement have not yet been determined upon with precision, because only a very small part of its revolution has been observed. We have only then to offer a few presumptions, some of which are, however, highly probable.

The consequence of this are:

1st- The heat and the cold alternating at the poles, and consequently the fusion of polar ice during half of the period of 25,000 years, and their new formation during another similar period; whence it must result that the poles are not destined to abide in everlasting sterility, but will enjoy in their turn the blessing of fertility.

2nd- The gradual displacement of the sea, which encroaches little by little upon the land, whilst it leaves bare other lands in order to abandon them again, and lie upon its former bed. This periodical movement indefinitely renewed would cover the whole Earth with water once every 25,000 years.

The slowness with which the seas thus operate renders it almost imperceptible to each generation; but after a few centuries it is very marked. It can cause no sudden inundation, because men retreat from it from age to age by measure as the sea advances, and they advance upon that land from which the sea retreats. It is to this cause that some wise men attribute the retreat of the sea upon certain shores, and its invasion upon others.

10. The slow, gradual, and periodical displacement of the sea is a fact proved by experience, attested by numerous examples at all points of the globe. In this manner it keeps in repair the productive forces of the Earth. This long immersion is a time of repose, during which the submerged Earth recuperates the vital principals exhausted by a no shorter period of production. The immense deposits of organic matter brought by the waters from age to age are natural composts periodically renewed; and generations succeed generations without perceiving these changes.[55]

---

[55] Among the most recent facts proving the displacement of the sea, one can cite the following: In the Gulf of Gascogne, between the old Souillac and the tower of Cordova, when the sea is calm, one discovers in the

FUTURE CATACLYSMS

11. The great commotions of the Earth have taken place when the crust, by reason of its thinness, offered only a feeble resistance to the effervescence of the incandescent substances in the interior. They diminished in intensity and generality as the crust consolidated. Numerous volcanoes are now extinguished; others have been recovered with rocks of a posterior formation.

There will still be local perturbations, in consequence of volcanic eruptions; also new volcanoes will open with the sudden inundations of certain countries. Some islands will spring out of the sea, and others will be engulfed by it; but the time of the general inundations, like those which have marked great geological periods is past. The Earth, henceforth, will take a position which, without being absolutely unchangeable, place human beings in shelter from general perturbation unless by unknown causes, strange to our globe, something should happen which cannot be foreseen.

12. As to comets, it has been decided that their influence is salutary, rather than hurtful; that they appear destined to refurnish with provisions (if such an expression be

---

water's depths pieces of wall. These are the remains of the great and ancient city of Noviomagus, invaded by the water A.D. 580. The rock of Cordova, which then joined the shore, is now twelve kilometers from it. By La Manche, upon the Havre side, the sea gains every day upon the earth, and undermines the cliffs of St. Andres, which are gradually crumbling. Two kilometers from the shore, between St. Andres and Cape Hague, exists the bank of L'Eclat, in olden time dry ground and united to terra firma. Ancient documents state that upon this ground where one can sail upon the water today was the village of St. Denis-chef-de-Caux. The sea having invaded the land during the fourteenth century, the church was engulfed in 1378. It is pretended that in a calm tide the remains of it can be seen in the waters. Upon nearly the whole extent of the coast of Holland the sea has been restrained only by dikes, which give way from time to time. The ancient Lake Fleno, united with the sea in 1255, forms today the Gulf of Zuyder-Zee. This eruption of the ocean submerged many villages. Judging from this,

allowable) worlds by carrying to them the vital principles which they have accreted during their journey through space in the neighborhood of suns. They would thus be sources of prosperity, rather than messengers of evil.

On account of their gaseous nature, which is now well understood (chap. VI, from item n° 28 on), a violent shock is not to be feared from them; for, in case they should collide with the Earth, the latter would pass through the comet as through a fog.

Their tails are not formidable, as they are formed only by the reflection of the solar light in the immense atmosphere surrounding them, and are constantly directed from the side opposed to the sun, and change their direction according to the sun's position. This gaseous matter would thus be able, in consequence of the rapidity of the comet's movement, to form a sort of coma like the foamy track which follow a ship, or the smoke of a locomotive. Besides, many comets have already approached the Earth without causing any damage; and, by reason of their respective density, the Earth will exercise a greater attraction upon the comet than the comet upon the Earth. The remains of an old prejudice can alone inspire fear of their presence.[56]

Paris and, indeed, all of France, will some day be again occupied by the sea, as it has already been many times, as geological observations prove. The mountainous regions will then form islands like Jersey, Guernsey, and England, formerly contiguous to the continent. The countries now traversed by railroads will then be sailed over. Ships will stop at Montmartre, at Mount Valerian, on the shore of St. Cloud and Meudon. The woods and forests through which we now promenade will be buried under water, covered again with earth, and inhabited by fish instead of birds. The biblical deluge cannot have been caused in this way, since the invasion of the waters was sudden and their sojourn short; otherwise, it would have lasted many thousand years, would still exist without men knowing of its occurrence.

[56] The comet of 1861 has traversed the same route as the earth twenty hours before the latter, without any accident resulting there from.
Note of SAB: COMET TEBBUTT, (C/1861 N1=1861 II). A naked-eye

13. It is necessary to banish from chimerical hypothesis the possibility of the encounter of the Earth with another planet. The regularity and unchangeableness of the laws which preside over the movements of celestial bodies take away all probability of a collision between them.

The Earth, however will have an end; but how? This is something upon which it is impossible to decide; but, as it is far from the perfection to which it will attain, and from the decay which will be a sign of its decline, its present inhabitants may well be assured that it will not be in their time (chap. VI, from item n° 48 on).

14. Physically the Earth has had convulsions from its infancy. It has, however, entered upon a career of relative stability, of peaceable progress, which is accomplished by the regular return of the same physical phenomena, and the intelligent concurrence of man. *But it is yet quite in the infancy of its work of moral progress:* there will be the cause of its greatest commotions. *Until humanity be sufficiently advanced toward perfection by intelligence and the practice of the divine laws, greater perturbations will be caused by man rather than by nature; that is to say, there will occur social and moral, rather than physical changes.*

INCREASE OR DIMINUTION OF THE VOLUME OF THE EARTH

15. Does the volume of Earth increase, decrease or remain the same?

To uphold the notion of the Earth's increase in volume,

---

object from discovery until mid-Aug., T=1861 June 12. Extraordinary display created by comet's close encounter with Earth. On June 24th, when near Rigel, zero magnitude. In conjunction with the Sun on June 29th. Earth passed through the comet's tail! In the Northern Hemisphere, appeared suddenly in Auriga at dawn - immense, brilliant object. Descriptions suggest the head was at least -1 or -2 magnitude. Source:http://encke.jpl.nasa.gov/bright_comet.html#pre1900

some people maintain that plants give to the soil more than they extract from it. This is both true and false. Plants nourish themselves just as much - even more in fact — from the gaseous substances they draw from the atmosphere, than they do from the absorption of their roots. Being that the atmosphere is an integral part of the globe; the gases it is comprised of come from the decomposition of solid bodies; and these solid bodies, upon their recomposition take back that which they had previously given out. It is an exchange or, better still, a perpetual transformation. In fact, the increase of animal and vegetal life is accomplished with the aid of constituent elements of the globe, that is, with their remains. Note that despite their considerable amount these remains do not add a single atom to the mass. If the solid part of the globe increased permanently as a result of this fact, it would have to entail a proportional decrease of the atmosphere. Such an occurrence would render the atmosphere unsuitable for the sustenance of life - if it did not recover, through decomposition of solid bodies that which it lost for their composition.

At the origin of the Earth the first geologic layers were formed by solid matter - momentarily volatilized by the effects of high temperature - condensed later on by the cooling of temperature, and then precipitated. Undeniably this caused the Earth's surface to increase slightly, though this did not add to the total mass of the globe, as this occurrence was simply a displacement of matter. When the atmosphere attained its normal state, by purging itself of the strange elements it contained within, things took their natural path. Today, a minor modification in the atmosphere's constitution would forcibly bring about the destruction of its current inhabitants. Though new races would probably be formed, under these other conditions.

Considering it from this viewpoint, the mass of the globe — which is the sum of the molecules that comprise the set of its solid parts, liquid and gaseous — has been unquestionably the same since its origin. If the globe experienced an expansion or contraction, its volume would increase or decrease without the mass, having to undergo any alteration. Therefore, if the Earth increased its mass, it would have to be the result of a foreign cause, as it could not extract from itself the necessary elements for such an increase.

There is an opinion saying that the globe could increase its mass and volume by the influx of cosmic interplanetary matter. This idea is not irrational, but it is too hypothetical to be accepted as a principle. It is no more than a hypothesis opposing another contrary hypothesis, about which science has not yet defined itself in either way. On this subject, we present herewith the opinion of the eminent Spirit who dictated the wise uranographic studies transcribed in chapter VI:

"Worlds wear out because of their old age and tend to dissolve in order to serve as constituent elements for the formation of other universes. Little by little they give back to the universal cosmic fluid that which they took for their formation. Additionally, all bodies wear out by attrition; the rapid and incessant movement of the globe, through the cosmic fluid, results in the constant decrease of its mass, though in quantities imperceptible to us at any given period of time. [57]

The existence of the worlds, as I see, can be divided into three periods: *First period*: condensation of matter; at this period the volume of the globe decreases considerably, though its mass remains the same. This is the infancy period. *Second Period*: contraction and solidification of the crust; eclosion of germs and development of life up to the appearance of the most perfectible type. At this moment the globe has all its plenitude, this is the virility epoch; it loses, though very little, its constituent elements. *Third period*: as its inhabitants *progress spiritually*, the globe enters its period of material decrease; it suffers losses, not only as a result of attrition, but also by the

---

[57] In its orbital movement around the Sun, the velocity of the Earth is 400 leagues per minute. Being that its circumference is 9,000 leagues, in its movement of rotation around its axis, each point of the equator traverses 9,000 leagues in 24 hours, or 6.3 leagues per minute.

dispersion of its molecules, similarly to a rock that, worn out by the passage of time, is reduced to dust. In its double movement of rotation and the orbiting of the sun, the globe gives back to space fluidic parcels of its substance, until the moment of its complete dissolution.

Then, as the power of attraction is directly related to its mass, and not to volume, upon the reduction of the globe's mass, its conditions of equilibrium in space are modified. Dominated by more powerful planets, to which it cannot counterbalance, it would experience deviation in its movements, causing thus profound changes in the conditions of life in its surface. Thus: birth, life and death; or, infancy, virility, decrepitude. These are the three phases through which all agglomeration of organic or inorganic matter goes through. Only the Spirit, which is not matter, is indestructible." (Galileo, Société de Paris, 1868)

Chapter X
ORGANIC GENESIS

First Formation of Living Beings – Vital Principle – Abiogenesis – Spontaneous Generation – Scale of Material Beings – Man.

FIRST FORMATION OF LIVING BEINGS

1. There was a time when animals did not exist, and also a time when they began to appear. Each species appeared as soon as the Earth acquired the conditions necessary to its existence; this we positively know. But how were the first individuals of each species formed? A first couple must have been formed. Many beings have sprung from them; but this first couple, whence did they spring? This is one of the mysteries of the beginning, about which one can form only hypothesis. If science cannot yet completely solve the problem, it can at least put us on the way to a solution.

2. The first question presenting itself is this: has each animal species sprung from a *single first* couple, or have many couples been created simultaneously in different places?

This last supposition is the most probable. One can even call it a result of observation. Accordingly, studies of the geological layers indicate the presence of the same species in great quantities — in terrains of identical formation — on points of the globe very distant from one another. Such generalized and somewhat contemporaneous multiplication would have been impossible with one single primitive type.

Moreover, the life of an individual, above all that of a growing child, is submitted to so many uncertainties, that an entire species would be endangered without a plurality of primitive types, which would not be in accordance with divine foresight. Besides, if one type has been able to form itself upon a certain point, there is no reason why it should not be formed in many places by the same cause.

All concur then in proving that there has been a simultaneous and multiple creation of the first couples of each animal and vegetable species.

3. The knowledge of the formation of the first living beings can be deduced by analogy from the same law, by means of which have been formed and are forming every day inorganic bodies. According as one studies the laws of nature, one sees the machinery which at first sight appears so complicated, become simplified, and blend into the great law of unit, which presides over the entire work of creation. One will comprehend it better if one will notice the formation of inorganic bodies, which is the first stage of it.

4. In chemistry are found a certain number of elementary substances, such as: —oxygen, hydrogen, nitrogen, carbon, chlorine, iodine, fluoride, sulfur, phosphorus, and all the metals. By their combination they form compound bodies: — the oxides, acids, alkalize, salts, and innumerable varieties resulting from combinations of these.

By the combination of two bodies, in order to form a third, a particular concurrence of circumstances is exacted, — either a determined degree of heat, dryness or humidity, movement or repose, or an electric current, etc. If these conditions do not exist, the combination does not take place.

5. When there is combination, the bodies composing it lose their characteristic properties, whilst the composition resulting from it possesses new ones, different from those of the first. It is thus, for example, that oxygen and hydrogen, which are invisible gases, being chemically combined, form water, which is liquid, solid or vaporous according to temperature. Water, properly speaking, is no more oxygen and hydrogen, but a new body. This water decomposed, the two gases, becoming again free, recover their properties and are no more water. The same quantity of water can thus be decomposed and recomposed *ad infinitum.*

6. The composition and decomposition of bodies take place according to the degree of affinity that the elementary principles possess for one another. The formation of water, for example, results from the reciprocal affinity of oxygen and hydrogen but, if one places in contact with the water a body having a greater affinity for oxygen than for hydrogen, the water is decomposed; the oxygen is absorbed, the hydrogen liberated, and there is no more water.

7. Compound bodies are always formed in definite proportions; that is to say, by the combination of a quantity determined by the constituent principles. Thus, in order to form water, one part of oxygen is needed and two of hydrogen. If you mix two volumes of hydrogen with more than one of oxygen, then cause them to unite, the hydrogen would only unite with one volume of oxygen; but, if in other conditions there are two parts of oxygen combined with two of hydrogen, in place of water, the dentoxide of hydrogen is obtained, — a corrosive liquid, formed, however, of the same elements as water, but in another proportion.

8. Such is, in few words, the law which presides at the formation of all natural bodies. The innumerable variety of these bodies is the result of a very small number of elementary principles combined in different proportions.

Thus oxygen, combined in certain proportions with sulfur, carbon, and phosphorus, forms carbonic, sulfuric, and phosphoric acids. Oxygen and iron form the oxide of iron, or rust; oxygen and lead, both inoffensive, give place to the oxides of lead, such as litharge, white lead, and red lead, which are poisonous. Oxygen, with metals called calcium, sodium, potassium, forms limestone, soda, and potassium. Limestone, united with carbonic acid, forms the carbonites of limestone, or calcareous stones, such as marble, chalk, building stones, the stalactites of grottos. United with sulfuric acid, it forms the sulfate of limestone, or plaster and alabaster; with phosphoric acid, the phosphate of limestone. The solid base of bones, hydrogen, and chlorine form hydrochloric acid. Hydrochloric acid and soda form the hydrochloride of soda, or marine salt.

9. All these combinations, and thousands of others, are artificially obtained on a small scale in chemical laboratories. They are operated on a large scale in the grand laboratory of nature.

The Earth, in its beginning, did not contain these combinations of matter, but only their constituent elements in a state of volatility. When the calcareous and other soils became after a long time stony, they had been deposited on its surface. They did not at first exist as formations, but in the air were found in a gaseous state. These substances, precipitated by the effect of cold under the sway of favoring circumstances, have been combined according to the degree of their molecular affinity. It is then that the different varieties of carbonates and sulfates, etc., have been formed, — at first in a state of dissolution in the water, then deposited on the surface of the soil.

Let us suppose that by some cause the Earth should return to its primitive incandescent state; all that we see would decompose; the elements would separate; all fusible substances would melt; all those which were volatile would return to a state of volatility; after which a second cooling process would lead to a new precipitation, and the ancient combinations would form anew.

10. These considerations prove how necessary is chemistry to give us an intelligent idea of Genesis.

Before the knowledge of the laws of molecular affinity, it was impossible to comprehend the formation of the Earth. This science has thrown an entirely new light upon the question, as astronomy and geology have done upon other points of view.

11. In the formation of solid bodies, one of the most remarkable phenomena is that of crystallization, which consists of the regular form which certain substances appropriate in their passage from the liquid or gaseous state to a solid condition. This form, which varies according to the nature of the substance, is generally that of geometrical solids, such as the prism, the rhomboid, cube, and pyramid. Everyone has seen the crystals of sugar candy, — rock crystals, or crystallized silica, which are prisms with six sides terminated by a pyramid equally hexagonal. The diamond is pure carbon, or crystallized coal. The designs which are produced upon window-panes in winter are due to the crystallization of the vapor from water under the form of prismatic needles.

The regular disposition of the crystals belongs to the particular form of the molecules of each body. These infinitely small particles occupy, nevertheless, a certain space, have been drawn toward one another by molecular attraction; they are arranged and in juxtaposition to one another, according to the exigency of form, in such a way that each one takes its place around the nucleus, or first center of attraction, and forms a symmetrical whole.

Crystallization only operates under the empire of certain favorable circumstances, without which it cannot take place. A right degree of temperature with repose is an essential condition. Too much heat, keeping the molecules separated, would prevent condensation; and, as agitation is opposed to their symmetrical arrangement, they would form only a confused and irregular mass under its influence, which is consequently not crystallization in the true sense of the word.

12. The law which presides at the formation of minerals leads naturally to the formation of organic bodies.

Chemical analysis shows us that all vegetable and animal substances are composed of the same elements as inorganic bodies. Of these elements those which play the principal role are: oxygen, hydrogen, nitrogen, and carbon; the others are only accessory to them. As in the mineral kingdom, the difference of proportion in the combination of these elements produces all varieties of organic substances and their various properties: such as, muscles, bone, blood, bile, nerves, cerebral matter, and fat among animals; and sap, wood, leaves, fruits, essences, oils, and resins in the vegetable kingdom. Thus no special body enters into the composition of animals and plants which is not also found in the mineral kingdom.[58]

13. A few common examples will show the transformations which take place in the kingdom of organic beings by the modification of the constituent element alone.

In the juice of the grape is found neither wine nor alcohol, but simply water and sugar. When this juice has arrived at maturity, and is placed in favorable circumstances, fermentation is produced. In this process a portion of the sugar is decomposed. Oxygen, hydrogen, and carbon are separated, and combined in the required proportions to form alcohol. By drinking the grape-juice when it is first formed, one does not drink alcohol, as it does not yet exist therein; thus, the alcohol is formed from the constituent parts of water and sugar existent therein, without adding or taking away one single molecule.

In bread and vegetables that we eat, there is certainly neither flesh, blood, bone, bile, nor cerebral matter; yet these articles of food produce them by decomposing and recomposing in the labor of digestion, and produce these different substances solely by the transmutation of their constitutive elements.

In the seed of a tree there is neither wood, leaves,

---

[58] The following table of analysis of a few substances shows the difference of properties resulting solely in the difference in the proportions of the constituent elements in 100 parts: —

	Carbon.	Hydrogen.	Oxygen	Nitrogen.
Sugar-cane	42.470	6.900	50.530	-
Grape-sugar	36.710	6.780	56.510	-
Alcohol	51.980	13.700	34.320	-
Olive-oil	77.210	13.360	9.430	-
Oil of nuts	79.774	10.570	9.122	0,534
Fat	78.996	11.700	9.304	-
Fibrin	53.360	7.021	19.685	19.934

flowers, nor fruit; and it is a puerile error to believe that the entire tree, in a microscopic form, is found in the seed. There is not even in this seed the quantity of oxygen, hydrogen, and carbon necessary to form a leaf of the tree. The seed encloses a germ which comes to light when, the necessary conditions are found. This germ grows by aid of the juices it draws from the Earth, and the gas that it inhales from the air. These juices, which are neither wood, leaves, flowers, nor fruit, by infiltrating themselves into the plant, form sap, as food with animals makes blood. This sap, carried by the circulation into all parts of the vegetable, according as it is submitted to a special elaboration, is transformed into wood, leaves, and fruits, as blood is transformed into flesh, bones, bile, etc.; and, although these are always the same elements, — oxygen, hydrogen, nitrogen, and carbon, — they are diversely combined.

14. The different combinations of the elements for the formation of mineral, vegetable and animal substances can then be formed only under propitious circumstances. Outside of these circumstances the elementary principles are in a sort of inertia; but, as soon as conditions are favorable, a work of elaboration commences. The molecules begin to move: they act, approach, and are drawn toward one another, and separate by virtue of the law of affinity, and by their multiple combinations compose the infinite variety of substances. If these conditions cease, the work is suddenly arrested, to recommence so soon as conditions are again furnished. Thus vegetation is active, retards, ceases, and resumes action under the power of heat, light, humidity, cold, and dryness; as some plants prosper in one climate or soil, and perish in another.

15. That which took place from the beginning is daily taking place under our eyes; for the laws of nature are always the same since the constituent elements of organic and inorganic beings are identical.

As we continually see them under the empire of certain circumstances form stones, flowers, and fruits, one can conclude that the bodies of the first living beings were formed as the first stones, — by the reunion of elementary molecules by virtue of the law of affinity, according as the conditions of vitality of the globe have been propitious to this or that species.

The similitude of form and color in the reproduction of individuals of each species can be compared to the similitude of form of each species of crystal. The molecules, being in juxtaposition under the dominion of the same law, produce an analogous whole.

VITAL PRINCIPLE

16. Though we say that plants and animals are formed of the same constituents as minerals, it is necessary to understand this statement in a purely material sense, as it has reference only to the body.

Without speaking of the intelligent principle, which is a question by itself, there is in organic matter a special indiscernible principle, which has never yet been defined: *it is the vital principle.* This principle, which is active in living beings, though *extinct* in beings deprived of life by death, nevertheless gives to them characteristic properties, distinguishing them from inorganic substances. Chemistry, which decomposes and recomposes the greater part of inorganic bodies, has power to decompose organic bodies, but has never known to reconstruct even a dead leaf, which is a conclusive proof that there is something in one which does not exist in the other.

17. Is the vital principle something distinct, having a separate existence before it enters the systematic unity of the generative element? Or is it only a particular state, one of the modifications of the universal cosmic fluid, which has become the principle of life, as light, fire, heat, electricity? It is in this last sense that the question is solved by the communications connected with this subject (chap. VI, "*General Uranography*").

But, whatever the opinion be concerning the nature of the vital principle, we know it exists as we see the effects of it. One can then admit logically that, in forming themselves from it, organic beings have assimilated the vital principle necessary to their existence as immortal beings; or, if one wishes to say that this principle has been developed in each individual through a combination of elements under the rule of certain circumstances, one sees heat, light, and electricity develop themselves.

18. Oxygen, hydrogen, nitrogen, and carbon, in combining themselves without the vital principle, form only a mineral or inorganic body. The vital principle, modifying the molecular constitution of this body, gives to it special properties. In place of a mineral molecule is found a molecule of organic matter.

The activity of the vital principle is sustained during life by the action of the organs, as is heat by the rotary movement of a wheel. As this action ceases with death, the vital principle is *extinguished*, as heat is when the wheel ceases to turn. But the *effect* produced upon the molecular state of the body by the vital principle lives after its extinction, just as the carbonization of wood continues after the extinction of heat. In the analysis of organic bodies, chemistry finds again the constituent elements, oxygen, hydrogen, nitrogen, and carbon; but it cannot reconstruct them, because the cause exists no more: and thus the *effect* cannot be reproduced, although it can reconstruct a stone.

19. We have taken as an illustration heat generated by the movement of a wheel, because it is a common effect known to all and easier to comprehend; but it had been more exact to say, that in the combination of elements needed to form organic bodies, they are developed by *electricity*. Organic bodies are therefore veritable *electric batteries* which operate to the extent that the elements composing them are in a condition to generate *electricity*, which is life. When these conditions are arrested, death ensues. The vital principle can be none other than a particular kind of electricity designated under the name of animal electricity, evolved during life by the action of the organs, of which the production is arrested by death owing to the cessation of this action.

ABIOGENESIS - SPONTANEOUS GENERATION[59]

20. One naturally asks: why have there not been formed more living beings in the same conditions as the first to appear on Earth?

The question of abiogenesis with which science is occupied today, although yet diversely decided upon, cannot fail to throw light upon this subject. The problem proposed is this: are there spontaneously formed in our day organic beings by the sole union of the constituent elements without previous germs produced by ordinary generation, i.e., without fathers or mothers?

The partisans of abiogenesis reply affirmatively, and are supported by direct observations, which seem conclusive. Others think that all living beings are reproduced by one another, and support this fact arrived at by experience, as the germs of certain vegetable and animal species, being dispersed, can preserve a latent vitality for a considerable time until circumstances are favorable to their birth. This opinion does not answer any question concerning the formation of the first parents of any species.

21. Without discussing the two systems, it is well to remark that the principle of abiogenesis can evidently be applied only to the inferior order of beings of the vegetable and animal kingdoms, to those on which life is commencing to dawn, their

---

[59] **Note of SAB**: ABIOGENESIS, in biology, the term, equivalent to the older term "spontaneous generation," Generatio acquivoca, Generatio primaria, and of more recent terms such as archegenesis and archebiosis, for the theory according to which fully formed living organisms sometimes arise from not-living matter. Source: http://www.avsands.com/abiogenesis-av.htm

organisms being extremely simple and rudimentary. These are probably the first which have appeared upon the Earth, of which the generation has been spontaneous. We could thus form an idea of a permanent analogous creation to this which has taken place in the first ages of the world.

22. Why, then, could not beings of a complex organization be formed in the same manner? That these beings have not always existed is a positive fact: then they must have had a beginning. If moss, lichens, zoophytes, infusorians, intestinal worms, and others can be spontaneously produced, why is it not the same with trees, fishes, dogs, and horses?

For a time investigations rest here. The conducting thread is lost, and, until that be found, the field is open to hypothesis. It would then be imprudent and premature to give any views on the subject as absolute truths.

23. If the fact of abiogenesis is proved, however limited it may be, it is no less a capital fact, a steady beacon-light on the way to new discoveries. If complex organic beings are produced in this manner, who knows how they have obtained their origin? Who knows the secret of all transformations? When one regards the oak and the acorn, who can say if a mysterious tie does not exist between the polyp and the elephant? (n° 25). From our current state of knowledge we cannot thus far establish the theory of permanent spontaneous generation, expect as a hypothesis; however a hypothesis that will perhaps in the future take a prominent place among the incontestable scientific truths.[60]

SCALE OF MATERIAL BEINGS

24. Between the vegetable and animal kingdom there are no distinctly traced boundaries. Upon the borders of the

---

[60] *"Revue Spirite,"* July 1868, page 201: Development of the Theory of Abiogenesis.

two are the *zoophytes*, or *animal plants*, of which the name indicates that they belong to both: they are the hyphen between the two.

Like animal, plants are born, live, grow, are nourished, breathe, reproduce their kind, and die. Like them they have need of light, heat, and water: if they are deprived of them, they wither and die. The absorption of vitiated air and deleterious substances poisons them. Their distinctive trait of character, the most defined, is of being attached to the soil, and, without leaving their place, drawing their nourishment from it.

The zoophyte has the exterior appearance of a plant. Like the plant it belongs to the soil, but seems to partake more of the nature of an animal. It draws its nourishment from the ambient midst.

An animal, being one degree above a zoophyte, is free to go and seek its food. Firstly, there are innumerable varieties of polyps with gelatinous bodies, without very distinct organs, and which differ from plants only by locomotion. Then come in the order of development those with organs of vital activity and instinct, — intestinal worms, mollusks, fleshly animals without bones, of which some are entirely destitute, as slugs or cuttle-fish; others are provided with shells, as snails and oysters; then shell-fish, of which the skin is invested with a hard shell, like crabs and lobsters; insects, who lead a very active life, and manifest an industrious instinct, like the ant, the bee, and the spider; a few submit themselves to a metamorphosis, as the caterpillar, which is transformed into an elegant butterfly. Then comes the order of vertebrates, — animals with a bony framework, — which comprises fish, reptiles, birds, and mammals, of which the organization is more complete.

25. If we consider only the two opposite ends of the chain, there is no apparent analogy in these beings. However, if we go from one ring to the other, without solution of continuity, we arrive, without any sudden transition, from plants to vertebral animals. One can then understand the possibility that animals of complex organization may be no more than a transformation, or if we prefer, a gradual development, unnoticeable at first, of the immediately inferior specie and thus successively down to the most elementary primitive being. Between the acorn and the oak tree, there is a great difference; nevertheless, if we follow step by step the development of the acorn, we will arrive at the oak tree, and then we will not be surprised to see that it originated from such a small seed. If the acorn encompasses, in latency, the elements appropriate to the formation of a gigantic tree, why then won't the same happen from the insect to the elephant? (n° 23)

From the above we conclude that there is no spontaneous generation, except for elementary organic beings; the superior species would be a product of successive transformations of these same beings, achieved as soon as atmospheric conditions were propitious for it. When each species acquired the ability to reproduce, their crossbreeding brought about innumerable varieties. Then, once the species were set in conditions of lasting vitality, who could say that the primitive germs from which they emerged did not disappear, for lack of usefulness? Who could say that our current day insect is not the same that, from transformation to transformation, produced the elephant? This would explain why there is no spontaneous generation among animals of complex organization.

Although not yet admitted as final, this theory tends evidently to prevail in Science today. It is the theory accepted by most serious observers, for being the most rational.

Man

26. At the corporeal and purely anatomical point of view, man belongs to the mammals, from which he differs only slightly in outward form. Beyond that he is of the same chemical composition as all animals, has the same organs, functions, modes of nutrition, respiration, secretion, and reproduction. He is born, lives, and dies in the same conditions; and at his death his body is decomposed like that of all other beings. There is not in his blood, flesh, or bone, an element more or less than in those of the lower animals. Like the latter, in dying he renders to the Earth oxygen, hydrogen, nitrogen, and carbon, which were combined in order to form him, and go towards forming new combinations, new mineral, vegetable, and animal bodies. The analogy is so perfect that man can study his own organic functions in certain animals when experiments cannot be made with himself.

27. In the family of mammals man belongs to the two _legged_ order of animals. Immediately below him comes animals with _four legs_, — the monkeys, of which a few, like the orangutan, chimpanzee, and the ape, have certain ways like men, so much so that for a long time they have been called _wild men of the woods_. Like him they walk erect, use a stick, and carry food to their mouths with their hands, which are characteristically human habits.

28. Although one can observe the scale of living beings at the point of view of organism, it is recognized that from the lichen to the tree, and from the zoophyte to man, there is a continuous chain elevating itself by degrees, in which all the links are joined together. _Following step by step the series of beings, one can say that each species is a transformation of the species immediately below it._ Since the body of man is in conditions identical with other bodies chemically and constitutionally, as he is born, lives, and dies in the same manner, he must have been formed in the same way.

29. Although it is humbling to his pride, man must be resigned to behold in _his material body_ only the last link of animality _upon the Earth_. The inexorable argument of facts compels him thus to regard himself, against which all protestation is vain.

But the more the body diminishes in value in his eyes,

the more the spiritual principle increases in importance. If the first puts him on a level with the brute, the second elevates him to an immeasurable height. We can see the point where the animal stops; but, we cannot see the limit to which the human spirit can attain.

30. Materialism can see by this that Spiritism, far from fearing the discoveries of science and its positivism, goes before and invites them, because it is certain that the spiritual principle, which has an existence of its own, can suffer no harm from them.

In the field of matter, Spiritism advances side by side with materialism. It admits everything the latter does, though it advances beyond the point whereat science stops. Spiritism and materialism are like two travelers going on a journey, leaving from the same point. After a certain distance, one tells the other: "I cannot go any further." The other however proceeds and discovers a new world. Why should the first traveler say that the second traveler is crazy? Only because, upon foreseeing new horizons, one decides to surpass the limits whereat the other decided to stop? Was not Christopher Columbus labeled crazy because he believed in the existence of a world beyond the ocean? How many of these crazy and sublime people, who propelled humanity forward and to whom we now render our praises — after throwing mud at them — does History register?

Spiritism, the idiocy of the 19th century, according to those who want to remain at the shores of Earth, reveals to us a whole new world. A world which is more important to mankind than America, as not everyone can go to America, whereas all of us, without exception, go to the Spirit world — usually making numerous trips from one world to the other.

Reaching the point wherein we currently find ourselves in Genesis, materialism comes to a halt, while Spiritism proceeds with its researches, in the realm of *Spiritual Genesis*.

Chapter XI
SPIRITUAL GENESIS

Spiritual Principle – Union of Spiritual Principle with Matter – Hypothesis upon the Origin of Human Bodies – Incarnation of Spirits - Reincarnation – Emigration and Immigration of Spirits – The Adamic Race – Doctrine of Fallen Angels.

SPIRITUAL PRINCIPLE

1. The existence of the spiritual principle is a fact needing no more demonstration than does the existence of the material principle. It is sort of axiomatic truth; it affirms itself by its effects as matter by those which are peculiar to it.

According to the maxim, "all effects have a cause; all intellectual effects must have an intelligent cause." There is no one who would not see a difference between the mechanical effect of a bell agitated by the wind and the movement of this · same bell destined to give a signal, a notice, attesting by that a thought, an intention. Now, as it can occur to no one to attribute the thought to a bell, one concludes that it is moved by an intelligence to which it serves as an instrument of manifestation.

For the same reason no one thinks of attributing thought to the body of a deceased man. If a living man thinks, it is because there exists something in him that is not destroyed by his death. The difference between him and the simple bell is that the intelligence that makes the bell ring is outside of it, whereas that which makes a man act comes from within.

2. The spiritual principle is the corollary of the existence of God. Without this principle God would forever remain unrevealed to man; for one could not conceive sovereign intelligence reigning eternally over only animal matter, or a terrestrial monarch reigning throughout his life only over stones. As one cannot admit God to be without the essential elements of divinity, justice, and goodness, these qualities would be useless if exercised only over matter.

3. On the other hand, one would not be able to conceive of a God sovereignly just and good creating intelligent and sensible beings, in order to condemn them to nothingness after a few years of suffering without compensation, enjoying a view of an indefinite succession of beings who are born without having demanded the gift of life, who are endowed with the power of thought only to learn pain, and are destroyed after an ephemeral existence.

Without the survival of the thinking being, the sufferings of life would be on the part of God cruelty without object. This is why materialism and atheism are consequences of one another. Denying the cause, one cannot admit the effect; denying the effect, one cannot admit the cause. Consequently materialism is not reasonable.

4. The idea of the perpetuity of the spiritual principle is innate in man. It is present in him through intuition and aspiration; he comprehends that there alone is compensation for the ills of life. That is why there always have been and always will be more spiritualists than materialists, more theists than atheists.

To the intuitive idea and to the power of reason Spiritism comes to add the sanction of facts - the material proof of the existence of a spiritual being, of its survival, immortality and individuality. It points directly to and defines that which was vague and abstruse in this thought. It shows us the intelligent being acting outside of matter either during or after the life of the body.

5. The spiritual and vital principle are by no means one and the same thing!

Commencing always with the observation of facts, if the vital principle were inseparable from the intelligent principle, there would be some sense in confounding them. But, as we see some beings who live without thinking, like plants - beings animated with organic life, who give no manifestation of thought; as there are produced in living beings active movements independent of the act of the will; as during sleep organic life is in all its activity, whilst intellectual life does not manifest itself by any exterior sign - we are induced to conclude that organic life resides in a principle inherent in matter, independent of the spiritual life which is inherent in Spirit. Consequently, as matter possesses vitality independent of Spirit, it is evident that this double vitality reposes upon two different principles (Chap. X, n° 16 to 19).

6. Does the spiritual principle have its source in the universal cosmic element? Can it be only a transformation of it? A mode of existence of this element, like light, heat, electricity, etc?

If it were thus, the spiritual principle would submit to the vicissitudes of matter. It would be extinguished by disintegration, as is the vital principle. An intelligent being would have a momentary existence, like unto the body; and at death it would be annihilated, or return into the universal whole, which is the doctrine of the materialists.

The properties *sui generis* which are found in the spiritual principle prove that it has an independent existence of its own; but, if it had its origin in matter, it would not have these properties. Consequently, as intelligence and thought cannot be attributes of matter, one arrives at the conclusion that the material and spiritual elements are the two constituent principles of the universe. The individualized spiritual element constitutes the beings called *Spirits*, as the individualized material element constitutes the different organic and inorganic bodies of nature.

7. Admitting there is a spiritual being, and its source found to be outside of matter, what is its origin? From whence does it come?

Here the means of investigation absolutely fail, as in all matters relating to the beginning of things. Man can ascertain only that which is material. Upon all else he can establish only hypothesis. Whether this knowledge is beyond the compass of his present intelligence or whether it is useless or inconvenient for him to possess it now, God does not give it to him even by revelation.

That which God reveals to him by his messengers, besides that which man is able to deduce for himself from the principle of sovereign justice, which is one of the essential attributes of divinity, is that all have the same starting-point; that all are created simple and ignorant, with an equal aptitude to progress by their individual activity; that all will attain the degree of perfection compatible with the creature by their personal efforts; that all, being children of the same Father, are objects of an equal solicitude; that there is no one more favored, or better endowed than another, or excused from the labor which would be imposed upon others in order to attain the end.

8. In the same way as God has created material worlds during all time, he has equally created spiritual beings for the same length of time; without this, the material worlds would have been useless. One could rather conceive of spiritual beings without material worlds, than the latter without spiritual beings. Material worlds must furnish to spiritual beings the elements of activity for the development of their intelligence.

9. Progress is the normal condition of spiritual beings and relative perfection the object to which they must attain. Now, as God has always created, and is always creating, there must be some spirits who have reached the highest point of the ladder of progress.

Before this world was created, worlds had succeeded to worlds, and, when sprang forth from the chaos the elements which form this globe, space was peopled with spiritual beings in all degrees of advancement, from those who were just born into life to those who through countless ages had ranked among the pure Spirits, commonly called angels.

UNION OF SPIRITUAL PRINCIPLE WITH MATTER

10. Matter being the object of the work of the spirit for the development of his faculties, it is necessary that it should be able to act upon matter; that is why man has come to inhabit it as the woodcutter lives in the forest. The former being at the same time the object and instrument of the labor, God, instead of uniting him to the rigid stone, created for his use organized flexible bodies, capable of receiving all the impulsions of his will, and of lending themselves to all his movements.

The body is then at the same time the envelope and the instrument of the Spirit; and, as the latter acquires new aptitudes, it is reinvested with an appropriate envelope for the new kind of work which it must accomplish, as a workman is given finer utensils for his work as he becomes capable of performing more difficult tasks.

11. In order to be more exact, it is necessary to say that it is the spirit itself which fashions its envelope, and appropriates it to its new needs. It brings it toward perfection, develops and completes the organism by measure as it experiences the need of manifesting new qualities. In a word, it makes him in accordance with his intelligence. God furnishes the materials for the work; it is up to the Spirit to put it to functioning. Thus advanced races have an organism or, one might say, utensils of a more refined order than the primitive races. Thus is explained the special seal which the Spirit imprints on the expression of the face and manner (Chap. VIII, n°7: *The Spirit of the Earth*).

12. As soon as the spirit is born into self-conscious life, it must for its advancement make use of its faculties, which are at first in a rudimentary state. That is why it is invested with a material envelope, appropriate to its state of intellectual infancy - an envelope which it quits in order to be reinvested with another suited to its enlarged forces. Now, as from all time worlds have existed, and as these worlds have given birth to organized bodies proper to be receptacle of Spirits, from all time Spirits have found what their degree of advancement was, and the necessary elements for their material life.

13. Bodies being exclusively material are subject to the vicissitudes of matter. After having for some time operated, it becomes disorganized and decomposed. The vital principle, no longer finding an element for its activity, is extinguished, and the body dies. The Spirit, for whom the body deprived of life is henceforth useless, leaves it as one moves away from a ruined house, or throws an article of wearing apparel aside, after it is no longer serviceable.

14. The body is then simply an envelope to receive the Spirit; consequently, its origin and the materials of which it is composed matters little. Let the body of man be a special creation or not, it is certainly formed from the same elements as that of animals, animated by the same vital principle, and one might say heated by the same fire, as it is lighted by the same luminary, subject to the same vicissitudes and to the same needs; this is a point upon which there can be no controversy.

Considering only matter and abstracting the Spirit, man has nothing which distinguishes him from the animal; but there is an immediate change of aspect when the distinction between the habitation and the inhabitant is made.

A great lord under his own roof, or dressed in the garments of a peasant, is a great lord. He is always the same man; it is not by his vestment that a man is elevated above the brute, and made a unique being, it is by his Spirit.

HYPOTHESIS UPON THE ORIGIN OF HUMAN BODIES

15. From the similitude which exists between the body of man and that of the monkey certain physiologists have contended that the former was only a transformation of the latter. In that there is nothing impossible, although, if it is so, the dignity of man will naturally suffer. Bodies of monkeys may have served very well for the vestment of the first human Spirits necessarily undeveloped, who have been incarnated upon the Earth, these garments being more appropriate to their needs and for the exercise of their faculties than the bodies of any other animal. Instead of a special robe having been made for the Spirit, it may have been dressed in the skin of the monkey without ceasing to be a human Spirit, as man is sometimes dressed in animal skins without losing his manhood.

It is well understood that this is only an hypothesis which is not based upon principle, but only given to show that such an origin of the body is not prejudicial to the Spirit, which is the principal being, and that similitude of the body of man to that of the monkey does not imply equality between their respective Spirits.

16. By admitting this hypothesis, one can say that, under the influence of and by the effect of the intellectual activity of its new inhabitant, the envelope has been modified, embellished in details, yet preserving the general form as a whole (n° 11). The improved bodies by procreating themselves have reproduced themselves in improved conditions, like grafted trees. They have given birth to a new species, which has been gradually removed from the primitive type according as the Spirit has progressed. The spirit of the monkey, which has not been annihilated, has continued to bring about bodies of monkeys for its use like wild fruit reproduced from wild fruit; and the human Spirit has produced bodies of men varying from the first established form. The trunk has become divided, forked. It has produced a sprout and this sprout has become an independent trunk.

As there are no sudden transitions in nature, it is probable that the first men appearing on Earth have differed little from monkeys in exterior form, and probably no more in intelligence. There are still in our day savages who, by the length of their arms and feet, and the formation of their heads, have so many ways like a monkey, that a hairy covering only is missing to complete the resemble.

INCARNATION OF SPIRITS

17. Spiritism teaches us the mode of union between Spirit and matter through incarnation.

The Spirit, due to its spiritual essence is an unlimited abstract being, which can have no direct action upon matter. An intermediary is necessary to it. This intermediary is the fluidic envelope which makes in some sort an integral part of the Spirit, a semi-material envelope, connecting matter with spirit by its ethereal nature. Like all matter, it is drawn from the universal cosmic fluid, which is submitted by this circumstance to a special modification. This envelope, designated *perispirit*, from an abstract being, makes of the spirit a concrete, defined being, seized by thought. It renders it apt to act over tangible matter the same as all imponderable fluids, which every one knows are the most potent forces.

The perispiritual fluid is, then, the bond between spirit and matter. During its union with the body it is the vehicle for transmitting thought to different parts of the organism, which acts under the impulsion of will; it also transmits to the spirit the sensation caused by external agents. Its conducting wires are the nerves which are used, as in telegraphing, when the electric fluid has metallic wire for conductor.

18. When the spirit must incarnate in a human body in process of formation, a fluidic connection, which is none other than an expansion of the perispirit, attaches it to the germ toward which it finds itself attracted by an irresistible force from the moment of conception. By measure, as the germ unfolds, the connection shortens. Under the influence of the *vital material principle of the germ*, the perispirit, which possesses certain properties of matter, is united *molecule by molecule* with the forming body; whence one can say that the Spirit, through the perispirit, takes root in the germ, like a plant in the Earth. When the germ is entirely developed, the union is complete, and then it is born into outward life.

By contrary effect this union of the perispirit and flesh, which was accomplished under influence of the vital principle of the germ, when the principle ceases to act in consequence of the decay of the body, death is the result. The union which was only maintained by an active force ceases when the force ceases to act; then the perispirit detaches itself molecule by molecule, as it was united, and the Spirit is rendered free. *It is then not the departure of the Spirit which causes the death of the body, but the death of the body which causes the departure of the Spirit.*

Therefore, instants after death the integration of the

spirit is complete; in fact, its faculties acquire a greater perspicuity, whereas the principle of life is extinguished in the body. This is by itself an evident proof that the vital principle and the spiritual principle are two different things.

19. Spiritism teaches us by the fact that it introduces to our observation the phenomena accompanying this separation. It is sometimes rapid, easy, gentle, and insensible. At other times it is very slow, laborious, horribly painful, according to the moral state of the spirit, and can endure for months.

20. A particular phenomenon equally signalized by observation always accompanies the incarnation of the Spirit. As soon as the latter is seized by the connecting fluid which joins it to the germ, trouble comes to it. This trouble increases by measure as the connection is shortened, and in the last moments the Spirit loses all consciousness of itself, in a way rendering it never a conscious witness of its birth. At the moment when the infant breathes, the Spirit begins to recover it faculties, which are developed according as the organs which must serve for their manifestation are formed and consolidated.

21. But at the same time the Spirit recovers its consciousness, it loses the remembrance of its past without losing the faculties, qualities, and aptitudes of anterior existences, aptitudes which momentarily remained in a latent state, and which, in resuming their activity, come to aid it, and make it more and better than it was before. It gives new birth to anterior work; it is for it a new starting point, a new ladder to climb, a new field of endeavor. Here again is manifested the goodness of the Creator; for the remembrance of a past often painful or humiliating, adding itself to the bitterness of a new existence, would trouble and detain man. He remembers only that which he has learned, because that is useful to him. If sometimes he preserves a vague recollection of past events, it is like the remembrance of a fugitive dream. He is then a new man, however ancient his Spirit may be; he marches over new fields aided by that which he has acquired. When he re-enters the spiritual life, his past is unrolled before his eyes, and he judges if he has well or ill employed his time.

22. There is no destruction of continuity in spirit-life, notwithstanding forgetfulness of a past. The Spirit is always his individual self before, during and after incarnation; incarnation being only a special phase of his existence. This forgetfulness has only place during the life of exterior relations. During sleep, the spirit partially disengages itself from fleshly bonds, is rendered free, and in spiritual life remembers itself. Its spiritual sight is not then so much obscured by matter.

23. Regarding humanity at the lowest rung of the intellectual ladder with the most undeveloped savages, one wonders if this is not the starting-point of the human soul.

According to the opinion of some spiritualist philosophers, the intelligent principle, distinct from the material, is individualized and elaborated by passing through the different degrees of animal life. It is there that the soul tries life and first develops its faculties by exercise; this would be, so to say, its time of incubation. Arrived at the degree of development comporting with this state, it receives special faculties, which constitute the human soul; there would thus be a spiritual affiliation, as there is a corporeal one.

This system, founded upon the grand law of unity, which presides in all creation, has much to commend it. It is agreeable to the justice and goodness of the Creator. It gives an issue, an object, a destiny to animals which are no more disinherited beings, but find in the future reserved to them a compensation for their sufferings. That which constitutes spiritual man is not his origin, but the special attributes with which he is endowed at his entrance into humanity, attributes which transform and make of him a distinct being, as the delicious fruit is distinct from the bitter root whence it sprang. Because he had passed through the experience of animality, man would be no less a man. He would be no more an animal than the fruit is a root, as the wise man not the fetus by which he has made his debut into the world.

But this system raises numerous questions, for which there is no more an opportunity of discussing whys and wherefores than of examining the different hypothesis which

have been made on this subject. Without then searching again
for the origin of the soul, and the vicissitudes through which
it has been able to pass, we take it at entrance into humanity,
at the point where, endowed with moral sense and free will,
it commences to realize the responsibility of its acts.

24. The necessity for the incarnated spirit to provide for
the nourishment of the body, for its security and well-being,
the constraint of applying its faculties in research, in exercising
and developing them, renders its union with matter useful for
its advancement; that is why *incarnation is a necessity*. Besides,
by the intelligent work it accomplishes to its profit over matter,
it aids in the transformation and material progress of the globe
it inhabits; thus, by progressing itself, it concurs with the work
of the Creator, of whom it is the agent.

25. But the incarnation of the spirit is neither constant
nor perpetual; it is only transitory. In leaving a body it does
not take another instantaneously. During a greater or less
considerable lapse of time, it lives the spiritual life, which is
its normal life, in such a way that the sum of the time passed
in the different incarnations is small, compared to that it
passes in the free spiritual state.

In the interval between incarnations the spirit progresses
in this sense, that he puts to profit for his advancement the
knowledge and experience acquired during material life. He
examines that which he has done during his terrestrial sojourn,
passes in review that which he has learned, recognizes his faults,
arranges his plans, forms resolutions with which he expects to
guide himself in a new existence by striving to do better. Thus
each existence is a step in advance in the way of progress, a
sort of school of application.

26. Incarnation is not then normally a punishment for
the spirit, as some have thought it, but an inherent condition
and a means of progress (*"Heaven and Hell,"* by Allan
Kardec, chap. III, from item n° 8 on).

By measure, as the spirit progresses morally, he
dematerializes himself; that is to say, that preserving himself
from the influence of matter, he purifies himself, his life becomes

spiritualized, his faculties and perceptions are extended, his happiness is by reason of accomplished progress. But, as he acts by virtue of his free will, he can, by negligence or bad desire, hold up his advancement. He prolongs, therefore, the duration of his material incarnations, which become then for him a punishment, since by his own fault he remains in the inferior ranks, obliged to recommence the same task. It depends then upon the spirit to abridge by its work of self-purification the duration of the period of its incarnations.

27. The material progress of a globe follows the moral progress of its inhabitants. Now, as the creation of worlds and spirits is incessant, as the latter progress with greater or less rapidity by reason of their free will, the result is, that there are some worlds of considerable antiquity, at different degrees of spiritual and physical advancement, where incarnation is more or less material, and where, consequently, the work for the spirit is more or less rude. At this point of view the Earth is one of the least advanced. Peopled by spirits relatively inferior, corporeal life is more painful than on many other worlds. On some planets things are still less developed. There life is more painful still than upon this Earth; and for the inhabitants of such worlds this Earth would be relatively a happy world.

28. When the spirits have acquired over a world the degree of progress comporting with the state of that world, they quit it in order to dwell upon another more advanced, where they acquire new knowledge, and so on in succession until incarnation, in a material body, being no longer of use to them, they live exclusively in the spiritual life, where they still progress in other ways and by other means. Arrived at the culminant point of progress, they enjoy supreme felicity. Admitted into the counsels of the Almighty, they have his thought, and become his messengers, his ministers for the government of worlds, having under their charge spirits of various degrees of advancement.

Thus all spirits, incarnated or discarnated, of whatever degree of the hierarchy to which they belong, from the lowest to the highest, have their attributions in the great mechanism of the universe. All are useful to the whole; at the same time they are useful to themselves. To the least advanced is incumbent a material task, a simple maneuver, at first unconscious, then gradually intelligent. Everywhere there is activity in the spiritual world; nowhere is there useless idleness.

The collective body of Spirits is, in a manner, the soul of the universe; it is the spiritual element which acts over all and through all, under the impulsion of the divine thought. Without this element, there is only inert matter, without object, without intelligence, without other motor power than material forces, which leave a crowd of insoluble problems. By the action of the individual spiritual element, all has an object, a reason for being; all explains itself; that is why, without spirituality, one is hurled against insurmountable difficulties.

29. When the Earth is found in climatic condition suited to the existence of the human species, spirits come to be incarnated there. Where did they come from? Whether these spirits may have been created at such moments or whether they may have come completely formed from space, from other worlds, or from the Earth itself, their presence on it, occurring from a certain epoch is a fact, as before them there existed only animals. They were covered with bodies suitable to their special needs and aptitudes, which physiologically pertained to animalism. Under their influence, and by the exercise of their faculties, their bodies were modified and perfected. This is what observation has proved. Leaving aside the question of origin, unsolved till now, and considering the Spirit, not at his point of origin but at the moment the first germs of free will and moral sense were manifested, we see him carrying out his humanitarian role, without concerning ourselves with the ambient in which he spent his infancy or his incubation period. Despite the analogy of his physical garment with those of the animals, due to his intellectual and moral faculties, which characterize his spirit, we will know how to differentiate him from the animal, just as we can distinguish a rustic man from a civilized when they are both wearing the same garments.

 30. Although, the first who came must have been very undeveloped, and were therefore enveloped in very imperfect bodies, there must have been between them appreciable difference in character and aptitude. Similar spirits are naturally grouped by analogy and sympathy. The Earth has thus been peopled with different categories of spirits, more or less desirous of or rebellious against progress. Bodies receiving the imprint of the character of the spirit, and these bodies reproducing themselves by reason of their respective type, the result are different races physically and morally (n° 11). Similar spirits, continuing to incarnate themselves by preference among their own kind, have perpetuated a distinctive moral and physical character among races and nations, who do not lose them except by the fusion and progress of spirits. ("*Revue Spirite*," July, 1860, p. 198: Phrenology and Physiognomy.")

 31. One can compare the spirits who have come to people the Earth to troops of emigrants of diverse origin who came to establish themselves on a virgin soil. They find there wood and stone with which to make habitations, and each one gives to his own a special seal, according to the degree of his knowledge and ingenuity. They group themselves by reason of analogy, of origin, and taste. These groups end in time by forming tribes, then nations, each having its own customs and characters.

 32. Progress has not then been uniform among all the human species. The most intelligent races have naturally advanced before others, without counting Spirits newly born into the spiritual life who, having come to incarnate themselves on Earth among the first arrivals, render the differences in progress more sensible. It would be impossible, indeed, to give the same antiquity of creation to savages, scarcely distinct from monkeys, as to the Chinese, and still less to civilized Europeans.

 These spirits of savages however belong also to humanity. They will attain some day the level of their elders; but this will certainly not be in the bodies of the same physical race, improper to certain intellectual and moral development. When the instrument will no more be en rapport with their development, they will emigrate from this place, in order to incarnate themselves in one of a superior character, and so on in succession until they have conquered all the terrestrial grades; after which they will quit the Earth to pass into worlds more and more advanced. (*"Revue Spirite,"* April, 1862, p. 97: "Perfection of the Black Race").

REINCARNATION

33. The principle of reincarnation is the natural consequence of the law of progress. Without reincarnation, how is it possible to explain the difference which exists between the present social state of the world and that of barbarous times? If souls have been created at the same time as bodies, those which are born today are all as new, all as primitive, as those who lived a thousand years ago. Let us add, that there is not between them any connection, no necessary relation; that they are completely independent of one another. Why, then, should the souls of today be better endowed by God than their predecessors? Why have they better comprehension, purer instincts, gentler manners? Why have they knowledge of certain things without having learned them? We defy anyone to dispute reincarnation without at least admitting that God created souls of diverse qualities, some superior to others, according to time and place - a proposition irreconcilable with sovereign justice (Chap. II, n° 19).

Say, to the contrary, that souls of today have already lived in remote times, that they have been barbarous as their age, but that have progressed; that to each new existence they carry the acquisition of anterior existences; that consequently the souls of civilized times are not which have been created superior, but which have perfected themselves with time, and will have the only plausible explanation of the cause of social progress. (*"The Spirits' Book,"* Chaps. IV and V).

34. Some people think that the different existences of the soul are accomplished by going from world to world, and not in one same world where each Spirit appears only once.

This doctrine would be admissible if all the inhabitants of the Earth were on the same intellectual and moral level. They would then be able to progress only by going to another world, and their reincarnation on this Earth would be useless. Now God does nothing uselessly. One finds all degrees of intelligence and morality, from the wildness of the animal to that of the most civilized people; it offers a vast field to progress. One would ask why the savage should have to seek elsewhere the degree above him, when he can find it beside ·him, and soon, from stage to stage in this world of human progress? Why should he go to another world for stages of progress which he can find in this, as there are different degrees of advancement not only between nation and nation, but in the same nation and in the same family? If it were thus, God would have done a useless thing in placing ignorance and knowledge side by side, barbarism and civilization, good and evil, as neighbors; while it is precisely this contact which makes the backward ones advance.

There is then no more necessity for souls to change worlds at each reincarnation, than there is for a student to change colleges in going from class to class. Far from being an incentive to progress, it would retard it; for the spirit would be deprived of the examples offered him by those of superior degree, and of the possibility of repairing wrongs he has done in the same place, and in respect to the persons whom he has injured - a possibility which is for him the most powerful means for moral advancement. After a short cohabitation spirits would disperse, and become strangers to one another. The ties of family and friendship, not having time to consolidate, would be broken.

To the moral inconvenience, one would also add a material one. The nature of the elements, the organic laws, and the conditions of their existence vary according to their worlds. On this aspect there are no two that are perfectly identical. Our strivings in physics, chemistry, anatomy, medicine, botanic, etc. would serve no purpose in other worlds, although what we have learned is never lost. In addition to enhancing the intellect, the ideas acquired from such knowledge helps us to foster new concepts. (Chapter VI, from item n° 61 on). If the spirit were to make only one appearance, frequently of a short duration, in the same world, at every migration he would find himself in conditions entirely different. Each time there would be a new knowledge to acquire, and new forces according to laws unknown to him. All this, before he has the time to elaborate upon familiar elements; of studying them, or being able to exercise them. The constant changes would be an obstacle to progress. The spirit should, then, remain in the same world, until he has acquired in that world the sum of knowledge and the degree of perfection that such a world encompasses (n° 31).

That the spirits leave a world when they can acquire nothing more upon it for one more advanced, must be a truth, and is so without doubt. If they leave before having thoroughly graduated from one stage to another, it is without doubt, in individual cases which God weighs in his wisdom.

All has an object in creation, else God would neither be prudent nor wise. Now, if the Earth were the theatre for only one incarnation of each soul, of what use would it be for children who die in infancy to come to pass only a few months, sometimes hours, during which they acquire nothing? – the same of idiots and fools. A theory is only good when it solves all the questions it raises. The question of premature deaths has been a stumbling block for all doctrines, except for the Spiritist Doctrine, which alone solves it rationally.

For those to whom is furnished a normal career on Earth there is a real advantage when finding themselves again occupants of the same place in order to continue there something they have left undone, often in the same family, or in contact with the same persons, in order to repair the evil they have done, or to submit to the law of retaliation.

EMIGRATION AND IMMIGRATION OF SPIRITS

35. In the interval between their material existences, spirits live in an erratic state, and compose the ambient spiritual population of the globe. By deaths and births those two populations are mingled. There is then daily emigration from the material to spiritual world, and immigrations from the spiritual into the material world. This is the normal state of existence.

36. At certain epochs regulated by divine wisdom, these emigrations and immigrations take place en masse in consequence of great revolutions, causing great numbers of human beings to change worlds, which are soon replaced by equivalent incarnations. It is then necessary to consider destructive scourges and cataclysms as collective arrival and departures - providential means of renewing the material population of the globe by replenishing it by the introduction of new and purer spiritual elements. If in these catastrophes there is a great destruction of bodies, they are only *torn vestments*; but no spirit perishes. They only change place. Instead of departing alone, they go in numbers, which is the whole difference from the ordinary. By one cause or another they must inevitably depart sooner or later.

The rapid and almost instantaneous renovations which take place in the spiritual element of the population, in consequence of destructive scourges, hasten social progress. Without emigrations and immigrations, which from time to time give a violent impulsion, it would march very slowly.

It is remarkable that all great calamities which decimate populations are always followed by an era of marked spiritual, intellectual and physical progress in the social state of the nations in which they occur. Their object is to produce a great change in the spiritual, which is the normal and active, population of the globe.

37. The transfusion, which takes place between the incarnated and spiritual population of the same globe, operates in the same way between different worlds, either individually in normal conditions or by masses in special circumstances. There are then collective emigrations and immigrations from one world to another. From there it results in the introduction into the population of the globe of entirely new elements, new races of spirits coming to mingle with existing races, constituting new races of men. Now, as spirits never lose anything they have once acquired, they carry with them intelligence and intuition of the knowledge they possess. They impress, consequently, their character on the corporeal race they came to animate. There is no need of new bodies created for especial use. Since the corporeal species exist, they find them ready to receive them; they are simply new inhabitants. In arriving upon the Earth, they are at first a part of its spiritual population; then incarnate themselves like others.

THE ADAMIC RACE

38. The Adamic race, according to the teachings of the spirits, is due to one of these great immigrations, where one of these great colonies of spirits came from another sphere, which has given birth to the race symbolized in the person of Adam, and for this reason named Adamic. When they arrived, the Earth had been peopled from time immemorial, *as America had been when Europeans reached it shores.*

The Adamic race, more advanced than those which had preceded it upon the Earth, is indeed the most intelligent. It is that race which has pushed all other races forward. Genesis shows us it from its debut to be industrious, apt in all the arts and sciences, without having passed through an intellectual infancy, which is not the experience of primitive races. This accords with the opinions of spirits that it had already progressed upon other worlds, all proves that it did not originate, and is not ancient, upon the Earth; and nothing opposes itself to the idea that it might have only been here since a few thousand years, which would be in contradiction neither to geological facts nor to anthropological observations, but would tend to the contrary to confirm them.

39. The doctrine which proceeds from the idea of human beings of one individuality alone six thousand years old is not admissible in the present state of knowledge. The principal considerations which contradict it are drawn from physical and moral order.

From a physiological point of view, certain races present

particular characteristics, which do not allow of a common origin being assigned to them. There are differences which are evidently not produced by climate variations, since white people who are born in a land of black people do not become black. The heat of the sun broils and burns the skin, but has never transformed a white man into a black man, flattened the nose, changed the form of the features of the face, or rendered the hair crimped and woolly, from that which was naturally long and silky. One knows today that the color of the black race is produced by a peculiar tissue under the skin, appertaining to the species.

It is necessary then to consider the Black, Mongolian, and Caucasian races as having each its own particular origin, and of having been born successively or simultaneously upon different parts of the globe; and their mingling has produced mixed secondary races. The physiological characters of primitive races are the evident indications that they are the result of special types. The same considerations apply then to man, as well as to animals, as to the plurality of origins (chap. X, from item 2 on).

40. Adam and his descendents are represented in Genesis as men essentially intelligent, since from the second generation they have built cities, cultivated the Earth, and worked with metals. Their progress in the arts and sciences was at all times rapid and constant. We cannot, therefore, conclude that a race so numerous could have proceeded, thus highly gifted, from a people of most rudimentary intelligence who were still in the days of simple animality, and at the same time have lost all trace of their descent, so that they had not even a traditional memory of their ancestors. A difference so radical in intellectual abilities, and also in moral development, proves, with no small degree of evidence, that this race had a distinct origin.

41. Independently of geologic facts, the proof of the existence of man upon the Earth before the epoch fixed by Genesis is drawn from the population of the globe.

Without alluding to Chinese chronology, which carries

men back, it is said, thirty thousand years, more authentic documents declare that Egypt, India, and other countries were populous and in a flourishing condition at least three thousand years B.C., consequently only one thousand year after the creation of the first man, according to biblical chronology. These documents, as well as recent observations, leave no room for doubt in our minds today that there were inhabitants at a remote period on both hemispheres, and that relations existed between America and ancient Egypt. From this we are forced to conclude that America was already peopled at that epoch. It would be folly to admit that in one thousand years the posterity of a single man could cover so large a portion of the Earth for such amazing fecundity is contrary to all the laws of anthropology.[61]

42. The impossibility of such multiplication is made still more evident, if we admit with Genesis that the deluge destroyed *the entire human race*, with the exception of Noah and his immediate family, which was not numerous in the year of the world 1656, or 2348 B.C. It cannot thus, in reality, be true that the present population of the globe dates only from Noah, or from about this time. According to the Hebrew records, they had established themselves in Egypt 612 years

---

[61] The universal Exposition of 1867 presented antiquities from Mexico, which left no doubt of the relationship the people of that country had with the ancient Egyptians. During the Exposition, on a note he posted at a Mexican temple, Leon Mechedin expressed himself as follows:
"It is not convenient to publish, before the appropriate time, the discoveries concerning the history of man, made during the recent scientific expedition of Mexico. However, nothing impedes that the public learns, at once, that the exploration revealed the existence of a great number of cities erased by the passage of time, but that, with the aid of a pickax and fire we can extract from its burial shroud. All around, the excavations discovered there are three layers of civilizations which give the American world a fabulous antiquity."
This is how, each day, science comes to deny the facts of a doctrine which limits to 6000 years the appearance of man on earth, making him appear to descend from a single origin or trunk.

after the deluge. It cannot be that this powerful empire could have been peopled in so short a time, besides other countries, in less than six centuries by the sole descendents of Noah; such a supposition is decidedly inadmissible.

Let us, moreover, observe that the Egyptians received the Hebrews as strangers. It would be contrary to reason to suppose that they had lost all remembrance of their common origin and of their reunion; for we know that at that time they religiously kept records and monuments of their history.

Exact logic, corroborated by stern facts, clearly shows in the most unequivocal manner that men have existed on Earth through an indefinitely long period of time - certainly that the origin of the race is greatly anterior to the epoch assigned by Genesis. It is the same with the doctrine of the diversity of primitive sources. In order to demonstrate the impossibility of a proposition being a correct one, it must be shown that a contrary proposition is demonstrable. If geology discovers authentic traces of the presence of man before the great deluge period the demonstration becomes still more absolute.

DOCTRINE OF FALLEN ANGELS AND OF PARADISE LOST[62]

43. Worlds advance physically by the transformations of matter, and morally by the purification of the spirits who inhabit them. Goodness can only be realized in the predominance of good over evil, and the predominance of good results from the moral progress made by spirits. Intellectual progress will not suffice, because with knowledge it is possible to work harm.

---

[62] When, in the "*Revue of January*," 1862, we published an article on the interpretation of the doctrine of fallen angels, we presented this theory only as an hypothesis, having in its support found no higher authority than controvertible personal opinion. From that time till the present we have lacked the necessary materials out of which to construct an

At the time then when a world has reached one of its transformation crises which mark the stages of its ascent in the hierarchy, changes of a marked character take place among its incarnated and discarnated inhabitants, causing extensive emigrations and immigrations (n° 34 and 35). Those who, notwithstanding their intelligence and knowledge, have continued in evil their revolt against God and his laws, would be henceforth obstacles in the path of further moral progress, a permanent source of trouble, disturbing the tranquility and well-being of the virtuous. For this reason are they sent forth into less advanced worlds - worlds in which they can utilize their intelligence and the results of their acquired knowledge in furthering the advancement of those among whom they are called to live, at the same time expiating in a series of laborious existences, by hard work, their past faults and their willful obstinacy.

How will it fare with them among colonies so strange to them, tribes still in barbaric infancy? Will not such surroundings make the lives of these exiled angels or spirits lives of expiation indeed? And the world from which they have been sent forth, will it not appear to them a lost paradise? Was it not to them a delightful place in comparison to that where they are banished for centuries, until they have merited deliverance from it? The vague intuitive remembrance they preserve is to them like a distant mirage, which recalls to them what they have lost by their fault.

44. But, while the wicked have departed from the world they inhabited, they are replaced by higher spirits, who have come, perhaps, from a less advanced world that their merits

---

absolute affirmative proposition. We gave this title to that essay for the sake of provoking research, fully determined either to abandon or modify the theory if necessity should rise. Today this theory has been submitted to the trial of universal control. Not only has it been endorsed by a great majority of spiritists as most rational and most in accord with the sovereign justice of God, but has been directly confirmed by the greater part of the instructions given by the Spirits on this subject. It is identical with that which explains the origin of the Adamic race.

have allowed them to leave, and for which their new abode is a recompense. The spiritual population being thus renewed and purged of its lower elements at the end of an age, the moral state of the world is improved.

These changes are sometimes partial; i.e., limited to a people, to a race. At other times they are general when a period of renovation for the globe has arrived.

45. The Adamic race has all the characteristics of a proscribed race. The spirits forming part of it have been exiled upon the already peopled Earth, but peopled by primitive men yet in ignorance, to whom their mission was to effect their progress by carrying among them the light of a developed intelligence. Is it not indeed the place that this race has filled until now? Their intellectual superiority proves that the world from which they came was more advanced than this Earth; but that world entering upon a new phase of progress, these spirit, by their obstinacy not placing themselves at the required heights, would have been a hindrance to the providential march of events. That is why they were expelled; while others who have merited them have taken their places.

By placing this race upon this Earth of trial and suffering, God was just in saying to it: "By the sweat of your brow you will eat your food." In his mercy he promised to send them a Savior; i.e., he who will enlighten them concerning the route from a state of misery, from this hell, to angelic felicity. This Savior he has sent to them in the person of Christ, who has taught the law of love and charity which was unknown to them, and who becomes to them the veritable anchor of salvation.

It is equally with a view to the advancement of humanity in a determined sense that some superior spirits who have not all the qualities of Christ incarnate from time to time on Earth, in order to accomplish definite missions which aid in their own advancement, if they fulfill them according to the will of the Creator.

46. Without reincarnation the mission of Christ, as well as the promise made by God, would be useless. Let us suppose that the soul of man is created at the birth of his body and that it only once appears, and then disappears from the Earth. There is no relation between those who have come from Adam to Jesus, neither between those who have been born since; they are all strangers to one another. The promise of a Savior made by God could not only apply to the descendents of Adam if their souls were not yet created. In order that the mission of Christ should fulfill the divine word, it was necessary that it should be applied to the same souls. If these are new souls, they cannot be stained with the fault of the first father, who is only the material and not the spiritual parent; otherwise God must have created souls stained with sin they could not have committed. The common doctrine of original sin implies the necessity of a connection between the souls living on Earth in the days of Christ and those of the time of Adam, and consequently of reincarnation.

Suppose that all these souls formed a part of the colony who came to Earth in the days of Adam, and that they were stained with the sin which had expelled them from a brighter world, and you will find a rational interpretation of original sin, each individual's own sin, and not the result of the fall of another, whom he has never known. Say that these spirits are reborn in different parts of the Earth into corporeal life, that they may progress and purify themselves; that Christ came to enlighten these same souls not only with reference to their past, but also with a view to their ulterior lives; and then only do you endow his mission with an object acceptable to reason.

47. A familiar example striking by its analogy will cause the principles just exposed to be better understood.

May 24, 1861, the frigate "Iphigenia" conducted to New Caledonia a company composed of two hundred and ninety-one men. The commander of the colony addressed them on their arrival an order couched in these words:

"At your entrance into this distant land, you already comprehend that work which is expected of you.

By the example of our brave soldiers of the marine service, serving under your eyes, you will aid us to carry with glare in the midst of the savage tribes of New Caledonia the torch of civilization. Is it not a beautiful and noble mission to which I call you? You will fulfill it worthily.

Listen to the voice and counsels of your leaders. I am at their head. Let my words be well understood.

The choice of your commander of your officers, of your under officers and corporals, is a sure guaranty of all the efforts which will be put forth to make of you excellent soldiers. I say more, to elevate you to the height of good citizens, and to transform you into honorable colonists, if you but desire it.

Your discipline is strict; it has to be so. Placed in our hands it will be firm and inflexible - you know it well - but also just and paternal. It shall know how to discover all error, vice, and degradation.

Here then are men expelled for their bad conduct from a civilized country, and sent for punishment among barbaric people. What says the chief to them? – "You have broken the laws of your country - you have caused trouble and scandal, and they have exiled you from it. They sent you here; but you can retrieve your past. You can by labor create for yourselves here an honorable position, and become honest citizens. You have a beautiful mission to fulfill here - that of carrying civilization among these savage tribes. The discipline will be severe but just; and we shall know how to distinguish those who will conduct themselves well. Your destiny is in your own hands; you can improve it if you so desire, for you have your free will."

For these men thus thrown upon the bosom of barbarism, is not the mother country a paradise lost to them by their rebellion against its laws? In this distant land are they not fallen angels? The language of the chief, is it not that which God makes spirits exiled upon the Earth to hear? You have disobeyed my laws; and it is for that offence that I have banished you from a world in which you could live happily and in peace. Here you will be condemned to work; but you will be able by your good conduct to merit your pardon, and re-enter the country you have forfeited by your sin – i.e., heaven.

48. At first the idea of a downfall would appear contradictory to that of the non-retrograde movements of the spirit; but it is necessary to consider that it carried them toward a return to the primitive state. The spirit, although in an inferior position, loses nothing he has once acquired. His moral and intellectual development remains, whatever may be the condition in which he finds himself. He is in the position of a man of the world condemned to the convicts' prison by his misdeeds. Certainly, he has fallen in a social sense; but the fall makes him neither imbecile nor ignorant.

49. Does anyone believe that the men sent to New Caledonia are to be suddenly transformed into models of virtue? That they will all at once abjure their past errors? One cannot know humanity if he supposed that. For the same reason the spirits of the Adamic race, once transplanted upon the soil of exile, have not been instantaneously despoiled of pride and depraved instincts; for a long time they have preserved the tendencies of their origin, the remains of the old leaven. Now, is this not original sin?

Chapter XII
MOSAIC GENESIS

Six Days — Paradise Lost

SIX DAYS

CHAP. I. – 1. In the beginning God created the heavens and the Earth.

2. Now the Earth was formless and empty, darkness was over the surface of the deep, and the Spirit of God was hovering over the waters.

3. And God said, "Let there be light," and there was light.

4. God saw that the light was good, and he separated the light from the darkness.

5. God called the light "day," and the darkness he called "night." And there was evening, and there was morning-the first day.

6. And God said, "Let there be an expanse between the waters to separate water from water."

7. So God made the expanse and separated the water under the expanse from the water above it. And it was so.

6. God called the expanse "sky." And there was evening, and there was morning-the second day.

9. And God said, "Let the water under the sky be gathered to one place, and let dry ground appear." And it was so.

10. God called the dry ground "land," and the gathered waters he called "seas." And God saw that it was good.

11. Then God said, "Let the land produce vegetation: seed-bearing plants and trees on the land that bear fruit with seed in it, according to their various kinds." And it was so.

12. The land produced vegetation: plants bearing seed according to their kinds and trees bearing fruit with seed in it according to their kinds. And God saw that it was good.

13. And there was evening, and there was morning - the third day.

14. And God said, "Let there be lights in the expanse of the sky to separate the day from the night, and let them serve as signs to mark seasons and days and years,

15. And let them be lights in the expanse of the sky to give light on the Earth." And it was so.

16. God made two great lights - the greater light to govern the day and the lesser light to govern the night. He also made the stars.

17. God set them in the expanse of the sky to give light on the Earth,

18. To govern the day and the night, and to separate light from darkness. And God saw that it was good.

19. And there was evening, and there was morning - the fourth day.

20. And God said, "Let the water teem with living creatures, and let birds fly above the Earth across the expanse of the sky."

21. So God created the great creatures of the sea and every living and moving thing with which the water teems, according to their kinds, and every winged bird according to its kind. And God saw that it was good.

22. God blessed them and said, "Be fruitful and increase in number and fill the water in the seas, and let the birds increase on the Earth."

23. And there was evening, and there was morning - the fifth day.

24. And God said, "Let the land produce living creatures according to their kinds: livestock, creatures that move along the ground, and wild animals, each according to its kind." And it was so.

25. God made the wild animals according to their kinds,

the livestock according to their kinds, and all the creatures that move along the ground according to their kinds. And God saw that it was good.

26. Then God said, "Let us make man in our image, in our likeness, and let them rule over the fish of the sea and the birds of the air, over the livestock, over all the Earth, and over all the creatures that move along the ground."

27. So God created man in his own image, in the image of God he created him; male and female he created them.

28. God blessed them and said to them, "Be fruitful and increase in number; fill the Earth and subdue it. Rule over the fish of the sea and the birds of the air and over every living creature that moves on the ground."

29. Then God said, "I give you every seed-bearing plant on the face of the whole Earth and every tree that has fruit with seed in it. They will be yours for food.

30. And to all the beasts of the Earth and all the birds of the air and all the creatures that move on the ground - everything that has the breath of life in it - I give every green plant for food." And it was so.

31. God saw all that he had made, and it was very good. And there was evening, and there was morning - the sixth day.

CHAP. II. — 1. Thus the heavens and the Earth were completed in all their vast array.

2. By the seventh day God had finished the work he had been doing; so on the seventh day he rested from all his work.

3. And God blessed the seventh day and made it holy, because on it he rested from all the work of creating that he had done.

4. This is the account of the heavens and the Earth when they were created. When the LORD God made the Earth and the heavens -

5. And no shrub of the field had yet appeared on the Earth and no plant of the field had yet sprung up, for the

LORD God had not sent rain on the Earth and there was no man to work the ground,

6. But streams came up from the Earth and watered the whole surface of the ground,

7. The LORD God formed the man from the dust of the ground and breathed into his nostrils the breath of life, and the man became a living being.

2. After the developments explained in the preceding chapters concerning the origin and constitution of the universe, according to knowledge furnished by science concerning the material part, and according to Spiritism for the spiritual, it is useful to place beside it the text of the Mosaic Genesis, in order that a comparison may be established, and one may judge by knowledge. Some supplementary clarification will suffice to make the parts which need special explanation to be understood.

3. Upon some points there is certainly a remarkable agreement between science and Moses; but it would be an error to imagine it sufficient to substitute for six days of twenty-four hours each, six periods of time (duration unknown) in order to find a complete analogy. It would be no less error to conclude that, save the allegorical sense of a few words, Genesis and science do not follow each other step by step, and are only a paraphrase of one another.

4. Let us remark at first, in addition to what has been said already (see chap. VII, n° 14), that the number of the geological periods is not arbitrarily six, since they include more than twenty-five very characteristic formations. This number marks only the great general phases. It has been adopted principally to approach to the letter of the biblical text as nearly as possible, at an epoch when it was believed to be a duty to control science by the Bible. That is why the authors of the great majority of theories of cosmogony, with a view to making their productions more easily accepted, have been forced to place themselves in accord with the sacred text. When science leans upon the experimental method, it feels stronger, and becomes emancipated. Today it is the Bible which is controlled by science.

On the other hand, exact geology, taking its point of departure only from the formation of granite rocks, does not include in the number of its periods the primitive state of the Earth. It does not occupy itself with sun, moon, and stars, nor with that portion of Genesis which belongs to astronomy. In order to deal fairly with Genesis, it agrees to add a primary period embracing this order of phenomena, which might be called *the astronomical period.*

Besides, the deluge period is not considered by all geologists as a distinct period, but as a transitory fact which has not notably changed the climate state of the globe, neither marked a new phase in the vegetable or animal species, since, with few exceptions, nearly the same species have been found to exist before and after the deluge. One can thus make an abstract without detracting from truth.

5. The following table of comparison, in which is a summary of the phenomena characterizing each one of the six periods, permits of embracing the whole, and enables one to decide between the statements of science and the Biblical Genesis:

SCIENCE.	GENESIS.
1. *Astronomical Period.*	*First Day.*
Agglomeration of universal cosmic matter upon a point of space in a nebula which has received birth by the condensation of matter from diverse points, from the sun, stars, moon, Earth, and all planets. Primitive fluid and incandescent state of Earth. Dense atmosphere charged with vapor and volatile matter.	The heavens and the Earth Light.
2. *Primary Period.*	*Second Day.*
Hardening of Earth's surface by cooling process; formation of granite beds. Atmosphere thick and burning, impenetrable to sun's rays. Gradual precipitation of water and solid volatile substances in the air. Absence of all organic life.	The firmament. Separation of waters under firmament from those above it.

3. Transition Period.	***Third Day.***
The waters cover all the surface of the globe. First deposits of sediment formed by waters. Humid heat. Sun commences to pierce the foggy atmosphere. First organized beings of most rudimentary constitution, — Lichens, mosses, ferns, lycopodes, herbaceous plants. Colossal vegetation. First marine animals, — zoophyte, polyps, crustaceans. - Coal deposits.	The waters under the firmament are gathered together. Dry land appears. The Earth and sea. Plants.
4. Secondary Period.	***Fourth Day.***
Surface of Earth little uneven, waters not very deep, and forming marshes on Earth. Temperature less burning, purer atmosphere; considerable calcareous deposits, vegetation less colossal; new species, woody plants; first trees. Fishes, jelly and shell; turtles, great aquatic and amphibious reptiles.	Sun, moon, stars.
5. Tertiary Period.	***Fifth Day.***
Great uprising of solid crust, formation of continents; retreat of waters into lower places, formation of seas. Purified atmosphere; present temperature by solar heat. Gigantic terrestrial animals; vegetables and animals as at present; birds. Universal deluge.	Fishes and birds.
6. Post-Deluge Period.	***Sixth Day.***
Alluvial beds. Present vegetables and animals. Man.	Terrestrial Animals - Man

6. The first fact which is brought to light by the above comparative table is that the work performed during the six comparative "days" does not correspond in an exact way, as many believe, to each of the six geological periods. The most remarkable agreement is in the order of succession of organic beings, which is nearly identical, and in the appearance of man at the last. Now that is an important concordance.

There is also a coincidence, not in the numerical order of periods, but in the passage where it is said that on the third day the waters under the firmament were gathered into one heap, and dry land appeared. It is the acknowledgment of what actually took place in the tertiary period, when, by the uprising of the solid crust, oceans and continents were formed. It was then that terrestrial animal first appeared, both according to Moses and geology.

7. When Moses declares that creation was perfected in six days, did he mean days twenty-four hours long? Or has he used the word in its sense of indeterminate time? The Hebrew word standing for "day" has this double acceptation: the first hypothesis is the more probable. The specification of day and night, which is attached to each of these six periods, gives reason for the supposition that he meant ordinary days. One cannot doubt this, when he says (verse 5), "God called the light "day," and the darkness he called "night." And there was evening, and there was morning - the first day." The latter can evidently apply only to a day of twenty-four hours divided by light and darkness. The sense is still more evident (verses 17 to 19), where, in speaking of sun, moon, and stars, "God set them in the expanse of the sky to give light on the Earth, to govern the day and the night, and to separate light from darkness. And God saw that it was good. And there was evening, and there was morning - the fourth day."

Besides, it is certainly stated that creation was effected in a miraculous manner; and, since the ancients believed in miracles, they could readily believe that the Earth was formed in a hundred and forty-four hours, particularly at a time when men were totally ignorant of natural laws. This belief has been shared by all civilized people, until geology has furnished documentary evidence in proof of its impossibility.

8. One of the most contested points in Genesis is that of the creation of the sun after light had appeared. They have sought to explain by means of geologic discoveries, by stating that, at the time of its first formation, the terrestrial atmosphere, being charged with dense and opaque vapors, did not allow of the sun's being visible, though the sun previously existed. This reason would perhaps be admissible had there been inhabitants to judge of the presence or absence of the sun. Now, according to Moses, at this epoch there were only plants

upon the Earth which could not grow and multiply without the action of solar heat.

There is evidently an anachronism in the order that Moses assigns to the creation of the sun; but involuntarily, or otherwise, he has stated facts correctly when declaring that light preceded the sun.

The sun is not the source of universal light, but a concentration of the luminous element at one point, otherwise called fluid, which in certain circumstances acquires luminous properties. This fluid, which is the cause, must necessarily exist prior to the sun, which is its effect. The sun is *a cause* for the light which it expands, but is an *effect* of that which it has received.

In an obscure chamber a lighted candle is a little sun. What has one accomplished by lighting the candle? He has developed the illuminating property of the luminous fluid, and has concentrated this fluid upon one point. The candle is the cause of the light expanded in the chamber; but, if the luminous principle had not existed before the candle, the latter could not have been lighted.

It is so with the sun. The error has arisen in the false idea that has long been conceived, that the entire universe began with the Earth, and it has not been understood how the sun could be created after light. It is known now, however, that, before our sun and Earth were created, millions of suns and Earths existed which enjoyed light. The assertion of Moses is, then, exact in principle; it is only false when it declares that the Earth was created before the sun. The Earth being subject to the sun in its movement of translation must have been formed after it. That is something of which Moses was ignorant, since he was ignorant of the law of gravitation.

The same thought is met with in the Genesis of the ancient Persians. In the first chapter of the Vendedas, Ormuzd, recounting the origin of the world, says, "I created light, which gave light to the sun, the moon, and the stars" ("*Dictionary of Universal Mythology*"). The form is here clearer and more scientific than that in the Pentateuch, and need no commentary.

9. Moses partook evidently of the most primitive beliefs concerning cosmogony. Like many of his time, he believed in the solidity of the celestial vault, and of superior reservoirs for water. This thought has been expressed without allegory or ambiguity in this passage (verses 6 and 7): And God said, "Let there be an expanse between the waters to separate water from water. So God made the expanse and separated the water under the expanse from the water above it." And it was so. (See chap. V, "*Systems of Ancient and Modern Worlds*," n° 3 to 5).

· An ancient belief made the water an element, the generative primitive element. Moses does not speak of the creation of waters, which seems to have existed previously to the first creation, according to his theory. "The darkness˙ covered the deep;" i.e.; the depths of space that the imagination vaguely depicted as dark watery wastes, before the creation of light. That is why the Spirit of God, according to Moses, moved upon the waters. The Earth's being formed in the midst of water necessitated its isolation. It was supposed that God made the firmament a solid vault, separating the waters above from those under the Earth.

In order to comprehend certain parts of Genesis, it is necessary to place ourselves at that point of view from which we can watch˙ the reflection of the ideas entertained on cosmogony at that time.

10. Since the advancement of the physical sciences and astronomy, such a doctrine cannot be supported.[63] Moses, however, attributes these words to God himself; but in doing so he is guilty of either one of two serious mistakes. Either he was deceived by God in the record he gave of his work, or this recital is not a divine revelation. The first supposition

---

[63] Much which is palpably erroneous must be the result of such a belief; but still, in our days, children's doubts are lulled to rest as they are told by their instructors that it is all a sacred verity. It is only with fear and trembling that their teacher will venture to give to these writings a timid interpretation. How can we wonder that incredulity has at last taken them by storm?

·

is inadmissible. We must therefore conclude that Moses simply gave utterance to his own ideas. (See chap. I, n° 3)

11. Moses is more nearly right when he says that God formed man out of the dust of the Earth.[64] Science proves to us, in fact (see chap. X) that the human body is composed of the elements gathered up in inorganic forms of matter, otherwise called the dust or mud of the Earth.

The formation of a woman from one of Adam's ribs is an allegory, apparently puerile if we consider only its letter, but profound in its significance. It undertakes to demonstrate that woman is of the same nature as man, consequently his equal before God, and not a creature designed to be his slave and treated with disrespect. Being taken out of his side, the image of equality is very much more startling than though she had been formed separately from the same dust. This is to say to man that she is his peer and not his servant, and that he must love and revere her as part of himself.

12. For uncultured minds, without any apprehension of universal laws, incapable of embracing the whole and of conceiving of the infinite, this miraculous and instantaneous creation was essentially calculated to take hold of the imagination. The picture of the universe created out of nothingness, in a few days, by a single act of creative will, was to them the most magnificent portrayal of the power of God. What painting, in fact, could be more sublime and more poetic than these words, illustrative of the divine power, God said: "Let there be light, and there was light!" Had they been told that God accomplished the creation of the universe by the gradual and slow working of universal laws, he would have appeared to them far less glorious and powerful. It was necessary to them that these things should appear marvelous, instead of being brought about in ordinary ways: otherwise they would have said that God was no more skillful than men. A scientific and rational theory would have been received by them with coldness and indifference.

---

[64]The Hebrew word haadam, "man", which gives us Adam, and the Hebrew word haadama, "earth", are from the same root.

Let us not reject the biblical Genesis; on the contrary, let us study it as an instructive history of infancy of people. It is an epic rich in allegories, in which we may find hidden wisdom; it must be commented upon with the aid of such light as reason and science can supply. Let us prize all its poetic beauties and the spiritual instructions veiled under its allegoric forms. It must be shown boldly wherein its errors lie in the interest of religion itself. We can respect it far more when its errors are no longer imposed upon our belief as truths; and God will but appear grander and more powerful when his name shall be no longer attached to misleading documents.

PARADISE LOST

13. — CHAPTER II. 8. Now the LORD God had planted a garden in the east, in Eden; and there he put the man he had formed. 9. And the LORD God made all kinds of trees grow out of the ground-trees that were pleasing to the eye and good for food. In the middle of the garden were the tree of life and the tree of the knowledge of good and evil. 10. A river watering the garden flowed from Eden; from there it was separated into four headwaters. 11. The name of the first is the Pishon; it winds through the entire land of Havilah, where there is gold. 12. (The gold of that land is good; aromatic resin and onyx are also there.) 13. The name of the second river is the Gihon; it winds through the entire land of Cush. 14. The name of the third river is the Tigris; it runs along the east side of Asshur. And the fourth river is the Euphrates. 15. The LORD God took the man and put him in the Garden of Eden to work it and take care of it. 16. And the LORD God commanded the man, "You are free to eat from any tree in the garden; 17. but you must not eat from the tree of the knowledge of good and evil, for when you eat of it you will surely die."

14. — CHAPTER III. — 1. Now the serpent was more crafty than any of the wild animals the LORD God had made. He said to the woman, 'Did God really say, 'You must not eat from any tree in the garden?' 2. The woman said to the serpent,

'We may eat fruit from the trees in the garden,' 3. But God did say, 'You must not eat fruit from the tree that is in the middle of the garden, and you must not touch it, or you will die.' 4. 'You will not surely die,' the serpent said to the woman. 5. 'For God knows that when you eat of it your eyes will be opened, and you will be like God, knowing good and evil.' 6. When the woman saw that the fruit of the tree was good for food and pleasing to the eye, and also desirable for gaining wisdom, she took some and ate it. She also gave some to her husband, who was with her, and he ate it. 7. Then the eyes of both of them were opened, and they realized they were naked; so they sewed fig leaves together and made coverings for themselves. 8. Then the man and his wife heard the sound of the LORD God as he was walking in the garden in the cool of the day, and they hid from the LORD God among the trees of the garden. 9. But the LORD God called to the man, "Where are you?" 10. He answered, "I heard you in the garden, and I was afraid because I was naked; so I hid." 11. And he said, "Who told you that you were naked? Have you eaten from the tree that I commanded you not to eat from?" 12. The man said, "The woman you put here with me - she gave me some fruit from the tree, and I ate it." 13. Then the LORD God said to the woman, "What is this you have done?" The woman said, "The serpent deceived me, and I ate." 14. So the LORD God said to the serpent, "Because you have done this, "Cursed are you above all the livestock and all the wild animals! You will crawl on your belly and you will eat dust all the days of your life. 15. And I will put enmity between you and the woman, and between your offspring and hers; he will crush your head, and you will strike his heel." 16. To the woman he said, "I will greatly increase your pains in childbearing; with pain you will give birth to children. Your desire will be for your husband, and he will rule over you." 17. To Adam he said, "Because you listened to your wife and ate from the tree about which I commanded you, 'You must not eat of it,' "Cursed is the ground because of you; through painful toil you will eat of it all the days of your life. 18. It will produce thorns and thistles for you, and you will eat the plants of the field. 19. By the sweat of your brow you will eat your food until you return to the ground, since from it you were taken; for dust you are and to dust you will return." 20. Adam named his wife Eve, because she would become the mother of all the living. 21. The LORD God made garments of skin for Adam and his wife and clothed them. 22 And the LORD God said, "The man has now become like one of us, knowing good and evil. He must not be allowed to reach out his hand and take also from the tree of life and eat, and live forever." 23. So the LORD God banished him from the Garden of Eden to work the ground from which he had been taken. 24 After he drove the man out, he placed on the east side of the Garden of Eden cherubim and a flaming sword flashing back and forth to guard the way to the tree of life.

15. Under a puerile and sometimes ridiculous image, if one regards its form only, allegory often conceals the greatest truths. Is this a more absurd fable than that of Saturn, who is represented as a god devouring stones whom he takes for his children? But at the same time what can be more profoundly philosophically true than this figure if we seek its moral? Saturn is the personification of time. All things being the work of time, he is the father of all that exists. Moreover, all is destroyed by time. Saturn devouring stones is the emblem of destruction by time of even the most enduring forms, which are his children since they are formed by time. And what escapes this destruction according to this same allegory? Jupiter, the emblem of superior intelligence, of the indestructible spiritual principle. This image is so natural, that in modern language, without allusion to the ancient fable, it is said of a thing defaced by time that it has been devoured, corroded, or ravaged by it.

All pagan mythology is in reality only a vast allegorical picture of the good and bad sides of humanity. He who seeks the spirit of it ever finds it a complete course in the highest philosophy, which is also true of our modern fables. The absurdity is to mistake the form for the moral of it.

16. It is so with Genesis, where it is necessary to see

great moral truths under material figures, which, taken
literally, are as absurd as any of our fables taken literally;
the scenes and dialogues attributed to animals, for instance.
Adam personifies humanity. His individual fault is but
a figure of the general feebleness of mankind, in whom the
material instincts predominate, which man knows not how to
resist.[65]

The tree of life is the emblem of spiritual life. As the tree
of knowledge represents the conscious knowledge of good
and evil, which man acquires by the growth of intelligence
and use of free will, by virtue of which he chooses between
the two; it marks the point at which the soul, ceasing to be
guided by instinct alone, takes possession of liberty, and incurs
responsibility for action.

The fruit of the tree emblematizes the object of the material desires of man. It is an allegory of temptation, and
employs under the same figure the influences which lure
toward evil. By eating, is meant his succumbing to the
temptation. It grows in the midst of a delightful garden, in
order to show that seduction accompanies pleasure, and to
recall to mind at the same time, that, if man allows material
joys to preponderate, he attaches himself to Earth, removing
himself far off from his spiritual destiny.[66]

The death with which he is menaced if he infringes the

---

[65] Today, it is a well known fact that the Hebrew word "haadam" is not
a proper noun, and that it means: "man in general, humanity;" that in
itself destroys all the structure created around Adam's personality.

[66] In no text is the fruit specially mentioned as an apple. This word
apple is only found in infantile versions of it. The Hebrew word is peri,
which means the same as in French ("fruit"), but without specification
of species, and can be taken in the material, moral, or figurative sense.
With the Israelites there is no obligatory interpretation. When a word
has many acceptations, each one understands it in his own way,
provided the interpretation is not contrary to the rules of grammar. The
word peri has been translated into the Latin malum, which signifies
"apples" and all other fruits. It is derived from the Greek mélon,
participle of verb mé'o, "to interest," "to take care," "to attract."

divine law is the warning of the inevitable physical and moral consequences which the violation of divine law entails upon him — the violation of those laws which God has engraved upon his conscience. It is very evident that corporeal death is not signified, since, after his fall, Adam lived on Earth many years; but spiritual death is unquestionably referred to the loss of acquisitions that result from moral advancement. The image employed is the loss he experiences by his expulsion from this delightful garden.

17. The serpent today passed for something quite other than deceit. It is in connection with its form, rather than with its character, that it is associated with wicked suggestions which glide into the mind with the noiseless subtlety of the serpent, and by which we are so often easily led into temptation. Besides, if the serpent on account of having deceived the woman has been doomed to crawl upon the Earth, it must formerly have had limbs when it could not have been a serpent. Why then impose upon the artless faith of childhood as truths allegories which are so evidently such, and which, in misleading judgment, cause children to regard the Bible later in life as a tissue of absurd fables?

We should remark that the Hebrew word *nahasch*, translated as the word *serpent*, originates from the root *nahasch*, which means: *to make enchantment; to practice divination; or the art of revealing occult things; it also means: enchanter, guesser.* This is the meaning found in Genesis, chapter XLIV: 5 and 15, regarding the instance when Joseph had someone hide a cup in Benjamin's sack: "Isn't this the cup my master drinks from and also uses for divination? (nahasch)[67]– "Don't you know that a man like me can find things out by divination?" (nahasch)?" From the Book of Numbers, chapter XXIII: 23 - "There is no sorcery (nahasch) against Jacob, no divination against Israel." Consequently, the word nahasch began to take the meaning of serpent - the reptile used by the enchanters in their rituals.

---

[67] Would this fact show that the Egyptians practiced mediumship through the use of a glass of water? (*"Revue Spirite,"* June of 1868, page 161).

It was not until the Septuagint's version that the word *nahasch* was translated *as serpent*. That version, according to Hutcheson, presents the Hebrew text corrupted in several passages. It was written in Greek, during the second century before the Christian era. Undeniably, that version's inaccuracies resulted from modifications the Hebrew language endured during the elapsed time. Note, still, that the Hebrew language of Moses' time was already a dead dialect, which differed from ordinary Hebrew, just like ancient Greek and literary Arabic differ from the Greek and the Arabic of modern times.[68]

It is possible that Moses may have deemed the indiscreet desire to know occult things, provoked by the spirit of divination, to be a seducement of women. This meaning is in agreement with the original meaning of the word nahasch - to guess - and with the words of this parable: "For God knows that when you eat of it your eyes will be opened, and you will be like God, knowing good and evil. When the woman saw that the fruit of the tree was good for food and pleasing to the eye, and also desirable for gaining wisdom (leaskil), she took some and ate it." We should not forget that Moses wanted to ban from amongst the Hebrews the art of divination, which was then practiced by the Egyptians; this fact is evident by his prohibition to question the dead and the spirit of Python. ("*Heaven and Hell*," chapter XII)

18. The passage that reads: "The Lord wandered through paradise after mid-day, when a light wind was blowing," is a naive and childish imagery, which critics did not fail to point out. This, however, has nothing that should cause surprise, if we consider the conception the Hebrews of primitive times had of the Divinity; for these frustrated intelligences, incapable of conceiving abstractions, God should embody a concrete form. For lack of any other point

---

[68]The word "Nahasch" existed in the Egyptian language, with the meaning of black, probably because black people had the gift of enchantment and of divination. This is perhaps the reason the sphinx, of Syrian origin were represented by an image of a black person.

of reference, they attributed human characteristics to God. Moses spoke to them as one would speak to children, through the use of tender images. In this instance, sovereign potency is personified, as the pagans personified it with the use of allegoric figures, with virtues, vices, and abstract ideas. Later on, man was able to disassociate the idea from the form, like a child who on becoming adult, looks for the moral meaning of the tales he heard throughout his infancy. One should therefore consider this passage as an allegory of the Divinity personally supervising the object of its creation. The great rabbi Wogue translated it as follows: "They heard the voice of the Eternal God echoing through the garden, from the direction where the day arises."

19. If the fault of Adam is literally that of having eaten fruit, the almost puerile nature of the sin cannot be justly condemned with the severity it has received. We cannot rationally admit what is generally considered to be the fact; otherwise God, considering this fault irredeemable, must have condemned his own work, since he had created man for the propagation of man. If Adam had understood in this sense that he was forbidden to touch the fruit of the tree, and if he had scrupulously obeyed the command, where would humanity be? And would not the designs of the Creator be frustrated?

God had not created Adam and Eve to remain alone upon the Earth. The proof of it is found in the words addressed to them immediately on their formation, when they were unfallen in the terrestrial paradise.

"God blesses them, and says to them, *Increase and replenish the Earth, subduing it*" (chap. I, v. 28). Since the multiplication of man was a law of the terrestrial paradise, his expulsion cannot be due to the supposed cause.

That which has given credit to this supposition is the feeling of shame with which Adam and Eve were seized at the sight of God, and which caused them to cover themselves. But this shame is a figure of comparison: it symbolizes the confusion that all culprits experience in the presence of him whom they have offended.

20. What then is the definition of this fault which has been able to strike forever with reprobation the descendants of him who committed it? Cain, the fratricide, was not treated so severely. No theologian has been able logically to define it, because all have followed the same circle of faulty ideas about it, departing not from the letter of the tale.

Today we know that this fault is not an isolated action, personal to an individual, but that it comprehends under one unique allegorical fact all the departures from the right which can render culpable all humanity, yet imperfect on Earth, who make *an infraction of the law of God*. That is why the fault of the first man, symbolizing humanity, is symbolized by an act of disobedience.

21. By saying to Adam that he will draw his nourishment from the Earth by the sweat of his brow, God symbolized the obligation of work; but why does he make work a punishment? What would the intelligence of man be if it were not developed by labor? What would the Earth be if it were not made fruitful, transformed, and rendered healthy by the intelligent work of man?

It is written (in chap. II, v. 5 and 7): "the LORD God had not sent rain on the Earth and there was no man to work the ground, the LORD God formed the man from the dust of the ground." This quotation, taken in connection with another, which is: "Replenish the Earth," proves that man was from the beginning destined to occupy *all the Earth, and to cultivate it*; moreover, that paradise was not a circumscribed place upon one corner of the globe. If the culture of the Earth was in consequence of Adam's fall, if Adam had not sinned, the Earth would not have been cultivated, and the views of God would not have been accomplished.

Why did he say to the woman, that, because she had committed this sin, she should bear children in sorrow? How can the pain of child-bearing be a chastisement, since it is a consequence of the organism, and has been physiologically proved to be necessary? How can anything which is according to the laws of nature be a punishment? This is what theologians have not yet explained, and that which they will not be able to do while they look at things from their present point of view. However, theses Bible quotations, which seem so contradictory, can be justified.

22. Lets us remark at first, that, if at the moment of the creation of Adam and Eve their soul had just been taken from nothing, as is taught us, they must have been novices in all things: they could have known nothing of death. Since they were *alone* upon the Earth, whilst they lived in their terrestrial paradise, they had never seen anyone die. How, then, could they comprehend the menace of death which God made to them? How could Eve comprehend that the pain of child-bearing would be a punishment when she had never borne children, and was, besides, the only woman in the world?

The words of God could have had to Adam and Eve no meaning. Just taken from nothing, they could neither have known why they were created, or whence they came. They could neither comprehend the Creator or his object in forbidding them to eat the fruit. With no experience of the conditions of life, they must have sinned like children who act without discernment, which renders more incomprehensible still the terrible responsibility which God has imposed upon them and the whole of humanity.

23. To that which theology fails to explain, Spiritism gives without difficulty a clear explanation in a rational manner by the anteriority of soul, and the plurality of existences, without which all is mystery and anomaly in the life of men. The admission that Adam and Eve had lived before, makes all things plain. God does not speak to them as children, but as to beings in a condition to comprehend, and who do comprehend him — an evident proof that this knowledge has been acquired in an anterior life. Let us admit also that they have lived in a more advanced world, which was less material than ours, where the work of the spirit took the place of manual labor; that by their rebellion against the law of God, figured by disobedience, they have been exiled as a punishment to this Earth, where man, in consequence of the nature of the globe, is compelled to labor,

God was right in saying to them, "By the sweat of your brow you will eat your food;" and to the woman, "I will greatly increase your pains in childbearing; with pain you will give birth to children." (Chap. XI, from item n° 31 on).

The terrestrial paradise for which they have so vainly sought the traces was then a description of the happy world, where Adam had once lived, or rather the race of spirits of whom he is the personification. The expulsion from paradise marks the moment when these spirits have come to incarnate themselves among the inhabitants of this world, and the change of situation which has succeeded to it. The angel armed with a flaming sword, who defends the gate of paradise, symbolizes the impossibility for spirits of lower worlds to penetrate into superiors ones, before having merited them by purification. (See chap. XIV, from item n° 8 on).

24. Cain, after the murder of Abel, said to the LORD, "My punishment is more than I can bear. Today you are driving me from the land, and I will be hidden from your presence; I will be a restless wanderer on the Earth, and whoever finds me will kill me." But the LORD said to him, "Not so; if anyone kills Cain, he will suffer vengeance seven times over." Then the LORD put a mark on Cain so that no one who found him would kill him. So Cain went out from the LORD's presence and lived in the land of Nod, east of Eden." Cain lay with his wife, and she became pregnant and gave birth to Enoch. Cain was then building a city, and he named it after his son Enoch. (Chap. IV, v. 13 to 17).

25. If one clings to the literal meaning of Genesis, behold to what consequences one arrives. From it we learn that Adam and Eve were alone in the world after their expulsion from the terrestrial paradise. It is subsequent to that that Cain and Abel were born. Now, Cain having killed his brother, and having been exiled of another country, saw his father and mother no more; and they were again alone. It is only a long time after, at the age of a hundred and thirty years, that Adam had a third son called Seth. After the birth of Seth, he still lived, according to biblical genealogy, eight hundred years, and begat sons and daughters.

When Cain established himself eastward of Eden, according to Genesis, there were only three persons upon the Earth — Adam, Eve, and Cain. However, he had a wife and child. Who could this woman have been? And where could he have found her? The Hebrew text says: *He was building a city*, and not he *built*, which indicates a present action and not an anterior one; but many inhabitants are necessary to make a city: for it is not possible or presumable that he made it for himself, wife, and son, or that he was able to construct it by himself alone.

It is necessary to infer, from this recital, that the country was peopled. Now this could not have been by the descendants of Adam, who then had no other children than Cain.

The presence of other inhabitants is also proved by this saying of Cain: "I will be a restless wanderer on the Earth, and whoever finds me will kill me," and from the reply God made to it. By whom could he have been killed? And for what good could the sign which god placed on his forehead have been needed if he was not to encounter anyone? If, then, there were upon Earth other men outside of the family of Adam, they must have been there before him, whence this sequence, drawn from even the text of Genesis, that Adam is neither the first not the only father of human beings (chap. XI, n° 34).[69]

26. There has come a necessity for the knowledge that Spiritism brings touching the connections between the spiritual and material principles and the nature of the soul; its creation in a state of simplicity and ignorance; its union with the body; its progressive, indefinite march through successive existences, and through worlds which are so many rungs of the ladder on the way to perfection; its

---

[69] This idea is not new. La Peyrère, the wise theologian of the seventh century in his book "*Préadamites*," written in Latin and published in 1655, extracted from the original biblical text, this being subsequently adulterated by the translations, the clear evidence that the Earth was inhabited before Adam; today this is the opinion of many enlightened ecclesiastics.

gradual release from the influence of matter by the use of its free will; the cause of its leanings toward good or evil and of its aptitudes; the phenomena of birth and death; the state of the spirit in the erraticity, and at length its future reward for efforts made in the improvement of its condition as incentive to its perseverance in well-doing, which throw light upon every part of the spiritual Genesis.

Thanks to this light, man knows henceforth whence he comes; where he goes, why he is upon Earth, and why he suffers. He knows that his future is in his own hands, and that the duration of his captivity here below depends upon himself. Genesis, which previously appeared as a mean and shallow allegory, now appears grand and majestic, worthy of the goodness and justice of the Creator. Considered from this point of view, Genesis will both confound and vanquish incredulity.

Chapter XIII

THE MIRACLES ACCORDING TO SPIRITISM

Nature of Miracles
Miracles according to Theology - Spiritism does not perform miracles - Does God perform miracles? - The supernatural and the religions.

MIRACLES ACCORDING TO THEOLOGY

1. In its etymological acceptation, the word "miracle," from *mirari* (Latin), *admirer* (French), signifies *"to wonder," an extraordinary or surprising thing*. The French Academy defines this word, *"an act of divine power contrary to the known laws of nature."*

In its acceptance, this word has lost, like so many others, its primitive significance. In general it was, and still is, limited to a particular order of facts. The general idea of masses is that a miracle is supernatural. In the liturgical sense it is a derogation of the laws of nature by which God manifests his power. Such is, indeed, its common acceptation, which is considered its proper sense. It is only by comparison and metaphor that it is applied to ordinary circumstances of life.

One of the characteristics of a miracle, properly speaking, is that of inexplicability, which implies its accomplishment by supernatural laws; and such is the idea that is attached to it, that, if it is possible to explain a miraculous fact, it is no more a miracle, people say, no matter how surprising it may be. For the church, that which gives merit to miracles is precisely its supernatural origin and the impossibility to explain them. It adheres so strictly to this point that it regards all associations of miracles with phenomena of nature as heresy, and attempt against faith. It has gone to the extreme point of excommunicating, and even burning those who did not believe in certain miracles. Another characteristic of a miracle is its unique or exceptional nature. From the moment when phenomenon is reproduced, be it spontaneously or by an act of will, it is implied that it is subject to a law; and thenceforth, be this law known or unknown, the event cannot be miraculous.

2. Science produces miracles every day before the eyes of the ignorant. If a really dead man be recalled to life by divine intervention, this would be a veritable miracle, because it is a fact contrary to the laws of nature; but if the man had only the appearance of death, if he has still in him the remains of *latent vitality*, and science or magnetic action succeeds in reanimating him, to enlightened people a natural phenomenon is presented, but to the eyes of the ignorant the fact will appear miraculous. When, in certain countries, a physicist flies an electric kite, and makes lightning strike a tree, this new Prometheus will certainly be credited with diabolical power; but Joshua arresting the movement of the sun, or rather of the Earth, by admitting this fact, we must admit a veritable miracle, for there exists no magnetizer endowed with such power to accomplish so prodigious a feat.

Centuries of ignorance have been fruitful in miracles, because all that was not understood passed for miracle. Measurably as science has discovered new laws, the circle of the marvelous has been narrowed; but, as it has not explored the whole of nature's field, there remains still quite a large place for the miraculous.

3. The marvelous, expelled from the material domain by science, has been entrenched in that of Spiritism, which has been its last refuge. Spiritism, by demonstrating that the spiritual element is one of the living forces of nature, a force continually acting concurrently with material forces, takes in the phenomena which arise in the circle of natural effects, because that like all others, they are subject to law. If the marvelous is to be expelled from the realm of spirit, it has then no more existence; then alone can we say that the age of miracles has passed (Chap. 1, n° 18).

SPIRITISM DOES NOT PERFORM MIRACLES

4. Spiritism comes, then, in its turn to do that which each science has done at its advent, to reveal new laws, and explain, consequently, the phenomena which are the result of these laws.

These phenomena, it is true, are connected with the existence of spirits, and with their intervention in the material world which has been called supernatural. But to make it really so it would be necessary to prove that spirits and their manifestations are contrary to the laws of nature, that not one of these laws produces their manifestation.

The spirit is none other than the human life or soul which survives the body. It is the real indestructible being which cannot die, while the body is only a destructible accessory. Its existence is, therefore, as natural after as during the incarnation. It is submitted to the laws governing the spiritual principle, as the body submits to those which rule the material universe; but as these two principles have a necessary affinity, as they incessantly react upon one another, as from their simultaneous action result the harmony and movement of the whole, it follows that the spiritual and material elements are parts of the same whole, one as natural as the other, and that the first is not an exception, an anomaly in the order of things.

5. During the incarnation the spirit acts upon matter through the intermediation of its fluidic body, or perispirit; it is the same when discarnated. It accomplishes as spirit, and by the measure of its capacities, that which it did when on Earth; only, as it has no longer for an instrument its mortal body, it serves itself, when necessary, with the material organs of an incarnate being who is what we call *a medium*. It does as he does, who, unable to write himself, employs a secretary, or who, not understanding a language, is served by an interpreter. A secretary and an interpreter are *mediums* for an incarnated being, as a medium is the secretary or the interpreter of a spirit.

6. The element in which spirits act, and the means of execution being different from those employed during the incarnation, the effects are different. These effects only appear supernatural because they are produced through agents, who are not those by means of which men serve themselves; but from the instant when it is known that these agents are natural, and that the manifestations occur in obedience to laws, there is nothing supernatural or marvelous about them. Before the properties of electricity were known, the electricity phenomenon was regarded as miraculous by certain people. As soon as the cause was known, the miracle vanished. It is the same with spiritual phenomena, which arise no more from the setting aside of nature's laws than do the electrical, acoustic, luminous, and other phenomena which have given rise to a crowd of superstitions.

7. However, will it not be said, you admit that a spirit can raise a table and maintain it in space without support? Isn't that a derogation of the law of gravity? Yes, to the known law; but are all laws known? Before men had experimented with the ascending force of certain gas, who had imagined that a heavy machine, carrying several men, could soar by force of attraction? To the vulgar eye the ascent of a balloon must have appeared miraculous or diabolical. He, who had proposed a hundred years ago to transmit a dispatch five hundred leagues, and receive an answer within a few minutes, would have passed for a fool. If he had performed the feat, it would have been commonly believed that he had the Devil under his control; for then no one but the Devil was thought capable of traveling so quickly. However, now the occurrence is not only regarded as possible, but is accepted as altogether natural. Why, then, should an unknown fluid not possess the property, under given circumstances, of counterbalancing the effect of weight, as hydrogen counterbalances the weight of the balloon? An occurrence indeed, similar to that, is which takes place in the case under our notice. (See *"The Mediums Book,"* chap. 4).

8. The spiritual phenomena, being natural, have been produced in all ages; but because their study could not be effected by material means, with which physical science arms itself, they have remained longest in the supernatural domain whence Spiritism rescues them.

The supernatural hypothesis based upon inexplicable appearances leaves the imagination wholly free, which, wandering into the unknown gives birth to superstitious beliefs. A rational explanation founded upon natural law, leading man to a foundation in reality, gives a place of rest to imaginative flights, and destroys superstition. Far from extending the supernatural domain, Spiritism reduces it to the narrowest limits, and robs it of its last refuge. If it makes possible belief in certain facts, it prevents belief in much else, because it demonstrates in the circle of spiritual being as science in a circle of materiality, that which is possible, and that which is not. Always, however, as it makes no pretension to say the final word upon all subjects, even upon those which belong to its own realm, it does not take the position of an absolute regulator of the possible, and reserves always some knowledge for future disclosures.

9. The spiritual phenomena consist in different modes of manifestation of soul or spirit during the incarnation, or in their discarnate state. It is by its manifestations that the soul reveals its existence, its survival, and its individuality; and it is judged by its effects. The cause being natural, the effect is equally so. These effects made the special object of research in the study of Spiritism, in order to arrive at knowledge as completely as possible of the nature and of the attributes of the soul, as well as of the laws which govern the spiritual principle.

10. For those who deny the independent existence of the spirit, and consequently that of the independent individuality of the surviving soul, all nature is simple tangible matter. All phenomena attaching to Spiritism are to them supernatural, and consequently chimerical. Failing to admit the cause, they cannot admit the effect; and, when the effects are patent, they are attributed by them to imagination, illusion, hallucination; they refuse to give credence to them. Their own preconceived opinions render them incapable of judging Spiritism fairly, because they deny all things which are immaterial.

11. Since Spiritism admits effects which are the consequence of the existence of the soul, it does not follow that it accepts all the qualified effects of the marvelous, or that it justifies and accredits them. To let it be the champion of all dreamers, of every utopian idea, of all systematic eccentricities, of all miraculous legends, one must have a very slight knowledge of it and its purposes. Its adversaries imagine that they can oppose it with arguments admitting no reply, when, after making learned researches, with the *convulsionaries* of St. Médard, the *Camisards* of Cevennes, or the recluses of Loudon, they have discovered patent cases of imposition that no one contests. But are these histories the gospel of Spiritism? Have its partisans denied that charlatanism has employed certain truths for its own profit that the imagination may have created, that fanaticism may have exaggerated much? Extravagances are not committed solely in its name. Is not true science abused by ignorance and true religion by excess of fanaticism? Many critics regard Spiritism as a fairy tale and popular legend, which are fictions worth no more than historical and tragic romances.

12. The spiritual phenomena are most often spontaneous, and are produced without any preparation through persons who bestow the least thought upon them; at other times they are provoked by agents known as mediums. In the first case the medium is *unconscious* of his mediumistic powers; in the second he acts by a knowledge of cause; hence the distinction between conscious and *unconscious* mediums. The latter are the more numerous, and are frequently found among obstinate and skeptical persons, who are made good witnesses in defense of Spiritism without their own knowledge or desire. The spontaneous phenomena constitute an important capital for Spiritism; for one cannot suspect the good faith of the parties through whom they are obtained, like somnambulism, which with some individuals is purely natural and involuntary, and with others induced by magnetic action.[70]

But let these phenomena be, or not be, the result of mental volition, the first cause is exactly the same in either instance, and detracts nothing from natural laws. Mediums, then, produce nothing absolutely supernatural; consequently they perform *no miracle*. The instantaneous cures often effected are no more miraculous than other effects; for they are due to the action of a fluidic agent performing the office of therapeutic agent, whose properties are no less natural because unknown until today. The title *thaumaturgist*, given to certain mediums by ignorant critics of the principles of Spiritism, is then altogether improper. The qualification of *miraculous* given to these kinds of phenomena can only give an erroneous idea of their true character.

13. The intervention of occult intelligences in spirit phenomena renders the later no more miraculous than other phenomena which are due to invisible agents, because that the occult beings populating space are one of the powers of nature — a power whose action upon the material world is incessant as well as upon the moral.

Spiritism, in enlightening us with regard to this power, gives us the key, to a crowd of mysterious things unexplained by any other means, and which in former times must have passed for amazing prodigies of knowledge. It reveals, as does magnetism, a law hitherto unknown, or at least poorly understood; or it is more correct to say that the effects were known; for they have been produced through all time before the law was discovered, and it is only the ignorance of this law which engendered superstition. This law being now known, the marvelous disappears, and the phenomena enter into the order of natural events. Thus, by moving a table or writing prescriptions under spirit guidance, spiritists perform no

---

[70] *"The Mediums' Book,"* chap. 5 – *"Revue Spirite,"* examples: December, 1865, p. 370; August, 1865, p. 231.

miracles any more than does the physician who restores a man almost dead to life, or than the scientist does by bringing lightning from the clouds. He who would pretend, with the aid of this science, to perform miracles would be either an ignorant or an impostor.

14. Since Spiritism repudiates all pretension to the miraculous, outside of it are there miracles only in the usual acceptance of the word?

Let us first declare, that of so-called miracles having taken place before the advent of Spiritism, and which still take place in our day, the greater part, if not all, find their explanation in the new knowledge of laws just revealed. These facts enter, then, although under a new name, into the order of spirit phenomena, and as such are not supernatural. It is well understood that it acts only with authentic facts, and not with those which, under the name of miracles, are the product of an unworthy jugglery in view of taking advantage of credulity, any more than it acts with certain legendary facts which can have had in the beginning a depth of truth, but which superstition has enlarged to absurdity. Upon these facts Spiritism comes to throw light by affording means to separate truth from error.

DOES GOD PERFORM MIRACLES?

15. As to miracles, properly speaking, nothing being impossible with God, he can perform them without doubt. Has he done it? Does he ever act contrary to the laws which he has established? It does not belong to man to prejudge the acts of divinity, and to subordinate them to the feebleness of his understanding. However, we have for criterion of our judgment, in regard to divine things, the attributes even of God. To sovereign power he joins sovereign wisdom, whence it is necessary to conclude that he does nothing uselessly.

Why then should he perform miracles? In order to attest his power, it is said. But the power of God, is it not manifested in a much more striking manner by the magnificent whole of the works of creation, by the foreseeing wisdom which presides in the smallest as well as the largest of his works, and by the harmony of the laws which rule the universe, than by a few little and puerile modification which all tricksters know how to imitate? What would we think of a learned mechanic who, in order to prove his skill, should disarrange the clock which he had constructed, a masterpiece of scientific skill, in order to prove that he can deface that which he has made? On the contrary, is his knowledge not displayed by the regularity and precision of its movements?

The question of miracles, then, is not, properly speaking, in the province of Spiritism; but, sustaining itself by the reasoning that God makes nothing uselessly, this idea can be educed: *that, miracles not being necessary to the glorification of God, nothing in the universe is diverted from the general laws. God does not perform miracles; since his laws are perfect, he has no need to derogate them.* If there are some facts which we do not understand, it is because we have not the necessary knowledge to comprehend them.

16. The admission that God may be able, for reasons which we cannot appreciate, derogate the laws which he has established, would make these laws no more immutable; but at least it is rational to think that God alone possesses this power. One could not admit, without denying totally that he is omnipotent, that it is allowed to the spirit of evil to eclipse the work of God by performing mighty works which may deceive even the very elect. This would imply the possession of a power equal to his own. That is a doctrine, however, which is or has been taught. If Satan has the power to interrupt the course of natural laws, whose work is the divine one? If Satan does it without the divine permission, he is more powerful than God. Moreover, God is not omnipotent if he delegates to him this power, as they pretend he does, in order to induce men more easily to commit wrong; and this theory denies sovereign goodness. In both cases it is a denial of one of the attributes of the Creator, without which he could not be God.

As to the Church, how does it distinguish the good miracles which come from God from evil ones which emanate from Satan? How can one draw the line between them? Let a miracle be official or not, it is not at least a derogation of the laws which emanate from God alone. If an individual is cured, as is said, miraculously, let it be by God or Satan, he is no less cured. It is necessary to have a very poor idea of human intelligence in order to expect that such doctrines can be accepted in our day.

The possibility of certain reputed miraculous facts being recognized, it is just to conclude, that, notwithstanding they are from the source which is attributed to them, they are natural effects which spirits or incarnated beings can employ, like all things, as their own intelligence or scientific knowledge allows them, for good or evil, according to their goodness or perversity. A perverted being can then do things which pass for prodigies to the eyes of the ignorant, by putting to profit his knowledge; but, when effects are good, it would be illogical to attribute to them a diabolical origin.

17. But it has been thought that religion leans upon facts which never have and never can be explained. Perhaps they never have been; but that they never can be, is another question. Does anyone know what knowledge and discoveries may be ours in the future, without alluding to the miracle of creation, the grandest of all beyond dispute, and which is now acknowledged to be within the domain of universal law? Can we not see already, under the empire of Spiritism, magnetism, somnambulism, the ecstasies, visions, apparitions, clairvoyance, instantaneous cures, trances, oral and other communications with beings of the invisible world, phenomena known from time immemorial, considered formerly as miraculous, now being demonstrated as belonging to the natural order of things in harmony with the universal laws of being? Sacred books are full of accounts of these things, which are qualified as supernatural; but, as analogous facts are found in all religious works of antiquity, some of which are more marvelous than any biblical accounts, if the truth of a religion depended upon the number and nature of these facts, Christianity could at once be swept away by Paganism.

THE SUPERNATURAL AND THE RELIGIONS

18. To pretend that the supernatural is the necessary foundation of all religion, that it is the key to the whole arch of the Christian edifice, is to sustain a dangerous thesis. If one makes the truth of Christianity rest solely upon the base of miracle, he gives it but a fragile support, from which stones are detached every day. This belief, of which some eminent theologians are defenders, conducts rightly to the conclusion that, in a given time, no religion will be possible, not even the Christian religion, if that which is regarded as supernatural be demonstrated as natural; for so many arguments will be heaped against it that no one will be able to maintain the miraculous character of any fact after its naturalness has been proved. Now, the proof that a fact is no exception to natural laws is, that it can be explained by these laws, and that, being able to be reproduced by the intermediation of any individual whatever, it ceases to be the exclusive property of saints. It is not the *supernatural* which is essential to religion, but the spiritual principle which has been so mischievously confounded with the marvelous, and without which religion is impossible.

Spiritism considers the Christian religion at a more elevated point; it gives to it a more solid base than miracles, that is, the immutable laws of God, which rule the spiritual equally with the material principle. This base bids defiance to time and science alike; for time and science will at length sanction it.

God is no less worthy of our admiration, gratitude, or respect, because he does not derogate his laws, grand beyond all else in their immutability. He needs not the supernatural as an element in his worship. Nature is sufficiently imposing of itself, without any additions, to prove the existence of the Supreme Power. Religion will find each time less incredulous ones, the more reason sanctions it. Christianity can lose nothing by this sanction: it, on the contrary, gains by it. If anything has destroyed it, in the opinion of certain people, it is the abuse of the marvelous or supernatural.

19. If we take the word "*miracle*" in its correct etymological sense, — in the sense simply of *a wonder*, — we behold incessant miracles before our very eyes. We breathe them in the air; they crowd upon our steps: for all nature is a wonder.

Can one give to the people, to the ignorant, to the weak-minded, an idea of God's power, without showing them infinite wisdom presiding in all things? — In the admirable organisms of all that live, in the fructification of plants, in the appropriation of every part of every being to its needs, according to the place of its abode. It is necessary to make them behold the divine action in producing a blade of grass, in the expanding flower. We must show them his goodness in the sun which vivifies all things, his goodness in his solicitude for all creatures however small or feeble they may be, his foresight, in the reason of existence of everything, none of them useless, his wisdom in the good which proceeds from momentary and apparent evil. Make them comprehend that evil is really man's own work, and that God has made everything good. Seek then, not to frighten them with pictures of endless flame, causing them to doubt the goodness of God; encourage them with the certainty of their ability to repair all the wrong they have done; show them the discoveries of science as revelations of divine law, and not as the work of Satan; finally, teach them to read the book of nature, incessantly open before them as an inexhaustible volume, wherein the wisdom and goodness of the Creator are inscribed on every page. Then they will comprehend that a Being so great, occupying himself with all, watching over all, foreseeing all, must be sovereignty powerful. The laborer will behold him while he ploughs a furrow, and the unfortunate will bless him in affliction, for he will know that unhappiness is his own fault. Then will man be truly religious, rationally so, which is far better than to encourage faith in stories of images which sweat blood, in statues which wink their eyes and shed tears.

Chapter XIV
FLUIDS

I. NATURE AND PROPERTIES OF FLUIDS: Fluidic Elements - Formation and Properties of the Perispirit - Action of the Spirits upon the Fluids - Fluidic Creations – Photograph of the Thought - Quality of the fluids.
II. EXPLANATION OF SOME FACTS REFUTED TO BE SUPERNATURAL: Spiritual or Psychic Sight - Second Sight – Somnambulism - Dreams - Catalepsy - Resurrection - Cures, - Apparitions -Transfiguration - Physical Manifestations - Mediumship - Obsessions and Possessions

I. Nature and Properties of Fluids
Fluidic Elements

1. Science has furnished the key to those miracles which proceed particularly from the material element, either by explaining them, or in demonstrating the impossibility of them by the laws which rule matter. But the phenomena where the spiritual element is the preponderating force, not being explainable solely by the laws of matter, escape the investigations of scientists. That is why they have more than other facts the apparent character of marvels. It is then only in the laws which rule spiritual life one can find the key for the miracles of this category.

2. The universal cosmic fluid is, as has been demonstrated, elementary primitive matter, of which the modifications and transformations constitute the innumerable varieties of the bodies of nature (Chap. X). So far as the elementary universal principle is concerned, it offers two distinct states; that of etherealization, or imponderability, that one can consider as the primitive and normal state, and that of materialization, or ponderability, which is in some sort only consecutive. The intermediary point is that of the transformation of the fluid into tangible matter; but there still is no sudden transition, for one can consider our imponderable fluids as a boundary between the two states (chap. IV, from n° 10 on).

Each one of these two states gives place necessarily to special phenomena. To the second belong those of the visible world, and to the first those of the invisible one. Those called *material phenomena* are, properly speaking, in the domain of science. The solution of the others, designated *spiritual or physical phenomena*, because they are allied more especially to the existence of spirits, is among the prerogatives of Spiritism. But, as spiritual and material life are in incessant contact, the phenomena of these two orders are presented often simultaneously. Man, in a state of incarnation, can have only the perception of the physical phenomena which are connected with the material life. Those which belong to the exclusive domain of spiritual life escape the eye of the material senses, and can be perceived only in the spiritual state.[71]

3. In an etherealized state the cosmic fluid is not uniform. Without ceasing to be ethereal, it is submitted to modifications as varied in their kind and more numerous than in a state of tangible matter. These modifications constitute distinct fluids, which, although proceeding from the same principle, are endowed with special properties, and give rise to particular phenomena of the invisible world.

---

[71] The name psychical phenomena expresses the idea better than spiritual does, as these phenomena rest upon the properties and attributes of the soul, or rather on the perispiritual fluids, which are inseparable from the soul. This qualification attaches them more intimately to the order of natural facts, regulated by laws. One can then admit them as psychical effects without allowing them the title of miracles.

All being relative, these fluids have for the spirits, who are themselves fluidic, an appearance as material as that of the objects for the incarnates, and are for them that which the substances of the terrestrial world are for us. They elaborate and combine them, in order to produce determined effects, as men do with their materials, yet by different processes.

But there, as here, it is only given to the most enlightened spirits to comprehend the role of the constitutive elements of their world. The ignorant people of the invisible world are as incapable of explaining the phenomena of which they are witnesses, and in which they cooperate often mechanically, as the ignorant of Earth are of explaining the effects of light or of electricity, or of explaining the process of seeing and hearing.

4. The fluidic elements of the spiritual world elude our instruments of analysis, and the perception of our senses. They are things suited to tangible and not to ethereal matter. Spiritual substances belong to a midst so different from ours that we can judge of them only by comparisons as imperfect as those by which a man born blind seeks to form an idea of the theory of color.

But among these fluids a few are intimately joined to corporeal life, and belong in a measure to the terrestrial universe. In default of direct perception of cause, it is possible to observe the effects of them as one can observe the fluids of a magnet, which no one has ever seen, and acquire some knowledge of their nature with precision. This study is essential; for it is the key to a multitude of phenomena, which are inexplicable by the laws of matter alone.

5. The starting-point of the universal fluid is the degree of absolute ethereality, of which nothing can give us an idea. Its opposite point is its transformation into material substance. Between these two extremes there exist innumerable transformations, which are allied more or less to one another. The fluids which are the nearest materiality – consequently the least pure – are composed of that which might be called the *spiritual terrestrial atmosphere*. In this midst are found the widely different degrees of ethereality whence the incarnated and discarnated inhabitants of the Earth draw the necessary elements for the economy of their existence. These fluids, however subtle and impalpable they may be to us, are nevertheless of comparatively gross nature to the ethereal fluids of the superior regions.

It is the same on the surface of all worlds, saving the differences of constitution and vitality proper to each. The less material life there is there, the less the spiritual fluids have of affinity with matter.

The name "*spiritual fluid*" is not rigidly accurate as it is really always matter more or less refined. There is nothing really *spiritual*, but the soul or intelligent principle. We designate fluids thus by comparison, and chiefly by reason of their affinity with spirits. They constitute the substance of the spiritual world. That is why they are called *spiritual fluids*.

6. Who understands the intricate constitution of tangible matter? It is, perhaps, compact only in relation to our senses; and that which seems to prove this is the facility with which it is traversed by spiritual fluids, and the spirits to whom it is no more of an obstacle than are transparent bodies to light.

Tangible matter, having for a primitive element the ethereal cosmic fluid, must be able, by *becoming disintegrated*, to return to a state of etherealization, as the diamond, the hardest of bodies, can be volatized into impalpable gas. *The solidification of matter is in reality only a transitory state of the universal fluid, which can return to its primitive state when the conditions of cohesion cease to exist.*

Who knows even if, in a tangible state, matter is not susceptible of acquiring a sort of etherealization which would give to it peculiar properties? Certain phenomena which appear authentic tend towards such a supposition as this. We do not yet posses all the beacon-lights of the invisible world; and the future has in reserve for us, without doubt, the knowledge of new laws, which will allow us to comprehend that which is still to us a mystery.

FORMATION AND PROPERTIES OF THE PERISPIRIT

7. The perispirit, or fluidic body of the spirits, is one of the most important products of the cosmic fluid: it is a condensation of this fluid around a focus of intelligence or soul. It is also seen that the fleshly body has also its origin in this same fluid transformed and condensed into tangible matter. In the perispirit the molecular transformation operates differently, for the fluid preserves its imponderability and its ethereal qualities. The perispiritual and carnal body have, then, their source in the same primitive element; both are of matter, although under two different states of it.

8. Spirits draw their perispirit from the place where they find themselves; that is to say, that this envelop is formed from the ambient fluids. The result is, that the constitutive elements of the perispirit must vary according to worlds. Jupiter, being a very advanced world, in comparison to the Earth, where corporeal life has not the materiality of ours, its perispiritual envelopes must be of a nature infinitely more ethereal than upon our Earth. Now, although we would not be able to exist in that world in our carnal bodies, our spirits would not be able to penetrate there with their terrestrial perispirit. In quitting the Earth the spirit leaves there its fluidic envelop, and is supplied with another appropriate to the world where he must go.

9. The nature of the fluidic envelope is always in accord with the degree of moral advancement of the spirit. Inferior spirits cannot change their inclination, and consequently cannot by desire transport themselves from one world to another. It is they whose fluidic envelope, although ethereal and imponderable as regards tangible matter, is still too heavy, if one can express it thus, in relation to the spiritual world to allow them to leave their place. It is necessary to include in this category those whose perispirit is gross enough to be confounded with their carnal body, which for this reason they believe is still alive. These spirits (and their number is great) remain on the surface of the Earth like the incarnated ones, believing themselves always to be attending to their occupations. Others, a little more dematerialized, are not sufficiently so to elevate themselves above the terrestrial regions.[72]

Superior spirits, on the contrary, can enter into inferior worlds, and even incarnate themselves there. They draw, from the constitutive elements of the world they enter, the materials for the fluidic and carnal envelopes appropriate to the midst where they find themselves. They, like the great lord who temporarily leaves his gilded garments to assume the peasant's garb, without being other than the titled character he is on account of the change, will not change thereby their high estate.

It is thus that spirits of the most elevated order can manifest themselves to the inhabitants of Earth, or incarnate themselves for a mission among them. These spirits carry with them, not the envelope, but the remembrance by intuition of the regions whence they came, and which they see in thought. These are people who see among the blind people.

10. The bed of spiritual fluids which surrounds the Earth can be compared to the inferior beds of the atmosphere, heavier, more compact, less pure than the superior beds. These fluids are not homogeneous, they are a mixture of molecules of diverse qualities, amongst which are necessarily found the elementary molecules which form the base, but more or less changed in different states. The effect produced by these fluids will be according to the number of pure parts which they enclose. Such is, by comparison, rectified or mixed alcohol in different proportions of water or of other substances. Its specific weight is augmented by this mixture; while, at the same time, its force and inflammability are diminished, although there may be pure alcohol in all.

The spirits called to live in this midst draw from there their perispirit; but, *according as the spirit becomes more or less purified, its perispirit is formed from the purest or grossest fluid of the world in which it is going to incarnate.* The spirit produces there, always by comparison and not by assimilation,

---

[72] Examples of spirits believing themselves still in this world: "Revue Spirite," Dec., 1859, p. 310; Nov., 1864, p. 339; April, 1865, p. 117.

the effect of a chemical re-agent which attracts to it the molecules assimilable to its nature.

This *capital* fact results from it: *that the inmost constitution of the perispirit is not identical with all incarnated or discarnated spirits which people the Earth or surrounding space.* It is not the same with carnal bodies, which, as has been demonstrated, have been formed of the same elements whatever the superiority or inferiority of their spirits may have been. Also with us the effects produced by bodies are the same, they have the same necessities, while they differ by all that which is inherent in the perispirit.

Another result is, that *the perispiritual envelope of the same spirit is modified with the moral progress of the latter at each incarnation, although incarnating himself in the same surroundings; that the superior spirits, incarnating themselves exceptionally by a mission into an inferior world, have a perispirit less gross than that of the natives of this world.*

11. A place is always in harmony with the nature of the beings who must live there. Fish are in water; winged beings are in the air; spiritual beings are in the spiritual or ethereal fluid, even upon the Earth. *The ethereal fluid is for the needs of the spirit, as the atmosphere is for the necessities of the body.* Now, as fishes cannot live in the air, and terrestrial animals cannot live in an atmosphere too rarefied for their lungs, inferior spirits cannot support the splendor and impression of the most ethereal fluids. They would not die, because spirit cannot die; but an instinctive force keeps them at a distance, as one keeps away from a fire which is too hot, or from a light which is too strong. This is the reason why they cannot go away from the midst appropriate to their nature. In order to change it, it is necessary first to change their nature, that they be despoiled of the material instincts which retain them in material midst. As they become purified and morally transformed, they gradually become identified with purer surroundings, which become a necessity to them, like the eyes of him who has remained a long time in darkness are habituated imperceptibly to the light of day and the splendor of the sun.

12. Thus all is united, all harmonize in the universe. All is submitted to the great and harmonious law of unity, from the most compact materiality to the purest spirituality. The Earth is like a vase whence escapes a thick smoke, which clears away as it ascends, the rarefied particles of which are lost in infinite space.

Divine power shines in all parts of this great whole. Who would desire that, in order better to attest his power, God, discontented with that which he has made, should disturb this harmony? That he should lower himself to the level of a magician by performing acts worthy of a prestidigitator? And in addition to this they dare to give him as a rival in skill Satan himself! Never, in truth, was divine Majesty more undervalued, and men are astonished at the progress of incredulity!

You are right in saying "Faith is departing!" But it is faith in all that chokes reason and good sense that is departing, – a faith similar to that which formerly induced persons to exclaim, "the Gods are departing." But faith in serious things, in God, and in immortality, is always alive in the hearts of men; and, if it has been stifled with the puerile histories with which it has been overloaded, it raises itself stronger as soon as it has been extricated, as the restrained plant rises again in the light of the sun of which it has been deprived.

All is wonderful in nature because all is admirable, and testifies of divine wisdom. These wonders are for all the world, for all those who have eyes to see and ears to hear, and not for the profit of a few. No, there are no miracles in the sense attached to this word, because all is amenable to the eternal laws of creation.

ACTION OF THE SPIRITS UPON THE FLUIDS – FLUIDIC CREATIONS – PHOTOGRAPH OF THE THOUGHT

13. The spiritual fluids, which constitute one of the states of the universal cosmic fluid, are then the atmosphere of spiritual beings. It is the element whence they draw the materials with which they operate, – the place where special phenomena take place, perceptible to the sight and hearing of the spirit, but which escapes the carnal senses which are impressed alone by tangible matter; the ambient wherein the light peculiar to the spiritual world is formed, this being different from the ordinary light because of its causes and effects. In short, they are the vehicle for thought, as the air is for sound.

14. Spirits act upon spiritual fluids, not by manipulating them as men manipulate gas, but by the aid of thought and will. Thought and will are to the spirit that which the hand is to man. By thought they impress these fluids into such and such directions; they agglomerate them, combine or disperse them; they form harmonious wholes of them, which have a definitive appearance, form, and color; they change the properties of them, as a chemist changes those of gas or other bodies by combining them by following certain laws.

Sometimes these transformations are the result of an intention; often they are the product of an unconscious thought. It is sufficient for the spirit only to think of a thing in order that this thing produces itself; it suffices for one to form a melody in one's mind for it to reverberate through the atmosphere.

Thus, for example, a spirit presents himself to the view of an incarnated being endowed with spiritual sight with the same appearance he had when living at the epoch of their acquaintance, although he may have had many incarnations since that time. He presents himself with the costume, the exterior signs, infirmities, wounds, amputated members, etc., that he had then. A person who has been beheaded will present himself with no head. We do not desire to convey the impression that he has preserved these appearances; no, certainly not; for as a spirit he is neither lame, maimed, blind, nor headless: but, his thought conveying the impression when he was thus, his perispirit takes instantaneously the appearance of it, but it can at the same time leave it instantaneously. If, then, he has been both a black and a white man, he will present himself according to which of these two incarnations may be evoked whence his thought will report itself.

By a similar effect, a spirit's thought creates fluidicly the objects which he often makes use of. A miser will manage his gold; a military man will have his guns and his uniform; a smoker, his pipe; a workman his plow and his cattle; and an elderly woman, her knitting utensils. These fluidic objects are as real for the spirit, who is also fluidic, as they were in the material state of the living man. However, because they are created by the thought, their existences are also as fleeting as the thought.[73]

15. Fluids being the vehicle of the thought, the latter acts upon them, as the sound does upon the air. They bring us the thought, just as the air brings us the sound. We can, then, say with all truth that in such fluids there are waves and rays of thoughts that cross each other without ever becoming entangled, as do the waves and sonorous rays in the air.

Moreover, the thought creates *fluidic images* and reflects itself back on its perispiritual body, as on a mirror; the thought takes on body and somehow *photographs* itself on it. Let us say, for example, that a man has the idea of murdering someone; although his material body is inactive, his fluidic body is - through the thought - put into action, reproducing from this all vibrations. The act he tried to practice is executed fluidicly. The thought creates the image of the victim and, similarly to a picture, the entire scene is drawn, precisely as it is in his spirit.

This is how the innermost secret movements of the soul are reverberated onto the fluidic body; and how one soul can read another, as one reads a book; and how it sees what is not perceptible by the eyes of the body. Yet, although the intention is seen and it can foresee the subsequent execution of the act, it cannot determine the moment it will take place; neither can it be exact with details, or even affirm whether it will indeed take place, as later circumstances can modify the plans and change the dispositions. The soul cannot see that which is

---

[73] *"Revue Spirite,"* July, 1859, p. 184, *The Mediums's Book*, chap. 8.

not yet in another person's thought. What it does see is the habitual preoccupation of the person, his desires, his projects, and his good or bad intentions.

QUALITY OF THE FLUIDS

16. The action of spirits upon spiritual fluids has consequences of a direct and capital importance for incarnated beings. From the instant that these fluids are the vehicle of thought, that thought can modify the properties of them. It is evident that they must be impregnated by the good or bad qualities of the thoughts which put them in vibration, modified by the purity or impurity of the sentiments. Bad thoughts corrupt the spiritual fluids, as deleterious miasmas corrupt the air we breathe. The fluids which surround or that project bad spirits are then vitiated, whilst those which receive the influence of good spirits are as pure as the degree of moral perfection to which they have attained.

17. It would be impossible to itemize or classify the good or bad fluids. Neither could we specify their respective qualities, considering that their diversity is as great as that of the thought.

Fluids do not have "sui generis" qualities, except those they acquire whereat they are elaborated; they are modified by the effluviums of the ambient, just as the air is modified by exhalations, and the water by the layers of salt it crosses. Depending on the circumstances, their qualities are, like those of the air and the water, either temporary or permanent, which makes them more suitable for the production of certain specific effects.

Neither do the fluids have special denominations. As with odors, they are designated by their properties, their effects and their original type. On a moral point of view, they bring the impressions of the sentiments of hatred, envy, jealousy, pride, selfishness, violence, hypocrisy, kindness, benevolence, love, charity, sweetness, etc. On a physical point of view, they are excitants, sedating, piercing, coercing, irritant, soothing, soporific, narcotics, toxics, replenishing, and expellants. They also become a means of transmission, propulsion, etc. The overall picture of the fluids would then be that of all passions, virtues and vices of humanity; and that of the properties of matter, corresponding to the effects they produce.

18. Men, being incarnate beings, have in part the attributes of the spiritual life; for they live in this life as well as in a corporeal one, always during sleep, and often in a conscious state. The spirit, incarnating itself, preserves its perispirit with the qualities which are proper to it, and which, as is known, is not circumscribed by the body, but envelops and radiates around it like a fluidic atmosphere.

By its intimate union with the body the perispirit plays a preponderating role with the organism. By its expansion it places the incarnated being more directly in contact with free spirits.

The thought of the incarnated mind acts upon the spiritual fluids as that of the discarnated spirit's thought acts. It is transmitted from spirit to spirit in the same way, and, according as it is good or bad, it holds a vicious or healthy relation to the surrounding fluids.

Since the fluids of an ambient are modified by the projection of the spirit's thoughts, his perispiritual body - which is a constituent part of his being, and which receives directly and in a permanent way the impressions of his thoughts - should receive even more so the impressions of his good or bad qualities. The fluids vitiated by the effluviums of the bad spirits can be purified by their removal. The perispirit however will always be that which it is, as long as the spirit does not modify itself.

The perispirit of incarnates, being of a nature identical to that of the spiritual fluids, assimilates itself with them readily, as a sponge absorbs water. These fluids have over the perispirit an action which is the more direct because of its expansion and radiation; it confounds itself with them.

These fluids acting upon the perispirit, the latter, in its turn, reacts upon the material organism with which it is in molecular contact. If the effluvia are of a good nature, the bodies receive a salutary impression; if bad, a painful one.

If the bad are permanent and energetic, they can cause physical disorders; certain maladies have no other cause.

The midst where bad spirits abound are then impregnated with bad fluids, which are absorbed through all the perispiritual pores, as by the pores of the body pestilential miasmas are absorbed.

19. It is the same in assemblies of incarnated beings. An assembly of people is a focus whence radiate diverse thoughts. An assembly of persons is, like an orchestra, a choir of thoughts, where each one produces his note. The result is a multitude of fluidic-flowing effluvia, of which each one receives the impression of the sounds by the spiritual sense, like in a music choir each one receives the impression of the sound through the sense of hearing.

But, as there are harmonious or discordant sounds, there are also harmonious or discordant thoughts. If all is harmonious, the impression is agreeable; if otherwise, painful. There is no need for the thought to be formed into words. The fluidic-radiation exists all the same, whether it is expressed or not.

Such is the cause of the sentiment of satisfaction that is experienced in a sympathetic reunion, animated by good and benevolent thoughts. It reigns there like a salubrious moral atmosphere, which one breathes with ease. One is strengthened there, because it is impregnated with salutary fluidic effluvia; but, if some evil thoughts are mingled with it, they produce the effect of a current of icy air in a warm atmosphere 'or of a wrong key note played in a concert. Thus is explained also the anxiety, the indefinable uneasiness, that one feels in antipathetically surroundings, where malevolent thoughts are called forth like currents of nauseous air.

20. Thought produces, then, a substantial effect, which reacts upon our moral being. Spiritism alone can explain it. Man instinctively feels it, since he seeks homogeneous and sympathetic reunions, where he knows that he can draw new moral forces. One could say that he retrieves there the fluid losses that he makes each day by the radiation of thought, as he makes up the losses of the material body by food. Thought, indeed, is an emission which causes a real loss in the spiritual fluids, and consequently in the material fluids, also in such a way that man has need of strengthening himself by the effluvia which he receives from outside.

When a doctor is said to cure his patient by pleasant words, it is an absolute truth; for the benevolent thought carries with it healing fluids, which act physically as well as morally.

21. It is possible, without doubt, to evade men of well-known malicious intentions; but how can we be preserved from the influence of undeveloped spirits which multiply around us, and glide everywhere without being seen?

The means are very simple; for it depends upon the will of the man himself, who carries within him the necessary instrument of protecting himself. Fluids unite by reason of the similitude of their nature, dissimilar ones repel each other. There is an incompatibility between good and bad fluids, as between oil and water.

What is done when the air becomes vitiated? They purify it by destroying the center of the miasma by chasing out the unhealthy effluvium by currents of salubrious air stronger than it. We need the good fluids in order to counteract the invasion of bad fluids; and, as each one has in his own perispirit a permanent fluidic-source, the remedy is within one's self. It acts only to purify this source or spring, and to give to it such qualities as are necessary to *repel* bad influences, in place of being an attractive force. The perispirit is, then, a breastplate to which it is necessary to give the best possible character. Now, as the qualities of the perispirit correspond with the qualities of the soul, it is necessary to work for its own improvement; for it is the imperfections of the soul which attract bad spirits.

Flies go where centers of corruption attract them. Destroy these centers, and the flies will disappear. In the same way bad spirits go where evil attracts them. Destroy the evil, and they will flee. *Spirits really good, whether incarnated or discarnated, have nothing to fear from the influence of bad spirits.*

II. EXPLANATION OF SOME FACTS REPUTED TO BE SUPERNATURAL
SPIRITUAL OR PSYCHIC SIGHT - SECOND SIGHT – SOMNAMBULISM - DREAMS.

22. The perispirit is the connecting link between corporeal and spiritual life. By it the incarnate is in continual rapport with the discarnate. In short, it is by it that special phenomena are accomplished in man, the first cause of which is not found in tangible matter, and which for this reason seem supernatural.

It is necessary to seek for the cause of *second or spiritual sight* in the properties and radiations of perispiritual fluids, which can also be called psychic sight, with which many persons are endowed, as well as another called somnambulic sight, often unknown to them.

The perispirit is the *sensitive organ* of the spirit. It is by its intermediation that the incarnate obtains the perception of spiritual things which escape carnal sense. By it the organs of the body – sight, hearing, and the diverse sensations – are localized and limited to the perception of material things. By the spiritual sense or *psychic*, they are generalized. The spirit sees, hears, and feels through all his being, that which is in the sphere of the radiation of his perispiritual fluid.

These phenomena are, with man, the manifestation of the spiritual life. It is the soul which acts outside the organism. In second sight, or perception by the psychic sense, objects are not seen by the material eye, although by habit it often directs them towards the point to which attention is diverted. The clairvoyant sees with the soul's eyes; and the proof of it is that he sees all as well with the eyes closed as open, and also beyond the compass of the visual radius. He reads the thought stamped in the fluidic radius (n° 15). [74]

23. Although, during life, the spirit is *chained* to the body by the perispirit, it is not such a slave that it cannot

---

[74] See facts in regard to double sight and somnambulic lucidity reported in the *"Revue Spirite"* of Jan., 1858, p. 25; Nov., 1858, p. 513; July, 1861, p. 197; Nov., 1865, p. 352.

lengthen its chain, and transport itself to afar in some point in space or upon the Earth. The spirit is only with regret attached to the body, because his normal life is liberty, whilst the corporeal one is like that of a serf bound to the soil.

The spirit is then as happy to leave his body as the bird is to leave its cage. It seizes all occasions for freeing itself from it, and profits by all instances where its presence is not necessary to the relation of life. It is the phenomenon designated under the name of *emancipation of the soul.* It takes place in sleep. Every time that the body reposes and the senses are inactive, the spirit releases itself. (See *"The Spirits' Book,"* chap. 8.)

In these moments the spirit sees spiritual life, whilst the body sees only vegetative life. It is partially in the state in which it will be after death; it passes through space, converses with friends, and other free or *incarnated* spirits like itself.

The fluidic-link which holds it to the body is not broken until death. A complete separation does not take place until the absolute extinction of the activity of the vital principle. So long as the body lives, the spirit, at whatever distance it may be, is instantly recalled to it as soon as its presence is necessary; then it resumes its relation with the course of exterior life. Sometimes, upon the awakening of the body, it preserves the remembrance of its peregrinations, – an impression more or less distinct, which constitutes a dream. It is, *en rapport,* in all cases, with the intuitions which are suggested to it by new thoughts and ideas, and justify the proverb, "Night brings counsel and advice."

Thus are also explained certain characteristic phenomena of natural and magnetic somnambulism, catalepsy, lethargy, ecstasy, etc., and which are none other than manifestations of spiritual life.[75]

24. Since spiritual sight is not given through the eyes of

---

[75] See examples of lethargy and catalepsy: *"Revue Spirite,"* Madame Schwabenhaus, Sept., 1858, p. 255; *"The Young Cataleptic of Souabe,"* Jan., 1866, p. 18.

the flesh, the perception of things is not given by any ordinary light; indeed, material light is made for the material world. For the spiritual world there exists a special luminary, the nature of which is unknown to us, but which is, without doubt, one of the properties of the ethereal fluid affected by the visual perceptions of the soul. There is, then, material and spiritual light. The first has circumscribed focuses from luminous bodies; the second has its focus everywhere; therefore, there are no obstacles to spiritual sight. It is neither arrested by distance nor by the opacity of matter, nothing dims it. The spiritual world is then illuminated by a spiritual light which has its characteristic power, as the material world has its solar light.

25. The soul enveloped in its perispirit carries thus in it its luminous principle. Penetrating matter by virtue of its ethereal essence, there are no opaque bodies to its vision.

However, the spiritual sight has not the same penetration or extent with all spirits. The pure spirits alone possess it in all its power. With inferior ones it is weakened by the coarseness of the perispirit, which interposes itself like a fog.

It manifests itself in different degrees with incarnates by the phenomenon of second sight, whether in a natural or magnetic somnambulism, or in a waking state. According to the power of the faculty is the lucidity, more or less great. By the aid of this faculty some persons see the interior of the organism, and describe the cause of maladies.

26. Spiritual sight gives, then, special perceptions, which, being not seated in the material organs, operate by conditions totally different from the corporeal sight. For the same reason one cannot expect identical effects, or experiment with it by the same means. Being accomplished outside of the organism, it has a mobility which baffles all foresight. It is necessary to study all its causes and effects, and not by assimilation with ordinary sight, which it is not intended to supply, except in exceptional cases, which must not be taken as a rule.

27. Spiritual sight is necessarily incomplete and imperfect with incarnates, therefore subject to aberrations.

Having its seat in the soul itself, the state of the soul must sway the perceptions it gives. According to the degree of its development, the circumstances and moral state of the individual, it can give either in sleep or in a waking state:

1st- The perception of certain material, real facts, as the knowledge of events that are happening afar; descriptive details of a locality, the causes of disease, and the proper remedies.

2nd- The perceptions of things equally real in the spirit world, as a sight of spirits.

3rd- Fantastic images created by the imagination, analogous to fluidic creations of thought (see item n° 14 of this chapter).

These creations are always in relation with the moral disposition of the spirit who gives birth to them. Thus, to persons very strongly imbued and preoccupied with religious beliefs, hell is presented with its furnaces, its tortures, its demons, such as they imagine them to be. Sometimes it is an epic poem. The pagans saw Olympus and the Tartarean depths, as the Christians see Paradise and Hell. If, upon awakening of coming out of ecstasy, these persons preserve a distinct remembrance of their visions, they take it for the reality and confirmation of their belief, while it is only a product of their own thoughts. [76] It is necessary to make a rigorous selection from amongst the visions we see in a state of ecstasy, before accepting them. On this subject, the remedy for an excessive credulity is the study of the laws which govern the spiritual world.

28. In their essence, dreams present all three characteristics of the visions described above. Prophetic dreams, presentments and warnings belong to the first two categories.[77] Under the third category, that is, in the fluidic creations of thought, we can find the causes for certain

---

[76] The visions of sister Elmerich can thus be explained, who, carrying herself back to the time of the passion of Christ, is said to have seen material things which have only existed in the books which she has read; also those of Madame Cantonille (*"Revue Spirite,"* Aug., 1866, p. 240), and a part of Swedenborg.

[77] See ahead, chapter XVI on Theory of Prescience, n° 1, 2 & 3.

fantastic images, which have nothing real for the corporeal life, but that has, for the spirit, such a clear reality that the body suffers the blows (upon being hit), and one's hair turn white under the impression of a dream. Such creations can be provoked by an exaggerated credulity, retrospective recollections, or by likes, desires, passions, fear, and remorse; it can also be caused by habitual worries, or because of the body's needs, or still by a malfunction of the organism; finally, it can also be caused by other spirits with good or bad intentions, according to their nature.[78]

Catalepsy - Resurrection

29. Inert matter is insensible. Perispiritual fluid is equally so; but it transmits the sensation to the sensitive center, which is the spirit. Painful injuries to the body reflect themselves then in the spirit like an electric shock, by the intermediation of the perispiritual fluid, of which the nerves appear to be the conducting threads. This is the nerve-power of the physiologists, who, knowing not the connection of this fluid with the spiritual principle, have not been able to explain all the effects.

An interruption can take place by the separation of a limb, or dissection of a nerve, but also partially, or in a general manner, without any injury, in moments of emancipation, over-excitability, or preoccupation of the spirit. In this state the spirit thinks no more of the body; and in his feverish activity he attracts, as it were, the perispiritual fluid to him, which, being withdrawn from the surface, produces there a momentary insensibility. We could still admit that in some circumstances a molecular modification is produced in the perispiritual fluid itself, temporarily disabling its ability of transmission. Thus, in the ardor of combat, a military man does not perceive he is wounded. A person whose attention is concentrated upon a work hears not the noise which is made around him. An

---

[78] *"Revue Spirite,"* June of 1866, pg. 172; September of 1866, pg. 284; *"The Spirit's Book,"* chapter VIII, question n° 400.

analogous effect, but more pronounced, takes place with somnambulists in lethargy and catalepsy. Thus, in short, can be explained the insensibility of convulsionaries and of certain martyrs ("*Revue Spirite*," January, 1868: *Study of the Aïssaouas*).

Paralysis does not proceed from the same cause. With it the effect is entirely organic. It is the nerves themselves, the conducting threads, which are unqualified for the fluid circulation; it is the chords of the instrument which are broken or injured.

30. In diseased states of the body, when the spirit is no longer in it, and the perispirit adheres to it only at a few points, the body has all the appearance of death; and one is absolutely correct in saying life hangs by a single thread. This state can continue for short or long time. Certain parts of the body can even decompose without life being entirely extinguished. As long as the last thread is not broken, the spirit can, either by an energetic action of its *own* will, or by a *strange fluidic influx, equally powerful*, be recalled to the body. Thus can be explained certain prolongations of life against all probability, and certain pretended resurrections. A plant sometimes puts forth only one sprout from its root; but when the last molecules of the fluidic body are detached from the carnal one, or when the latter is in a state of irreparable decay, all return to life becomes impossible.[79]

CURES

31. The universal fluid is, as has been seen, the primitive element of the carnal body and of the perispirit, which are only transformation of it. By the sameness of its nature this fluid can furnish to the body the principal reparative. Being condensed in the perispirit, the propelling power is the spirit, incarnated or discarnated, which infiltrates into a deteriorated

---

[79] Examples: "*Revue Spirite*," Dr. Cardon, Aug., 1863, p. 251; "*The Woman Corse*," May, 1866, p. 134.

body a part of the substance of its fluid-envelope. The cure is performed by the substitution of an unhealthy molecule for a healthy one. The curative power will then be drawn from the purity of the inoculated substance. It depends also upon the energy of the will, which provokes a more abundant fluid-emission, and gives to the fluid a greater force of penetration. In short, it is the intentions of he who desires to cure, *let him be man or spirit*. The fluids which emanate from an impure source are like defective medical substances.

32. The effects of the fluidic-action upon illnesses varied according to circumstances. Its action is sometimes slow, and requires a prolonged treatment, as in ordinary magnetism. At other times it is rapid as an electric current. There are some persons endowed with such a magnetic power, that they perform upon certain ill people instantaneous cures only by the laying-on of hands, or sometimes by the sole act of will. Between the two extreme poles of this faculty there is an infinite variety of distinctive shades. All the cures of this kind are from the different varieties of magnetism, and differ only in the power and rapidity of their action. The principle is always the same: it is the fluid which plays the role of therapeutic agent, the effect of which is subordinated to its quality and to special circumstances.

33. Magnetic action can be produced in many ways:

1st By the fluid of the magnetizer·himself; properly speaking, magnetism, or *human magnetism*, the action of which is subordinate to the power, and above all to the quality of the fluid.

2nd By fluid from the spirit acting directly and *without intermediation* upon an incarnate being, either to cure or to calm suffering, to provoke spontaneous somnambulistic sleep, or to exercise over the individual any moral or physical influence whatever. That is *spiritual magnetism*, of which the quality is determined by the quality of the spirit.[80]

3rd By the fluid which the spirits shed upon the

---

[80] Examples: *"Revue Spirite,"* Feb., 1863, p. 64; April, 1865, p. 133; Sept., 1865, p. 264.

magnetizer, to which the latter serves as a conductor. This is mixed magnetism, semi-spiritual, or human-spiritual. The spiritual fluid, combined with the physical, gives to the latter the qualities which are wanting to it. The meeting of spirits for a like circumstance is sometimes spontaneous, but more often it is brought about by the call of the magnetizer.

34. The faculty to cure by the fluidic-influx is very common, and can develop itself by exercise; but that of curing instantaneously by the laying-on of hands is rare and its power can be considered as exceptional. However, it has been seen at diverse epochs, and in nearly every nation there are some individuals who possess it to an eminent degree. Lately many remarkable examples have been seen of it, the authenticity of which cannot be contested. Since these kinds of cures rest upon a principle of nature, the power of performing them is not a preference shown, or a departure from nature's laws. They can only be miraculous in appearance.[81]

APPARITIONS - TRANSFIGURATION

35. The perispirit is invisible to us in its normal state; but, as it is formed of ethereal matter, the spirit can, in certain cases, make it submit by an act of the will to a molecular modification, which renders it momentarily visible. Thus *apparitions* are produced which no more than other phenomena are outside of the laws of nature. The latter are no more extraordinary than that of vapor, which is invisible when it is rarefied, and which becomes visible when it is condensed.

According to the degree of condensation of the

---

[81] Examples of instantaneous cures reported in the *"Revue Spirite:"* The Prince of Hohenlohe, Dec., 1866, p. 368; Jacob, Oct. and Nov., 1866, pp. 312 and 345; Oct. and Nov., 1867, pp. 306 and 339; Simonet, Aug., 1867, p. 232; Caid Hassan, Oct., 1867, p. 303; The Curate Gassner, Nov., 1867, p. 331.

perispiritual fluid, the apparition is sometimes vague and vaporous; and at other times it is more distinctly defined; at others it has quite the appearance of tangible matter. It can even reach tangibility sufficiently to be mistaken for a person in the flesh.

Vaporous apparitions are frequent; and it often happens that some individuals present themselves thus, after death, to persons whom they have loved. Tangible apparitions are rare, although there have been numerous examples of them which are perfectly authentic. If the spirit can make itself recognized, it will give to its envelope all the exterior signs which it had in life.[82]

36. Let us remark that tangible apparitions have only the appearance of carnal matter, but would not know how to obtain its qualities. By reason of their fluidic nature, they cannot have the same cohesion, because in reality they are not of the flesh. They are instantaneously formed, and disappear in the same manner, or are evaporated by the disintegration of the fluidic-molecules. Beings which present themselves by these conditions are neither born nor die like other men; they appear and vanish without knowing whence they come, how they have come, or where they will go. They could not be killed, chained, or incarcerated, because they have no carnal body. By attempting to strike them, one would only strike into space.

Such is the character of the spirits (agénères) with whom we can communicate without doubting their true individuality, yet who never make long visits, cannot become habitual boarders in a house, nor figure among the members of a family.

There is besides in all their person, in their manner, something strange and unusual which divides spirituality from materiality. The expression of their eyes, vaporous and penetrating at the same time, has not the distinctness of those of the flesh; their language brief, and nearly always

---

[82] *"The Mediums Book,"* chap. 6 and 7.

sententious, has nothing of the brilliancy and volubility of human language; their approach makes us experience a particular, indefinable sensation of surprise, which inspires a sort of fear; and it is involuntarily said by all who compare them with human beings, "Here is a singular being."[83]

37. The perispirit being the same among incarnates and discarnates, by a completely identical effect an incarnate can appear in a moment, when he is freed from the flesh at another point than that where his body is reposing, with his habitual features and all the signs of his identity. It is this phenomenon, of which authentic examples are given, which has caused belief in double or dual men.[84]

38. A particular effect of this kind of phenomena is, that the vaporous and even tangible apparitions are indistinctly perceptible to everybody. The spirits show themselves only when they desire, and to whom they desire. A spirit would then be able to appear in an assembly to one or more persons, and not be seen by all. This is because these kinds of perceptions are processed through the spiritual, rather than the corporeal vision. Accordingly, spiritual visions are not awarded to everyone, and the communicating spirit can, at his exclusive discretion, if necessary, disable it in those whom he does not wish to be seen by. Likewise it can, momentarily, be awarded to someone, if the communicating spirit deems it necessary.

The condensation of the perispiritual fluid of apparitions, extending even to its tangibility, lacks the properties of ordinary matter. If it were not so, apparitions would be perceptible

---

[83] Examples of vaporous or tangible apparitions and agénères: *"Revue Spirite:"* Jan., 1858, p. 24; Oct., 1858, p. 291; Feb., 1859, p. 38; March, 1859, p. 80; Jan., 1859, p. 11; Nov., 1859, p. 303; Aug., 1859, p. 210; April, 1860, p. 117; May, 1860, p. 150; July, 1861, p. 199; April, 1866, p. 120; the laborer Martin presented to Louis XVIII., complete details; Dec., 1866, p. 353.

[84] Examples of apparitions of living persons: *"Revue Spirite:"* Dec., 1858, pp. 329 and 331; Feb., 1859, p. 41; Aug., 1859, p. 197; Nov., 1860, p. 356.

through the corporeal eyes, and thus perceived by everyone present.[85]

39. The spirit being able to accomplish transformations by means of his perispiritual envelope, and this envelope having the power to radiate around bodies like a fluidic-atmosphere, a phenomenon analogous to that of apparitions can be produced even on the surface of bodies. Under the fluidic-film the real figure of the body can be effaced more or less completely and be reinvested with other features; or, rather, the original features seen through a modified fluidic-film, as through a prism, can assume another expression. If the incarnate spirit, in going from Earth to Earth, identifies itself with things of the spiritual world, the expression of a homely face can become beautiful, radiant, and sometimes even luminous; if, on the contrary, it is prey to bad passions, a beautiful face can take a hideous aspect.

Thus are *transfigurations* performed, which are always a reflection of the qualities and predominating sentiments of the spirit. This phenomenon is, then, the result of fluidic transformation. It is a kind of perispiritual apparition which is produced even upon living bodies, and sometimes at the moment of death, instead of producing itself at a distance, as apparitions are generally seen. That which is distinguishing peculiarity of this kind of apparitions is, that they are generally perceptible to all present by the eye of the flesh, because they are based upon visible, carnal matter, whilst in purely fluidic displays of the same there is no tangible matter employed.[86]

---

[85] We must be very cautious in accepting as facts strictly individual recitals of apparitions, which in certain cases may have been the effect of an over-excited imagination, or an invention for some selfish end. It is well, then, to gain a careful account of the circumstances, of the respectability of the person, as well as the interest they might have in abusing the credulity of too-confiding individuals.

[86] Example and theory of transfiguration: "*Revue Spirite*:" March, 1859, p. 62; "*The Mediums' Book*," chap. 7, p. 142.

PHYSICAL MANIFESTATIONS - MEDIUMSHIP

40. The phenomena of moving and communicating by means of turning tables, the ethereal raising of heavy bodies, of mediumistic writing (as ancient as the world, but common today), give the key to many spontaneous, analogous phenomena, to which, by ignorance of the law which governs them, they attribute to a supernatural and miraculous character. These phenomena rest upon the properties of the perispiritual fluid of either incarnate beings or free spirits.

41. It is by the aid of its perispirit that the spirit acts upon his living body. It is with this same fluid that it manifests itself by acting upon inert matter; that it produces sounds, movement of tables, and raises, overturns, or transports other objects. There is nothing surprising in these phenomena if one considers that with us the most powerful motors are found in the most rarefied and even imponderable fluids, like air, vapor, and electricity.

It is equally by the aid of his perispirit that the spirit enables mediums to speak, write, or sketch. Having no tangible body to manifest, he serves himself with the body of the medium, from which he borrows the organs and uses as if it were his own, obtaining possession of it by the fluidic-effluvium which he throws around it.

42. By the same means the spirit acts upon the table, either to make it simply to move, or give intelligent raps, indicating the letters of the alphabet, in order to form words or phrases, a phenomenon named "typtology." Here the table is only an instrument for use, as a pencil in writing. It gives to it a momentary vitality by the fluid with which it penetrates it; but it *does not identify itself with it.* Persons who, in their emotion at being able to communicate with spirits dear to them, embrace the table perform a foolish act; for it is absolutely the same as if they should embrace the stick which a friend uses to make the raps. It is equivalent to saying that the spirit was enclosed in the wood of the table, or that the wood had become a spirit.

When communications like these take place, it is necessary to represent the spirit as not in the table, but beside us as he was in life; and thus they would see him if their spiritual eyes were open. The same takes place when one obtains communications by writing; one would see the spirit beside the medium, directing or transmitting to him his ideas by a fluidic-current.

43. When the table is detached from the ground and floats in space without support, the spirit does not raise it by arm-strength, but by enveloping and penetrating it with a sort of fluidic-atmosphere, which neutralizes the effect of gravitation, as the air does for balloons and kites. The fluid with which it is permeated gives a momentarily greater specific lightness. When it is nailed to the ground, it is in a condition analogous to that of the pneumatic receiver under which the air is exhausted. These comparisons here are only to show the analogy of effects, and not the absolute similitude of causes (*"The Mediums' Book,"* chap. 4).

One can comprehend, after this, that it is no more difficult to raise a person than a table, to transport an object from one place to another, than to throw it somewhere. These phenomena are produced by the same law.[87]

When the table pursues a person, it is not the spirit who runs, for he can remain calmly in the same place; but,

---

[87] Such is the principle of the phenomena of levitation, or the rising of bodies upwards, and suspension in the air, with no visible means of support, – an actual phenomenon, but which must be accepted with extreme reserve; for it is one which lends itself the most to imposture and jugglery. The absolute worthiness of the person who obtains them, his entire material and moral disinterestedness, and the cooperation of accessory circumstances, must be taken into serious consideration. It is necessary to distrust the too great facility with which these effects are produced, and to be doubtful of those who renew them too frequently, as it were, by willpower. The prestidigitators do most extraordinary things. The raising of a person into mid-air is a fact no less positive, but much more rare, perhaps, because it is more difficult to imitate. It is generally known that Mr. Home has been more than once elevated to the ceiling in this manner, making the tour of the hall. St. Cupertin is said to have had this same power, which is no more miraculous in one than in the other.

by the aid of his will, he gives the fluidic-current an impulsion.

When the raps are heard on a table or elsewhere, the spirit does not rap with his hand or with any instrument whatever; he directs upon the point whence the noise proceeds a stream of fluid, which produces the effect of an electric shock. He changes the sound, as sounds produced by air can be modified.[88]

44. A phenomenon which is very common in mediumship is the aptitude of certain mediums to write in a language which is unknown to them, – to speak or write upon subjects outside their knowledge. It is not rare to see those who write rapidly without having learned to write; others still who become poets, without ever having before composed a line of poetry; others sketch, paint, sculpt, compose music, play on an instrument, without having previously known anything of either accomplishment. Very frequently the writing-medium reproduces the writing and signature of the spirits communicating by him, although he had never known them in Earth-life.

This phenomenon is not more wonderful than to see a child write when someone conducts his hand. One can thus perform all that one wishes. Any person could write in any language whatever by dictating the words letter by letter. It is the same with mediumship. Mediums are only passive instruments in the spirit's hands. But if the medium possesses a knowledge of the mechanism of it, if the expressions are

---

[88] Examples of material manifestations and perturbations by the Spirits: *"Revue Spirite,"* Young Girl of Panoramas, Jan., 1858, p. 13; Miss Clairon, Feb., 1858, p. 44; Spirit-Rapper of Bergzabern, complete account, May, June, and July of 1858, pp. 125, 153, 184; Dibbelsdorf, Aug., 1858, p. 219; Boulanger of Dieppe, March, 1860, p. 76; Merchant of St. Petersburg, April 1860, p. 115; Noyers St., Aug., 1860, p. 236; Spirit-Rapper of Aube, Jan., 1861, p. 23; id., in the 16th century, Jan., 1864, p. 32; Poitiers, May, 1864, p. 156, and May, 1865, p. 134; Sister Mary, June, 1864, p. 185; Marseilles, April, 1865, p. 121; Fives, Aug., 1865, p. 225; The Rats of Equihem, Feb., 1866, p. 55.

familiar to him, if he has, in short, in his brain the elements of that which the spirit desires him to execute, he is in the position of the man who knows how to read and write rapidly. The work is easier and more rapid. The spirit has only to transmit the thought that his interpreter reproduces by means at his disposal.

The aptitude of a medium in things which are strange to him is often caused by the knowledge he has obtained in another existence, of which his spirit has preserved the intuition. If he has been a poet or a musician, for example, his mind will the more readily grasp the poetical and musical ideas which they wish to reproduce. The language of which he is now ignorant may have been familiar to him in another existence; hence he has a greater aptitude as a writing-medium in this language.[89]

OBSESSIONS AND POSSESSIONS

45. Bad spirits increase most abundantly around the Earth on account of the moral inferiority of its inhabitants. Their wrongdoing in a measure is the cause of the plagues to which humanity is exposed here below. Obsession, which is one of the effects of this action, like maladies and all tribulations of life, must then be considered as a trial or expiation, and accepted as such.

Obsession is the persistent action which a bad spirit exercises over an individual. It presents many different characters, from the moral influence without any distinct exterior signs, to complete disturbance of the organism and of the mental faculties. It destroys all mediumistic faculties. In

---

[89] The aptitude of certain persons for languages which they have never learned is caused by an intuitive remembrance of that which they have learned in another existence. The example of the poet Mery, reported in the *"Revue Spirite"* of Nov., 1864, p. 328, is a proof of it. It is evident, that, if Mr. Mery had been a medium in his youth, he would have written in Latin as easily as in French, and would have been called a prodigy.

hearing and psychographic mediumship an obstinate spirit manifests to the exclusion of all others.

46. Just as maladies are the result of physical imperfections which render the body accessible to pernicious exterior influences, obsession is always that of a moral imperfection, which gives place to a bad spirit. To a physical cause one opposes a physical force; to a moral cause it is necessary to oppose a moral force. In order to preserve one's self from maladies, one must fortify the body; in order to guarantee one's self against obsession, one must fortify the soul: hence for the obsessed the necessity for working for his own betterment, which is often sufficient to cure obsession without external aid. This aid becomes necessary when obsession degenerates into complete subjugation and possession; for then the patient sometimes loses his volition and free will.

Obsession is nearly always due to a vengeance, exercised by a spirit, and which most often has its source in connections which the obsessed has had with it in a previous existence.

In case of grave obsession the obsessed is enveloped and impregnated with a pernicious fluid, which neutralizes the action of the salutary fluids, and repels them. It is necessary to remove this fluid. Now a bad fluid cannot be repelled by a bad fluid. By an action similar to that of a healing medium in a case of *illness, it is necessary to expel the bad fluid by the aid of a better one.*

The latter, which is mechanical action, does not always suffice. It is necessary, above all, *to act upon the intelligent being*, to whom it is necessary *to speak with authority*, and this authority is given only to moral superiority. The greater the latter is, the greater the authority.

That is not all, however. It is necessary to lead the perverse spirit to renounce his bad designs; to awaken within him a desire to do good, and true repentance, by the aid of cleverly directed instructions, by the evoking of particular spirits to aid him in his moral education. Then one can have the double satisfaction of delivering an incarnated being and of converting an imperfect spirit.

The task is rendered easier if the obsessed, comprehending his situation, joins his will and prayers with yours. It is not thus when the latter, seduced by the deceiving spirit, is deluded in regard to the qualities of his ruler, and delights in the error into which the latter plunges him; for then, far from seconding, he repels all assistance. Such are cases of fascination always vastly more obstinate than the most violent subjugation. (See *"The Mediums' Book,"* chap. 23.)

In all cases of obsession prayer is the most powerful auxiliary to act against the obsessing spirit.

47. In obsession the spirit acts exteriorly by the aid of its perispirit, which he mingles with that of the incarnates. The latter finds himself bound as if in a network, and constrained to act against his will.

In taking possession of a human organism, the free spirit substitutes itself, as it were, for that of the incarnated one, instead of acting exteriorly; he chooses a home in his body, although its owner does not leave it entirely, which can take place only with death. The possession is then only temporary and intermittent, for a discarnate has not the power to take exclusive possession of a human organism, only when the molecular union of the perispirit and body can be performed at the moment of conception (chap. XI, n° 18).

The spirit in momentary possession of the body uses it as his own. He speaks through its mouth, sees with its eyes, moves its arms as he had done in life. It is not as in mediumship when the incarnate speaks the thoughts of a discarnate, which are transmitted through him. It is the latter who speaks; and, if one has known him in life, one recognizes him by his language, voice, and gestures, even to the expression of his face.

48. Obsession is always due to the influence of a malevolent spirit. Possession can be taken of a human being by a good spirit, who desires to speak in order to make a deeper impression upon his auditors, borrows the medium's body, as the latter loans it to him voluntarily as he would lend his coat. This is done without any trouble or bad effect; and during this time the medium's spirit is free as in a state of emancipation, and he frequently remains beside his substitute in order to listen to him.

When the spirit in possession is a bad one, all is otherwise; he does not borrow the body, but forcibly takes possession of it if the owner has *not the moral force to resist him*. He does it for malice towards the latter, whom he tortures and torments in every way, desiring to kill him either by strangulation, or by throwing him in the fire or other dangerous places. Using the limbs and organs of the unhappy patient, he blasphemes, injures, and maltreats those who surround him, – delivers him to eccentricities of action, which have the character of an insane person.

Cases of this kind, of different degrees of intensity, are very numerous; and many cases of insanity have had no other cause. Often it is joined to pathological disorders which follow the course of time, and against which medical treatment is powerless as long as the first cause exists. Spiritism, by giving a knowledge of the source of a part of human suffering, indicates the means for curing it. This remedy is to act upon the author of the evil, who, being an intelligent being, must be treated intelligently.[90]

49. Obsession and possession are mostly individual cases, but sometimes they are epidemic. When a troop of undeveloped spirits take up their abode in a locality, it is as when a troop of enemies come to surround it. In this case the number of individuals attacked by them can be many.[91]

---

[90] Examples of cures by obsession and possession: *"Revue Spirite:"* Dec., 1863, p. 373; Jan., 1864, p. 11; June, 1864, p. 168; Jan., 1865, p. 5; June, 1865, p. 172; Feb., 1866, p. 38; June, 1867, p. 174.

[91] It was an epidemic of this kind which took place some years ago in the village of Morzine, Savoy. See the complete history of this epidemic in the "Revue Spirite" of Dec., 1862, p. 353; Jan., Feb., April, and May, 1863, pp. 1, 33, 101, 133.

Chapter XV

THE MIRACLES OF THE GOSPEL

Superiority of the Nature of Jesus — Dreams — The Star of the Wise Men of the East — Second Sight — Cures — Possessed Persons — Resurrections — Jesus Walks upon the Water — Transfiguration — The Tempest Stilled — Marriage at Cana — Making of the Loaves of Bread — Temptation of Jesus — Wonderful Things at the Death of Jesus — Appearance of Jesus After his Death — Disappearance of the Body of Jesus.

SUPERIORITY OF THE NATURE OF JESUS

1. The facts reported in the Gospels, and which have been considered until recently miraculous, belong for the most part to the order of *psychic phenomena*, — those which arise from the faculties and attributes of the soul. By comparing them with those which have been described and explained in the preceding chapter, one recognizes between them an identity of cause and effect. History shows analogous instances in all times and among all nations, for the reason that, ever since souls have been incarnated and discarnated, the same effects must have been produced. One can, it is true, contest the veracity of history upon this point; but now they are produced under our eyes, as it were, by will-power, and by individuals who have nothing exceptional about them. The fact alone of the reproduction of a phenomenon in identical conditions suffices to prove that it is possible, and governed by a law of nature, and that it therefore is not miraculous.

The principle of the psychic phenomena reposes, as has been seen, upon the properties of the perispiritual fluid, which constitutes the magnetic agent upon the manifestations of the spiritual life during life and after death, — in short, upon the constitutive state of the spirits and their role as the active force of nature. These elements known, and their effects ascertained, the result is, that certain facts must be admitted as such which were formerly rejected when attributed to a supernatural origin.

2. Without prejudging anything of the nature of Christ, which is not in the compass of this book, let us consider him as nothing other than a superior spirit, — one of those of the highest order; and let him be placed only by his virtues above the rest of terrestrial humanity. By the great results which he produced, his incarnation into this world could have been only one of those missions which are confided alone to direct messengers from the Most High for the accomplishment of his designs. By supposing that he was not God himself, but an ambassador of him for the transmission of his word, he would be more than a prophet: he would be a divine Messiah.

As man, he had the organization of organized beings; but as a pure spirit, detached from matter, he must have lived in the spiritual life more than in the carnal, of which he had not the weaknesses. *His superiority over men was only of his spiritual nature, which absolutely controlled matter, and his perispirit, which was formed of the most refined of earthly fluids* (chap. XIV, n° 9). His soul must have been attached to the body only by the most indispensable links; constantly separated from one another, it must have endowed him with a double sight, not only permanent, but of an exceptional penetration, very superior to that of ordinary men. It must have been the same with all the phenomena which depend upon the perispiritual or psychic fluids. The quality of these fluids gave to him an immense magnetic power, seconded by a constant desire to do good.

In the cures which he performed, did he act as a *medium*? Can he be considered as a powerful healing medium? No; for the medium is an intermediary, an instrument which discarnate spirits use. Now, Christ had no need of assistance, he who assisted others; he acted, then, by himself, by virtue of his personal power. Thus can incarnated beings, in certain cases, do according to their strength. What other spirit would have dared to inspire him with his own thoughts, and charge him to transmit them? If he received a strange influx, it could only be from God. According to a definition given of him by a spirit, he was a *medium from God*.

DREAMS

3. Joseph, the Gospel narrative states, was warned by an angel who appeared to him in a dream, and who said to him, "Get up, take the child and his mother and go to the land of Israel, for those who were trying to take the child's life are dead." (Matthew, 2: 19 to 23).

Warnings by dreams play an important part in the sacred works of all religions. Without guaranteeing the exactitude of all facts reported, and without discussing them, the phenomenon has nothing in itself anomalous when one knows that in sleep, the spirit frees itself from its imprisonment in matter, and enters again momentarily into the spiritual life, where it finds itself with those whom it has known. It often happens that this moment is chosen by guardian angels to manifest themselves to their protégés, in order to give them more direct counsel. Authentic examples of warnings by dreams are numerous; but it is not necessary to infer that all dreams are warning, and still less that all have a signification. It is well to reckon the art of interpreting dreams among superstitious and absurd beliefs (chap. XIV, n° 27 and 28).

THE STAR OF THE WISE MEN OF THE EAST

4. It is written that a star appeared to the wise men who came to worship Jesus; that it went before them to indicate the route to them, and stood still when they had arrived at their destination (Matthew, 2: 1 to 12).

The question is asked, not to ascertain if the statement given by St. Matthew is true, or if it is only a figure of speech to indicate that the wise men were mysteriously guided to the young child, because no means exist whereby it can be examined, but simply to ask if such a thing were possible.

One thing is certain, that the light referred to could not have been a star. They could believe it at that epoch where the stars were thought to be luminous points attached to the firmament, which could fall upon the Earth; but not now, when their nature is known.

The right cause may now be attributed to it: the fact of a light in appearance like a star is possible. A spirit can appear under a luminous form, or transfer a part of his perispiritual fluid to a luminous point. Many facts of this kind, recent and perfectly authentic, have no other cause; and this cause has nothing supernatural about it. (Chap. XIV, from item n° 3 on)

SECOND SIGHT
ENTRY OF JESUS INTO JERUSALEM

5. As they approached Jerusalem and came to Bethphage on the Mount of Olives, Jesus sent two disciples, saying to them, "Go to the village ahead of you, and at once you will find a donkey tied there, with her colt by her. Untie them and bring them to me. If anyone says anything to you, tell him that the Lord needs them, and he will send them right away." This took place to fulfill what was spoken through the prophet: "Say to the Daughter of Zion, 'See, your king comes to you, gentle and riding on a donkey, on a colt, the foal of a donkey.'

The disciples went and did as Jesus had instructed them. They brought the donkey and the colt, placed their cloaks on them, and Jesus sat on them. (Matthew, 21: 1 to 7 and Zechariah, 9: 9 and 10).

THE KISS OF JUDAS

6. "Rise, let us go! Here comes my betrayer!" While he was still speaking, Judas, one of the Twelve, arrived. With him was a large crowd armed with swords and clubs, sent from the chief priests and the elders of the people. Now

the betrayer had arranged a signal with them: "The one I kiss is the man; arrest him." Going at once to Jesus, Judas said, "Greetings, Rabbi!" and kissed him. Jesus replied, "Friend, do what you came for. (Matthew, 26: 46 to 50).

MIRACULOUS DRAUGHT OF FISHES

7. One day as Jesus was standing by the Lake of Gennesaret, with the people crowding around him and listening to the word of God, he saw at the water's edge two boats, left there by the fishermen, who were washing their nets. He got into one of the boats, the one belonging to Simon, and asked him to put out a little from shore. Then he sat down and taught the people from the boat. When he had finished speaking, he said to Simon, "Put out into deep water, and let down the nets for a catch." Simon answered, "Master, we've worked hard all night and haven't caught anything. But because you say so, I will let down the nets. When they had done so, they caught such a large number of fish that their nets began to break. So they signaled their partners in the other boat to come and help them, and they came and filled both boats so full that they began to sink. (Luke, 5: 1 to 7).

VOCATIONS OF PETER, ANDREW, JAMES, JOHN, AND MATTHEW

8. As Jesus was walking beside the Sea of Galilee, he saw two brothers, Simon called Peter and his brother Andrew. They were casting a net into the lake, for they were fishermen. "Come, follow me," Jesus said, "and I will make you fishers of men." At once they left their nets and followed him. Going on from there, he saw two other brothers, James son of Zebedee and his brother John. They were in a boat with their father Zebedee, preparing their nets. Jesus called them, and immediately they left the boat and their father and followed him. (Matthew, 4: 18 to 22).

As Jesus went on from there, he saw a man named

Matthew sitting at the tax collector's booth. "Follow me," he told him, and Matthew got up and followed him. (Matthew, 9: 8 to 10)

9. These facts are not surprising when one knows the power of second sight, and the natural cause of this faculty. Jesus possessed it in a supreme degree; and he can also have been at the time in his normal state, as a great number of his acts testify, and which is explained today by the magnetic phenomena and Spiritism.

The miraculous draught of fishes is equally well explained by second sight. Jesus did not produce fishes spontaneously there where they did not exist. He has seen, as a lucid would have been able to do, by the eyes of the soul, the place where they were found; and he has been able to say with assurance to the fishers: "Put out into deep water, and let down the nets for a catch."

The power to fathom thought, by which foresight can be obtained, is the result of second sight. When Jesus called Peter to him, as well as Andrew, James, John, and Matthew, he must have known their dispositions intimately in order to know that they would follow him, and that they were capable of fulfilling the mission with which he must charge them. It was also necessary that they themselves should have an intuition of this mission in order to give themselves up to him. Again, it is the same at the Lord's Supper, when he announces that one of the twelve will betray him, and when he designates him by saying it is he who is placing his hand in the dish with him, and also when he says that Peter will deny him.

In many places in the Gospels we read: "But Jesus, knowing their thoughts, said unto them." Now, how could he know their thoughts if it was not at the time in the fluidic-radiance which carried their thoughts to him, and also the spiritual sight, which gave him power to read the mind of individuals?

Then, often when one believes an idea profoundly shrouded in the depth of the soul, one doubts not that there is a mirror within which reflects it, — a revelator in its own fluidic-radiance which is impregnated with it. If we could see the mechanism of the invisible world which surrounds us, the ramifications of these conducting threads of thought which bind all intelligent beings, incarnated and otherwise, the fluidic-effluvia charged with imprints of the moral world, and which like aerial currents traverse space, one would be less surprised at certain effects that ignorance attributes to chance (chap, XIV, from item n° 22 on).

CURES
THE WOMAN WHO HAD THE ISSUE OF BLOOD

10. A large crowd followed and pressed around him. And a woman was there who had been subject to bleeding for twelve years. She had suffered a great deal under the care of many doctors and had spent all she had, yet instead of getting better she grew worse. When she heard about Jesus, she came up behind him in the crowd and touched his cloak, because she thought, "If I just touch his clothes, I will be healed." Immediately her bleeding stopped and she felt in her body that she was freed from her suffering. At once Jesus realized that power had gone out from him. He turned around in the crowd and asked, "Who touched my clothes?" "You see the people crowding against you," his disciples answered, "and yet you can ask, 'Who touched me?' " But Jesus kept looking around to see who had done it. Then the woman, knowing what had happened to her, came and fell at his feet and, trembling with fear, told him the whole truth. He said to her, "Daughter, your faith has healed you. Go in peace and be freed from your suffering." (Mark, 5: 25 to 34).

11. These words, "*At once Jesus realized that power had gone out from him,*" are significant. They express the movement of the fluid which Jesus transferred to the sick woman. Both have felt the action which has just been produced. It is remarkable that the effect has not been

provoked by any will-power of Jesus. Neither magnetism
nor laying-on of hands were employed. The normal fluidic-
radiance was sufficient to effect the cure.

But why was this radiance directed to the woman rather
than to others, since Jesus did not think of her, and he was
surrounded by a multitude of people?

The reason is very simple. The fluid, being given as
therapeutic matter, must reach organic disorder in order to
repair it. It can be directed upon the evil by the will of the
healing medium, or attracted by the ardent desire, the
confidence, or, in one word, the faith of the sick one. In regard
to the fluidic-current the first is the effect of forcing it, and
the second of suction. Sometimes the simultaneousness of
the effects is necessary; at others one alone suffices. The
second has taken place in this circumstance.

Jesus was then right in saying, "Your faith has healed
you." The faith expressed here is not the mystical virtue
which some believe it to be, but a veritable *attractive force*; while he who has it not, opposes to the fluidic-current
a repelling force, or at least an inert one, which paralyzes
action. Knowing this, one can comprehend how two sick
persons attacked by the same illness, in the presence of a
healing medium, one can be cured, and the other not. This
is one of the most important principles of healing
mediumship, and which explains, by a very natural cause,
certain apparent anomalies (chap. XIV, n° 31 to 33).

THE HEALING OF A BLIND MAN AT BETHSAIDA

12. They came to Bethsaida, and some people brought
a blind man and begged Jesus to touch him. He took the blind
man by the hand and led him outside the village. When he
had spit on the man's eyes and put his hands on him, Jesus
asked, "Do you see anything?" He looked up and said, "I
see people; they look like trees walking around." Once more
Jesus put his hands on the man's eyes. Then his eyes were
opened, his sight was restored, and he saw everything

clearly. Jesus sent him home, saying, "Don't go into the village." (Mark, 8: 22 to 26).

13. Here the effect of magnetism is evident. The cure has not been instantaneous but gradual, and in consequence of sustained and reiterated action, although more rapid than in ordinary magnetization. The first sensation of this man is that which blind men experience in recovering sight. By an optical illusion, objects appear to them of an inordinate size.

JESUS HEALS A PARALYTIC

14. Jesus stepped into a boat, crossed over and came to his own town. Some men brought to him a paralytic, lying on a mat. When Jesus saw their faith, he said to the paralytic, "Take heart, son; your sins are forgiven." At this, some of the teachers of the law said to themselves, "This fellow is blaspheming!" Knowing their thoughts, Jesus said, "Why do you entertain evil thoughts in your hearts? Which is easier: to say, 'Your sins are forgiven,' or to say, 'Get up and walk'? But so that you may know that the Son of Man has authority on Earth to forgive sins...." Then he said to the paralytic, "Get up, take your mat and go home." And the man got up and went home. When the crowd saw this, they were filled with awe; and they praised God, who had given such authority to men. (Matthew, 9: 1 to 8).

15. What could these words signify, "Yours sins are forgiven?" And how could they help the cure? Spiritism gives the key to them, as well as to an infinite number of other sayings misunderstood till now. It teaches us, by the law of the plurality of existences, that the evils and afflictions of life are often expiations of the past, and that we submit in the present life to the consequence of faults that we have committed in an anterior existence; the different existences being connected with one another, until we pay off the debt of our imperfections.

If, then, the malady of this man was a punishment for evil which he had committed, by saying to him: "your sins are forgiven," was equal to saying: "You have paid your debt. The cause of your malady is effaced by your faith; consequently you merit to be delivered from your malady." He therefore said to the scribes: "It is as easy to say, Your sins are forgiven, as to say: arise, and walk;" the cause ceasing, the effect must cease also. The case is the same with a prisoner to whom they would go and say: "Your crime is expiated and pardoned;" which is equivalent to saying: "You can leave prison."

Ten Healed of Leprosy

16. Now on his way to Jerusalem, Jesus traveled along the border between Samaria and Galilee. As he was going into a village, ten men who had leprosy met him. They stood at a distance and called out in a loud voice, "Jesus, Master, have pity on us!" When he saw them, he said, "Go, show yourselves to the priests." And as they went, they were cleansed. One of them, when he saw he was healed, came back, praising God in a loud voice. He threw himself at Jesus' feet and thanked him - and he was a Samaritan. Jesus asked, "Were not all ten cleansed? Where are the other nine? Was no one found to return and give praise to God except this foreigner?" Then he said to him, "Rise and go; your faith has made you well." (Luke, 17: 11 to 19).

17. The Samaritans were schismatic, as Protestants stand in regard to Catholics, and despised by the Jews as heretics. Jesus, by curing indiscriminately the Samaritans and the Jews, gave at the same time a lesson and an example of tolerance; and, by showing that the Samaritan alone returned to give glory to God, it proved that there was in him more true faith and gratitude than with those who were called orthodox. By saying: "Your faith has made you well," he shows that God regards the feeling of the heart, and not the exterior form of adoration. However, the others have been cured; it was necessary for the lesson which he wished to give, and to prove their ingratitude. But who knows the result of it, and if they have profited by the favor which was accorded them? By saying to the Samaritan: "Your faith has made you well," Jesus gives us to understand that it will not be the same with the others.

THE WITHERED HAND

18. Another time he went into the synagogue and a man with a shriveled hand was there. Some of them were looking for a reason to accuse Jesus, so they watched him closely to see if he would heal him on the Sabbath. Jesus said to the man with the shriveled hand, "Stand up in front of everyone." Then Jesus asked them, "Which is lawful on the Sabbath: to do good or to do evil, to save life or to kill?" But they remained silent. He looked around at them in anger and, deeply distressed at their stubborn hearts, said to the man, "Stretch out your hand." He stretched it out, and his hand was completely restored. Then the Pharisees went out and began to plot with the Herodians how they might kill Jesus. Jesus withdrew with his disciples to the lake, and a large crowd from Galilee followed. When they heard all he was doing, many people came to him from Judea, Jerusalem, Idumea, and the regions across the Jordan and around Tyre and Sidon. (Mark, 3: 1 to 8).

A CRIPPLED WOMAN HEALED ON THE SABBATH

19. On a Sabbath Jesus was teaching in one of the synagogues, and a woman was there who had been crippled by a spirit for eighteen years. She was bent over and could not straighten up at all. When Jesus saw her, he called her forward and said to her, "Woman, you are set free from your infirmity." Then he put his hands on her, and immediately she straightened up and praised God. Indignant because Jesus had healed on the Sabbath, the synagogue ruler said to the people, "There are six days for work. So come and be healed on those days, not on the Sabbath." The Lord answered him, "You hypocrites! Doesn't each of you on the Sabbath untie his ox or donkey from the stall and lead it out to give it water? Then should not this woman, a daughter of Abraham, whom Satan has kept bound for eighteen long years, be set free on the Sabbath day from what bound her?" When he said this, all his opponents were humiliated, but the people were delighted with all the wonderful things he was doing. (Luke, 13: 10 to 17).

20. This fact proves that at this epoch the greater number of maladies were attributed to demons, and that they confounded victims of obsession with people ill from other causes, but in an inverse sense; that is to say, now, those who do not believe in bad spirits think obsession is a pathological malady.

THE HEALING AT THE POOL

21. Some time later, Jesus went up to Jerusalem for a feast of the Jews. Now there is in Jerusalem near the Sheep Gate a pool, which in Aramaic is called Bethesda and which is surrounded by five covered colonnades. Here a great number of disabled people used to lie, the blind, the lame, the paralyzed. One who was there had been an invalid for thirty-eight years. When Jesus saw him lying there and learned that he had been in this condition for a long time, he asked him, "Do you want to get well?" "Sir," the invalid replied, "I have no one to help me into the pool when the water is stirred. While I am trying to get in, someone else goes down ahead of me." Then Jesus said to him, "Get up! Pick up your mat and walk." At once the man was cured; he picked up his mat and walked. The day on which this took place was a Sabbath, and so the Jews said to the man who had been healed, "It is the Sabbath; the law forbids you to carry your mat." But he replied, "The man who made me well said to me, 'Pick up your mat and walk.' " So they asked him, "Who is this fellow who told you to pick it up and walk?" The man who was healed had no idea who it was, for Jesus had slipped away into the crowd that was there. Later Jesus found him at the temple and said to him, "See, you are well again. Stop sinning or something worse may happen to you." The man went away and told the Jews that it was Jesus who had made him well. So, because Jesus was doing these things on the Sabbath, the Jews persecuted him. Jesus said to them, "My Father is always at his work to this very day, and I, too, am working." (John, 5: 1 to 17).

22. Pool (from the Latin pisces, fish) was with the Romans a reservoir or nurse-pond for fish. Later, it was understood to be a public bathing-place.

The Pool of Bethesda, at Jerusalem, was a cistern near the Temple, fed by a natural spring, the water of which possessed healing properties. It was doubtless a circulating fountain, which, at certain times, burst forth with strength, and moved the water. According to common belief, this moment was the most favorable for cures. Perhaps, in reality, at the moment it gushed out, it had more active properties, or that the agitation produced by the gushing water stirred the mud at the bottom, which was beneficial for certain diseases. These effects are natural and perfectly well known now. But then there was but little advance in science, and they saw a supernatural cause for all or the most part of unknown phenomena. The Jews attributed the agitation of this water to the presence of an angel; and this belief seemed to them so much the more reasonable, as at this moment the water was more salutary.

After having cured this man, Jesus said to him: "See, you are well again. Stop sinning or something worse may happen to you." By these words he makes him to understand that his disease was a punishment, and that, if he did not cease sinning, he would be again punished more severely than ever. This doctrine conforms entirely to that which Spiritism teaches.

23. Jesus appears to have taken pains to perform cures on the Sabbath, in order to have occasion to protest against the rigorous observance of the Pharisees of this day. He wished to show them that true piety consisted, not in the observance of forms and of outside things, but in the true worship of the heart. He justifies himself by saying: "My Father is always at his work to this very day, and I, too, am working," that is to say, that God does not suspend the workings of nature on the Sabbath. He continues to produce that which is necessary to your nourishment and health; and I am here to do his will.

THE MAN BORN BLIND

24. As he went along, he saw a man blind from birth. His disciples asked him, "Rabbi, who sinned, this man or his parents, that he was born blind?" "Neither this man nor his parents sinned," said Jesus, "but this happened so that the work of God might be displayed in his life. As long as it is day, we must do the work of him who sent me. Night is coming, when no one can work. While I am in the world, I am the light of the world." Having said this, he spit on the ground, made some mud with the saliva, and put it on the man's eyes. "Go," he told him, "wash in the Pool of Siloam" (this word means Sent). So the man went and washed, and came home seeing. His neighbors and those who had formerly seen him begging asked, "Isn't this the same man who used to sit and beg?" Some claimed that he was. Others said, "No, he only looks like him." But he himself insisted, "I am the man." "How then were your eyes opened?" they demanded. He replied, "The man they call Jesus made some mud and put it on my eyes. He told me to go to Siloam and wash. So I went and washed, and then I could see." "Where is this man?" they asked him. "I don't know," he said. They brought to the Pharisees the man who had been blind. Now the day on which Jesus had made the mud and opened the man's eyes was a Sabbath. Therefore the Pharisees also asked him how he had received his sight. "He put mud on my eyes," the man replied, "and I washed, and now I see." Some of the Pharisees said, "This man is not from God, for he does not keep the Sabbath." But others asked, "How can a sinner do such miraculous signs?" So they were divided. Finally they turned again to the blind man, "What have you to say about him? It was your eyes he opened." The man replied, "He is a prophet." The Jews still did not believe that he had been blind and had received his sight until they sent for the man's parents. "Is this your son?" they asked. "Is this the one you say was born blind? How is it that now he can see?" "We know he is our son," the parents answered, "and we know he was born blind. But how he can see now, or who opened his eyes, we don't know. Ask him. He is of age; he will speak for himself." His parents said this because they were afraid of the Jews, for already the Jews had decided that anyone who acknowledged that Jesus was the Christ would be put out of the synagogue. That was why his parents said, "He is of age; ask him." A second time they summoned the man who had been blind. "Give glory to God," they said." We know this man is a sinner." He replied, "Whether he is a sinner or not, I don't know. One thing I do know. I was blind but now I see!" Then they asked him, "What did he do to you? How did he open your eyes?" He answered, "I have told you already and you did not listen. Why do you want to hear it again? Do you want to become his disciples, too?" Then they hurled insults at him and said, "You are this fellow's disciple! We are disciples of Moses! We know that God spoke to Moses, but as for this fellow, we don't even know where he comes from." The man answered, "Now that is remarkable! You don't know where he comes from, yet he opened my eyes. We know that God does not listen to sinners. He listens to the godly man who does his will. Nobody has ever heard of opening the eyes of a man born blind. 33. If this man were not from God, he could do nothing." To this they replied, "You were steeped in sin at birth; how dare you lecture us!" And they threw him out. (John, 9: 1 to 34).

25. This recital, so simple and artless, carries in itself an evident character of truth. There is nothing marvelous or fantastic about it; it is a scene from real life. The language of this blind man is that of one in which good, natural common sense supplies the place of knowledge, and who combats the arguments of his adversaries with simplicity, yet with an ability which is not wanting in justice. Is not the speech of the Pharisee like that of proud men who think there is no knowledge outside of their own, and that a man of the people is unworthy of a single thought or remonstrance? Barring the name, we have the same kind of people in our day.

To be expelled from the synagogue was equivalent to being excommunicated from the Church. The Spiritists, whose doctrines are those of Christ, interpreted according to the progress of the present light, are treated as the Jews who recognized Jesus as the Messiah. By excommunicating them, they place them outside of the Church, as the scribes and the Pharisees did in regard to the followers of Jesus. In this narrative the man is expelled because he can believe only in him who has cured him, whether he be a sinner or one possessed by a demon, and because he glorifies God for his cure! Is not the same thing done to Spiritists? Because they obtain wise counsel from spirits, have returned to goodness and God, and perform cures, it is said to be the work of the Devil, and anathema is cast at them. Have we not heard priests from the high altar say, "*It is better to remain an incredulous than to return to the faith by Spiritism?*" Have we not heard them tell the sick ones that they must not be cured by Spiritists who possess this gift, because it is a gift from Satan? Have we not heard them telling the sick to reject the bread given by Spiritists, for it is the bread of the devil? What did and said the Jewish priests and Pharisees more than that? Moreover, it is written that the same unbelief must be felt by some at this epoch of the world's history, as in the time of Christ.

This question of the disciples — viz., "Is this man blind because of sin?" — indicates the knowledge of an anterior existence; otherwise no sense could be made of it; for the sin which would be the cause of an infirmity, *which is born with a person*, must have been committed before this birth, and consequently in an anterior existence. If Jesus had recognized a false idea in the question, he would have said to them, "How could this man have sinned before birth?" Instead of that, he replies, that, if this man is blind, it is not because he has sinned, but that the glory of God may be shown in him; i.e., that he must be the instrument of a manifestation of the power of God. If it were not an expiation of the past, it was an experience which must have advanced him towards perfection; for God's laws are just, we have no suffering without compensation.

As to the means employed to cure him, it is evident that the clay formed of soil and saliva obtained its healing properties from the healing fluid with which it was impregnated. Thus the most simple agents — water, for example — can acquire powerful and effective qualities under the action of the spiritual or magnetic fluid, to which they serve as vehicle, *or reservoir.*

The Numerous Cures performed by Jesus

26. Jesus went throughout Galilee, teaching in their synagogues, preaching the good news of the kingdom, and healing every disease and sickness among the people. News about him spread all over Syria, and people brought to him all who were ill with various diseases, those suffering severe pain, the demon-possessed, those having seizures, and the paralyzed, and he healed them. Large crowds from Galilee, the Decapolis, Jerusalem, Judea and the region across the Jordan followed him (Matthew, 4: 23 to 25).

27. Of all the acts which testify to the power of Jesus, without doubt the cures he performed are the most numerous. He wished to prove by that that true power is that which does good; that his object was to render himself useful, and not to satisfy indifferent curiosity by the performance of extraordinary things.

By alleviating suffering, he touched the hearts of men, and made more proselytes than if he had alone gratified their curiosity. By this means he made himself beloved. Whilst, if he had limited himself to producing surprising material effects, as the Pharisees demanded of him, the greater part of the people would have seen in him only a sorcerer or skillful juggler with whom idlers had been amused.

Thus, when John the Baptist sends to him his disciples

to ascertain if he is the Christ, he does not say, "I am he;" for every impostor could have been able to say as much. He does not tell them of the marvelous things he has accomplished, but simply replies, "Go say to John, the blind see, the lame walk, the deaf hear, and the Gospel is preached to the poor." It was equivalent to saying: "recognize me in my works; judge the tree by its fruit:" for there is found the veritable character of the divine mission.

28. It is also by the good it does that Spiritism proves its divine mission. It cures physical evils, but, above all, moral maladies, which are the most important works by which it affirms itself. Its most sincere adepts are not only those who have been astonished by the sight of its extraordinary phenomena, but those who have been touched to the heart by the consolation it gives; those who have been delivered from the tortures of doubt; those whose courage has been sustained by it in affliction, who have drawn strength from the certitude of the future which it has brought to them, with a knowledge of their spiritual being and destiny; those whose faith is unchangeable because they feel it and comprehend.

Those who see in Spiritism only material effects cannot comprehend its moral power; as incredulous, who know it only by its phenomena of which they do not admit its first cause (God), see in Spiritists only jugglers and charlatans. It is then, not by the performance of wonderful works that Spiritism will triumph over incredulity; it is by multiplying its moral benefits. For, if they will not believe in the mighty works it accomplishes, they experience, like all the world, sufferings and afflictions, and no one refuses alleviation and consolation.

THOSE POSSESSED BY AN EVIL SPIRIT

29. They went to Capernaum, and when the Sabbath came, Jesus went into the synagogue and began to teach. The people were amazed at his teaching, because he taught them as one who had authority, not as the teachers of the law. Just then a man in their synagogue who was possessed by an evil spirit cried out, "What do you want with us, Jesus of Nazareth? Have you come to destroy us? I know who you are—the Holy One of God!" "Be quiet!" said Jesus sternly. "Come out of him!" The evil spirit shook the man violently and came out of him with a shriek. The people were all so amazed that they asked each other, "What is this? A new teaching—and with authority! He even gives orders to evil spirits and they obey him." News about him spread quickly over the whole region of Galilee. (Marc, 1: 21 to 28).

30. While they were going out, a man who was demon-possessed and could not talk was brought to Jesus. And when the demon was driven out, the man who had been mute spoke. The crowd was amazed and said, "Nothing like this has ever been seen in Israel." But the Pharisees said, "It is by the prince of demons that he drives out demons." (Matthew, 9: 32 to 34).

31. When they came to the other disciples, they saw a large crowd around them and the teachers of the law arguing with them. As soon as all the people saw Jesus, they were overwhelmed with wonder and ran to greet him. "What are you arguing with them about?" he asked. A man in the crowd answered, "Teacher, I brought you my son, who is possessed by a spirit that has robbed him of speech. Whenever it seizes him, it throws him to the ground. He foams at the mouth, gnashes his teeth and becomes rigid. I asked your disciples to drive out the spirit, but they could not." "O unbelieving generation," Jesus replied, "how long shall I stay with you? How long shall I put up with you? Bring the boy to me." So they brought him. When the spirit saw Jesus, it immediately threw the boy into a convulsion. He fell to the ground and rolled around, foaming at the mouth. Jesus asked the boy's father, "How long has he been like this?" "From childhood," he answered. "It has often thrown him into fire or water to kill him. But if you can do anything, take pity on us and help us." " 'If you can'?" said Jesus. "Everything is possible for him who believes." Immediately the boy's father exclaimed, "I do believe; help me overcome my unbelief!" When Jesus saw that a crowd was running to the scene, he rebuked the evil spirit. "You deaf and mute spirit," he said, "I command you, come out of him and never enter him again." The spirit shrieked, convulsed him violently and came out. The boy looked so much like a corpse that many said, "He's dead." But Jesus took him by the hand and lifted him to his feet, and he stood up. After Jesus had gone indoors, his disciples asked him privately, "Why couldn't we drive it out?" He replied, "This kind can come out only by prayer." (Marc, 9: 14 to 29).

32. Then they brought him a demon-possessed man who was blind and mute, and Jesus healed him, so that he could both talk and see. All the people were astonished and said, "Could this be the Son of David?" But when the Pharisees heard this, they said, "It is only by Beelzebub, the prince of demons, that this fellow drives out demons." Jesus knew their thoughts and said to them, "Every kingdom divided against itself will be ruined, and every city or household divided against itself will not stand. If Satan drives out Satan, he is divided against himself. How then can his kingdom stand? And if I drive out demons by Beelzebub, by whom do your people drive them out? So then, they will be your judges. But if I drive out demons by the Spirit of God, then the kingdom of God has come upon you. (Matthew, 12: 22 to 28).

33. The deliverance of those possessed by evil spirits figure, with the cures, among the most numerous acts of Jesus. Among the facts of this nature there is one that is reported above in n° 30, where the proof of his obsession is not evident. It is probable that then, as now, they attributed to the influence of demons all maladies, of which the cause was unknown, mainly to dumbness, epilepsy, and catalepsy. But there are some cases of it where the action of undeveloped spirits is very evident. They have with those to which we have been witness such a striking analogy, that one recognizes with them all the symptoms of this kind of affection. The proof of the participation of an occult intelligence in similar cases is from the fact that a number of radical cures have been made in some spiritist centers, solely by the evocation and enlightenment of the spirit obsessors, without magnetism or medicine, and often in the absence and at a distance from the patient. The immense superiority of Christ gave to him such authority over imperfect spirits, then called demons, that it was sufficient for him command them to retire; for they could not resist his will (Chap. XIV, n° 46).

34. The narrative of the evil spirits having been sent into the herd of swine is contrary to all probability. Incidentally, it would hardly be explainable the presence of such a numerous amount of pigs in a country wherein that animal was seen as horrendous and useless for nutritional purposes. An evil spirit is no less a human spirit still, though imperfect enough to do evil after death as he did it before; and it is contrary to the laws of nature that he can animate the body of an animal. One sees there the amplification of a real common fact of the ignorance and superstition, or perhaps an allegory to characterize the impure inclinations of certain spirits.

35. Obsession and possession by evil spirits seem to have been very common in Judea in the time of Jesus, which gave him the opportunity of curing many. The undeveloped spirits had no doubt invaded this country, causing an epidemic of the disease (chap. XIV, n° 49).

Without being epidemic, the obsession of individuals is extremely frequent, and presents itself under various aspects which a profound knowledge of Spiritism makes easily recognizable. The health of the individual is often sadly affected by it, either by aggravating organic affections or causing them. Obsessions will some day be inevitably ranged among pathological causes requiring by their special nature special curative means. Spiritism, by making known the cause of the evil, opens a new way for the art of curing, and furnishes to science the means of success where it fails only by a lack of knowledge of the original cause of the evil (*"The Mediums Book,"* chap. 23).

36. Jesus was accused by the Pharisees of exorcising

demons by demons. Even the good he did was, according to them, the work of Satan. They did not reflect that it would make no sense for the Devil to expel his own self. It is well known that the Pharisees of that time already considered all transcendental faculties as supernatural and consequently, as the work of the devil. According to them, Jesus himself received from the Devil such powers. This same doctrine is that which the Church upholds today against spiritual manifestations.[92]

RESURRECTIONS
JAIRUS' DAUGHTER

37. When Jesus had again crossed over by boat to the other side of the lake, a large crowd gathered around him while he was by the lake. Then one of the synagogue rulers, named Jairus, came there. Seeing Jesus, he fell at his feet and pleaded earnestly with him, "My little daughter is dying. Please come and put your hands on her so that she will be healed and live." So Jesus went with him.

While Jesus was still speaking, some men came from

---

[92] All theologians are far from professing absolute opinions upon the subject of demons. Here is that of an ecclesiastic, the value of which the clergy would not know how to call into question. The following passage is found in *"Conferences upon Religion,"* by Monseigneur Freyssinous, Bishop of Hermopolis, vol. II. p. 341. Paris, 1825: "If Jesus had employed evil spirits to cast out demons, the latter would then have been working to destroy their own empire, and Satan would have been employing power against himself. It is certain that a demon who would seek to destroy the reign of vice in order to establish that of virtue must be a strange demon. That is why Jesus replied to the absurd accusation of the Jews, 'If I perform mighty works in the name of the demons, his kingdom must then be divided against itself!' — an answer which admits of no reply." This is precisely the argument which the Spiritists oppose to those who attribute to the evil spirits the good counsels which they receive. The demon would act like a professional thief who would return all that which he had stolen, and engage other thieves to become honest men.

the house of Jairus, the synagogue ruler. "Your daughter is dead," they said. "Why bother the teacher any more?" Ignoring what they said, Jesus told the synagogue ruler, "Don't be afraid; just believe." He did not let anyone follow him except Peter, James and John the brother of James. When they came to the home of the synagogue ruler, Jesus saw a commotion, with people crying and wailing loudly. He went in and said to them, "Why all this commotion and wailing? The child is not dead but asleep." But they laughed at him. After he put them all out, he took the child's father and mother and the disciples who were with him, and went in where the child was. He took her by the hand and said to her, "Talitha koum!" (which means, "Little girl, I say to you, get up!"). Immediately the girl stood up and walked around (she was twelve years old). At this they were completely astonished. He gave strict orders not to let anyone know about this, and told them to give her something to eat. (Marc, 5: 1 to 24 and 35 to 43).

SON OF THE WIDOW OF NAIN

38. Soon afterward, Jesus went to a town called Nain, and his disciples and a large crowd went along with him. As he approached the town gate, a dead person was being carried out—the only son of his mother, and she was a widow. And a large crowd from the town was with her. When the Lord saw her, his heart went out to her and he said, "Don't cry." Then he went up and touched the coffin, and those carrying it stood still. He said, "Young man, I say to you, get up!" The dead man sat up and began to talk, and Jesus gave him back to his mother. They were all filled with awe and praised God. "A great prophet has appeared among us," they said. "God has come to help his people." This news about Jesus spread throughout Judea and the surrounding country. (Luke, 7: 11 to 17).

39. The fact of the return to corporeal life of an individual really dead would be contrary to the laws of nature, and consequently miraculous. Now it is not necessary to go over this order of facts in order to explain the resurrections performed by Jesus.

If among us the appearance of death sometimes deceives our most celebrated physicians, accidents of this nature must have been much more frequent in a country where no precaution in regard to it was taken, and where burials were immediate.[93] In all probability, in the two cases cited above, the disease was syncope or lethargy. Jesus himself tells it positively of the daughter. *"The child,"* said he *"is not dead but asleep."*

With the fluid power which Jesus possessed, there is nothing surprising in the fact that the vivifying fluid, directed by a strong will, should have reanimated the benumbed senses; that he should have been able to recall the spirit to the body which it was ready to leave, as the perispiritual connection was not broken. For men of that time, who believed a person dead when he ceased to breathe, there were resurrections, and they have been able to affirm it in good faith; but they were in reality cures, and not resurrections in the true acceptation of the word.

40. The resurrection of Lazarus, whatever they may say, disaffirms nothing in regard to this principle. He was, they say, for four days in the sepulcher. But it is well known that some attacks of lethargy last eight days or more. They add that he smelt badly, which is a sign of decomposition.

---

[93] A proof of this custom is found in Acts, 5: 5 to 10. When Ananias heard this, he fell down and died. And great fear seized all who heard what had happened. 6. Then the young men came forward, wrapped up his body, and carried him out and buried him.7About three hours later his wife came in, not knowing what had happened. 8Peter asked her, "Tell me, is this the price you and Ananias got for the land? "Yes," she said, "that is the price." 9Peter said to her, "How could you agree to test the Spirit of the Lord? Look! The feet of the men who buried your husband are at the door, and they will carry you out also." 10At that moment she fell down at his feet and died. Then the young men came in and, finding her dead, carried her out and buried her beside her husband.

This allegation proves nothing more, as with some persons there is partial decomposition of the body before death, which is attended by a disagreeable odor. Death arrives only when the organs essential to life are attacked.

And who could be able to know if a disagreeable odor attended him? It was his sister Martha who said it; but how did she know? Lazarus having been buried four days, she could suppose it, but have no certitude of it.[94]

JESUS WALKS UPON THE WATER

41. Immediately Jesus made the disciples get into the boat and go on ahead of him to the other side, while he dismissed the crowd. After he had dismissed them, he went up on a mountainside by himself to pray. When evening came, he was there alone, but the boat was already a considerable distance from land, buffeted by the waves because the wind was against it. During the fourth watch of the night Jesus went out to them, walking on the lake.[95] When the disciples saw him walking on the lake, they were terrified. "It's a ghost," they said, and cried out in fear. But Jesus immediately said to them: "Take courage! It is I don't be afraid." "Lord, if it's you," Peter replied, "tell me to come to you on the water." "Come," he said. Then Peter got down

---

[94] The following fact proves that decomposition sometimes precedes death: In the convent of bon-Pasteur, founded at Toulon by the Abbot Marin, chaplain of the convict-prison for repentant females, was found a young woman who had endured the most terrible suffering with the calmness and impassibility of an expiatory victim. In the midst of the pain she seemed to smile, as if in a celestial vision. Like St. Theresa, she asked to suffer more. Her flesh was in shreds; the gangrene gained upon her limbs. By a wise foresight the doctors recommended the burial of the body immediately after decease. Strange enough! Hardly had she rendered the last sigh than all work of decomposition arrested itself, the death-like exhalations ceased, and during thirty-six hours she remained exposed to the prayers and veneration of the community.

[95] The lake of Gennesaret.

out of the boat, walked on the water and came toward Jesus. But when he saw the wind, he was afraid and beginning to sink, cried out, "Lord, save me!" Immediately Jesus reached out his hand and caught him. "You of little faith," he said, "why did you doubt?" And when they climbed into the boat, the wind died down. Then those who were in the boat worshiped him, saying, "Truly you are the Son of God." (Matthew, 14: 22 to 33).

42. This phenomenon finds its natural explanation in the principles previously explained in chap. XIV, n°43.

Analogous examples prove that it is neither impossible nor miraculous, since it is in the laws of nature. It can be produced in two ways.

Jesus, although living, appeared upon the water under a tangible form, whilst his body was elsewhere. This is the most probable hypothesis. One can even recognize in the recital certain characteristic signs of tangible apparitions (chap. XIV, n° 35 to 37).

On the other hand, his body could have been sustained and weight neutralized by the fluidic-force which maintains a table in space without support. The same effect has many times been produced over human bodies.

TRANSFIGURATION

43. After six days Jesus took Peter, James and John with him and led them up a high mountain, where they were all alone.[96] There he was transfigured before them. His clothes became dazzling white, whiter than anyone in the world could bleach them. And there appeared before them Elijah and Moses, who were talking with Jesus. Peter said to Jesus, "Rabbi, it is good for us to be here. Let us put up three shelters—one for you, one for Moses and one for Elijah." (He did not know what to say, they were

---

[96] The Mount Tabor is located at Southwest of the Lake Tabarich, and 11 km Southeast of Nazareth; it is approximately 1000 meters high.

so frightened.) Then a cloud appeared and enveloped them, and a voice came from the cloud: "This is my Son, whom I love. Listen to him!" Suddenly, when they looked around, they no longer saw anyone with them except Jesus. As they were coming down the mountain, Jesus gave them orders not to tell anyone what they had seen until the Son of Man had risen from the dead. They kept the matter to themselves, discussing what "rising from the dead" meant. (Mark, 9: 2 to 10).

44. The reason for this phenomenon can be found in the properties of this same perispiritual fluid. The transfiguration (explained in chap. XIV, n° 39) is an ordinary circumstance enough, which, in consequence of fluidic-radiation, can change the appearance of an individual; but the purity of the perispirit of Jesus has given to his spirit an exceptional brilliancy. As to the apparitions of Moses and Elijah, they can be accounted for in the same way as similar ones (chap. XIV, from item n° 35 on).

Of all the faculties which have been revealed to us in Jesus, there is not one which is outside or beyond the conditions of humanity, because they are gifts of nature; but, by the superiority of his moral essence and of his fluidic qualities, they attained with him proportions above that of the common. He represented to us, aside from his carnal envelope, the state of pure spirits.

THE TEMPEST STILLED

45. One day Jesus said to his disciples, "Let's go over to the other side of the lake." So they got into a boat and set out. As they sailed, he fell asleep. A squall came down on the lake, so that the boat was being swamped, and they were in great danger. The disciples went and woke him, saying, "Master, Master, we're going to drown!" He got up and rebuked the wind and the raging waters; the storm subsided, and all was calm. "Where is your faith?" he asked his disciples. In fear and amazement they asked one another, "Who is

this? He commands even the winds and the water, and they obey him." (Luke, 8: 22 to 25).

46. We do not yet know enough of the secrets of nature to affirm if there are or not occult intelligences which preside at the action of the elements. In this hypothesis the phenomena in question would be the result of an act of authority over these same intelligences, and would prove a power which has not been given to any man to exercise.

At all events, Jesus, sleeping quietly during the tempest, attests a security which can be explained by this fact, that his spirit saw there was no danger, and that the storm was going to be allayed.

Marriage at Cana - Turning of Water into Wine

47. This miracle, mentioned only in the Gospel of St. John, is indicated as being the first that Jesus had performed; and under this title it ought to have been so much to more remarked upon; but it seems to have produced very little sensation, as no other evangelist mentions it. Such an extraordinary fact ought to have astonished the guests to the highest degree, and, above all, the host himself, who, it seems, had not even perceived it.

Considered by itself, this fact has little importance comparatively with those which truly testify of the spiritual qualities of Jesus. By admitting that things have taken place as they are reported to have done, it is remarkable that it is the sole phenomenon of this kind which he has produced. He was of a nature too elevated to attach himself to purely material effects, calculated solely to attract the curiosity of the crowd, who would have confounded him with a magician. He knew that useful things would obtain him more sympathy, and obtain for his cause more converts than those which could pass for a juggler's tricks, and touch not the heart (n° 27).

However, the act may be clearly explained up to a certain point, to which fluidic-action as well as magnetism offers some examples of having the power of changing the properties of water by giving it the taste of wine; but this hypothesis is not very probable, as in a case of this kind the water has not been of the color of wine, which could not have failed in being remarked. It is more rational to see in it one of those parables so frequent in the teachings of Jesus, like that of the "prodigal son," "the marriage feast," "the dry fig-tree," "the parable of the bad rich man," and many others. He made during the repast an allusion to the wine and water, whence he would have evoked a moral. That which justifies this opinion are the words which have been spoken in regard to it by the ruler of the feast, — "Everyone brings out the choice wine first and then the cheaper wine after the guests have had too much to drink; but you have saved the best till now."

Between these two hypothesis, one should prefer the most rational; Spiritists are not so credulous as to see manifestations everywhere, neither are they so conclusive in their opinions as to wish to explain everything by means of fluids.

THE MIRACLE OF THE MULTIPLICATION OF BREAD

48. This miracle of the bread is one of those which have puzzled commentators, and diverted the imagination of the incredulous. Without giving themselves the trouble to look for the allegorical sense of it, the latter have seen in it only a puerile history; but the greater number of serious men have seen in this recital, although under a form different from the ordinary one, a parable comparing the spiritual nourishment of the soul with the nourishment of the body.

One can see in it, however, more than one metaphor, and admit at a certain point of view the reality of a material effect, without resorting to belief in the miracle of it. One knows that in great preoccupation of mind, caused by giving undivided attention to a certain thing, hunger is forgotten. Now, those who followed Jesus were people greedy to hear him. There is nothing astonishing in the fact, that, having been fascinated by his words, and perhaps also by the powerful magnetic action which he exercised over them, they had not felt the need of eating.

Jesus, who foresaw this result, has been able to tranquilize his disciples by saying, in the figurative language which was habitual to him, that they had really brought some bread with them, and that this would satisfy the needs of the multitude. At the same time he gave to the latter a lesson: "You give them something to eat," said he. He taught them by that, that they also must nourish them by the word.

Thus, beside the moral allegorical sense, he has been able to produce a well-known, natural, psychological effect. The wonderful part in this case is the great power of his words, which have captivated the attention of an immense crowd to such a point as to make them forget the necessities of the body. This moral power testifies the superiority of Jesus much more than the purely material fact of the multiplication of bread, which must have been considered as an allegory.

This explanation is found confirmed by Jesus himself in the following passages:

The Yeast of the Pharisees and Sadducees

49. When they went across the lake, the disciples forgot to take bread. "Be careful," Jesus said to them. "Be on your guard against the yeast of the Pharisees and Sadducees." They discussed this among themselves and said, "It is because we didn't bring any bread." Aware of their discussion, Jesus asked, "You of little faith, why are you talking among yourselves about having no bread? Do you still not understand? Don't you remember the five loaves for the five thousand, and how many basketfuls you gathered? Or the seven loaves for the four thousand, and how many basketfuls you gathered? How is it you don't understand that I was not talking to you about bread? But be on your guard against the yeast of the Pharisees and Sadducees." Then they understood that he was not telling them to guard against the

yeast used in bread, but against the teaching of the Pharisees
and Sadducees. (Matthew, 16: 5 to 12).

JESUS THE BREAD OF LIFE, OR MANNA

50. The next day the crowd that had stayed on the
opposite shore of the lake realized that only one boat had
been there, and that Jesus had not entered it with his disciples,
but that they had gone away alone. Then some boats from
Tiberias landed near the place where the people had eaten
the bread after the Lord had given thanks. Once the crowd
realized that neither Jesus nor his disciples were there, they
got into the boats and went to Capernaum in search of Jesus.
When they found him on the other side of the lake, they asked
him, "Rabbi, when did you get here?" Jesus answered, "I
tell you the truth, you are looking for me, not because you
saw miraculous signs but because you ate the loaves and had
your fill. Do not work for food that spoils, but for food that
endures to eternal life, which the Son of Man will give you.
On him God the Father has placed his seal of approval."
Then they asked him, "What must we do to do the works
God requires?" Jesus answered, "The work of God is this:
to believe in the one he has sent." So they asked him, "What
miraculous sign then will you give that we may see it and
believe you? What will you do? Our forefathers ate the
manna in the desert; as it is written: 'He gave them bread
from heaven to eat.'" Jesus said to them, "I tell you the truth,
it is not Moses who has given you the bread from heaven, but
it is my Father who gives you the true bread from heaven.
For the bread of God is he who comes down from heaven
and gives life to the world." "Sir," they said, "from now on
give us this bread." Then Jesus declared, "I am the bread of
life. He who comes to me will never go hungry, and he who
believes in me will never be thirsty. But as I told you, you
have seen me and still you do not believe. I tell you the truth,
he who believes has everlasting life. I am the bread of life.
Your forefathers ate the manna in the desert, yet they died.

50. But here is the bread that comes down from heaven, which a man may eat and not die. (John, 6: 22 to 36 and 47 to 50).

51. In the first passage, Jesus, by recalling the effect previously produced, gives us clearly to understand that he was not acting with material bread; otherwise the comparison which he established with the yeast of the Pharisees had been without object. "Don't you remember the five loaves for the five thousand, and how many basketfuls you gathered? Or the seven loaves for the four thousand, and how many basketfuls you gathered? How is it you don't understand that I was not talking to you about bread? But be on your guard against the yeast of the Pharisees and Sadducees." This reproach was given them for having had a material idea of the multiplication. The act had been extraordinary enough in itself to have struck the imagination of his disciples, who however appeared not to have remembered it.

This idea is set forth no less clearly from the speech of Jesus upon the bread from heaven, or manna, in which he tries to make them comprehend in the true sense the value of spiritual nourishment. "Work," said he, "not for food that spoils, but for food that endures to eternal life, which the Son of Man will give you." This nourishment is his word, which is the bread descended from heaven, and which gives life to the world. "I am the bread of life," said he: *"he who comes to me will never go hungry, and he who believes in me will never be thirsty."*

But these distinctions were too subtle for these rough natures, who could comprehend only tangible things. The manna which had fed their ancestors was the true bread from heaven to them: there was the miracle. If, then, the act of producing bread had taken place materially, why should these same men, for whose profit it was produced a few days before, say to Jesus: "What miraculous sign then will you give that we may see it and believe you? What will you do?" It is evident they understood miracles to be the mighty works which the Pharisees demanded; i.e., signs from heaven as commanded with the wand of an enchanter. Those which Jesus did were too simple, and did not depart enough from the laws of nature. The cures even were not sufficiently extraordinary. The spiritual miracles were not material enough for them.

TEMPTATION OF JESUS

52. Jesus transported by the Devil to the pinnacle of the temple, from thence to the summit of a mountain, and tempted by him, is one of these parables so common with him, which public credulity has transformed into material fact.

53. The following explanation is taken from a teaching given by a spirit on this subject:

"Jesus was not carried by an evil spirit, as above affirmed; but he wished to make men comprehend that humanity is subject to failure, and that it must always be on guard against the bad inspirations to which its weak nature is subjected. The temptation of Jesus is, then, a figure of speech, and one must be blind to take it literally. Why would you desire that the Messiah, the 'Word' of God incarnate, should be submitted for a time, however short, to the suggestions of the Devil; and that, as the evangelist Luke writes, the Devil had quitted him for a time, which would make one imagine that he would yet be submitted to his power? No; comprehend better the teachings which have been given you. The Spirit of Evil had no power over the Spirit of Goodness. No one has been said to have seen Jesus upon the temple or upon the mountain. Certainly, if it had been a fact, it would have been noticed by the people. The temptation was then not a material or physical act. As to the moral side of it, could you admit that the spirit of darkness could tempt him who knew his origin and power with the words: 'Adore me, and I will give you all the kingdoms of the Earth?' The devil in that case must have been ignorant of who he was, to whom he made such offers, which is not probable. If he knew him, his proposition was nonsensical; for he must have well known that he would repel one who came to ruin his empire over men.

"Comprehend the sense of this parable; for it is one, as well as the '*Prodigal Son*' and the '*Good Samaritan*.' One shows us the dangers men run if they resist not this inmost voice, which constantly cries, 'you can be more than you are; you can possess more than you now possess; you can grow great, increase, acquire. Listen to the voice of ambition, and all your wishes will be fulfilled.' It shows to you the danger and the means of evading it, by saying to the evil inspirations, '*Away from me, Satan!*' or, in other words: '*go away from me, temptation.*'

The other two parables show what hope there is for him who, too feeble to cope with temptation, has succumbed to it. It shows you the father blessing the repentant child, and according to him with love the pardon implored. They show you that the guilty, the schismatic, the man who is repelled by his brother, as being worth more in the eyes of the Supreme Judge than those who despise him because that he practices the virtues taught by the law of love.

"Weigh well the teachings given in the Gospels; learn to distinguish the proper sense from the figurative; and the errors which have blinded you so many centuries will, little by little, be effaced, in order to make place for the brilliant light of truth." — Bordeaux, 1862, by St. John the Evangelist.

Remarkable Phenomena at the Death of Jesus

54. From the sixth hour until the ninth hour darkness came over all the land. About the ninth hour Jesus cried out in a loud voice, "Eloi, Eloi, lama sabachthani?"- which means, "My God, my God, why have you forsaken me?" At that moment the curtain of the temple was torn in two from top to bottom. The Earth shook and the rocks split. The tombs broke open and the bodies of many holy people who had died were raised to life. They came out of the tombs, and after Jesus' resurrection they went into the holy city and appeared to many people. (Matthew, 27: 45 and 51 to 53).

55. It is strange that such mighty works, being accomplished at the moment even when the attention of the city was fixed upon the anguish of Jesus, which was the event of the day, should not have been remarked upon. As no historian mentions it, it seems impossible that an earthquake and darkness for three hours covered the face of the Earth, in a country where the heavens are in a constant state of limpidness, should have passed unnoticed.

The duration of this obscurity is about that of the eclipse of the sun; but this kind of an eclipse is produced only with the new moon, and the death of Jesus took place during the full moon, the 14th of the month of Nissan, the Passover of the Jews.

The obscuration of the sun may have been produced also by the spots which are observed upon its surfaces. In similar cases the brilliancy of the light is sensibly affected, but never to the point of producing obscurity and darkness. To suppose an obscuration of this kind took place at this epoch would be to assign to it a perfectly natural cause.[97]

As to the dead having been raised from their graves, perhaps *some persons* have seen visions or apparitions, which is not exceptional; but, as then they knew not the cause of these phenomena, they imagined the individuals who appeared came out of their sepulchers.

The disciples of Jesus, excited by the death of their master, have, without doubt, attached some particular facts to it, attention to which would not have been drawn at any other time. To men predisposed to the marvelous, a fragment of rock being detached at this time would have given them ample cause to say the rocks were mysteriously rent.

Jesus is great by his works, but not in the fantastical

---

[97] There are constantly on the surface of the sun fixed spots, which follow its rotational movement, and have served to determine the duration of it. But these spots sometimes increase in number, extent, and intensity, at which times a diminution in light and heat is produced. This augmentation in the number of spots appears to coincide with certain astronomical phenomena and the relative position of some planets, which occasions its periodical return. The duration of this obscuration is very variable. Sometimes it is only for two or three hours, but in 535 A.D. there was one which lasted fourteen months.

pictures with only an unenlightened enthusiasm must have
surrounded him.

APPEARANCES OF JESUS AFTER DEATH

56. "They have taken my Lord away," she said, "and
I don't know where they have put him." At this, she turned
around and saw Jesus standing there, but she did not realize
that it was Jesus. "Woman," he said, "why are you crying?
Who is it you are looking for?" Thinking he was the gardener,
she said: "Sir, if you have carried him away, tell me where
you have put him, and I will get him." Jesus said to her:
"Mary." She turned toward him and cried out in Aramaic:
"Rabboni!" (which means Teacher). Jesus said: "Do not hold
on to me, for I have not yet returned to the Father. Go instead
to my brothers and tell them, I am returning to my Father
and your Father, to my God and your God." Mary
Magdalene went to the disciples with the news: "I have
seen the Lord!" And she told them that he had said these
things to her. (John, 20: 14 to 18).

57. Now that same day two of them were going to a
village called Emmaus, about seven miles from Jerusalem.
They were talking with each other about everything that had
happened. As they talked and discussed these things with each
other, Jesus himself came up and walked along with them:
but they were kept from recognizing him. 17. He asked them,
"What are you discussing together as you walk along?" They
stood still, their faces downcast. One of them, named Cleopas,
asked him: "Are you only a visitor to Jerusalem and do not
know the things that have happened there in these days?"
"What things?" he asked. "About Jesus of Nazareth," they
replied. "He was a prophet, powerful in word and deed before
God and all the people. The chief priests and our rulers handed
him over to be sentenced to death, and they crucified him;
but we had hoped that he was the one who was going to redeem
Israel. And what is more, it is the third day since all this took
place. In addition, some of our women amazed us. They went

to the tomb early this morning but didn't find his body. They came and told us that they had seen a vision of angels, who said he was alive. Then some of our companions went to the tomb and found it just as the women had said, but him they did not see." He said to them: "How foolish you are, and how slow of heart to believe all that the prophets have spoken! Did not the Christ have to suffer these things and then enter his glory?" And beginning with Moses and all the Prophets, he explained to them what was said in all the Scriptures concerning himself. As they approached the village to which they were going, Jesus acted as if he were going farther. But they urged him strongly: "Stay with us, for it is nearly evening; the day is almost over." So he went in to stay with them. When he was at the table with them, he took bread, gave thanks, broke it and began to give it to them. Then their eyes were opened and they recognized him, and he disappeared from their sight. They asked each other: "Were not our hearts burning within us while he talked with us on the road and opened the Scriptures to us?" They got up and returned at once to Jerusalem. There they found the Eleven and those with them, assembled together and saying: "It is true! The Lord has risen and has appeared to Simon." Then the two told what had happened on the way, and how Jesus was recognized by them when he broke the bread. While they were still talking about this, Jesus himself stood among them and said to them: "Peace be with you." They were startled and frightened, thinking they saw a ghost. He said to them: "Why are you troubled, and why do doubts rise in your minds? Look at my hands and my feet. It is I myself! Touch me and see; a ghost does not have flesh and bones, as you see I have." When he had said this, he showed them his hands and feet. And while they still did not believe it because of joy and amazement, he asked them: "Do you have anything here to eat?" They gave him a piece of broiled fish, and he took it and ate it in their presence. He said to them: "This is what I told you while I was still with you: Everything must be fulfilled that is written about me in the Law of Moses, the Prophets and the Psalms." Then he opened their minds so they could understand the Scriptures. He told them: "This is what is written: The Christ will suffer and rise from the dead on the third day, and repentance and forgiveness of sins will be preached in his name to all nations, beginning at Jerusalem. You are witnesses of these things. I am going to send you what my Father has promised; but stay in the city until you have been clothed with power from on high." (Luke, 24: 13 to 49).

58. Now Thomas (called Didymus), one of the Twelve, was not with the disciples when Jesus came. So the other disciples told him, "We have seen the Lord! "But he said to them, "Unless I see the nail marks in his hands and put my finger where the nails were, and put my hand into his side, I will not believe it." A week later his disciples were in the house again, and Thomas was with them. Though the doors were locked, Jesus came and stood among them and said, "Peace be with you!" Then he said to Thomas, "Put your finger here; see my hands. Reach out your hand and put it into my side. Stop doubting and believe." Thomas said to him, "My Lord and my God!" Then Jesus told him, "Because you have seen me, you have believed; blessed are those who have not seen and yet have believed." (John, 20: 24 to 29).

59. Afterward Jesus appeared again to his disciples, by the Sea of Tiberias. It happened this way: Simon Peter, Thomas (called Didymus), Nathanael from Cana in Galilee, the sons of Zebedee, and two other disciples were together. "I'm going out to fish," Simon Peter told them, and they said, "We'll go with you." So they went out and got into the boat, but that night they caught nothing. Early in the morning, Jesus stood on the shore, but the disciples did not realize that it was Jesus. He called out to them, "Friends, haven't you any fish?" "No," they answered. He said, "Throw your net on the right side of the boat and you will find some." When they did, they were unable to haul the net in because of the large number of fish. Then the disciple whom Jesus loved said to Peter, "It is the Lord!" As soon as Simon Peter heard him say, "It is the Lord," he wrapped his outer garment around him (for he had taken it off) and jumped into the water. The other disciples followed in the boat, towing the net full of fish, for they were not far from shore, about a hundred yards. (John, 21: 1 to 8).

60. When he had led them out to the vicinity of Bethany, he lifted up his hands and blessed them. While he was blessing them, he left them and was taken up into heaven. Then they worshiped him and returned to Jerusalem with great joy. And they stayed continually at the temple, praising God. (Luke, 24: 50 to 53).

61. The appearance of Jesus after death is reported by all the evangelists with circumstantial details, which will not allow us to doubt the reality of the fact. They are, besides, perfectly explained by the fluidic laws and properties of the perispirit, and present nothing anomalous to the phenomena of the same kind of which ancient and contemporaneous history offers numerous examples, without excepting the tangibility of the form presented. If one observes the circumstances which have attended his diverse appearances, one recognizes in him at these moments all the characters of a fluidic being. He appeared and disappeared unexpectedly; he was seen by some, and not by others, under a guise not recognized even by his disciples; he appeared to them in closed rooms, where a carnal body could not have penetrated; his language even has not the animation of a corporeal being; he has the tone which is brief and sententious, peculiar to spirits who manifest in this manner. His whole manner, in short, is not that of a denizen of the terrestrial sphere. The sight of him causes at the same time surprise and fear. His disciples, in seeing him, speak no more to him with the old freedom; they feel that he is a man no more.

Jesus then showed his perispiritual body to them, which explains why he was seen only by those to whom he desired to make himself known. If he had worn his carnal body, he would have been seen by the first comer as in life. His disciples, being ignorant of the first cause of the phenomenon of apparitions, took no account of these peculiarities, which were not probably remarked. They saw Jesus, and touched him; for them it was the resurrected body (chap. XIV, n° 14 and 35 to 38).

62. Whilst incredulity rejects all facts accomplished by Jesus having a supernatural aspect, and considers them without exception as legends, Spiritism gives the greater part of them a natural explanation. It proves their possibility, not alone by the theory of the fluidic laws, but by their identity with analogous facts produced by a multitude of persons in the most common conditions. Since these facts are in some respects public property, they prove nothing, in principle, touching the exceptional nature of Jesus.[98]

63. The greatest miracle Jesus has performed — that which truly attests his superiority — is the revolution his teachings have made in the world, notwithstanding his limited field of action.

Jesus was indeed poor, obscure, born in a most humble condition among a despised people, very ignorant, and without political, artistic, or literary influence. He preached only three years. During this time, so short in duration, he was despised and persecuted by his fellow-citizens, calumniated and treated as an impostor; he was often obliged to flee, in order to escape stoning; he was betrayed by one

---

[98] The numerous contemporaneous facts of cures, apparitions, possessions, second sight, etc., which are related in the "Revue Spirite," and recalled in the above notes, offer, even to circumstances of detail, such a striking analogy to those which the evangelist reports, that their similarity in cause and effect are evident. One naturally asks why the natural cause of today should be a supernatural one in another epoch of the world's history, — diabolical with some, and divine with others. If it had been possible to have compared the two together here at greater length, the comparison would have been easier; but their number, and the elaborate explanations which the greater part necessitate, have not permitted of it.

of his own apostles, denied by another, and forsaken by all at the moment when he fell into the hands of his enemies. He did only good; but that did not shelter him from malevolence, which turned against him even the blessings which he bestowed. Condemned to the death reserved for criminals, he died ignored by the world; for contemporary history is silent in regard to him.[99] He has written nothing himself; however, aided by some obscure men like himself, his words have been sufficient to regenerate the world. His doctrine has killed all-powerful paganism, and has become the torch of civilization. He had against him all that can possibly foil men in an earthly career. This is the reason why we say that the triumph of his doctrine is the greatest of his miracles; at the same time, it proves his divine mission. If, in place of social and regenerative principles, founded upon the spiritual future of man, he had offered to posterity only a few marvelous facts, scarcely would his name be mentioned today.

DISAPPEARANCE OF THE BODY OF JESUS

64. The disappearance of the body of Jesus after his death has been the subject of many controversies. It has been attested by the four evangelists, upon the evidence of the women who presented themselves at the sepulcher the third day, and did not find him there. Some have seen in this disappearance a miraculous occurrence; while others have supposed a clandestine removal to have taken place.

According to another opinion, Jesus could not ever have been invested with a common carnal body, but only with a fluidic one; that he could have been during his whole life only partly tangible, — in a word, a sort of *agénère*. His birth, judged from his stand-point, his death, and all the acts of his life must have been only appearances. Thus they say his body returned

---

[99] The Jewish historian, Josephus, is the only one who speaks of him, and he writes very little in respect to him.

to the fluidic state, and was able to disappear from the sepulcher; and with this same body he appeared to friends after death.

Without doubt, a similar fact is not radically impossible, after that which one knows today of the properties of fluids; but it would be at least entirely exceptional, and in formidable opposition to the usual character of the *agénères* (chap. XIV, n° 36). The question then is, if such a hypothesis is admissible, if it is confirmed or contradicted by facts.

65. There are two periods in the sojourn of Jesus upon the Earth, — that which preceded, and that which followed his death. In the first, from the moment of conception until birth, all things occur, with respect to his mother, as in ordinary conditions of life.[100] From his birth until death, in all his acts, languages, and the diverse circumstances of his life, there are presented unmistakable evidences of corporeity. The phenomena of the psychic order which were produced through him were only occasional, and were not anomalous, since they are explained by the properties of the perispirit, and are developed in different degrees of power in other individuals. After his death, to the contrary, he is revealed to us as a fluidic being. The difference between the two states is so distinctly defined, that it is not possible to assimilate them.

Properly speaking, the carnal body has the inherent properties of matter, which differ essentially from those of the ethereal fluids. Disintegration is brought about by rupture of molecular cohesion. A sharp instrument by cutting into the material body divides its tissues. If the essential organs of life are attacked, the exercise of the functions is arrested, and death ensues; that is to say, the death of the body. This cohesion, existing not in the fluidic body, life reposes not on the play of special organs, and cannot be affected by analogous disorders. A sharp instrument, or any other, penetrates it, as it would vapor, without occasioning any harm. This is the reason why

---

[100] We do not speak here of the mystery of the incarnation, which will subsequently be examined.

this kind of body can *never die*, and why fluidic beings, designated by the name of *agénères*, can never be killed.

After the crucifixion of Jesus, his body remained inert and without life. It was buried like an ordinary corpse; and all could see him and touch him. After his resurrection, when he desires to quit the Earth, he does not die. He is raised, he vanished, disappeared, without leaving any trace behind, — an evident proof that this body was of another nature than that which perished upon the cross; whence it is necessary to conclude, that, if Jesus died, he had a carnal body.

In consequence of its material properties, the carnal body is the seat of the sensations and physical pains which are echoed in the sensitive center, or spirit. It is not the body which suffers: it is the spirit which receives the rebound of the injury or wounds to the organic tissues. A body deprived of spirit sensation feels absolutely no sensation; while the spirit, which has no material body, cannot experience sufferings which are the result of injury to matter; whence it is necessary to conclude, that if Jesus suffered materially, as one cannot doubt, it was because he had a material body in nature similar to our own.

66. To the material facts many powerful moral considerations must be added.

If Jesus had been, during his life, in the condition of fluidic being, he would have experienced neither pain nor any of the necessities of the material body. To suppose him to have been thus is to take away from him all the merit of a life of suffering and privation, which he chose as an example of resignation. If all this in him was only appearance, all the acts of his life — the reiterated announcement of his death, the sad scene in the garden of Gethsemane, his prayer to God to let, if possible, the cup pass from his lips, his passion, his agony, all, even to his last sigh at the moment of rendering up the spirit — would only be a vain show, a mockery of nature, making an illusory sacrifice of his life appear real. Such would be a comedy unworthy of a simple, honest man, and one much more unworthy of so superior a being; in short, it would have been the abuse of the good faith of his contemporaries and of posterity. Such are the logical sequences of this system of belief, sequences which are not admissible; for it lowers it morally instead of elevating it.

Jesus must then have had, like everybody else, a carnal and a spiritual body, which the material and physic phenomena of his life attest.

67. This idea upon the nature of the body of Jesus is not new. In the fourth century Apollinarius of Laodicea, chief of the sect of the *Apollinarists*, assumed that Jesus had not taken a body like ours, but one incapable of *harm or pain*, which had descended from heaven on the breast of the Virgin Saint, and was not born of her, that thus Jesus had been born, had suffered, and was dead only in *appearance*. The Apollinarists were anathematized at the Council of Alexandria in 360, in that of Rome in 374, and in that of Constantinople in 381.

The *Docetists*, (from the Greek *dokein*, to appear), a numerous sect among the Gnostics, had the same belief; this cult subsisted during the first three centuries A.D.

Chapter XVI
PROPHECIES IN THE LIGHT OF SPIRITISM

THEORY OF FOREKNOWLEDGE

1. How is it possible to obtain a knowledge of the future? One comprehends how to predict events which are a consequence of the present state of things, but not of those which have no connection with this, and still less of which are attributed to chance. Future things, they say, do not exist. They are still in nothingness. How then can one know that they will come? The examples of verified predictions are, however, numerous enough, from whence it is necessary to conclude it is a phenomenon of which we have not the key; for there is no effect without a cause. It is this cause we are seeking; and it is Spiritism, the key to so many mysteries, which will furnish it to us. Moreover, we will show that the fact of the predictions themselves is not obtained by a departure from the natural laws.

Let us take, as a comparison, an example in common things, which will aid us to make the principle which we have to develop better understood.

2. Let us suppose a man placed upon a high mountain, and considering the vast extent of the plain. In this situation the distance of a league, or three miles, will be a very short distance seemingly and he will easily embrace with a glance of the eye all the undulations of the Earth from commencement to the end of the route. The traveler who follows this route for the first time knows that by marching he will arrive at the end. There is a simple foreknowledge of the consequence of his march; but the unevenness of the route, the ascents and descents, the rivers to cross, the woods to traverse, the precipices from which he may fall, the places where thieves may be stationed to waylay him, the inns where he will be able to repose – all this is independent of his personal knowledge. It is for him the unknown, the future, because his sight extends not beyond the little circle which surrounds him. As to the continuance of it, he measures it by the time that it takes him to go from one point to another of the route. Take away from him the knowledge of the data of the route, and his knowledge of its continuance is effaced. For the man who is on the mountain, and who follows with the eye of the traveler, all this is the present. Let us suppose that he comes down, and says to the traveler, "At such a moment you will encounter such a thing; you will be attacked and delivered." He will predict the future to him; for it is the future to the pedestrian, but the present to the man of the mountain.

3. If we depart now from the circle of things purely material, and if we enter by thought into the domain of spiritual life, we will see this phenomenon produced upon a grander scale. The dematerialized spirits are like the man of the mountain. Space and duration of time are to them no more; but the extent and penetration of their sight are in proportion to their purification and to their elevation in the spiritual hierarchy. They are in connection with inferior spirits, like the man armed with a powerful telescope beside him who has only his eyes to see with. With the latter their view is circumscribed, not only because it can only with difficulty go far away from the globe to which they are attached, but because the coarseness of their perispirit veils distant things, as the fog does for the eyes of the body.

One understands then that, according to the degree of perfection to which a spirit has attained, it can foretell the events of a period of a few years; for what is a century in the presence of infinitude? The events do not successively unroll themselves like the incidents on the route of the traveler. He sees simultaneously the commencement and the end of the period. All the events, which in this period are the future for the man of the Earth, are for him the present. He will be able to tell us with certitude: such a thing will happen at this epoch, because he sees this thing, as the man of the mountain sees that which awaits the traveler on his route. If he does not inform him of it, it is because the knowledge of the future would be hurtful to the man; it might trammel his free will; it might paralyze him in the work which he must accomplish for his progress. The good and the evil which await him, being unknown to him, are the trial for him.

If such a faculty, even in a limited state, can be one of the attributes of the creature, to what a degree of power must it not be elevated in the Creator, who embraces infinitude? For him time does not exist; the commencement and the end of worlds are the present. In this immense panorama, what is the duration of the life of a man, of a generation, of a people?

4. However, as man must concur in the general progress, and as certain events must result from his cooperation, he can be useful in certain cases if he has a knowledge of these events, in order that he may prepare the way for them, and hold himself ready to act when the right moment comes. That is the reason God permits sometimes a corner of the veil to be lifted; but it is always for a useful object, and never to satisfy a vain curiosity. This mission can then be given not to all spirits; for there are some who know the future no better than men, but to some spirits sufficiently advanced for that. Now, it is well to observe that this kind of revelation is always made spontaneously, and never, or very rarely at least, in response to a direct demand.

5. This mission can equally be given to certain men in this manner:

He, to whom is confided the care of revealing a concealed fact, can receive in his ignorance, the inspiration of the spirits who know it, and then he transmits it mechanically, without rendering an account of them to himself. It is known besides that either during sleep, in a waking state, or in the ecstasies of second sight, the soul leaves the body, and is possessed in a greater or less degree with the faculties of the free spirit. If he is an advanced spirit, if he has, above all, like the prophets, received a special mission for this effect, he enjoys, in the moments of emancipation of the soul, the faculty of embracing by himself a greater or less extent of time, and sees as present the events of this period. He can then reveal them at the same instant, or preserve the memory of them for his awakening. If these events must remain a secret, he will lose the remembrance of them, or there will remain with him only a vague intuition of them sufficient to guide him.

6. Thus is this faculty seen developed on providential occasions, in imminent dangers, in great calamities, in revolutions; and the greater numbers of sects which have been persecuted have had numbers of *prophets*. Thus inspired by these visions, great captains are seen resolutely marching towards the enemy with a certitude of victory, that men of genius, like Christopher Columbus, for example, have pursued an object, predicting the moment when they will attain it. The reason for this is, they have seen this object accomplished in prophetic vision.

The gift of prophecy is then no more supernatural than a multitude of other phenomena. It is based upon the properties of the soul, and the law of connection between the spiritual and material worlds, which Spiritism has come to explain.

This theory of foresight does not solve, perhaps, in an absolutely correct manner, all cases which can be presented as revelations of the future; but one cannot deny that it is based on a truly fundamental principle.

7. Frequently, the person gifted with a faculty capable of foreseeing the future, either in ecstasy or in a somnambulistic state sees the events as if they were being drawn on a picture. The idea of a photograph of the thought could also explain this occurrence. Let us suppose an event is in the thought of a spirit responsible for its accomplishment, or in the thought of those whose acts should provoke them. Such thought, upon crossing the space, as sound crosses the air, can form an image which is visible by the clairvoyant. However, because its accomplishment can be either hastened or delayed depending upon the circumstances, he sees the facts without being able to determine the moment of its accomplishment. Perhaps this thought could be only a projection, a desire, which could not be translated into reality. Hence, we have the frequent errors regarding facts and dates in such previsions (Chap. XIV, from item n° 13 on).

8. In order to comprehend spiritual things – that is to say, to form as distinct an idea as that we make of a landscape before our eyes – there truly fails us a sense, exactly as the necessary sense is wanting to the blind man to comprehend the effects of light, of colors, and of sight, without contact with them. Thus it is only by an effort of the imagination we attain to it, and by the aid of comparisons drawn from familiar things. But some material things can give only very imperfect ideas of spiritual ones. On this account it is best not to take the comparisons which have been drawn too literally, and believe, for example, that the spirit is held at such an elevation as has been stated in one comparison, or that they are obliged to be upon mountains, or above the clouds, in order to see into time and space.

This faculty is inherent to a state of spiritualization or of dematerialization: that is to say, that spiritualization produces an effect which can be compared, though very imperfectly, with that view of the whole which a man has on the mountain-top. The object of this comparison was simply to show that some events, which are in the future to some, are in the present for others, and thus can be predicted which does not imply that the effect is produced in the same manner.

In order to enjoy this perception it is not necessary that the spirit should transport himself to any point in space whatever. He who is on Earth at our side can possess it in its plentitude as well as if he were a thousand miles away, although we see nothing beyond the horizon of our material vision. Sight, with spirits, not being produced in the same manner or with the same elements as with man, their visual horizon is entirely different; this is something that we have not the sense to conceive. *The spirit beside the incarnated one is a person with good eyes beside a blind man.*

9. It is also necessary to figure to one's self that this perception is not limited by extent of space, but that it comprehends penetration in all things. It is, we repeat, an inherent faculty proportioned to the state of dematerialization. This faculty is *weakened* by incarnation, but not completely deadened, because the soul has not been enclosed in the body as in a box. The incarnated being possesses it, although in a lesser degree than when free from matter; it is this that gives to some men a penetrating power, which is totally lacking in others, greater justice in a moral point of view, and a quicker comprehension of things beyond the material world.

Not only the mind perceives, but it remembers that which it has been seen in a spiritual state; and this remembrance is like a picture traced on its thoughts. In incarnation it sees but vaguely, as through a veil; in a liberated state, it sees and conceives clearly. *The principle of sight is not outside itself,* but within it: thus there is no need of our exterior light. By moral development the circle of our ideas and conception is enlarged. By the gradual dematerialization of the perispirit the latter is purified of the coarse elements which affect the delicacy of the perceptions, whence it is easy to comprehend that the extension of all the faculties follow spiritual progress.

10. It is the degree of extension of the spiritual faculties which, in incarnation, render it more or less apt to conceive of spiritual things. At the same time this aptitude is not the necessary consequence of the development of intelligence; common science does not give it. Thus we see men of great learning as blind in spiritual things as others are in material ones; they are stubborn in regard to spiritual things, because they do not understand them. The reason for which is, their progress in this respect is not yet accomplished; whilst one sees persons of an inferior intelligence and knowledge grasp them with the greatest facility, which proves that the latter have obtained the necessary preliminary intuition of it. It is with them a retrospective remembrance of that which they have seen and known either as a wandering spirit, or in their anterior existences, as others have the intuition of languages and sciences which they have possessed.

11. As to the future of Spiritism, the spirits are

unanimous in affirming the near triumph of it, notwithstanding the opposition it receives. This foresight comes easy to them, firstly, because that its propagation is their own personal work. Concurring in the movement or directing it, they know, consequently, what they must do. Secondly, it is sufficient for them to know that it is within a short time, and in this period they see upon the way the powerful auxiliaries which God raises up for them, and which will not be tardy in manifesting themselves.

Without being discarnated spirits, let the Spiritists carry themselves by thought thirty years in advance of this time, to the bosom of the generation which is now being educated by it; let them from that point consider what is taking place today; follow this main spring of action, and they will see those who think they are called to overturn it worn out in their vain endeavors. They will see them gradually disappear from the scene, while this tree, constantly increasing in magnitude, will take deeper root each day.

12. The common events of private life are nearly always governed by the different traits of character manifested by each individual. Some will succeed according to his capacities, his knowledge of things, his energy and perseverance, while another will fail by want of these traits; whilst we can truly say that each one is the "architect of his own future," which is never submitted to a blind fatality independent of his personal supervision. Knowing the character of an individual, one can easily predict for him his future.

13. The events which touch upon the general interests of humanity are regulated by Providence. When God designs a thing to be accomplished, it will be done in one way or another. Men concur in its execution; but no one is indispensable to it; otherwise God himself would be at the mercy of His creatures. If he, to whom the mission is entrusted fails to execute it, another is entrusted with the charge of it. There is not an unaccomplished mission. Man is always free to fulfill that which has been confided to him, and which he has voluntarily accepted. If he does not perform it, he loses its reward, and he assumes the responsibility of delays, which can be caused by his negligence or bad desire. If he becomes an obstacle to its accomplishment, God can cast him down with a breath.

14. The final result of an event can then be certain, because that it is in the designs of God; but, as most frequently the details and mode of execution are subordinate to circumstances and to the free will of men, the ways and means of doing it can be uncertain. The spirits can give us a general idea of its future accomplishment, if it is necessary that we be foretold of it; but in order to particularize in regard to it, giving date and place, a knowledge in advance of the determination of such and such individuals would be necessary. Now, if this determination is not yet in his mind, according to that which it will be, it can hasten or delay the announcement, thereby changing the secondary means of action, but all ending in the same result. Thus spirits can, judging from existing circumstance, predict that a war is more or less near, that it is inevitable, without being able to predict the day when it will commence, nor the detailed incidents which can be changed by the will of men.

15. In order to fix a time for future events, it is necessary also to take account of a circumstance inherent to the nature even of spirits.

With them time, as well as space, cannot be estimated only by aid of points of comparison or data which divides it into periods which they can count. Upon the Earth the natural division of time into days and years is marked by the rising and setting of the sun, and by the duration of the movement of translation of the Earth. The united measure of time must vary according to worlds, since the astronomical periods are different. Thus, for example, in Jupiter one day is equivalent to ten of our hours, and one year to nearly twelve of our years.

There is, then, in each world a manifest difference in computing time according to the nature of the astral revolutions which take place in it. This would make it difficult for a spirit unacquainted with our Earth to give dates. But outside of worlds these means of distinguishing time do not exist. For a spirit in space, there is for him no rising or setting of the sun marking the days, nor a periodic revolution marking the years. There is for him only duration of time and infinite space (chap. VI, from item n° 1 on). He, then, who had never come to the Earth could have no knowledge of our calculations, which besides would be useless to him. Moreover, he who had never been incarnate upon any world would have no notion of the fractions of duration of time. When a stranger spirit comes to this Earth to manifest, he cannot assign dates to events only by identifying himself with our usages, which is without doubt in his power, but that which the most frequently he judges useless to do.

16. However, the spirits which form the invisible population of our globe, where they have already lived, and still continue to remain in our midst, are naturally identified with our habits, of which they retain the remembrance in their free, wandering state. They have, then, less difficulty than the others in placing themselves at our point of view in regard to that which concerns terrestrial usages. They would therefore more easily assign a date to future events if they knew it; but, beyond that, it is not always allowed them to give data. They are hindered by this reason, that every time circumstances of detail are subordinate to the free will and eventual decision of man. The precise date really exists only when the event is accomplished.

For this reason circumstantial predictions cannot be offered as certitudes, and must be accepted only as probabilities. Then, even, they will carry with them a seal of *justifiable suspicion*. For this reason the truly wise spirits never give a fixed date to any event. They are limited to predict to us the issue of things which it is useful for us to know. To insist upon having fixed dates to events is to expose ourselves to the mystifications of inferior spirits, who predict what they wish without concerning themselves about the truth of it, and amuse themselves with the frights and deceptions they cause.

17. The forms generally enough employed till now for predictions makes of them veritable enigmas, often undecipherable. This mysterious and cabalistic form, of which Nostradamus offers the most complete type, give to them a

certain prestige to the common eye, which attribute so much
the more value as they are the more incomprehensible. By their
ambiguity they end themselves to very different interpretations,
in such a way that, according to the sense attributed to certain
allegorical words or those of convention, the manner of
computing the calculation, oddly complicated with dates, with a
little patience one finds there nearly all that one desires.

Whatever it may be, one cannot deny that some are
of a serious character, and are confounded by their truth.
It is probable that this veiled form has had some time its
use, and even its necessity.

Today circumstances are no more the same; the
positivism of the century would not accommodate itself to
sibylline language. Thus the predictions of our day affect no
more these strange forms. Those which the spirits give have
nothing mystical about them. They speak in common language,
as they did when living, because they have not ceased to belong
to humanity. They predict to us future things, personal or general, as this can be useful to us, according to the clear-
sightedness with which they are endowed, as counselors or
friends would do. Their predictions are, then, rather warnings,
which take nothing away from the free will, than predictions
which properly speaking, would imply an absolute fatality.
There is nearly always also a motive assigned for their opinion,
because they do not wish to annihilate man's reason under a
blind faith which permits them to appreciate the justice of it.

18. Contemporaneous humanity has also its prophets.
More than one writer, poet, *litterateur*, historian, and
philosopher has predicted in his writings the future march
of things which is realized around us today.

This aptitude comes often, without doubt, from a
rectitude of judgment which deduces logical consequences
from the present; but often, also, it is the result of a special
unconscious clairvoyance, or of a strange inspiration. That
which these men have done in life, they can for a much
stronger reason do, and with more exactitude, in the spiritual
state, when the spiritual sight is no more obscured by matter.

Chapter XVII

PREDICTIONS OF THE GOSPELS

No One is a Prophet in his Own Country – Death and Passion of Jesus – Persecution of the Apostles – Impenitent Cities – Ruin of the Temple of Jerusalem – Maledictions on the Pharisees – "My Word Will Not Pass Away" – The Cornerstone – The Parable of the Tenants – "One Flock and One Shepherd" – Coming of Elias – Announcement of the Consoler – Second Coming of Christ – Signs Foretold – "Your Sons and Your Daughters Shall Prophesy" – Last Judgment.

No One is a Prophet in his Own Country

1. Coming to his hometown, he began teaching the people in their synagogue, and they were amazed. "Where did this man get this wisdom and these miraculous powers?" they asked. "Isn't this the carpenter's son? Isn't his mother's name Mary, and aren't his brothers James, Joseph, Simon and Judas? Aren't all his sisters with us? Where then did this man get all these things?" And they took offense at him. But Jesus said to them, "Only in his hometown and in his own house is a prophet without honor." And he did not do many miracles there because of their lack of faith. (Matthew, 13: 54 to 58)

2. Jesus announced there a truth which passed into a proverb, which, from the beginning of time has been true as now, and to which one can still add: *"That no one is a prophet during life."*

In the present acceptation of this maxim, it is understood to be the credit which a man enjoys among his own people, and among those in whose midst he lives, by

the confidence in his superior knowledge and intelligence
with which he inspires them. If there are some exceptions,
they are rare; and in all cases they are never absolute. The
principle of this truth is a natural consequence of human
weakness, and can be explained thus:

The habit of seeing them from infancy up, in the common
circumstances of life, establishes between men a sort of material equality which makes one often refuse to recognize a moral superiority in him of whom one has been the companion
and comrade, who has sprung from the same place, and of
whom one has seen the first weakness. Pride suffers from the
superiority which one is obliged to submit to. Whoever is
educated above the common level is always a motive for
jealousy and envy. Those who feel themselves unable to attain
to his height must perforce try to lower him by slander and
calumny. They cry out against him so much the louder as they
see themselves inferior to him, believing by so doing to
aggrandize themselves, and eclipse him, by the noise they make.
Such has been, and such will be, the history of humanity as
long as men will not comprehend their spiritual nature, and
will not enlarge their moral horizon. This is also a prejudice
characteristic of narrow-minded and common spirits who yield
to all this in their selfishness.

On the other hand, they make generally of men whom
they do not know personally, only by their mind, an ideal
which increases by distance, time, and place. They nearly
despoil them of humanity. It seems to them that they must
not speak or feel like the rest of the world, that their language
and thoughts must constantly be at the height of sublimity,
without thinking that the mind cannot be incessantly strained
and in a perpetual state of excitability. In the daily contact of
private life they see too many men who live for the greater
part of the material plane, in whom is nothing to distinguish
them from the common man. The man who lives on the material plane, who impresses the senses, eclipses nearly always
the spiritual one, who interests the spirit. *From afar one only
sees the lightning of genius; nearer, they see the spirit at rest.*

After death, the comparison existing no more, the spiritual part of man alone is left; and he appears so much the grander as the remembrance of the corporeal man has been put farther away. That is the reason why men, who have marked their passage upon the Earth by works of real value, have been better appreciated after death than in life. They have been judged with more impartiality, because, the envious and jealous having disappeared, personal antagonisms exist no more. Posterity is a disinterested judge, which appreciates the work of the spirit, – accepts it without blind enthusiasm if it is good, and rejects it without hatred if it is bad. A separation from the individuality that has produced it has taken place.

Jesus suffered the more from the consequences of this principle, inherent in human nature, because he lived among people who were much unenlightened, and among men who lived entirely upon the material plane. His compatriots saw in him only the son of the carpenter, the brother of men as ignorant as themselves; and they demanded why he could be superior to them, and where he obtained the right to censure them. Therefore, seeing his words had less power over his own people, who despised him, than over strangers, he went to preach among those who would listen to him, and give him that sympathy which he needed.

One can judge somewhat of the feelings which his relatives entertained of his action by reading the account where his mother, accompanied by his brothers, came into an assembly where he was, and tried to induce him to go home with them, accusing him of being deranged in mind (Mark, 3: 20, 21, and 31-35; *"The Gospel According to Spiritism," chap. 14*).

Thus on one side priests and Pharisees accused Jesus of being influenced by evil spirits, and on the other he was accused of insanity by his nearest relatives. Is this not the same treatment that Spiritists receive in our day? And must they complain if they are not better treated by their fellow-citizens than Jesus was? That which was not astonishing among an ignorant people two thousand years ago is more so now in this nineteenth century of a more advanced civilization.

DEATH AND PASSION OF JESUS

3. (After the cure of the lunatic.) – While everyone was marveling at all that Jesus did, he said to his disciples, "Listen carefully to what I am about to tell you: The Son of Man is going to be betrayed into the hands of men." But they did not understand what this meant. It was hidden from them, so that they did not grasp it, and they were afraid to ask him about it. (Luke, 9: 44 and 45)

4. From that time on Jesus began to explain to his disciples that he must go to Jerusalem and suffer many things at the hands of the elders, chief priests and teachers of the law, and that he must be killed and on the third day be raised to life. (Matthew, 16: 21)

5. When they came together in Galilee, he said to them, "The Son of Man is going to be betrayed into the hands of men. 23. They will kill him, and on the third day he will be raised to life." And the disciples were filled with grief. (Matthew, 17: 22 and 23)

6. Now as Jesus was going up to Jerusalem, he took the twelve disciples aside and said to them, "We are going up to Jerusalem, and the Son of Man will be betrayed to the chief priests and the teachers of the law. They will condemn him to death And will turn him over to the Gentiles to be mocked and flogged and crucified. On the third day he will be raised to life!" (Matthew, 20: 17 to 19)

7. Jesus took the Twelve aside and told them, "We are going up to Jerusalem, and everything that is written by the prophets about the Son of Man will be fulfilled. He will be handed over to the Gentiles. They will mock him, insult him, spit on him, flog him and kill him. On the third day he will rise again." The disciples did not understand any of this. Its meaning was hidden from them, and they did not know what he was talking about. (Luke, 18: 31 to 34)

8. When Jesus had finished saying all these things, he said to his disciples, "As you know, the Passover is two days away—and the Son of Man will be handed over to be crucified." Then the chief priests and the elders of the people assembled in the palace of the high priest, whose name was Caiaphas, And they plotted to arrest Jesus in some sly way and kill him. "But not during the Feast," they said, "or there may be a riot among the people." (Matthew, 26: 1 to 5)

9. At that time some Pharisees came to Jesus and said to him, "Leave this place and go somewhere else. Herod wants to kill you." He replied, "Go tell that fox, 'I will drive out demons and heal people today and tomorrow, and on the third day I will reach my goal." (Luke, 13: 31 and 32)

PERSECUTION OF THE APOSTLES

10. "Be on your guard against men; they will hand you over to the local councils and flog you in their synagogues. On my account you will be brought before governors and kings as witnesses to them and to the Gentiles." (Matthew, 10: 17 and 18)

11. "All this I have told you so that you will not go astray. They will put you out of the synagogue; in fact, a time is coming when anyone who kills you will think he is offering a service to God. They will do such things because they have not known the Father or me. I have told you this, so that when the time comes you will remember that I warned you. I did not tell you this at first because I was with you." (John, 16: 1 to 4)

12. You will be betrayed even by parents, brothers, relatives and friends, and they will put some of you to death. All men will hate you because of me. But not a hair of your head will perish. By standing firm you will gain life." (Luke, 21: 16 to 19)

13. *Martyrdom of St. Peter.* – Jesus said, "Feed my sheep. I tell you the truth, when you were younger you dressed yourself and went where you wanted; but when you are old you will stretch out your hands, and someone else will dress you and lead you where you do not want to go." Jesus said this to indicate the kind of death by which Peter would glorify God. Then he said to him: "Follow me!" (John, 21: 18 and 19).

Impenitent Cities

14. Then Jesus began to denounce the cities in which most of his miracles had been performed, because they did not repent. "Woe to you, Korazin! Woe to you, Bethsaida! If the miracles that were performed in you had been performed in Tyre and Sidon, they would have repented long ago in sackcloth and ashes. But I tell you, it will be more bearable for Tyre and Sidon on the day of judgment than for you. And you, Capernaum, will you be lifted up to the skies? No, you will go down to the depths. If the miracles that were performed in you had been performed in Sodom, it would have remained to this day. But I tell you that it will be more bearable for Sodom on the day of judgment than for you." (Matthew, 11: 20 to 24)

Ruin of the Temple and of Jerusalem

15. Jesus left the temple and was walking away when his disciples came up to him to call his attention to its buildings. "Do you see all these things?" he asked. "I tell you the truth, not one stone here will be left on another; every one will be thrown down." (Matthew, 24: 1 and 2)

16. As he approached Jerusalem and saw the city, he wept over it and said, "If you, even you, had only known on this day what would bring you peace—but now it is hidden from your eyes. The days will come upon you when your enemies will build an embankment against you and encircle you and hem you in on every side. They will dash you to the ground, you and the children within your walls. They will not leave one stone on another, because you did not recognize the time of God's coming to you." (Luke, 19: 41 to 44)

17. "In any case, I must keep going today and tomorrow and the next day—for surely no prophet can die outside Jerusalem! O Jerusalem, Jerusalem, you who kill the prophets and stone those sent to you, how often I have longed to gather your children together, as a hen gathers her chicks under her wings, but you were not willing! Look, your house is left to you desolate. I tell you, you will not see me again until you say, 'Blessed is he who comes in the name of the Lord." (Luke, 13: 33 to 35)

18. Then let those who are in Judea flee to the mountains, let those in the city get out, and let those in the country not enter the city. For this is the time of punishment in fulfillment of all that has been written. How dreadful it will be in those days for pregnant women and nursing mothers! There will be great distress in the land and wrath against this people. They will fall by the sword and will be taken as prisoners to all the nations. Jerusalem will be trampled on by the Gentiles until the times of the Gentiles are fulfilled. (Luke, 21: 20 to 24)

19. A large number of people followed him, including women who mourned and wailed for him. Jesus turned and said to them, "Daughters of Jerusalem, do not weep for me; weep for yourselves and for your children. For the time will come when you will say, 'Blessed are the barren women, the wombs that never bore and the breasts that never nursed!' Then they will say to the mountains, "Fall on us!" And to the hills, "Cover us!" For if men do these things when the tree is green, what will happen when it is dry?" (Luke, 23: 27 to 31)

20. The faculty of foretelling the future is one of the attributes of the soul, and is explained by the theory of foresight or prophecy. Jesus possessed it, like all the other gifts of the soul, to an eminent degree. He has then been able to foretell the events which would follow his death, without in this act doing anything supernatural, since we have instances of it in the most common conditions of life. It is not rare for individuals to announce with precision the moment of their death, because their soul, for the time emancipated from the body, is like the man of the mountain (chap. XVI, n° 1); it can see the road passed over, and the end.

21. It must have been thus with Jesus, who, being conscious of the mission which he came to fulfill, knew that a violent death was the necessary consequence of it. Spiritual sight, which was permanent with him, as well as power to read thought, must have shown him the circumstances and fatal time. For the same reason he could foretell the ruin of the temple, that of Jerusalem, the misfortunes which would overtake its inhabitants, and the dispersion of the Jews.

MALEDICTIONS ON THE PHARISEES

22. *John the Baptist.* – But when he saw many of the Pharisees and Sadducees coming to where he was baptizing, he said to them: "You brood of vipers! Who warned you to flee from the coming wrath? Produce fruit in keeping with repentance. And do not think you can say to yourselves, 'We have Abraham as our father.' I tell you that out of these stones God can raise up children for Abraham. The ax is already at the root of the trees, and every tree that does not produce good fruit will be cut down and thrown into the fire." (Matthew, 3: 7 to 10)

23. "Woe to you, teachers of the law and Pharisees, you hypocrites! You shut the kingdom of heaven in men's faces. You yourselves do not enter, nor will you let those enter who are trying to. Woe to you, teachers of the law and Pharisees, you hypocrites! You travel over land and sea to win a single convert, and when he becomes one, you make him twice as much a son of hell as you are. Woe to you, blind guides! You say, 'If anyone swears by the temple, it means nothing; but if anyone swears by the gold of the temple, he is bound by his oath.' You blind fools! Which is greater: the gold, or the temple that makes the gold sacred? You also say, 'If anyone swears by the altar, it means nothing; but if anyone swears by the gift on it, he is bound by his oath.' You blind men! Which is greater: the gift, or the altar that makes the gift sacred? Therefore, he who swears by the altar swears by it and by everything on it. And he who swears by the temple swears by it and by the one who dwells in it. And he who swears by heaven swears by God's throne and by the one who sits on it. Woe to you, teachers of the law and Pharisees, you hypocrites! You give a tenth of your spices—mint, dill and cumin. But you have neglected the more important matters of the law—justice, mercy and faithfulness. You should have practiced the latter, without neglecting the former. You blind guides! You strain out a gnat but swallow a camel. Woe to you, teachers of the law and Pharisees, you hypocrites! You clean the outside of the cup and dish, but inside they are full of greed and self-indulgence. Blind Pharisee! First clean the inside of the cup and dish, and then the outside also will be clean. Woe to you, teachers of the law and Pharisees, you hypocrites! You are like whitewashed tombs, which look beautiful on the outside but on the inside are full of dead men's bones and everything unclean. In the same way, on the outside you appear to people as righteous but on the inside you are full of hypocrisy and wickedness. Woe to you, teachers of the law and Pharisees, you hypocrites! You build tombs for the prophets and decorate the graves of the righteous. And you say, 'If we had lived in the days of our forefathers, we would not have taken part with them in shedding the blood of the prophets.' So you testify against yourselves that you are the descendants of those who murdered the prophets. Fill up, then, the measure of the sin of your forefathers! "You snakes! You brood of vipers! How will you escape being condemned to hell? Therefore I am sending you prophets and wise men and teachers. Some of them you will kill and crucify; others you will flog in your synagogues and pursue from town to town. And so upon you will come all the righteous blood that has been shed on Earth, from the blood of righteous Abel to the blood of Zechariah son of Berekiah, whom you murdered between the temple and the altar. I tell you the truth, all this will come upon this generation." (Matthew, 23: 13 to 36)

My Words Will Not Pass Away

24. Then the disciples came to him and asked, "Do you know that the Pharisees were offended when they heard this?" He replied, "Every plant that my heavenly Father has not planted will be pulled up by the roots. Leave them; they are blind guides." (Matthew, 15: 12 to 14)

25. "Heaven and Earth will pass away, but my words will never pass away." (Matthew, 24: 35)

26. The words of Jesus will not pass away, because they will be true always. His moral code will be eternal, because that it contains conditions of well-doing which conduct man to his eternal destiny. But have his words been studied over, and purified of all alloy false interpretations? Have all the Christian sects seized the spirit of them? Has no one misconstrued the true sense of them in consequence of prejudices and ignorance of the laws of nature? Has no one made them an instrument of power to serve ambition and material interests, a stepping-stone, not for elevation to heaven, but for earthly elevation? Have they not all been given for a guide to the practice of the virtues which are made the express conditions upon which salvation depends? Are they not all exempt from the reproaches which he addressed to the Pharisees of his time? In short, are they not all, in theory and practice, the pure expression of his doctrine?

Truth, being one, it cannot be found in contrary affirmations. Jesus has not desired to give a double meaning to his words. If, then, the different sects contradict one another, if some consider as true that which others condemn as heresies, it is impossible that they are all right. If all had taken the true sense of the evangelical teaching, they would have taken the same ground of belief, and not formed different sects.

That which will not *pass away* is the true sense of the words of Jesus; that which will *disappear* is that false sense which men have built upon his words.

Jesus' mission being that of bringing to men God's thoughts, his pure doctrine alone can be their expression; for that reason he has said: "*Every plant that my heavenly Father has not planted will be pulled up by the roots.*"

THE CORNERSTONE

27. Jesus said to them: "Have you never read in the Scriptures: "The stone the builders rejected has become the capstone; the Lord has done this, and it is marvelous in our eyes'? "Therefore I tell you that the kingdom of God will be taken away from you and given to a people who will produce its fruit. He who falls on this stone will be broken to pieces, but he on whom it falls will be crushed." When the chief priests and the Pharisees heard Jesus' parables, they knew he was talking about them. They looked for a way to arrest him, but they were afraid of the crowd because the people held that he was a prophet. (Matthew, 21: 42 to 46)

28. The teachings of Jesus have become the cornerstone; that is to say, the stone which is the foundation of the new edifice of faith, elevated upon the ruins of the ancient one of old. The Jews, princes, priests, Pharisees, having rejected this word, it has crushed them, as it will crush those who since that time have slighted it, or misconstrued the sense of it, to aid ambition.

THE PARABLE OF THE TENANTS

29. "Listen to another parable: There was a landowner who planted a vineyard. He put a wall around it, dug a winepress in it and built a watchtower. Then he rented the vineyard to some farmers and went away on a journey. When the harvest time approached, he sent his servants to the tenants to collect his fruit. "The tenants seized his servants; they beat one, killed another, and stoned a third. Then he sent other servants to them, more than the first time, and the tenants treated them the same way. Last of all, he sent his son to them. 'They will respect my son,' he said. "But when the tenants saw the son, they said to each other, 'This is the heir. Come, let's kill him and take his inheritance.' So they took him and threw him out of the vineyard and killed him. "Therefore, when the owner of the vineyard comes, what will he do to those tenants?" "He will bring those wretches to a wretched end," they replied, "and he will rent the vineyard to other tenants, who will give him his share of the crop at harvest time." (Matthew, 21: 33 to 41)

30. The Father is God; the vine which he has planted

is the law which he has established; the tenants, to whom he has rented his vine, are the men who must teach and practice his law; the servants, whom he sent to them, are the prophets whom they have killed; his son, whom he has at length sent, is Jesus whom they have in like manner destroyed. How, then, will the Lord treat the prevaricating attorneys of his law? He will treat them as they have acted towards his ambassadors; he will fill their places with others, who will render better account of his goodness, and of the conduct of his flock.

Thus has it been with the scribes, with the princes, priests, and Pharisees; thus will it be when he will come again to ask an account of each one of that which he has made of his doctrine. He will take away authority from him who may have abused it; for he desires that justice be administered in his vineyard according to his law.

After nineteen centuries of growth, humanity, arrived at the virile age, is ripe to comprehend that which Christ has only touched upon, because, as he says himself, it could then not have been comprehended. What has been effected by those who during this long period have been charged with its religious education? To see indifference be supplanted by faith in it, and incredulity, or unbelief in God, erect a faith upon it. At no other epoch, indeed, has skepticism and disbelief in God been more manifested than today.

If a few of the sayings of Christ have been veiled in allegory, in respect to all that which concerns the rule of conduct, the connection of man with man, the moral principles of whom he makes the express condition of salvation, it is clear, explicit, and without ambiguity. *("The Gospel According to Spiritism," chap. 15)*

What have men done with his maxims of charity, of love, and of tolerance? With the exhortations he has given his disciples to convert men by gentleness and persuasion, by simplicity, humility, by unselfishness, and all the virtues of which he has been the example? The anathema and malediction have been cast at men for acknowledging him as their Master. They have been slain in the name of him who has said: "All men are brothers." They have made a jealous, cruel, vindictive, and partial God of him whom he has proclaimed infinitely just, good, and merciful. They have sacrificed to this God of peace and of truth thousands more of victims at the stake, by tortures and persecutions, than the pagans have ever sacrificed to false gods. They have sold prayers and favors from heaven in the name of him who has chased those who sold from the Temple, and who has said to his disciples: "Freely you have received, freely give."

What would Christ say to all this if he lived among us today? If he saw his representatives ambitious for the honors, the riches, the power and pomp of the princes of this world, whilst he, more kingly than the kings of the Earth, made his entrance into Jerusalem seated upon a donkey? Would he not do right if he said to them, "What have you made of my teachings, you who worship the golden calf, and address the greater part of your prayers to the rich, and the meager part to the poor? As I have said to you: the last shall be first, and the first last, in the kingdom of heaven." If it is not so carnally, it is so spiritually; and, as the master of the parable, he will come to demand an account of his tenants of the product of the vine when the harvest shall come.

ONE FLOCK AND ONE SHEPHERD

31. I have other sheep that are not of this sheep pen. I must bring them also. They too will listen to my voice, and there shall be one flock and one shepherd. (John, 10: 16)

32. By these words Jesus announces clearly that some day men will have only one religious belief. But how can this unity be effected? The thing appears difficult, if one considers the difference which exist between religions, the antagonism which exists between their respective adepts, their obstinacy in believing themselves in exclusive possession of the truth. All desire unity of faith; but all flatter themselves that it will be made to their profit, and no one understands how to make concessions to his beliefs.

However, unity will be in religion, as well as in all social, political, and commercial affairs, by the lowering of the barriers which separate nations, by the assimilation of manners, laws, and language. The nations of the entire world fraternize already, like the provinces of the same empire. They hasten this unity; they desire it. It will be done by the force of things, because it will become a necessity to tighten the bonds of fraternity between nations. It will be done by the development of human reason, which will make them comprehend the puerility of these differences; by the progress of the sciences, which demonstrates each day the material errors upon which they lean, and detaches little by little the decayed stones of their foundations. If science demolishes in religions that which is the work of men, and the fruit of their ignorance of the laws of nature, it cannot destroy, notwithstanding the opinion of some, that which is the work of God and of eternal truth. By clearing away the accretions of error it prepares the way of unity, religions must meet upon a neutral ground, however common to all.

In order to bring this about, all will have to make concessions and sacrifices, more or less great, according to the multiplicity of particular dogmas. But, by virtue of the principle of immutability that they all possess, the initiative concession should come from the official camp. Instead of taking their starting point from on high, it will be taken below by the initiative individual. It has been operating some time by a movement of decentralization, which is tending towards the acquisition of an irresistible force. The principle of immutability, which religions have hitherto considered as an aegis conservatrix, will become a destructive element on account of the unchangeable creeds. Whilst society marches ahead of them, they will be overflowed, and then absorbed in the current of progressive ideas.

The immobility, contrary to being a source of strength, becomes a cause of weakness and ruin for those who do not follow the general movement; it tears down the unity, because those who want to move forward separate from those who are obstinate in staying behind.

Judging from the present state of opinion and knowledge,

the religion which must one day attract all men under the same banner shall be that which will the best satisfy the reason and legitimate aspirations of the heart and mind; which shall not at any point conflict with positive science; which, instead of being immovable, will follow humanity in its progressive march without allowing itself to ever be outrun; which shall be the emancipator of intelligence by admitting only a reasonable faith, that of which the moral code shall be the purest, the most rational, the most in harmony with social needs; in short, that which is the best adapted to found upon the Earth the reign of goodness by the practice of charity and universal fraternity.

That which supports antagonisms between religions is the idea that each one has its particular god, and their pretension to having the only true and most powerful one which is in constant hostility with the gods of the other creeds, and occupied in combating their influence. When they shall have become convinced that there is only one God in the universe, and that he is the same that they adore under the names of Jehovah, Allah, or Deus; when they shall be in accord upon his essential attributes – they will comprehend that one being alone can have only one will; they will extend their hands to one another as servants of the same Master, and as children of the same Father; and they will have made a great stride towards unity.

ADVENT OF ELIAS

33. The disciples asked him, "Why then do the teachers of the law say that Elijah must come first?" Jesus replied, "To be sure, Elijah comes and will restore all things. But I tell you, Elijah has already come, and they did not recognize him, but have done to him everything they wished. In the same way the Son of Man is going to suffer at their hands." Then the disciples understood that he was talking to them about John the Baptist. (Matthew, 17: 10 to 13)

34. Elijah was already returned in the person of John the Baptist. His new advent has been announced in an explicit manner. Now, as he can only return in a new body, it is a formal consecration of the principle of the plurality of existences ("*The Gospel According to Spiritism*," chap. 4, item 10).

ANNOUNCEMENT OF THE CONSOLER[101]

35. "If you love me, you will obey what I command. And I will ask the Father, and he will give you another Counselor to be with you forever. The Spirit of truth. The world cannot accept him, because it neither sees him nor knows him. But you know him, for he lives with you and will be in you. But the Counselor, the Holy Spirit, whom the Father will send in my name, will teach you all things and will remind you of everything I have said to you. (John, 14: 15 to 17 and 26) ("*The Gospel According to Spiritism*," chap. 6)

36. But I tell you the truth: It is for your good that I am going away. Unless I go away, the Counselor will not come to you; but if I go, I will send him to you. When he comes, he will convict the world of guilt in regard to sin and righteousness and judgment: in regard to sin, because men do not believe in me; In regard to righteousness, because I am going to the Father, where you can see me no longer; And in regard to judgment, because the prince of this world now stands condemned. "I have much more to say to you, more than you can now bear. But when he, the Spirit of truth, comes, he will guide you into all truth. He will not speak on his own; he will speak only what he hears, and he will tell you what is yet to come. He will bring glory to me by taking from what is mine and making it known to you. (John, 16: 7 to 14)

37. This prediction, without doubt, is one of the most

---

[101] **Note of SAB**: "*The Bible*" quotation utilizes the word Counselor (advisor), but it is our understanding that the word Consoler (comforter) reflects better the nature of the Promised Consoler that Christ mentioned was going to come to teach us all things and to call to mind all that He had said. (See "*The Gospel According to Spiritism*" chap. 6 items 3 and 4, translated into English by J. A. Duncan, 1987) (See also Chapter 1, item 27 of the present book).

important, in a religious point of view, because it verifies in the most conclusive manner that *Jesus has not said all that he had to say*, because that he would not have been comprehended even by his apostles, since it is to them he addresses his words. If he had given secret instructions to them, they would have mentioned it in the Gospels. Since he has not told everything he knew to his apostles, their successors have known no more than themselves of it. They themselves have been able to misconstrue the sense of his words, to give a false impression of his ideas, often veiled under the form of parables. The religions founded upon the Gospels can then not be said to be in possession of all the truth, since the completion of them has been postponed to a subsequent time. Their principle of immutability is a protestation against even the words of Jesus.

He announces, under the name of *"Consoler"* and *"Spirit of Truth,"* he who *must teach all things* and make them recall that which he has said; then his teaching was not complete. Moreover, he predicted that they will have forgotten that which he has said, and that they will have altered the nature of it, since the Spirit of Truth must make them *recall it*, and in concert with Elias *reestablish all things*; that is to say, according to the true idea of Jesus.

38. When ought this new revelator to come? It is very evident, that, if at the epoch where Jesus spoke, men were not in a state to comprehend the things which remained for him to say, in a few years they could not acquire the necessary light. For intelligence in regard to certain parts of the Gospel, with the exception of its moral precepts, a knowledge which progress in the sciences alone could give was necessary, which must be a work of time and of many generations. If, then, the new Messiah had come shortly after Christ, he would not have found the ground prepared for him, and he would not have accomplished more than Christ. Now, from the time of Christ to our day, no one great revelation has been produced which might have completed the knowledge of the Gospel, and which might have elucidated the obscure parts of it, – a certain indication that the Messenger had not yet appeared.

39. Who must this Messenger have been? By Jesus saying: "And I will ask the Father, and he will give you another Consoler," indicates clearly that it is not himself; otherwise he would have said: "I will return to complete that which I have taught you." Then he adds: "*to be with you forever.*" The latter would not grasp the idea of an incarnated being who can live eternally with us, and still less be in us, but is comprehended very well of a doctrine which, when it has been assimilated, can be eternally in us. The *Consoler* is, then, in the thought of Jesus, the personification of a sovereignly consoling doctrine, of whose inspirer will be the *Spirit of Truth.*

40. Spiritism realizes, as has been demonstrated (chap. I, n° 30), all the conditions of the Consoler promised by Jesus. It is not an individual doctrine – a human conception. No one can tell the creator of it. It is the product of the collective teachings of the spirits, at which presides the Spirit of Truth. It suppresses nothing of the Gospel; it completes and elucidates it. By the aid of the new laws that it reveals, joined to that of science, it enables us to comprehend that which was unintelligible to admit, the possibility of that which incredulity regarded as inadmissible. It has had its prophets and harbingers, who have predicted its coming. By its moralizing power it is preparing for the reign of goodness upon the Earth.

The doctrine of Moses, incomplete, has remained circumscribed to the Jewish people. That of Jesus, more complete, has been spread all over the Earth by Christianity, but has not converted the whole world. Spiritism, more complete, still having roots over all the Earth, will convert all.[102]

41. Christ's saying to the apostles: "But the Consoler,

---

[102] All philosophical and religious doctrines bear the name of the individual founder. They say, the Mosaic, Christianity, Mohammedanism, Buddhism, etc. The word Spiritism, to the contrary, recalls no personality; it encloses a general idea, which indicates at the same time the character and multiple source of the doctrine.

will teach you all things and will remind you of everything I have said to you," proclaimed by that the necessity of reincarnation. How could these men profit, then, by the more complete teaching which must be given subsequently? How would they be more apt to comprehend it if they were not to live again? Jesus would have said an inconsistent thing if the future men were, according to the common doctrine, to be a new men, of souls which arose from nothingness to birth. Admit, to the contrary, that the apostles and the men of their time have lived since, *that they still live again today*, the promise of Jesus is found justified. Their intelligence, which must have been developed by contact with social progress, can bear now that which it could not then. Without reincarnation the promise of Jesus would have been an illusory one.

42. If they say that this promise was realized on the day of Pentecost by the descent of the Holy Spirit one would reply that the Holy Spirit has been able to inspire them, that he has opened their intelligence, developed in them medianimic aptitudes which were to facilitate their mission; but as nothing more, other than Jesus had taught them, has been given to them, one can find no trace of a special teaching. The Holy Spirit has, then, not realized that which Jesus announced as the Consoler; otherwise the apostles would have elucidated, while living, all which has remained obscure in the Gospels to this day, and the contradictory interpretation of which has given rise to innumerable sects, which have been divided, in regard to Christianity, since the first century.

SECOND COMING OF CHRIST

43. Then Jesus said to his disciples, "If anyone would come after me, he must deny himself and take up his cross and follow me. For whoever wants to save his life will lose it, but whoever loses his life for me will find it. What good will it be for a man if he gains the whole world, yet forfeits his soul? Or what can a man give in exchange for his soul? For the Son of Man is going to come in his Father's glory with his angels, and then he will reward each person according to what he has done. I tell you the truth, some who are standing here will not taste death before they see the Son of Man coming in his kingdom." (Matthew, 16: 24 to 28)

44. Then the high priest stood up before them and asked Jesus: "Are you not going to answer? What is this testimony that these men are bringing against you?" But Jesus remained silent and gave no answer. Again the high priest asked him: "Are you the Christ, the Son of the Blessed One?" "I am," said Jesus. "And you will see the Son of Man sitting at the right hand of the Mighty One and coming on the clouds of heaven." The high priest tore his clothes. "Why do we need any more witnesses?" he asked. "You have heard the blasphemy. What do you think?" (Mark, 14: 60 to 63)

45. Jesus announces his second coming; but he does not say he will return with a carnal body, neither that the *Consoler* will be personified in him. He presents himself as coming in spirit, in the glory of his Father, to judge the good and wicked, and render to each one according to his works, when the time shall be accomplished.

This saying, "I tell you the truth, some who are standing here will not taste death before they see the Son of man coming in his kingdom," seems a contradiction, since it is certain that he has not come during the life of anyone of those who were present. Jesus could not, however, be deceived in a prophecy of this nature, and above all in a contemporary fact which concerned him personally. At first it is necessary to demand if his words have always been faithfully rendered. One can doubt it when one thinks that he has written nothing himself; that a compilation of his teachings has not been made until after his death. And, when one sees the same discourse nearly always reproduced in different terms by each evangelist, it is an evident proof that they are not the textual expressions of Jesus. It is also probable that the sense has been sometimes altered in passing through successive transitions.

On the other hand, it is certain, that, if Jesus had said all that he could have said, he would have explained all things in a distinct and precise manner which had not given place to any equivocation, as he does it for moral principle; whilst he must have veiled his thoughts upon subjects which he has not judged proper to propose to them. The apostles, persuaded that the present generation must be the witness of that which he announced, must have interpreted the thought of Jesus according to their idea. They have been able, consequently, to draw from it a more absolute sense of the present than he has perhaps intended to convey himself. Whatever it may be, the fact is there, which proves that the circumstances have not happened as they have believed they would.

46. A capital point which Jesus has not been able to develop, because that men of his time were not sufficiently prepared for this order of ideas and its consequences, but of which he has, however, based the principle, as he has done for all things: this is the great and important law of reincarnation. This law, studied and brought to the light of day by Spiritism, is the key of many passages of the Gospel, which without that would appear nonsensical.

It is in this law that one can find the rational explanation of the above words by admitting them as textual. Since they cannot be applied to any one of the apostles, it is evident they refer to the future reign of Christ; that is to say, in the time when his doctrine, better comprehended, will be the universal law. By telling them that *anyone of those who were present* would see his coming, could not be understood in the sense that he would inhabit the carnal body at this epoch. But the Jews imagined they were to see all that Jesus announced, and took his allegories literally.

Finally, a few of his predictions have been accomplished in their time, – such as the ruin of Jerusalem, the misfortunes which followed it, and the dispersion of the Jews; but he saw farther, and, in speaking of the present, he makes constant allusion to the future.

PRECURSORY SIGNS

47. You will hear of wars and rumors of wars, but see to it that you are not alarmed. Such things must happen, but the end is still to come. Nation will rise against nation, and kingdom against kingdom. There will be famines and earthquakes in various places. All these are the beginning of birth pains. (Matthew, 24: 6 to 8)

48. "Brother will betray brother to death, and a father his child. Children will rebel against their parents and have them put to death. All men will hate you because of me, but he who stands firm to the end will be saved." (Marc, 13: 12 and 13)

49. "So when you see standing in the holy place 'the abomination that causes desolation,' spoken of through the prophet Daniel—let the reader understand—then let those who are in Judea flee to the mountains.[103] Let no one on the roof of his house go down to take anything out of the house. Let no one in the field go back to get his cloak. How dreadful it will be in those days for pregnant women and nursing mothers! Pray that your flight will not take place in winter or on the Sabbath. For then there will be great distress, unequaled from the beginning of the world until now—and never to be equaled again. If those days had not been cut short, no one would survive, but for the sake of the elect those days will be shortened." (Matthew, 24: 15 to 22)

50. "Immediately after the distress of those days 'the sun will be darkened, and the moon will not give its light; the stars will fall from the sky, and the heavenly bodies will be shaken.' "At that time the sign of the Son of Man will appear in the sky, and all the nations of the Earth will mourn. They

---

[103] The expression: the abomination of desolation, despite being meaningless, is also ludicrous. Ostervald's translation that says: "The abomination that causes desolation," is quite different. The meaning then becomes perfectly clear, as one comprehends that abomination brings desolation as punishment. Jesus said: "when abomination comes to a saintly place, so does desolation, and that will be a sign that the times are near."

will see the Son of Man coming on the clouds of the sky, with power and great glory. And he will send his angels with a loud trumpet call, and they will gather his elect from the four winds, from one end of the heavens to the other. "Now learn this lesson from the fig tree: As soon as its twigs get tender and its leaves come out, you know that summer is near. Even so, when you see all these things, you know that it is near, right at the door. I tell you the truth, this generation will certainly not pass away until all these things have happened." (Matthew, 24: 29 and 34)

As it was in the days of Noah, so it will be at the coming of the Son of Man. For in the days before the flood, people were eating and drinking, marrying and giving in marriage, up to the day Noah entered the ark. (Matthew, 24: 37 and 38)

51. "No one knows about that day or hour, not even the angels in heaven, nor the Son, but only the Father." (Marc, 13: 32)

52. I tell you the truth, you will weep and mourn while the world rejoices. You will grieve, but your grief will turn to joy. A woman giving birth to a child has pain because her time has come; but when her baby is born she forgets the anguish because of her joy that a child is born into the world. So with you: Now is your time of grief, but I will see you again and you will rejoice, and no one will take away your joy. (John, 16: 20 to 22)

53. And many false prophets will appear and deceive many people. Because of the increase of wickedness, the love of most will grow cold, But he who stands firm to the end will be saved. And this gospel of the kingdom will be preached in the whole world as a testimony to all nations, and then the end will come. (Matthew, 24: 11 to 14)

54. This picture of the end of time is evidently allegorical, as the greater part of them are which Jesus presented. The images which they contain are colored in a way to make a deep impression upon intelligences corroded with sin and ignorance. In order to strike these clouded spirits, it was necessary to paint vigorously with glaring colors.

Jesus addressed himself particularly to the people who were the least enlightened, those incapable of comprehending metaphysical abstractions, and of seizing the delicacy of forms. In order to reach the heart it was necessary to speak to the eyes by the aid of material signs, and to the ears by the vigor of language.

As a natural consequence of this disposition of mind, supreme power could not, according to the belief then, manifest itself only by extraordinary or supernatural things. The more impossible they were, the more ready were they to accept them.

The Son of man coming in the clouds of heaven with great majesty, surrounded by his angels, and with the sound of trumpets, seemed to them much more imposing than a being invested with moral power alone. So the Jews, who expected the Messiah to be a king of the Earth, mighty above all kings, to place their nation in the first rank among them, to raise up again the throne of David and Solomon, would not recognize him in the humble son of the carpenter without material authority. However, this poor, despised man of Judea has become the greatest among the great. He has conquered by his sovereignty more kingdoms than the most powerful potentates.

With his word alone, and with the aid of a few miserable fishermen, he has revolutionized the world; and it is to him that the Jews will owe their rehabilitation. He then had the truth when he replied to this question of Pilate: "Are you the king of the Jews?" "Yes, it is as you say," Jesus replied.

55. Allow us to observe, that among the ancients, earthquakes and the eclipse of the sun were necessary symbols of all events and all sinister presages. One finds them at the death of Jesus, of Caesar, and in a multitude of times in the history of paganism. If these phenomena were produced as often as has been related, it would appear impossible that men had not preserved the memory of them by tradition. To this is added that of the stars having fallen from heaven, which is evidently a fiction, as one knows now stars cannot fall.

56. However, under these allegories are concealed great truths. Firstly, it is the announcement of calamities of all kinds, which will strike and decimate humanity, – calamities engendered by a great contest between good and evil, faith and incredulity, progressive and retrogressive ideas. Secondly, that of the diffusion over all the Earth of the Gospel reestablished in its primitive purity. Then the reign of goodness, which will be that of peace and universal fraternity, will arise from the code of evangelical morals put in practice by all nations. This will truly be the reign of Jesus, since he will preside at its establishment, and men will live under the aegis of his law – a reign of goodness; for, said he, "Now is your time of grief, but I will see you again and you will rejoice, and no one will take away your joy."

57. When will these things be accomplished? "No one knows," says Jesus, *"not even the Son of man;"* but, when the moment shall have come, men will be warned of it by precursory indication. These signs will not take place in the sun or in the stars, but in the social state, as well as in phenomena which partake more largely of the moral quality than the physical, which one can in part deduce from his allusions to it.

It is very certain that this change could not have been operated during the life of the apostles; otherwise Jesus would not have been ignorant of it. Moreover, such a transformation could not take place in a few years. However, he speaks to them as if they were to be witness of it. He meant by it that they were to be reborn into life for this epoch, and to work themselves at the transformation. Sometimes he speaks of the approaching end of Jerusalem, and takes this fact as a point of comparison for the future.

58. Is it the end of the world which Jesus announces by his second coming, and when he says: "The end of the world will come when the Gospel shall have been preached over all the Earth?"

It is not rational to suppose that God will destroy the world precisely at the moment when it will enter into the way of moral progress by the practice of evangelical teachings. Nothing, moreover, in the words of Christ indicates a universal destruction, which, under such conditions, would not be justified.

The general practice of evangelical truths must lead to an amelioration of the moral state of men, will lead of itself to the reign of good, and will lead the downfallen from the errors of his ways. He refers, then, to the end of the old world, of the world governed by prejudices, pride, selfishness, fanaticism, incredulity, cupidity, and all the bad passions to which Christ alludes when he says: "And this gospel of the kingdom will be preached in the whole world as a testimony to all nations, and then the end will come;" but this will lead to a struggle from which will proceed the evils which he predicts.

Your Sons and Daughters shall prophesy

59. "In the last days," God says, "I will pour out my Spirit on all people. Your sons and daughters will prophesy, your young men will see visions, your old men will dream dreams. Even on my servants, both men and women, I will pour out my Spirit in those days, and they will prophesy." (Acts, Chap. II: 17 and 18 - Joel, Chap.2: 28 and 29))

60. If one considers the present state of the moral and physical world, the tendencies, aspirations, and presentiments of the masses, the decadence of old ideas which have struggled in vain for a century against new ideas, one cannot doubt that a new order of things is being prepared, and that the old world is reaching its end.

If now, by taking the true sense of the allegorical form of certain of his pictures, inquiring upon the innermost meaning of the words of Jesus, and comparing them with the present state of society and of the world, one cannot deny that many of his predictions are receiving their accomplishment today; whence it is reasonable to conclude that we are on the borders of the time announced, which confirmed at all points of the globe by the spirits who manifest themselves.

61. Thus, as one has seen (chap. I, n° 32), the advent

of Spiritism, coinciding with other circumstances, realizes one of the most important predictions of Jesus by the influence which it must forcibly exercise over ideas. It is, besides, clearly announced in this passage of the Acts of the Apostles: "In the last days, God says: I will pour out my Spirit on all people. Your sons and daughters will prophesy."

This is an unmistakable announcement of the prevalence of mediumship, which is revealed in our day in individuals of all ages, sexes, and conditions, and in consequence of the universal manifestations of the spirits; for without the spirits there would not be mediums. This, it has been said, will arrive in the latter days. Since it is not the end of the world, but its regeneration, we must understand this prophecy to imply, the last days of the moral world which is at an end. (*"The Gospel According to Spiritism,"* chap. 21)

THE LAST JUDGMENT

62. "When the Son of Man comes in his glory, and all the angels with him, he will sit on his throne in heavenly glory. All the nations will be gathered before him, and he will separate the people one from another as a shepherd separates the sheep from the goats. He will put the sheep on his right and the goats on his left. Then the King will say to those on his right, 'Come, you who are blessed by my Father; take your inheritance, the kingdom prepared for you since the creation of the world. "(Matthew, 25: 31 to 34) (*"The Gospel According to Spiritism,"* chap. 15)

63. The reign of goodness being established upon the Earth, it is necessary that spirits hardened in evil, and those who would be able to bring trouble to it, should be excluded. God has given them the necessary time for their improvement; but the moment when the globe must elevate itself into the hierarchy of worlds by the moral progress of its inhabitants, being arrived, the sojourn of spirits and incarnated beings, will be forbidden to those who have not profited by the instructions which they have been received in this world. They will be exiled into inferior worlds, as were formerly those of the adamic race upon our Earth, whilst their places will be filled by better spirits. It is this separation at which Jesus will preside, which is represented by these words of the last judgment: "The good will be on my right hand and the wicked on my left" (chap. XI, from item n° 31 on).

64. The doctrine of a last judgment, unique and universal, putting an end to humanity, conflicts with reason in this sense: that it would imply the inactivity of God during the eternity which has preceded the creation of the Earth, and the eternity which will follow its destruction. One would naturally demand of what use the sun, the moon, and stars would be, which, according to Genesis, have been made for the illumination of this Earth. One is astonished that a work so immense should have been made for such a short space of time, and for the profit of beings of whom the greater part were condemned in advance to eternal suffering.

65. Materially speaking, the idea of a unique judgment was, to a certain point, admissible to those who sought not the reason of things, when they believed all humanity concentrated upon this Earth, and that the whole universe was made for its inhabitants. It is inadmissible since it is known there are millions of similar worlds in which humanity is perpetuated during all eternity, and among which the Earth is an imperceptible point.

One sees by this fact alone that Jesus was right in saying to his disciples: "I have much more to say to you, more than you can now bear;" for the progress of science was indispensable to the healthy interpretation of some of his words. Assuredly the Apostles, St. Paul and the first disciples of them, would have established otherwise certain dogmas if they had known the principles of astronomy, geology, physics, chemistry, physiology, and psychology, which are known today. Thus Jesus has postponed the complement of his instructions, and announced that all things were to be reestablished.

66. Morally speaking, a positive judgment to which there is no appeal is irreconcilable with the infinite goodness of the Creator, whom Jesus constantly presents to us as a good Father, leaving always a way open for repentance, and ready ever to extend his arms to the prodigal son. If Jesus had understood the judgment in this sense, he would have contradicted his own words.

Then, if the last judgment must surprise men suddenly in the midst of their ordinary work, and mothers at the point of childbirth, one asks what object God has in it. He who does nothing uselessly or unjustly, why should he cause children to be born and *create new souls* at this supreme moment of the extermination of humanity, in order to make them pass into judgment from their mothers' bosoms before they were conscious beings, while others have had thousands of years to acknowledge him? On which side, right or left, will pass these souls who are not yet either good or bad, and to whom the way of all subsequent progress is henceforth closed, since humanity will exist no longer? (Chap. II, n° 19)

Let those whose reason is contented with similar beliefs preserve them. It is their right, and no one should blame them; but let them not expect the rest of the world to join them in their belief.

67. The judgment looked at in the emigration point of view is rational, (see n°63). It is founded upon the most rigorous justice, as it leaves eternally to the spirit its free will, as by it no partiality is shown to anyone, as an equal latitude is given by God to all his creatures, without exception, to progress; for the door of heaven is always open for those who are worthy of entering therein; but the annihilation of the world would bring no interruption to the progressive march of the spirit. Such is the consequence of plurality of worlds and of existences.

According to this interpretation, the name *last judgment* is not correct, since spirits pass by similar spheres to each renewal of worlds which they inhabit, until they have attained a certain degree of perfection. There is then, properly speaking, not a *last judgment*; but there are general *judgments* at all the epochs of partial or total renewal of the population of worlds, in consequence of which great emigrations and immigrations of spirits are brought about.

Chapter XVIII
THE TIME HAS ARRIVED

Signs of Time – The New Generation

SIGNS OF TIME

1. The time appointed by God has arrived, is said to us on all sides, where great events have been accomplished for the regeneration of humanity. In what sense is it necessary to understand these prophetic words? To the incredulous they are of no importance; to their eyes, it is only the expression of a puerile belief without foundation; for the greater number of the believing, they have something mysterious and supernatural, which seems to be the harbinger of the overturning of the laws of nature. These two interpretations are equally erroneous, – the first, in that which implies a denial of Providence; the second, in that these words announce no perturbation of the laws of nature, but their accomplishment.

2. All is harmony in creation. All reveals a foresight, the effects of which are wanting neither in the smallest nor largest of God's works. We must then, firstly, discard irreconcilable caprice with the divine wisdom. Secondly, if our epoch is marked for the accomplishments of certain things, it is because there is a reason for their accomplishment in the onward march of all things.

Our globe, like all which exists, is submitted to the law of progress. It progresses physically by the transformation of the elements which compose it, and morally by the purification of the incarnated and discarnated spirits who people it. The progress of the two is a parallel one; for the habitation becomes perfected according to the degree of perfection of its inhabitant. Physically, the globe has been submitted to transformations, ascertained by science, which have successively rendered it habitable for beings more and more perfected; morally, humanity progresses by the development of intelligence of the moral sense and gentleness of manners. At the same time, as the improvement of the globe has been accomplished under the empire of material forces, men have concurred in it by the efforts of their intelligence. They have learned how to make unwholesome localities healthy, rendering communications with one another easier and the soil more productive.

This double progress is accomplished in two ways, one slow, gradual, and insensible; the other by sudden changes, to each one of which has been operated a more rapid upper movement, which mark, in distinct characters the progressive periods of humanity. These movements, subordinate in details to the free will of man, are in a measure necessary or inevitable in their relation to the whole, because they are submitted to laws like those operated in the germination, growth, and maturity of plants. This is why the progressive movement is sometimes partial – that is to say, limited to a race or one nation – at other times general.

The progress of humanity is effected then by virtue of a law. Now, as all laws of nature are the eternal work of wisdom and divine prescience, all which is the effect of these laws is the result of the will of God – not of an accidental, capricious will, but an immutable one. Then, when humanity is ripe to take a higher degree in progression, one can say that the time appointed by God has arrived, as one speaks of the harvest season as having arrived with the maturity of its fruit.

3. While this progressive movement of humanity is inevitable, because it is natural, it does not follow that God is indifferent to it, and that, after having established laws, he is now in an inactive state, leaving things to take care of themselves. His laws are eternal and immutable without doubt, but only because his will itself is eternal and constant, and that his thought animates constantly all things. His thought which penetrates all things is the intelligent and permanent force which keeps all in harmony. If this thought should one moment cease to act, the universe would be like a clock without a pendulum. God watches, then, incessantly over the execution of his laws; and the spirits who populate space are his ministers charged with the details according to the unfoldment of their functions in their degree of advancement.

4. The universe is at the same time an incommensurable mechanism, conducted by a number no less incommensurable of intelligences, an immense government, where every intelligent being has his active part assigned him under the eye of the Sovereign Master, whose unique will maintains unity everywhere. Under the empire of this vast regulating power, all moves, all operates in perfect order. That which seems like perturbations to us are partial and isolated movements, which appear irregular only because our sight is circumscribed. If our vision could embrace the whole, we would see that these irregularities are only apparent, and that they harmonize with all.

5. Humanity has already accomplished incontestable progress. Men by their intelligence have attained to a knowledge of the sciences, arts, and material comforts never reached before. An immense progress still remains for them to realize, which is to make *charity, fraternity, and union reign among them in order to assure to them their moral well-being.* They could never accomplish this progress with their present beliefs, their superannuated institutions, which are remains of another age, good for a certain epoch, sufficient for a transitory state, but which, having given all that it has to give, would only be a hindrance now. It is not only the development of intelligence which is necessary to men, it is the elevation of sentiment; and for that reason it is necessary to destroy all that which excites in them undue selfishness or pride.

Such is the period upon which they are entering, and which will mark one of the most important phases of humanity. This phase, which is being elaborated at this moment, is the necessary complement of the preceding state, as the manly age is that of youth. It could then be foreseen and predicted in advance, and thus they say that the times appointed by God have come.

6. In these times a partial change is not being enacted, a renovation limited to one country, to one people or nation, or one race. It is a universal movement which is operating in moral progress. A new order of things is being established, and the men the most opposed to it are in their ignorance working for it. The future generation, rid of the dross of the old world, and formed of purer elements, will find itself animated with ideas and sentiments entirely different from the present one, which is passing away with gigantic strides. The old world will die, and live in history, as that of the Middle Ages, with its barbaric customs, is remembered in the present.

Each one knows that we all desire something different from the present order of things. After having exhausted in some respects the good which is the product of intelligence, one comes to comprehend that the complement of this well-being can be only in moral development. The more one advances, the more one feels that which is missing, without, however, being able to define it clearly. It is the effect of the interior work which is being effected for regeneration. We have desires and aspirations which are the prelude to a better condition.

7. But change as radical as that which is being elaborated cannot be accomplished without commotion. There will be an inevitable conflict in ideas. From this conflict will forcibly arise temporary perturbations, until the rubbish be cleared away, and the equilibrium be re-established. It is, then, from a battle of ideas that these grave events will arise, and not from cataclysms, or purely material catastrophes. The general cataclysms were the consequence of the state of formation of the Earth. *Now it is no more the center of the globe which is agitated, but that of the humanity.*

8. If the Earth no longer has to fear general cataclysms, it is nevertheless still subject to periodical revolutions; their causes, from a scientific point of view, are explained by the following instructions given by two eminent spirits:[104]

---

[104] Extracted from two communications given at the Société de Paris and published in the *"Revue Spirite,"* October 1868, pg. 313. They are consequence of Galileo's message, reproduced in Chapter VI and complementary of Chapter IX about the Globe's revolutions.

"In addition to obeying the ordinary laws that preside over the division of days and nights, seasons, and the like, each celestial body is subject to revolutions that require thousands of centuries to reach full completion. Analogous to brief revolutions, these long-term upheavals pass through all periods, from birth until those phases of utmost effect. After reaching such potential a decrease to the lowest limit occurs; then the cycle starts all over again.

Humanity only apprehends the phases of relatively short duration whose periodicity can be proved. Some of these revolutions, however, embrace lengthy creations of beings and even successions of races; consequently, their effects have the appearance of novelty and spontaneity. But if man could project his vision back some thousands of centuries he would see amidst these causes and effects a correlation he could hardly anticipate. Nevertheless, these periods, which confound the human imagination due to their relatively long duration, last only instants in the everlasting duration of eternity.

In a planetary system each body that constitutes the system reacts with the others, and all physical influences are mutually dependent of each other. In fact, there aren't any effects that you would consider as great disturbances that are not the consequence of the set of influences of the system as a whole.

I go further and say that planetary systems also react with each other; this is because of the proximity or distance resulted from their orbital movement through the myriads of systems comprising our nebula. In addition, our nebula, which is like an archipelago in the immensity of space, having also its own orbital movement through a large number of other nebula, is also subject to the influences of those nebula it approaches.

Therefore, nebula react on nebula and systems react on systems; planets react on planets, and the elements of each planet react with each other; and thus successively down to the atom. Whence in each world we have local or general revolutions that do not appear to be disturbances only because life's brevity allows us to perceive only their partial effects.

Organic matter could not escape these influences; the disturbances it suffers can thus alter the physical state of living beings and, in general, determine some of the diseases that attack plants, animals and humanity. We remark that these diseases, like all plagues, act as stimulants to propel the human intelligence, by need, to search for means to combat them and to discover the laws of nature.

Organic matter in turn has an effect on the spirit; through its contact and inner connection with the material elements, the spirit also suffers influences that modify its dispositions. This fact, however, does not deprive it of its free will, but rather accelerates or attenuates its activities, thus contributing to its development. The effervescence manifested from time to time in a population, among people of the same race, is neither a fortuitous occurrence nor the result of a whim, but has its origin in the laws of nature. This effervescence, which is unconscious at first and only a vague desire, a non-definite aspiration towards something better or a need for change, is characterized by a silent agitation; later on, however, it brings about acts that lead to social revolutions. As everything is interconnected in the universe, be certain that these revolutions, like physical revolutions, also have their periodicity. If your spiritual vision were not restricted by the veil of matter, you would see the fluidic currents that, like thousands of conductive wires, links together things of the spiritual world to those of the material world.

When you are told that humanity has arrived at a period of transformation, and that the Earth must rise within the hierarchy of worlds, do not find anything mystical in these words but, on the contrary, see it as the fulfillment of one of the greatest fatal laws of the universe, against which all ill-disposition of humanity collapses."

Arago

9. Yes, certainly, humanity changes, as it has changed at other times; and each transformation is marked by a crisis which is, for mankind, similar to the crises of the growth of individuals. These transformations are frequently sorrowful and painful, and take along with them generations of people and institutions; nevertheless, they are always followed by a phase of material and moral progress.

"Because earthly Humanity has reached one of these periods of growth, it has been working vigorously at its transformation for nearly a century. Whence we see it stirring from side to side, as if captured by some kind of fever and propelled by an invisible force. In such a state it will remain until it has again stabilized itself on its new foundation. Whoever shall see it then will find it greatly changed in its habits and character, in its laws and beliefs; in short, in all its social state.

One thing that will seem strange to you, although it is the absolute truth, is that the world of the spirits, a world that surrounds you, experiences the aftershocks of all commotions that agitate the world of incarnate beings. I even say that the former takes an active role in these commotions. This fact should bring no surprise to those who know that the Spirits comprise of one body with humanity; that they may leave it, but must eventually return to it. It is thus natural that they should take an interest in the movements that occur among mankind. Be certain that when a social revolution takes place on Earth, it agitates the invisible world alike, wherein all passions, good and bad, are intensified. Just as it happens among yourselves, inexpressible effervescence starts to reign among the community of spirits that still belong to your world and that await the moment to return to it.

As everything is linked together in Nature, to the agitation of incarnate and discarnate beings, quite often, it is added the disturbances of the physical elements as well. Whence, for a while there exists a true general confusion, which passes through like a hurricane. Henceforward heaven reacquires its usual serenity and Humanity, reconstituted on its new basis and imbued with new ideas, proceeds with its new phase of progress.

It is within this period that is now in progress that

Spiritism will flourish and bear its fruits. Thus, you are working more for the future than for the present. Still, it was necessary to prepare the work in advance, as it prepares the way for regeneration, through unification and rationality of beliefs. Blessed are those who profit from it today. So much will be gained and so many sorrows avoided."

Dr. Barry

10. From what precedes above we conclude that in consequence of their orbital movement through space, the celestial bodies exert upon each other a greater or lesser influence, according to their mutual proximity and respective positions; and that this influence can cause momentary disturbances to their constituent elements and modify the conditions of vitality for their inhabitants. Additionally, the regularity of these movements determines the periodical return of the same causes and effects; that while some periods are too short to be perceived by men, other periods go through generations and races who do not perceive them and consider them to be the normal state of things. In contrast, generations contemporary to these transitions suffer their effect and feel that everything is beyond the ordinary laws; they believe them to have a supernatural, marvelous, and miraculous cause, albeit they are simply the fulfillment of the laws of Nature.

If by the sequence and reciprocity of causes and effects these periods of moral renovation of Humanity shall also coincide with the physical revolutions of the globe, as everything leads us to think, then such periods can be accompanied or preceded by natural phenomena, which appear strange to those who are not accustomed to them, by the appearance of strange meteors and by the recrudescence and unusual intensification of deadly plagues. Still, these occurrences are neither a cause nor a supernatural omen; instead, they are the result of the general movement that takes place on the physical and moral world.

When predicting the era of restoration that would open to Humanity and mark the end of the old world, Jesus affirmed that it would be announced by extraordinary phenomena and by earthquakes, by a variety of plagues and by signs from the skies – these being simply meteors, without any abrogation of the natural laws. Nevertheless, ordinary and unaware people saw in these words a prediction of miraculous facts[105].

11. The prediction of Humanity's progressive movements offers no surprise for dematerialized beings who foresee the purpose and tendency of all things; considering, still, that some of them have direct knowledge of God's thoughts. Through partial movements these beings are able to predict the time that such generalized movements could occur; like a man can calculate beforehand the time a tree will take to bear fruits; and an astronomer can predict the time of an astronomical phenomenon by the time a celestial body takes to achieve its revolution.

12. Humanity is a collective being, in whom is operated at the same moral revolutions as in each individual being, with this difference: one is accomplished from year to year, the other from century to century. Let one follow it in its evolutions through time, and one will see the life of the diverse races marked by periods which give to each epoch a particular physiognomy.

13. The progressive march of humanity is operated in two ways – the gradual, slow, and insensible, if one considers well the epochs which have drawn to a close, which is expressed by successive ameliorations in manners, laws, and customs, which do not fully unfold themselves until after a long space of time, like the changes which currents of water bring to the

---

[105] An extraordinary and abundant rain of shooting stars occurred in 1866 which terrified the inhabitants of Maurice Island. This occurrence preceded the terrible epidemic that from 1866 to 1868 decimated the population of the Island. The illness that was spreading in a benign way for a few months developed into a devastating plague. This was a real sign from the skies; it is perhaps in this meaning that we must understand the phrase "stars falling from the sky," which is said in the Gospel as being one of the signs of the times. (Details of the epidemic of Maurice Island: *"Revue Spirite"* of July of 1867, pg. 208, and November of 1868, pg. 321).

face of the globe; the other, by movements relatively sudden and rapid, similar to a torrent breaking its barriers, which enables it to jump over in a few years the time which it otherwise would have taken centuries to go over. It is, then, a moral cataclysm which engulfs in a few instants the institutions of the past, and to which succeed a new order of things which little by little become fixed by measure as tranquility reestablishes itself, and becomes positive.

To him who lives long enough to embrace the two sides of the new phase, it seems that a new world is sprung from the ruins of the ancient one. The character, manners, customs, all are changed. It is true that new men, or better still, regenerate ones, have sprung up. The ideas swept away by the generation which is extinct have made place for new ideas in the generation which is being educated.

14. Humanity is becoming adult. With new needs, more elevated and larger aspirations, it comprehends the emptiness of the ideas with which it has been fed and the insufficiency of its institutions for its well-being. It finds no more, in the existing state of things, the legitimate satisfactions to which it has been called. For this reason it shakes off its swaddling-clothes, and bounds, aided by an irresistible force, towards unknown shores to the discovery of new horizons less limited.

It is one of those periods of transformation, or of moral growth, which has reached humanity. From adolescence it passes to the manly or virile age. Past ideas cannot suffice for its new aspirations, for its new needs. It can no more be led by the same means. It pays no more for illusions and magical unrealities. For its ripe reason something more substantial is necessary. The present is too ephemeral. It feels that its destiny is more vast, and that corporeal life is too restrained to enclose it entirely. For this reason it looks deeply into the past, and into the future also, to discover the mystery of its existence, and draw from it a consoling security.

It is at this moment, when its material sphere is too narrow for it, when the intellectual life outruns it, when the sentiment of spirituality expands itself, that men calling themselves philosophers hope to fill up the void left by belief in nothing beyond this life and in materialism, strange aberration! These same men, who pretend to be pushing on in advance, are striving to circumscribe the limits of the narrow circle of matter from whence humanity aspires to extricate itself. They shut off the view of the infinite life, and say to it, as they point to the tomb: "*There is nothing beyond.*"

15. Whoever has meditated upon Spiritism and its consequences, and circumscribes it not to the production of a few phenomena, comprehends that it opens to humanity a new way, and unrolls to it infinite horizons. By initiating it into the mysteries of the invisible world, it shows to it its true role in creation, a *perpetually active one*, as well to the spiritual state as to the corporeal one. Man marches blindly no more. He knows from whence he came, where he is going, and why he is on Earth. The future show its reality to him, rid of the prejudice of ignorance and superstition. It is no more a vague hope; it is a palpable truth, as certain to him as the succession of day and night. He knows that his being is not limited to a few instants of an ephemeral existence; that the spiritual life is not interrupted by death; that he has already lived, that he will live again, and that of all he has acquired in perfection by labor nothing has been lost. He finds in his anterior existences the reason for that which now he is; and, *by that which man is doing now, he can conclude that which he will be someday.*

16. The idea that individual cooperation and activity in the general work of civilization have been limited to the present life, that one has been nothing and will be nothing, gives to man no incentive for the present or future. What matters it to him that in the future man will be better governed, happier, more enlightened, kinder to one another, since it bears no fruit for him? Is not this progress lost upon him? What good will it do him to work for posterity if he will never be acquainted with it, if it is composed of strangers who will, after a little, enter themselves into nothingness? Under the empire of a denial of a future for the individual, all forcibly shrinks to the narrow proportions of the moment and of personality.

But, on the contrary, what amplitude is given to the thought of man by *a certainty* of the perpetuity of his spiritual being? What can be more rational, grander, more worthy of the Creator, according to which the spiritual and corporeal life are only two modes of existence which alternate themselves for the accomplishment of progress? What can be more just, more consoling, than the idea of the same beings progressing without ceasing, at first through generations on the same Earth, afterwards, from world to world onward and upward to perfection, *without solution of continuity*? All actions have, then, an object; for, by working for all, one works for himself, and reciprocally. As long as individual or general progress is never sterile in its results, it is profitable to future generations and individuals, who are none other than the past generations and individualities arrived at a higher degree of advancement.

17. Fraternity must be the cornerstone of the new social order. But there is no real, solid, and effective fraternity if it has not been supported upon an unchangeable base. This base is faith, – not the faith in such and such particular dogmas, which change with time and people, and at which the stone is cast, and in anathematizing it they sustain the antagonism to it, but the faith in fundamental principles which all the world can accept, – *God, the soul, the future, individual progress as well as indefinite, the perpetuity of connection between individuals.* When all men shall be convinced that God is the same to all; that this God, sovereignly just and good, can will no injustice; that evil comes from men, and not from him – they will regard themselves as children of the same Father, and will extend to him the hand.

It is this faith which is given to Spiritism, and which will henceforth be the pivot upon which human beings will move, whatever be their mode of adoration and their particular beliefs.

18. The vast proportion of intellectual progress which has been accomplished is a great step, and marks the first phase of humanity; but alone, it is impotent to regenerate it. So long as man will be governed by pride and selfishness he will use his intelligence and his knowledge for the profit of his passions and personal interests. For this reason he applies them to the perfection of means for injuring others and of destroying them.

19. Moral progress alone can assure the happiness of men upon the Earth by putting a rein upon their bad passions. It alone can make harmony, peace, and fraternity reign between them.

It is this which will break down the barriers between them, which will destroy the prejudices of caste, silence the antagonisms of sects, by teaching men to regard themselves as brothers called to aid one another, and not to live at the expense of one another.

It is moral progress, seconded by the progress of intelligence, which will lead men to one belief established upon the eternal truths, not subject to discussion; and for this accepted by all.

The unity of belief will be the most powerful bond of union, the most solid foundation for universal fraternity, which has always been broken by religious antagonisms, which divides people and families, which makes one see in a neighbor a person to avoid – one to combat, exterminate – instead of a brother whom we should love.

20. Such a state of things supposes a radical change in the sentiment of the masses, a general progress which could be accomplished only by departing from the circle of narrow ideas, and quitting the ground which fosters pride. At different epochs superior men have sought to lead men into this way; but humanity, yet too young, has remained deaf, and their teachings have been like good seed fallen among stones.

Now humanity is capable of looking higher then it has done, in order to assimilate larger ideas, and comprehend that which it had never before comprehended.

This generation which will disappear will carry with it its prejudices and errors; the generation which is being educated has drunk at a purer spring, is imbued with healthier ideas, will impress on the world the ascensional movement by way of moral progress, which must mark the new phase of humanity.

21. This phase is already revealed by unmistakable signs, by attempts at useful reforms, by grand and generous ideas which are brought to light, and which commence to find echoes. Multitudes of protective, civilizing, and emancipating institutions are founded under the management and by the introductory movement of men evidently predestined to the work of regeneration; while each day the penal laws seem to be impregnated with a more humane sentiment. The prejudices of race are weakened. Nations commence to regard themselves as members of one great family. By the uniformity and facility of the means of transaction, they abolish the barriers which divide them. In all parts of the world they unite in universal assemblages for pacific interchange of sentiments.

But to those reforms a base is missing to complete, develop, and consolidate them – a more general moral predisposition in order to bear fruit, and to be accepted by the masses. It is no less a characteristic sign of the time, the prelude of that which will be accomplished upon a larger ladder by measure, as the ground will become more propitious.

22. A sign no less characteristic of the period upon which we enter is the evident reaction in spiritualistic ideas. An instructive repulsion is manifested against materialistic ideas. The spirit of unbelief, which was carrying away the masses, ignorant or enlightened, and had made them reject with the form even the true basis of all faith, seems to have been asleep, on the awakening from which one experiences a need of breathing a more life giving air. Involuntarily, where the void has been made, one seeks something, a support, a hope.

23. If one supposes the majority of men imbued with these sentiments, one can easily figure the changes it would bring on social relations – charity, fraternity, kindness towards all, and tolerance for all beliefs: such will be their motto. It is the end towards which humanity is evidently tending without being very sure of the means of realizing them, it tries, it counts the pulse, but is arrested by active resistance, or the force of the inertia of the prejudices of stationary beliefs which are opposed to progress. These are resisting forces, which it must vanquish; and it will be the work of the new generation. If one follows the present course of things, one will recognize that all seems predestined to prepare the way for it. There will be the double power of number and of ideas, and, moreover, the explosion of the past.

24. The new generation will march them to the realization of all compatible humanitarian ideas with the degree of advancement to which it will have reached. Spiritism marching towards the same end, and realizing its views, they will meet each other in the same ground. Men of progress will find in the ideas of the spiritists a powerful lever, and Spiritism will find in men new minds entirely disposed to welcome it. With this state of things, what will those do who would desire to place an obstacle in its way?

25. It is not Spiritism which creates social renovation; it is the maturity of humanity which makes this renovation a necessity. By its moralizing power, by its progressive tendencies, by the liberality of its views, by the generality of the questions which it embraces, Spiritism is, more than any other doctrine, qualified to second the regenerative movement; for that reason it is contemporary with it. It has come at the moment when it could be useful; for it also is the time arrived. Sooner, at an earlier date, it would have encountered insurmountable obstacles. It would have inevitably succumbed, because men, satisfied with that which they had, had not experienced a need for that which it brings. Now, born with the movement of fermenting ideas, it finds the Earth prepared to receive it. Spirits, tired of doubt and of incertitude, frightened by the gulf that opens before them, welcome it as an anchor of salvation and a supreme consolation.

26. The number of those who have not joined our ranks is still great without doubt; but what can they do against the rising wave, except to throw a few stones at it? This wave is the generation which is being educated by it, while those who do not believe will disappear with the generation which is rapidly passing away. Until that they will defend every step of the ground. There is then an inevitable contest, but an unequal one; for it is that of a

decrepit past, which falls into fragments against the juvenile future; of stagnation against progress; of the creature against the will of God – for the times appointed by him are come.

THE NEW GENERATION

27. In order that man shall be happy upon the Earth, it is necessary that it be peopled with good spirits, incarnate or discarnate, who desire only good. This time has arrived; a great emigration is being accomplished at this moment among those who inhabit it. Those who return evil for evil, and in whom the desire to do right is not felt, being unworthy of the transformed state of the Earth, will be banished from it, because they will bring only trouble and confusion, and would be an obstacle to progress. They will go to expiate their hardness of heart, some into inferior worlds, and others with terrestrial races behind them in development, which will be the equivalent of inferior worlds, where they will carry their acquired knowledge, and where it will be their mission to teach undeveloped beings this knowledge. They will be replaced by better spirits, who will make justice, peace, and fraternity rule among them.

The Earth, according to the intelligence gained from the spirits, must not be transformed by a cataclysm which would suddenly annihilate a generation. The present generation will gradually disappear, and the new one succeed in the same manner without anything having been changed in the natural order of things.

All externally will pass along as is usual, with this difference alone, which is an important one, that a part of the spirits which are incarnated here now will no more be incarnated here. The children who will then be born, instead of being underdeveloped and inclined to evil, will be more advanced spirits inclined towards righteousness.

It acts then much less upon a new corporeal generation than upon the new generation of spirits. It is undoubtedly within this context that Jesus understood things when he said: "I tell you the truth, this generation will certainly not pass away until all these things have happened." Thus, those who will expect to see the transformation brought about by supernatural or miraculous effects will be disappointed.

28. The present epoch is a transition one; the elements of the two generations are mingling together. Placed at the intermediary point, we assist at the departure of one and at the arrival of the other. Each one signalized itself by its own proper character.

The two generations which follow each other have views and ideas totally opposed to one another. By the nature of the moral disposition, but more particularly by the intuitive and *innate* disposition, it is easy to distinguish to which of the two each individual belongs.

The new generation, being the founder of the era of moral progress, is distinguished generally by a precocious intelligence and reasoning powers, joined to the *innate* sentiment of goodness and of spiritualist beliefs, which is the unmistakable sign of a certain degree of anterior advancement. It will not be composed exclusively of eminently superior spirits, but of those who, having progressed already, are predisposed to embrace all the progressive ideas, and apt to second the regenerative movement.

That which distinguishes, on the contrary, undeveloped spirits is, firstly, the revolt against God by refusing to recognize any power superior to humanity; then the instinctive propensity to the degrading passions, to the anti-fraternal sentiments of selfishness, of pride, of the attachment for all that which is material; sensuality, cupidity and avarice.

These are the vices of which the Earth must be purged by the removal of those who refuse to amend, because they are incompatible with the reign of fraternity, and as good men will suffer always by contact with them. When the Earth shall have been delivered from them, men will march without hindrance towards that better future which has been reserved for them here below as the recompense for their efforts and perseverance, looking forward to a purification still more complete, which will open to them the entrance to superior worlds.

29. By this emigration of spirits it is not necessary to understand that all undeveloped spirits will be expelled from Earth, and condemned to live in inferior worlds. Many, on the contrary, will return here – those who have yielded to temptation by the force of circumstances and example; those who appeared to be much worse than they really were. Once delivered from the influence of matter, and the prejudices of the corporeal world, the greater part of them will see things in an entirely different light than when living, as we have numerous examples of it. In this they are aided by benevolent spirits who are interested in them, and who try to enlighten them by showing them the wrong in the way they have pursued. By our prayers and exhortations we can ourselves contribute to their improvement, because there is a perpetual connection, an unbroken chain, between the dead and living.

The transformation is very simple, entirely a moral one, which is according to the laws of nature.

30. Allowing that the spirits of the new generation are new ones, but better, more advanced than the preceding ones, or ancient developed spirits, the result is the same. From the instant that they become inspired by better desires, the renovation takes place. There are then two categories of incarnated spirits, which are formed according to their natural dispositions – on one side those tardy in progression who depart, and on the other the progressive ones who arrive. The condition of society in a nation or in the entire world will be according to the preponderance which one of these two categories has over the other.

31. A common comparison will make this better comprehended. Let us suppose a regiment composed of a great majority of undisciplined and unruly men, those who in constant disorder are brought to feel the severity of the penal laws. These men are the stronger, because they are the more numerous; they are sustained, encouraged, and stimulated by example. The few good ones among them are without influence; their counsels are despised, they are scoffed at, badly treated by the others, and suffer from this contact. Is this not an emblem of society at present?

Let us suppose that these men are withdrawn from this regiment one by one, ten by ten, hundred by hundred, and that they are replaced by an equal number of good soldiers, even by those who have become seriously amended. At the end of some greater or less period of time, there will be the same regiment, but a transformed one; good order will have succeeded to disorder. Thus will it be with regenerated humanity.

32. The great collective departures have not alone for object the acceleration of the different departures, but they also transform more rapidly the minds of the masses by removing the bad influences from the way, and by giving a greater ascendancy to new ideas, because many are ready for this transformation, notwithstanding their imperfections, while many depart to strengthen themselves at a purer source.

Should they have remained in the same midst and under the same influences, they would have persisted in their opinions, and in their manner of seeing things. A sojourn in the spirit-world suffices to open their eyes to the truth, because they see there that which they could not see on Earth. The incredulous, the fanatic, the absolutist, will then be enabled to return with innate ideas of faith, of tolerance, and of liberty. On their return they will find things changed, and will submit to the ascendancy of the new midst in which they will be born. Instead of making opposition to new ideas, they will be helpers towards them.

33. The regeneration of humanity does not absolutely require the complete renewal of the spirits. A modification in their moral dispositions suffices. This modification takes place with all those who are predisposed to it when they shall have freed themselves from the pernicious influence of the world. Those who return, then, are not always other spirits, but often the same ones, thinking and feeling otherwise.

When this amelioration is isolated and individual, it passes unperceived, and is without ostensible influences upon the world. Entirely different is the effect when it operates simultaneously over great masses of people; for then, according to the proportions of it in one generation, the ideas of a nation or a race can be profoundly modified by it.

This is observed after great accidents which decimate a population. The destructive scourges do not destroy the spirit, but only the body; they accelerate the coming-and-going movement between the corporeal and spiritual world, and consequently the progressive movement of incarnate and discarnate spirits. It has been observed, at all historical epochs that great social crises have been followed by an era of progress.

34. It is one of these general movements which is operating at this time, and which must lead to the repairing of humanity. The multiplicity of the means of destruction is a characteristic sign of the times; for they must hasten the expansion of the new germs. They are the leaves of autumn which must fall, but to which will succeed new leaves full of life; for humanity has its season, as individuals have their ages. The dead leaves of humanity fall, carried away by the tempestuous blasts of life, only to be reborn with still greater strength, with the same breath of life which is not annihilated, but purified.

35. To the materialist, destructive scourges are calamities without compensation, without useful results, since, according to him, they annihilate the beings forever. But for him who knows that death destroys only the envelope, they have not the same consequences, and cause not the least bit of fear. He comprehends the object of it, and knows that men lose no more by dying together than separately, since, in one way or another, it is necessary to arrive there.

Incredulous will laugh at these things, and treat them as chimerical dreams; but, whatever they may say, they cannot escape the common law. They will fall in their turn like the others; and then what will occur? They say: nothing! but they will live in spite of themselves, and be forced some day to open their eyes to the truth.

THE END

GENESIS INDEX

ALLAN KARDEC'S BIOGRAPHY

Born in Lyon, France, on October 3, 1804, of a traditional family, greatly distinguished in the legal profession and court system, Allan Kardec (Hippolyte Léon Denizard Rivail) did not pursue these careers. From his youth, he was inclined toward the studies of science and of philosophy. Educated in the renown School of Pestalozzi, in Yverdun (Switzerland), he became one of that celebrated teacher's most eminent pupils and one of the most zealous propagandists of the Educational system that exercised a great influence in the reform of the Educational system in France and in Germany.

Endowed with a notable intelligence, he was drawn to teaching, due to his character and his special aptitudes. Being thoroughly knowledgeable in the German language, he translated into German a variety of works on education and on morals and, what is uniquely characteristic of him, the works of Fénelon that had seduced him in an intriguing way.

From 1835 to 1840, he established, in his home, in Paris, free study courses on Chemistry, Physics, Anatomy, Astronomy, etc., an accomplishment worthy of commendation at any time, but, above all, at this time in which only a few illuminated minds dared to follow that path. It can be seen that even before Spiritism had become popularized Allan Kardec through his Celtic pseudonym, had already become well known, through the varied nature of his accomplishments in the educational system. About the year 1855, the spotlight focused on the subject of the manifestations of the Spirits, and Allan Kardec became dedicated to persevering on the observations of that phenomenon, and cogitating mainly in deducing its philosophical consequences. He could see, at once, that these phenomena were the beginning of new natural laws: the ones that govern the relationships between the visible and the invisible world. He recognized in the action of the invisible world one of the forces of Nature, whose knowledge would throw light on the immense problems that until then had been considered insoluble, and he understood its reach, under the religious point of view.

His main works written on this subject are: The Spirit's Book (1857); The Mediums' Book (1861); The Gospel According to Spiritism (April of 1864); Heaven and Hell, or The Justice of God According to Spiritism (1865); Genesis, the Miracles and Predictions According to Spiritism (1868); Revue Spirite, a monthly newspaper of psychological studies, that had begun on January 1st, 1858.

He demonstrated that the facts, which previously had erroneously been considered supernatural, were actually subject to the universal laws. He classified them under the phenomena of Nature, thereby eliminating the last refuge of the wonder and one of the elements of superstition.

The date of the launching of The Spirit's Book was the foundation of Spiritism. Starting from that moment, the doctrine attracted the attention of the serious-minded people and took a rapid development. In few years, those ideas overtook numerous followers in all social circles around the world. Instead of the postulate: "Without the Church there is no Salvation, which fosters separation and animosity between the different religious sects that have been responsible for so much bloodshed, Spiritism has as its emblem: Without Charity there is no Salvation, which enhances equality among men, tolerance, freedom of conscience and mutual benevolence in the eyes of God.

Instead of blind faith, which annuls free thinking, Spiritism says: Unshakable faith is only that which can meet reason face to face in every human epoch. In order to have faith a base is necessary; and, this base is the perfect intelligence of that which one believes. It is in fact due to the dogma of blind faith that today we still have such a great number of non-believers; as it tries to impose itself by annulling one of man's most precious abilities, that of reasoning, and of free-will.

A tireless worker, always the first to take on a task and the last one to leave it, Allan Kardec died on March 31st, 1869. He died as he lived: working.

SPECIAL THANKS

HAVE YOU HEARD OF FABIANO DE CRISTO HOME?

Special thanks to *Lar Fabiano de Cristo* for the support in publishing this book.
Fabiano de Cristo Home, started as a *"Dream of Love."* This non-profit organization has fought since its creation in 1958 to break the chains of moral, social and material poverty, which imprison families in the situation of social exclusion with tragic consequences for all society.

Since its early start in Brazil, the founders believed that the true sense of a charitable organization should be based on its educational features, and not only on giving away some clothes today, some food tomorrow, or some toys by Christmas time. It would be important to learn the true causes of material, social, moral and spiritual misery, in order to fight them directly.

Such direct action on the misery causes implies in searching the origin of the physical, moral and spiritual dependencies that afflict people. The program develops assistance and promotional methodology after a diagnosis of the situation of families in social risk. From this starting point, each attended family is given an individual *Life Quality Plan*, estimated to reach its target within 5 years. Reaching the target means having the family break the misery chain, with dignity. Once this goal is reached, the family steps aside, so that more families may join the program.

Fabiano de Cristo Home's Social Inclusion Plan is part of the Collective Consultation Body of Non-Governmental Organizations of Unesco's Basic Education and Literacy Program.

In order to face such wide scope of needs, this program was established considering 5 main groups:

Group 1 - Abandoned or orphan children, in need of a replacing home;

Group 2 - Children that for some reason need to be temporarily separated from their families or placed in temporary shelter;

Group 3 - Families in extreme poverty that require full promotion;

Group 4 - Response to emergency needs;

Group 5 - Attention to the elderly, especially those in extreme poverty.

FABIANO DE CRISTO HOME'S WORK IN ACTION:

✓ 233 social Promotion Units supporting 11,359 families in all Brazilian states.

✓ Children Education (0 to 6 years old) - Attendees: 2,755.

✓ Creativity Development and Scholastic Support (7 to 13 years old) - Attendees: 5,887

✓ Professional Formation (Teenagers and adults) - Attendees: 2,755

✓ Educational and Social Follow-Up - Attendees: 35,283

✓ Basic Needs Support- Including co-participants that are regularly given food (28,806) and medicines (3,521) - Attendees: 49,467

✓ Citizenship - Attendees: 25,032

✓ 102,218 Medical/Dental appointments attended at the units

✓ 341 Social Groups that involve 13,591 participants taking part in the Social-Family Orientation Program.

To become a volunteer, a donor or for further information, please visit:

www.lfc.org.br

LET'S WORK TOGETHER, TO SET UP PEACE FOR A BETTER WORLD.
HELP US HELP MORE FAMILIES!

Printed in format 18, 14x21 cm, Times font, 408 pages, 25 stacks, using 75g Sulfite paper inside and 250g Supreme paper for cover.